PROTECTIVE LABOR LEGISLATION

STUDIES IN HISTORY, ECONOMICS AND PUBLIC LAW

EDITED BY THE FACULTY OF POLITICAL SCIENCE
OF COLUMBIA UNIVERSITY

Volume CXVI] **[Number 2**

Whole Number 259

PROTECTIVE LABOR LEGISLATION

With Special Reference to Women in the State of New York

BY

ELIZABETH FAULKNER BAKER

AMS PRESS
NEW YORK

COLUMBIA UNIVERSITY
STUDIES IN THE
SOCIAL SCIENCES

259

This Series was formerly known as
Studies in History, Economics and Public Law.

Reprinted with the permission of Columbia University Press
From the edition of 1925, New York
First AMS EDITION published 1969
Manufactured in the United States of America

Library of Congress Catalogue Card Number: 76-82239

AMS PRESS, INC.
NEW YORK, N. Y. 10003

To

MY MOTHER

HATTIE BEARCE FAULKNER

WHOSE UNDERSTANDING HAS BEEN A CONSTANT SOURCE OF STRENGTH
DURING THE DEVELOPMENT OF THIS STUDY

PREFACE

The steadily increasing numbers of women in industry, both married and single, and their slow but continued emergence into the ranks of skilled workers force fresh inquiry into their needs. Since women have become an integral part of our economic society, of that part of the population which is gainfully employed, the problems concerning them are no longer confined to the family but they are problems of economic status as well. This fact tends to narrow the divergence between the interests and requirements of men and women. It urges careful examination of the common and separate difficulties of men and women as wage earners as well as of their common and separate relations to the family. This set of circumstances is in sharp contradistinction to that of yesterday when woman's work was confined to her home or when her presence in industry was viewed as an emergency measure, a temporary result of the introduction of machinery.

This study attempts, therefore, to analyse some of the actual conditions as they appear today in regard to women workers, and to urge further analysis and further search for facts. Those who chiefly desire a general discussion of the subject of special protection of women in industry, including the opposing views, will prefer to read only the Introduction and the final chapter—The Controversy.

I am indebted to Professor Henry R. Seager and Mr. John A. Fitch who have read my manuscript and have given continuous guidance and encouragement; to Miss Frances Perkins and Miss Nelle Swartz of the New York State Department of Labor who read parts of the study and offered criticism and suggestions; to my senior colleagues at Barnard College, Professor William F. Ogburn and Professor Emilie J. Hutchinson, and to Miss Clara Eliot, each one of whom has given invaluable aid throughout the course of my study; to my sister-in-law, Mrs. Frank B. Patterson, who, with me, has seen this book through the press. And finally, I owe deep gratitude to my friend Mrs. Louise Herrick Wall whose criticism has been an immeasurable help.

E. F. B.

New York, November, 1924.

CONTENTS

AGE

PART II

CHAPTER III

INFLUENCES BEARING UPON LEGISLATION FOR WOMEN IN NEW YORK STATE

CHAPTER IV

INFLUENCES CONTINUED

CHAPTER V

ENFORCEMENT OF LEGISLATION

PART I

PART II

PAGE

CHAPTER VI

Some Effects of Protective Legislation for Women

PART I

PART II

CHAPTER VII

The Controversy

INTRODUCTION

Protective labor legislation is a by-product of the machine age in which we live. With the growth of large-scale industry dominated by the desire for profit, the bargaining power of wage-earners has become disproportionately weak, and along with organization into labor unions for self-protection has developed a growing system of protection by the State. For example, practically all important industrial states in America have made legal provision for compensation to workmen for industrial accidents, and the daily hours of labor are regulated for large groups of employees such as those in public service and in hazardous industries. This is to say nothing of the mass of codified and statutory regulations for the improvement of working conditions for the safety of employment and the health of workmen.

Society has reacted to the tyranny of the machine system to maintain and promote citizenship and the welfare of the race. Factors retarding action have been the acquisitiveness of employers, the hesitation of the courts to interfere with the freedom of contract, and our traditional resistance to the usurpation of control by the State. Nevertheless interference by the State in the relations between employer and employee increases each year, and probably it is safe to predict that it will continue to increase if present indications are reasonably trustworthy as a basis for judgment.

Within this larger problem of the legal protection of wage earners falls that of the special protection of women which has developed steadily as the numbers of women in industry have grown. Here is a special problem which becomes more complicated from year to year as the problem of women in our changing society presses ever more insistently for adjustment. Women's position is unsettled by the slow passing of the home and family life of an agricultural people into the home and family life of an industrial people. But despite this lagging adjustment the constant element has been the increase in numbers of women in industrial employment. According to the last census eight and one-half million women in the United States were gainfully occupied. This number was more than one-fifth of all females ten years of age and over and one-fifth of the gainfully employed population. Comparing these figures with previous census data, the facts are as follows:

	Number women employed	Per cent of females 10 years of age and over	Per cent of gainfully employed population 10 years of age and over
1880	2,647,157	14.7	15.2
1890	4,005,532	17.4	17.2
1900	5,319,397	18.8	18.3
1910	8,075,772	23.4	21.2
1920	8,549,511	21.1*	20.5*

It is significant also to observe the changing distribution of women, to see that the occupations which have in the past claimed women more particularly appear to attract them relatively less. For example, in 1910 nearly one-third of all women gainfully employed were in domestic and personal

* This decrease in the proportion of women ten years of age and over who were gainfully employed in 1920 compared with 1910 is attributed to three causes: (1) The change in the census date from April to January, eliminating a busy farming season; (2) different instructions to census gatherers; (3) reduction in the employment of girls from ten to fifteen years of age. See *Bulletin No. 27*, Women's Bureau of the United States Department of Labor, p. 8.

service, while in 1920 one-quarter were so employed. In clerical occupations on the other hand, the number of women employed in 1920 was more than double that of 1910. The distribution is as follows:

	1910 Per cent	1920 Per cent
All women	100 (8,075,772)	100 (8,549,511)
Agriculture, forestry and animal husbandry	22.4	12.7
Manufacturing and mechanical industries	22.5	22.6
Transportation	1.3	2.5
Trade	5.8	7.8
Public service	0.2	0.3
Professional service	9.1	11.9
Domestic and personal service	31.3	25.6
Clerical occupations	7.3	16.7

Thus there appears to be a definite disinclination on the part of women to continue in domestic service although this occupation still holds a greater proportion of women than any other. Moreover, analysis of these and more specific census figures indicates that while women have not gone into occupations new to them in large numbers, they are now seen more commonly in occupations in which their presence heretofore has been exceptional. Furthermore the Federal Woman's Bureau, in comparing the figures for men and women, points out that the rate of increase of women " in by far the greater number of cases " was in excess of that of men. Numerically, of course, men are far in advance of women in most occupations, " but these huge increases none the less indicate that more and more industrial opportunities are being offered to women." [1]

With the growing importance of women in industry, the problems concerning their position in the family and in society become more complicated by problems concerning

[1] *Op. cit.*, p. 4.

their economic position. New demands upon them in industry obviously call for a shift in their responsibilities outside of industry unless women are to be permitted to break under a double load. Special legal protection in industry is a problem concerned both with women's economic position and with their changing position in the family and society. Thus while we are more particularly concerned with the industrial significance of legislation, social implications must also be considered if an analysis of this subject is to be of value. The State of New York has been selected for intensive study, not because all types of protective laws have been enacted there, but because its legislation is representative. New York is the most important industrial state in the Union with one-tenth of all gainfully occupied persons concentrated within its jurisdiction. There are in New York 8,402,786 persons ten years of age and over, 54 per cent of whom (4,504,791) are gainfully employed. One-fourth of these gainfully employed, or 1,135,948, are women and they constitute more than one-fourth of the total number of women inhabitants in the state. Thus problems which affect these women, employed in a state of such diversified industrial interests, may be considered fairly representative of problems affecting the other seven-eighths of the working women of the country.

To establish a broad base for analysis of the growth of protection of women workers in New York it has been necessary to study the environment in which all protective legislation developed—the attitude of the courts and the trend of legislation for all persons. Of the following chapters, therefore, the first will suggest the forms and extent of legislation in the United States for both men and women as the constitutionality of specific acts has been tested in the courts. We will then proceed to describe the growth of legislation for both men and women in New York State; this leads naturally to the discussion of special legislation principally in New York, attempting to look into the influences which prompted legislation specifically for women, the extent to which these laws are actually enforced, and their effects upon the women for whose benefit they are enacted. Finally, an attempt will be made to consider the views of the increasing body of women who object to this form of protection on the ground that it is prejudicial to them rather than advantageous. The number of women holding this view, though proportionately not large, suggests the importance of opening up for consideration a subject which seems to have been settled but discussion of which may have just begun. Indeed the shifting position of women would seem to demand repeatedly renewed inquiries into these important problems, lest emphasis properly placed yesterday be misdirected to-day.

CHAPTER I

Protective Labor Legislation in the United States as Reviewed by the Courts

It is essential to an adequate analysis of protective labor legislation in New York State, that the attitudes of the courts, both federal and in the several states, toward these laws be shown and that the growth, extent and trend of such legislation in the United States be indicated.

As acts of the legislature reflect our changing folkways, so also, if more reluctantly, do the decisions of the courts reflect such change. The task of the courts is two-fold, however, for while the legislatures need only act upon the progressive demands of their respective constituents, the courts must consider not only the will of the legislatures, but they must weigh that will against the constitution written by "the fathers" which demands equal protection for the whole of the people. Thus, acts of legislatures and decisions of courts must be frequently at variance.

Moreover, diversity of opinion arises not only between legislatures and courts but among the individual members who compose these respective bodies. As bills are won or lost in a legislative struggle, so are laws affirmed or annulled in a conflict of judicial opinions. Some discussion of the legislative battle will be made in a later chapter; at present it is pertinent to examine briefly into the cause of friction within the courts and between the courts and the legislature.

On July 28, 1868, the Fourteenth Amendment to the Federal Constitution was adopted. Section One of this amendment—the judicial storm center in the litigation of labor cases—reads as follows:

No State shall make or enforce any law which shall abridge the privileges or immunities of citizens of the United States; nor shall any State deprive any person of life, liberty, or property, without due process of law; nor deny to any person within its jurisdiction the equal protection of the laws.

Prior to this time, the several states decided their own questions of domestic policy, and the decisions of their respective tribunals were final. The result of the new amendment was to accord uniform federal protection to individuals against encroachments by the separate states,— to bring about a harmony in or of this protection by subjecting issues involving it to the ultimate determination of the United States Supreme Court. The Fourteenth Amendment thus insures to individuals as against state action immunities corresponding to those which, under the Fifth Amendment, they enjoy against federal action.

The very vagueness of the Fourteenth Amendment has lent it elasticity. In it is found support for the advocates of laissez faire on the one hand, and for those who would have the government interfere in the labor contract on the other hand. In deciding upon the validity of a statute, some judges retain the doctrines of individualism as a guide, while others have developed a socialized attitude toward life, society and government which influences them in their judgments. A conflict of opinion within the court room is thus inevitable. But a controlling decision regarding the constitutionality of a statute need not wait for universal agreement on the part of the justices. On the contrary, a bare majority which in the Federal Supreme Court means only five out of nine votes, can decide the fate of a law in spite of vigorous dissent from the minority. Furthermore a majority vote may become a minority vote by a shift in viewpoint or by the absence of a justice, while the points in question may remain the same.[1]

Thus laws are dependent for their lives as much upon the social viewpoint of judges as upon the precepts of the constitution to which judges are bound to defer.

Labor laws have most frequently been declared unconstitutional on these grounds: restriction of the freedom of contract which is implied in the property right; class legislation which abridges constitutional " privileges and immunities "; deprivation of " the equal protection of the laws." However, it is true that laws which restrict these rights are frequently declared valid because the restriction is considered necessary for the public welfare, the greater liberty of all the people, and thus a proper exercise of the police power. In other words abridgment of rights is likely to be sanctioned by the courts if such abridgement is established through the legitimate exercise of the police power and by " due process of law."

Due process of law has been defined on the procedural side as that which " merely requires such tribunals as are proper to deal with the subject in hand. Reasonable notice and a fair opportunity to be heard before some tribunal before it decides the issues are the essentials of due process of law." [2] Probably there would be no objection to this definition for the reason that the terms used are highly elastic. " Proper," " reasonable," and " fair " are all relative words and would necessarily be interpreted according to the social outlook of the judges involved. A close sense

[1] *Cf.* Holden *v.* Hardy, 169 U. S. 366 (1898) and Lochner *v.* New York, 198 U. S. 45 (1905); Ritchie *v.* People, 155 Ill. 198 (1895) and Ritchie & Co. *v.* Wayman, 244 Ill. 509 (1910); also The Children's Hospital of the District of Columbia *v.* Jesse C. Adkins, *et al.*, 284 Fed. Rep. 613 (1922).

[2] Stettler *v.* O'Hara, 69 Ore. 519 (1914).

of the meaning of the due process clause is only attainable, therefore, by an examination of judicial decisions which we are about to undertake. It has been well said that "the Court seems inclined to hold that a law of a state is not invalid under the due process clause unless it transgresses certain theories of government nowhere defined precisely in the law but existing in the minds of the judges who render the opinion." [1]

The extent and meaning of the police power is also incapable of being absolutely defined. Blackstone's definition as summoned for use in a state court was:

> the due regulation and domestic order of the kingdom, whereby the inhabitants of the state, like members of a well governed family, are bound to conform their general behavior to the rules of propriety, good neighborhood and good manners, and to be decent, industrious and inoffensive in their respective stations.[2]

Justice Holmes in speaking the opinion of the Federal Supreme Court in a non-labor case, once said, "The police power may be put forth in aid of what is sanctioned by usage, or held by the prevailing morality, or strong and preponderant opinion, to be greatly and immediately necessary to the public welfare." [3] The United States Supreme Court elsewhere says, "under the powers inherent in every sovereignty, a government may regulate the conduct of its citizens toward each other, and when necessary for the public good, the manner in which he shall use his own property." [4] In one of the most celebrated labor decisions of the Federal

[1] Beard, *American Government and Politics* (1924), p. 484.

[2] State *v.* Buchanan, 29 Wash. 603, 605 (1902).

[3] Noble State Bank *v.* Haskell, 219 U. S. 104 (1911).

[4] Munn *v.* Illinois, 94 U. S. 113 (1876). This was the first decision which declared the right of the public to interfere in private business. See Professor Ernst Freund, "Constitutional Limitations and Labor Legislation," 4 Ill. Law Rev. 609, or *Publications of the American Association for Labor Legislation*, 1910, pp. 51-71.

Supreme Court the constitutional interpretation of liberty and property rights was postulated as follows:

While the cardinal principles of justice are immutable, the methods by which justice is administered are subject to constant fluctuation, and . . . the Constitution of the United States which is necessarily and to a large extent inflexible and exceedingly difficult of amendment, should not be so construed as to deprive the States of the power to so amend their laws as to make them conform to the wishes of the citizens as they may deem best for the public welfare without bringing them into conflict with the supreme law of the land.[1]

But these instances are all drawn from opinions which seem to look with favor upon an expanding use of the police power, and it is quite essential to realize that this phrase has powers of contraction as well. One well known example of this possibility is that in which the court held that cigar making "in any building" (presumably regardless of the state of its sanitation) has no relation to the public health and that such manufacture cannot be prevented as a proper exercise of the police power.[2] Also in a more recent case, it was urged that "the tendency of the hour to socialize property rights under the subterfuge of police regulation is dangerous and if continued will prove destructive of our free institutions."[3]

So although the concept of the general purpose of the police power may be relatively clear, it is just as clear that this power has limits that expand and contract. Moreover, this elasticity seems inevitable, for, in any case, no one can foresee the ever-changing social and industrial conditions which may call for interference by the State. The question

[1] Holden *v.* Hardy, 169 U. S. 366 (1896), see post, p. 36.

[2] *In re* Jacobs, 98 N. Y. 98 (1885), see *infra*, p. 27.

[3] Children's Hospital of the District of Columbia *v.* Adkins, see p. 86, *infra*.

continually recurs as to what is the degree of social change which justifies new legislation with the accompanying restriction of individual rights or the demarcation of a social class? And on this question views vary and there is rarely a unanimous reply by the judiciary. One keen observer summarizes that " police power, like that other vague phrase 'due process of law', is wholly within the keeping of the judicial conscience, and its interpretation depends upon the general, social and political theories of the judiciary." [1]

The issue regarding the jurisdiction of court and legislature also arises. Is the need for legislation to be judged by the people through their respective legislatures, or by the whole people through the United States Supreme Court? Is the expediency or propriety of a statute the concern of the courts? To this Judge Learned Hand has answered, traditionally, no. The courts have always professed that matters of expediency lie with the legislature alone. But Judge Hand explains that this tradition is also in the process of change. At first, action of the legislatures was construed to be within due process of law if it were "actually and not merely colorably" for the public health, morals or safety, and the courts required that public health and safety be construed in the fair meaning of those terms. But the meaning became defined as including public "good" or "welfare" in general, and even public "prosperity" or "convenience".[2] This gave the legislature the power to make "welfare" and "convenience" the mere color for statutes by which corrupt interests meant to accomplish no result of the kind, or by which legislatures may have found expressions for a particular bias. So the courts "heroically took the 'bull by the horns'" declaring in favor of what they have traditionally

[1] Beard, *American Government and Politics* (1924), p. 488.

[2] See 21 Harvard Law Rev. 495, April, 1907-1908, citing Lochner *v.* New York (198 U. S. 45) and other cases.

held to be false,—that the courts have the power to examine the expediency of a measure and to determine whether in their judgment it has any relation to the purposes declared and to the purposes and objects which the court recognises as legitimate. The result, continues Judge Hand, is a "great divergence of constitutional decision and an apparent absence of actual principle upon which such cases can be determined. . . ."

A vote of the court necessarily depends not upon any fixed rules of law, but upon the individual opinions upon political and economic questions of the persons who compose it, and though in the course of time precedents will be established upon a large number of questions, to which presumably thereafter all members of the court will give the deference due to decisions, those precedents will not have the force of instances of a general principle, but of precedents upon precisely the questions which were decided.[1]

Thus there appears due explanation for the recurring clash of opinions respecting the jurisdiction of court and legislature, as well as for the clash of opinions within the judiciary itself. With this clue to the minds and to some of the problems presented to the country's tribunals, it is necessary to analyse their conclusions in specific cases. Practically speaking, the courts can make or break laws and the effects of their interpretations are momentous.

PART I: LEGISLATION FOR ALL ADULTS AS REVIEWED BY THE COURTS

Protective labor laws enacted in the United States which have been carried into the courts on the charge of unconstitutionality fall, roughly speaking, into three general categories,—those restricting hours of labor, those relating to wages, and those in respect to workmen's compensation.

[1] *Ibid.*, p. 501.

Workmen's compensation laws are the most recent type of legislation and have been increasingly sanctioned by the courts. Hour laws in so far as they have applied to dangerous occupations, have been pretty generally upheld. In so-called non-dangerous employments they have fared much less uniformly, however, and constitutionality has often turned upon whether men or women were the objects of protection. Statutes limiting the working hours of women have been upheld more commonly than those for men. Acts relating to hours and wages have, for the most part, been declared constitutional when they have applied to public employees. In private employment, statutes securing proper payment of wages have received irregular treatment in the courts of the several states and all important decisions affirming provisions for minimum wages in private employment have applied to acts relating to women and minors.

As judicial reasoning regarding protection of women takes a different turn from that relating to men, it will be discussed separately in Part II. Decisions relating to all adults, but more generally to men owing to the type of employment involved, will be considered at this time.

Less than fifty years ago no judicial interpretation had been made of the United States Constitution in its specific bearing upon the rights of industrial workers. The "principle of public control of economic interests" when those interests affected the public, was established in the Granger cases beginning in the late seventies.[1] The first decision of an American court against the power of the state to interfere with the freedom of laborers was declared in regard to New York cigar makers in the middle eighties.[2] The

[1] Munn *v.* Illinois, 94 U. S. 113 (1876) and cases following. See Ernst Freund, "Constitutional Limitations and Labor Legislation," 41 Ill. Law Review 609, or *Publications of the American Association for Labor Legislation*, 1910, p. 52.

[2] *In re* Jacobs, 98 N. Y. 98 (1885). See Fred R. Fairchild, "The Factory Legislation of the State of New York, *Publications of the American Economic Association*, vol. vi, 1905.

economic relation between employer and employee received first attention at bar in the truck acts of the eighties.[1] And beginning with these initial cases, the courts, high and low, have been increasingly pressed by advocates of labor legislation for a broader interpretation of the constitution, and have been met on every hand by the claims of the conservatives.

TENEMENT HOUSE LABOR

The act of the New York State legislature in 1883 prohibiting tenement house cigar manufacture, was declared unconstitutional on purely technical grounds. The title was insufficient to cover the body of the law. The revised bill fathered by the Cigar Makers' International Union, as also the first had been, was presented and adopted by the legislature in 1884. A manufacturer named Jacobs violated this act and upon his application for a writ of habeas corpus the case came again to the state's highest court. Able counsel was engaged by the manufacturers on the one side and the cigar-makers' union on the other, but in the absence of counsel for the union (who is reported to have accepted a retaining fee of $1000 in advance),[2] the case was argued and won by the manufacturers in May, 1885. The counts against the measure were that it interfered with private liberty and property in the disguise of an effort to promote public health, that it had " no relation whatever to the public health " and was therefore void.

The reasoning of the tribunal in this case of Jacobs was that liberty in America consists of the free use of one's faculties where and how one wishes, and any legislative attempt to restrain this right, unless as a proper exercise of the police power, is an infringement upon the rights of liberty

[1] Godcharles *v.* Wigmen, 113 Pa. St. 431 (1885); Millet *v.* People, 117 Ill. 294 (1886) and other cases.

[2] F. R. Fairchild, *op. cit.*, pp. 21-22.

which are under constitutional protection. That the court had little knowledge of the unsanitary conditions under which these people lived and worked is apparent as the delivery of the opinion continues:[1]

This law was not intended to protect the health of those engaged in cigarmaking, as they are allowed to manufacture cigars everywhere except in the forbidden tenement houses. It cannot be perceived how the cigarmaker is to be improved in his health or his morals by forcing him from his home and its hallowed associations and beneficent influences, to ply his trade elsewhere. It was not intended to protect the health of that portion of the public not residing in the forbidden tenement-houses, as cigars are allowed to be manufactured in private houses, in large factories and shops in the two crowded cities [New York and Brooklyn], and in all other parts of the State. What possible relation can cigarmaking in any building have to the health of the general public? . . . It is plain that this is not a health law, and that it has no relation whatever to public health. . . . Such governmental interferences disturb the normal adjustments of the social fabric, and usually derange the delicate and complicated machinery of industry and cause a score of ills while attempting the removal of one.

This decision made it clear that the evil of tenement house labor could not be abolished because of deleterious effects upon the workers themselves—at least during the existing state of mind of the judiciary. Later laws in New York State have attacked the problem indirectly as regulative measures with the explicit purpose of protecting consumers. The hope of those actively interested has been that laws

[1] There would seem to be some explanation for the adverse decree, however, for the Board of Health had declared that after a careful investigation they considered "that the health of the tenement population is not jeopardized by the manufacture of cigars in those houses; that this bill is not a sanitary measure and that it has not been approved by the board." *Report of the New York Factory Investigating Commission*, 1913, vol. i, p. 121.

framed to protect public health may be extended gradually to secure prohibition of tenement house labor and that the judiciary, as it changes to represent a more enlightened public, will approve. The later regulative laws have not been contested as yet except in one instance which was favorable to regulation.[1] There is increasing reason to believe, however, in the light of this single instance and of the expanded exercise of the police power in many other instances, that the attitude of the courts has already undergone such a change that the Jacobs decision would not be rendered today.

THE TRUCK ACTS

The early truck act cases which opened the discussion of the relation between employer and employed arose in the mining states of Pennsylvania and Illinois in the eighties. These statutes which forbade payment of wages in store orders were pronounced "an insulting attempt to put the laborer under a legislative tutelage, which is not only degrading to his manhood, but subversive of his rights as a citizen of the United States." The law prevented "persons who are *sui juris* from making their own contracts" and therefore it could not be constitutional.[2] Here then, were the time, the place, and the creators of "the novel doctrine of freedom of contract between capital and labor," [3] a doctrine which has become a cardinal consideration in the litigation of labor cases.

The guarding of this legacy has not necessitated inflexibility on the part of the courts however. For, while the

[1] People *v.* Balofsky, 167 N. Y. App. Div. 913 (1915). This was an appeal from the court of special sessions which decided in favor of the prohibition of making food and children's clothing in tenements. The judgment was affirmed with no opinion delivered.

[2] Godcharles *v.* Wigeman, 113 Pa. St. 431 (1886); Millet *v.* People, 117 Ill. 294 (1886).

[3] Ernst Freund, "Constitutional Limitations and Labor Legislation," *op. cit.*, p. 52.

principle of the right of free contract has led some state tribunals to invalidate acts on the ground that they interfered with the wage contract, that same principle has led other tribunals to declare such acts valid. For example, Ohio, Kansas, and Texas condemned protective acts relating to freedom of contract as also did Missouri,[1] while conclusions favorable to protection were reached in the courts of Colorado, Kentucky, and Tennessee, and in the United States Supreme Court.[2] In the decisions which affirmed the laws, the state was recognized to have the right to interfere in the relations between employer and employee to the extent of strengthening the bargaining power of the latter. The supreme court of Tennessee held that a statute which permits the employee to demand and receive his wages "in money rather than in something less valuable" tends even though to a slight degree "to place the employer and employee upon equal ground in the matter of wages." And further the court held that this was an act toward the suppression of strife which may even become bloodshed, and for the promotion of the public peace and order. The Supreme Court of the United States upheld these views. About two-thirds of the states in this country now have laws that deal with the time and method of wage payment but many of these laws have not been tested in the courts.[3]

SUNDAY CLOSING ACTS AND ONE DAY OF REST IN SEVEN

Judicial approval of the Sunday closing law for barbers was granted for New York in 1896. The New York

[1] Ohio: *re* Preston, 63 Ohio St. 428; Kansas: State *v.* Haun, 61 Kan. 146; Texas: Jordan *v.* State, 51 Tex. Cr. 531; Missouri: State *v.* Loomis, 115 Mo. 307; State *v.* Miss. Tie & Timber Co., 181 Mo. 536.

[2] Colorado: 48 Pac. Reporter 512 (1897); Kentucky: 58 S. W. Reporter 441 (1900); Tennesse: 53 S. W. Reporter 955 (1899); Knoxville Iron Co. *v.* Harbison, 183 U. S. 13 (1901); McLean *v.* Arkansas, 211 U. S. 539 (1908).

[3] Commons & Andrews, *Principles of Labor Legislation* (1920), p. 91.

decision was one of a group of conflicting decrees on this subject that were handed down within a few years,— New York and Minnesota upheld the acts and California and Illinois disaffirmed them.[1] The Minnesota case was carried to the United States Supreme Court and sustained.[2] The state court had recognized a peculiar need for legislative protection of men in the barbers' trade and thereby surmounted the constitutional barrier in respect to class legislation. The decision was in accordance with Professor Ernst Freund's view of justifiable class legislation,— "where a restraint is confined to a special class of acts or occupations, that class must present the danger dealt with in a more marked and uniform degree than the classes omitted." [3] Chief Justice Fuller, writing the opinion of the Federal Supreme Court, elaborated upon the view expressed in the state decision,

Upon no subject is there such concurrence of opinion, among philosophers, moralists, and statemen of all nations, as on the necessity of periodical cessations from labor. . . . The prohibition of secular business on Sunday is advocated on the ground that by it the general welfare is advanced, labor protected and the moral and physical well-being of society promoted.

For the New York court in respect to the "Barber's Statute," Judge Vann declared Sunday to be the reasonable day for rest from work not simply on religious grounds, but because "as a day of rest and recreation Sunday has been recognized from time out of mind both by the legislature and the courts", while we were still a British colony as well as since we have enjoyed our independence. His argument ran thus:

[1] New York, People *v.* Havnor, 43 N. E. 541 (1896); Minnesota, State *v.* Petit, 77 N. W. Rep. 225 (1898); California, *Ex. parte* Jentzsch, 44 Pac. 803 (1896); Illinois, Eden *v.* People, 43 N. E. 1108 (1896).

[2] 177 U. S. 164 (1899).

[3] Ernst Freund, *The Police Power*, p. 755.

It is to the interest of the state to have strong, robust, healthy citizens, capable of self support, of bearing arms, and of adding to the resources of the country. Laws to effect this purpose, by protecting the citizen from overwork, and requiring a general day of rest to restore his strength and preserve his health, have an obvious connection with the public welfare.

As though conscious of an error in judgment at the expense of society in the Jacob's case, the judge continued:

Independent of any question relating to morals or religion, the physical welfare of the citizen is a subject of such primary importance to the state, and has such a direct relation to the general good, as to make laws tending to promote that object proper under the police power, and hence valid under the constitution. . . . This [the statute under discussion] affords an opportunity, recurring at regular intervals, for rest, needed both by the employer and the employed, and the latter, at least, may not have the power to observe a day of rest without the aid of legislation. As Mr. Tiedeman says, in his work on Police Powers: "If the law did not interfere, the feverish, intense desire to acquire wealth, . . . inciting a relentless rivalry and competition, would ultimately prevent not only the wage earners, but likewise the capitalists and employers themselves, from yielding to the warnings of nature, and obeying the instinct of self-preservation, by resting periodically from labor." . . . As barbers generally work more hours each day than most men, the legislature may well have concluded that legislation was necessary for the protection of their health. We think that this statute was intended and is adapted to promote the public health, and thereby to serve a public purpose of the utmost importance, by promoting the observance of Sunday as a day of rest. It follows, therefore, that it does not go beyond the limits of legislative power by depriving any one of liberty or property within the meaning of the constitution.

This interpretation by the court of appeals forms an odd

contrast to that which struck so hard a blow at the cause of the cigar makers. In that instance the manufacture of cigars in unregulated tenement houses was deemed to have "no relation whatever to public health," while in this instance the relation between private and public health was considered vital, and a just ground for interference by law. The opinion of the court in the barbers' case could well be recalled more frequently than it has been in the adjudication of later laws for the protection of workers.

Consistent with its view in People *v.* Havnor, the New York court of appeals affirmed a legislative order issued nearly twenty years later (1913) for the general extension of the day-of-rest provision to employees in factories and mercantile establishments. Judge Hiscock, for the court explained:

> The doctrine that personal liberty must yield to what is supposed to be the public welfare has not waned any during recent years, and if the statute now before us comes within the principles which sanction and regulate such legislation it is not subject to the attack made upon its constitutionality. . . . Our only inquiry must be . . . whether it can fairly be believed that its [the statute's] natural consequences will be in the direction of betterment of public health and welfare, and, therefore, that it is one which the state for its protection and advantage may enact and enforce. It seems to me very clear that we may answer that it is such an one. . . .

Judge Hiscock then bore admirable witness to what seems a growing conviction that protective laws for women and children may also be necessary for men:

> The laws which have been passed and sustained with general approval in almost every jurisdiction limiting the hours of labor for women and children and for those engaged in especially trying employments, such as mining and operation of the railroads, amply testify to the widespread belief that in certain fields the

public health and welfare are subserved by generous opportunities for relaxation and recuperation. A constantly increasing study of industrial conditions I believe leads to the conviction that the health, happiness, intelligence and efficiency even of an adult man laboring in such employments as those mentioned in this statute will be increased by a reasonable opportunity for rest, for outdoor life and recreation, for attention to his own affairs, and, if he will, study and education.

Dwelling upon the relative jurisdiction of court and legislature, the Judge continued:

Then we come to the question what is a reasonable opportunity, and within wide limits that problem is for the legislature. Anybody would probably say that one day in thirty or sixty would be too little and one day in each two days extravagant. Between these extremes none can safely assert that the mean adopted by the legislature of one day in seven is unreasonable.[1]

This act has the distinction of being the only one-day-of-rest-in-seven act of general application that has been contested in a higher court.[2] It is even more notable, as it stands in contrast to an earlier invalidation of a rest-day act by the supreme court of Missouri, whose decision was based upon the reasoning of the Federal Supreme Court in regard to limiting hours of bakers in New York State, an act which the New York court had affirmed.

The grounds for the adverse decision in the Missouri case were not new:

We think that a law like the one before us involves neither

[1] People *v.* Klinck Packing Co., 214 N. Y. 121 (1915), sustaining the decision of the appellate division in 164 App. Div. 97.

[2] Commons & Andrews, *Principles of Labor Legislation*, p. 283. The Minnesota one-day-of-rest-in-seven law has recently been declared unconstitutional in a lower court because of the many exceptions it afforded: State *v.* Rand, district court, fourth judicial district, Minnesota, September 9, 1924. See 6 Law and Labor 300.

the safety, the morals nor the welfare of the public, and that the interest of the public is not in the slightest degree affected by such an act. The law must be upheld, if at all, as a law pertaining to the health of the individual engaged in the occupation of a baker. . . . Clean and wholesome bread does not depend upon whether the baker works but ten hours per day or only sixty hours a week. . . . The case at bar falls directly within the rules announced in the Lochner case.[1]

And as the Supreme Court of the United States would have jurisdiction over this case, the principles heretofore announced by the Supreme Court " furnish a rule to govern as well as to guide, hence it follows that the Lochner case must be treated as decisive." [2]

Thus in pronouncing invalid the one-day-in-seven legislation, the Missouri court, in 1909, followed the reasoning of the United States Supreme Court, in 1905, regarding the hours of New York bakers, as well as of the New York court of more than twenty years before regarding tenement house cigar manufacture. Nevertheless this decision in Missouri failed to stand as precedent for New York, in 1913, when the rest-day legislation was challenged there, and so far the affirmance of the New York court has not been appealed from.

EXTRA HAZARDOUS INDUSTRIES

Hours of Labor

Parallel with the contests in tribunals over the restriction of working times to give a weekly day of rest, began the series of appeals from the fiat of legislatures in their effort to protect men from being employed an excessive number of hours in extra-hazardous industries. With one exception these statutes were affirmed by state courts. And the

[1] Discussed, *infra*, p. 41.

[2] State *v.* Miksicek, 225 Mo. 561 (1909).

affirmance of the Utah decision by the United States Supreme Court marked growing sensitiveness to an economic demand on the part of the judiciary which proved to be as enduring as it was unequivocal.

1. *Mines*

The congeries of cases in respect to hours worked in hazardous industries began with that of Utah in 1896,[1] in review of an act passed in March of that year limiting the hours of men in mines, smelters, and ore-reduction works to to eight a day. Utah had been admitted to statehood in January and with foresight as to the growing needs of industrial workers for state protection, she had expressly included in her constitution an article applying specifically to labor. Thus when the supreme court of the state was asked to pronounce judgment upon the validity of this shortened day, the decision came promptly that the act was constitutional. Two years later, the decision was appealed from to the nation's highest tribunal, and sustained with but two justices dissenting.

The reasoning of the Federal Supreme Court evidenced an appreciation of the peculiar need of protection of underground workers for the preservation of public health and morals as well as of life:

> The enactment does not profess to limit the hours of all workmen, but merely those who are employed in underground mines, or in the smelting, reduction or refining of ores or metals. These employments, when too long pursued, the legislature has judged to be detrimental to the health of the employés, and, so long as there are reasonable grounds for believing that this is so, its decision upon this subject cannot be reviewed by the Federal courts. . . .
>
> But if it be within the power of the legislature to adopt such means for the protection of the lives of its citizens, it is difficult

[1] Holden *v.* Hardy, 14 Utah 71 (1896).

to see why precautions may not also be adopted for the protection of their health and morals. It is as much for the interest of the State that the public should be preserved as that life should be made secure. . . .

Upon the principles above stated, we think the act in question may be sustained as a valid exercise of the police power of the State. . . .

And continuing, the judges showed a clear recognition of an inequality of bargaining power between employer and employee which forms the cardinal reason for labor legislation.

The legislature has also recognized the fact, which the experience of legislators in many States has corroborated, that the proprietors of these establishments and their operatives do not stand upon an equality, and that their interests are, to a certain extent, conflicting. The former naturally desire to obtain as much labor as possible from their employés, while the latter are often induced by the fear of discharge to conform to regulations which their judgment, fairly exercised, would pronounce to be detrimental to their health or strength. In other words, the proprietors lay down the rules and the laborers are practically constrained to obey them. In such cases self-interest is often an unsafe guide, and the legislature may properly interpose its authority . . . or where the public health demands that one party to the contract shall be protected against himself. "The State still retains an interest in his welfare, however reckless he may be. The whole is no greater than the sum of all the parts, and when the individual health, safety and welfare are sacrificed or neglected, the State must suffer." . . .

The question in each case is whether the legislature has adopted the statute in exercise of a reasonable discretion, or whether its action be a mere excuse for an unjust discrimination, or the oppression, or spoliation of a particular class.[1]

This was not considered to be true of the case in point.

[1] Holden *v.* Hardy, 169 U. S. 366 (1898).

Here, as in the instance of the barbers, with the realization of the unequal bargain together with an intelligently directed aim for public benefit, the court passed over "from the theory of class legislation to the theory of reasonable classification. . . . That which is class legislation at one time may become reasonable classification at a later time, if the court perceives that what it once thought was equality is really inequality and what it once thought was merely private benefit is also public benefit." [1] This decision not only manifested a knowledge of economic conditions in mines, but it also recognized a need for reinterpretation of the constitution in respect to private property which it is our will to protect. For the institution of private property in modern society, in the wide scope of its present meaning is a conception alien to that of society before the Industrial Revolution.[2]

Three other decisions relating to restrictive hour laws for miners were handed down in the next five years—two favorable and one unfavorable. In the year following the decisive document in Holden *v.* Hardy, the supreme court of Colorado pronounced the death sentence upon a practically identical act with unfaltering voice.[3] Immune to the reasoning of the federal tribunal, the jurists appeared curiously sympathetic with the mind of the New York court of the middle eighties! How familiar is the sound:

> Indeed, the only object that can rationally be claimed for it [the statute] is the preservation of the health of those working in the smelters. Were the object of the act to protect the public

[1] Commons and Andrews, *op. cit.*, p. 30 (1920).

[2] With this new recognition of a less new need, it would seem that a judicial mile-post had been reached from which there would be no movement backwards. But it is well to keep in mind that the decision had not been unanimous and that the dissenting minority became the leading majority in an important case seven years later, viz., Lochner *v.* New York, 198 U. S. 45, *infra*, p. 42.

[3] *Re* Morgan, 26 Colo. 415 (1899).

health, and its provisions reasonably appropriate to that end, it might be sustained; for in such a case even the constitutional right of contract may be reasonably limited. But the act before us is not of that character. In selecting a subject for the exercise of the police power the legislature must keep within its true scope. The reason for the existence of the power rests upon the theory that one must so use his own as not to injure others, and so as not to interfere with, or injure, the public health, safety, morals or general welfare. How can one be said injuriously to affect others, or interfere with these great objects, by doing an act which confessedly visits its consequences on himself alone? And how can an alleged law, that purports to be the result of an exercise of the police power, be such in reality, when it has for its only object, not the protection of others or the public health, safety, morals or general welfare, but the welfare of him whose act is prohibited, when, if committed, it will injure him who commits it, and him only? . . .

As if to outwit the reasoning of the New York judges in the early case, the argument was reduced to an absurdity:

If, to protect the health of workmen engaged in these two [mining and smelting] occupations, the legislature may limit them to eight hours' per day, it may hereafter, upon the ground that idleness, resulting from short hours of labor, leads to drunkenness and gambling; and industry, promoted by longer hours, to happiness and health, enact that workmen must labor at these occupations fourteen or sixteen hours per day. . . .

The Colorado course was the only detour, however, in this straight advance of the judiciary, for the Missouri and Nevada courts followed closely in the path of Holden *v.* Hardy. The Missouri court, decrying the refusal of some jurists to observe facts pertinent to the case in hand which experts had submitted for their use, commented,

If the constitutionality of all laws enacted for the protection of public health and safety can be assailed in this manner, truly and sadly would it be declared that our laws rest upon a very weak and unstable foundation.[1]

The court of Nevada continued:

While we are not forgetful of the important rights and constitutional guarantees of the individual, they are, at the most, only branches of the common tree, while the welfare of the state, which includes the protection of the health and lives of the people in their various industrial pursuits, is the trunk, without which the tree could not stand or bear fruit. The public good and the health of a considerable portion of our population, when placed in the balance, must outweigh and turn the scale, regardless of slight inconveniences and reasonable restrictions which individuals may suffer. . . .

We cannot close our eyes and deny that employment in the places named in the statute is unhealthful. . . .[2]

And here is cited expert testimony, foreshadowing the high importance attached to scientific facts relative to health presented by counsel in recent years.

2. *Railroads*

Regulative acts applying to railway employees also have been upheld by the courts for the most part on the grounds of giving needed protection in an extra-hazardous industry. Protection to the traveling public cannot be assured independently of the physical welfare of employees connected with the running of trains. This was the import of a decision of the United States Supreme Court in 1911.[3] In spite of this, New York's eight-hour day for train despatchers, approved by the state court, was declared void by the Federal Supreme Court in 1914.[4] The New York judiciary

[1] State *v.* Cantwell, 179 Mo. 245 (1903).

[2] *Re* Boyce, 27 Nev. 299 (1904).

[3] Baltimore & Ohio Ry. *v.* I. C. C., 221 U. S. 612 (1911).

[4] People *v.* Erie R. R. Co., 198 N. Y. 369 (1910); Erie R. R. Co. *v.* New York, 233 U. S. 671 (1914).

had declared the act " simply supplemented " the act of Congress prescribing a nine-hour day as " a general minimum limit of safety applicable to average conditions throughout the country." The federal judiciary in sustaining the dignity of its position held that the federal act " admits of no supplement " and " when Congress acts in such a way as to manifest its purpose to exercise its constitutional authority, the regulating power of the state ceases to exist." Following this settlement of a jurisdictional dispute, the New York provision for twenty-four hours of rest for trainmen twice a month without reduction of pay, was declared invalid by the state appellate division. The dictum was that " there can be no valid state legislation covering the same field where the federal authority has asserted its right to act." [1]

The decision of the United States Supreme Court in 1917 [2] validating the Adamson law is the latest important ruling regarding the hours of this industrial group. This was an emergency act to preserve interstate commerce, however, rather than to limit hours for the greater safety of workmen and travelers. The result was to be found more in a substantial increase in earnings than in the reduction of hours. Four justices dissented from the opinion of the majority.

NON-HAZARDOUS INDUSTRIES

Hours of Labor

The progress in the courts of general laws restricting the hours of labor of adults in employments considered non-hazardous has been halting and indecisive. A number of such laws applying to various industries have been enacted in the several states, but many have not been taken seriously and where they have been subjected to court review more

[1] People *v.* New York Central and H. R. R. R. Co., 163 App. Div. 79 (1914).

[2] Wilson *v.* New, 243 U. S. 332.

have been annulled than affirmed. The two instances in which far-reaching acts that limit the working hours of adults have passed through the judicial fire and emerged living are those of Mississippi and Oregon in 1912 and 1914, the latter having survived action by the United State Supreme Court.[1] A brief judicial history of this type of legislation will serve to show its character.

The Nebraska legislature passed an act in 1891 placing a severe economic penalty upon the employers of mechanics and laborers (including all but farm and domestic labor) who permit more than eight hours of work a day. The supreme court of the state declared the statute unconstitutional as being both class legislation and interference with the freedom of contract,[2] and this decision has remained final for Nebraska.

The judicial story of the New York bakers has become as well known as that of the Utah miners, though from the point of view of epoch-making legislative history, not so classic. Lochner, proprietor of a bakery, violated the act of 1896 that restricted the number of hours in bakeries and confectionery establishments to ten a day and sixty a week. Carried first into the lower and then into the higher courts of the state, the act was declared constitutional as a health measure under the police power.[3] The law was the subject of vehement discussion by the justices of the court of appeals, and authorities were quoted on the nature and causes of phthisis in elaboration of grounds for sustaining the act. The opinion of Justice J. Vann may be quoted in part to give the spirit of the majority:

While the mortality among those who breathe air filled with minute particles of flour is less than among those who work in

[1] Bunting *v.* State of Oregon, 243 U. S. 426 (1917), *infra*, p. 48.

[2] Low *v.* Rees Printing Co., 41 Neb. 127 (1894).

[3] People *v.* Lochner, 177 N. Y. 145 (1904).

stone, metal or clay, still it seems to be demonstrated that it is greater than in avocations generally. . . . The evidence while not uniform leads to the conclusion that the occupation of a baker or confectioner is unhealthy and tends to result in diseases of the respiratory organs. As statutes are valid which provide that women or children shall not be employed in any manufacturing establishment more than a certain number of hours in a single day, so I think an act is valid which provides that in an employment which the legislature deems, and which is in fact, to some extent detrimental to health, no person, regardless of age or sex, shall be permitted or required to labor more than a certain number of hours per day or week. Such legislation, under such circumstances, is a health law and is a valid exercise of the police power.[1]

From the decision of the state court the case was appealed to the Supreme Court of the United States where it was finally declared violative of the Fourteenth Amendment by a five to four decision. An excerpt from the majority opinion characterizes the prevailing attitude:

Clean and wholesome bread does not depend upon whether the baker works but ten hours per day or only sixty hours a week. . . . The act is not, within any fair meaning of the term, a health law, but is an illegal interference with the rights of individuals, both employers and employés, to make contracts regarding labor upon such terms as they may think best, or which they may agree upon with the other parties to such contracts. Statutes of the nature of that under review, limiting the hours in which grown and intelligent men may labor to earn their living, are mere meddlesome interferences with the right of the individual. . . .[2]

Perhaps there has been no important decision of a high court on a labor law that has brought down as much un-

[1] People *v.* Lochner, 177 N. Y. 145 (1904).

[2] Lochner *v.* People of the State of New York, 198 U. S. 45 (1905).

favorable comment by the legal profession as this one relating to bakers in New York, coming as it did but seven years after the more liberal views of the same tribunal in Holden *v.* Hardy.[1] Severe disapproval appeared in law journals as well as in the press. Sir Frederick Pollock asked from England after declaring the Supreme Court to have overstepped its province, how can the Supreme Court at Washington have conclusive judicial knowledge of the conditions affecting bakeries in New York?[2] Professor Ernst Freund pronounced the decision "a serious check" to the advance of labor legislation and regretted that the Supreme Court "should have deemed it proper to impugn the good faith of the state legislature." He reminds us that this is an unprecedented invasion into the affairs of state courts and legislatures in a case not involving interstate relations, enforcing "a constitutional right of liberty of contract against the exercise of the police power on the part of the state, in opposition to the judgment of the courts of that state that such power was legitimately exercised."[3]

The court implied no economic basis for its decree—that

[1] It is pertinent to analyse the source of the opinion. Justice Peckham now spoke for the majority of the bench although he had been one of the two vociferous dissenters from the favorable ruling on the Utah eight-hour law for miners. Also, two justices who helped form the majority in the Utah case now joined the majority in the Lochner case (Justices Brown and the Chief Justice). Moreover, Groat informs us that a "count of judges of the various courts which passed upon the case shows that the total number was twenty-two. Of these, twelve cast their vote in favor of the validity of the law. In the final hearing by the United States supreme court the decision was carried by a majority of one vote only. The closeness of the decision indicates how near to the borderline the principles involved really were." G. G. Groat, *Attitude of American Courts in Labor Cases*, pp. 331-312 (1911).

[2] Sir Frederick Pollock, "The New York Labour Law and the Fourteenth Amendment," 21 Law Quart. Rev. 211.

[3] Ernst Freund, "Limitation of Hours of Labor and the Federal Supreme Court," 17 Green Bag 411-417.

the reduced number of hours worked would endanger profits or the supply of bread. But its decision rested upon the impairment of the liberty of contract by the limitation of hours where health and safety are not in jeopardy. And yet, it may be recalled, the sanction of this highest tribunal of the eight-hour law for employees in mines had in view, not immediate health and safety, but a social aim,—recognition of the need for a better standard of living with all that such a standard connotes. A dissenting opinion, driving home his understanding of the function of laws and of courts, was given at length by Mr. Justice Holmes:

> I think that the word liberty in the Fourteenth Amendment is perverted when it is held to prevent the natural outcome of a dominant opinion, unless it can be said that a rational and fair man necessarily would admit that the statute proposed would infringe fundamental principles as they have been understood by the traditions of our people and our law. It does not need research to show that no such sweeping condemnation can be passed upon the statute before us. A reasonable man might think it a proper measure on the score of health. Men whom I certainly could not pronounce unreasonable would uphold it as a first instalment of a general regulation of the hours of work. . . . .
>
> Some of these laws embody convictions or prejudices which judges are likely to share. Some may not. But a constitution is not intended to embody a particular economic theory, whether of paternalism and the organic relation of the citizen to the State or of *laissez faire*. It is made for people of fundamentally differing views, and the accident of our finding certain opinions natural or familiar or novel and even shocking ought not to conclude our judgment upon the question whether statutes embodying them conflict with the Constitution of the United States.

Doubtless this far-famed decision, from which Mr. Justice Holmes had sharply dissented and which was in exact opposition to what had appeared to be the direction social legislation was taking, has dampened the faith of industrial workers in the efficacy of laws and has engendered a growing hostility to the courts. It has forced doubt among all concerned of the power of their legislatures to act for their economic and social interest.

As if to vindicate the New York state courts in their affirmance of protection for bakers, and to criticize the reversal of the Federal Supreme Court, came the judicial sanction in Mississippi in 1912 of a law limiting the hours of employees in establishments of manufacture and repair. Moreover, this decision was reaffirmed after a rehearing in the following year. The constitutional basis for the affirmance was that legislatures of the states have the right under their exercise of the police power to enact proper laws to regulate and provide for the "safety, the health, the morals, and the general welfare of the public."

It is well known that, in the work connected with the running of machinery, the operator is subjected to a mental as well as physical strain. In many cases the nearness to machinery makes the work dangerous in case of an overtaxing of the strength of the worker, or any lessening in his alertness. . . . [And furthermore] it would not be unreasonable for the legislature to decide that it would promote the health, peace, morals and general welfare of all laborers engaged in the work of manufacturing or repairing if they were not permitted to extend their labor over ten hours a day, and the legislature could also decide that the best interests of the people in the state would be promoted by limiting the time of work of this numerous class of its citizenry to the time mentioned. In fact, when we consider the present manner of laboring, the use of machinery, the appliances, requiring intelligence and skill, and the general present day manner of life, which tends to nervousness, it seems to us quite reasonable, and in no way improper, to pass such law so limiting a day's labor.[1]

[1] State *v.* J. J. Newman Lumber Co., 102 Miss. 802 (1912) and 103 Miss. 263 (1912).

The Mississippi courts, upon rehearing the argument, advanced the novel idea that "Some day, perhaps, the inalienable right to rest will be the subject of litigation." This thought came with the court's observation "that it is rare for the seller of labor to appeal to the courts for the preservation of his inalienable rights of labor. This inestimable privilege is generally the object of the buyer's disinterested solicitude." A similar implication in Holden *v.* Hardy was that "the argument would certainly come with better grace and greater cogency from the latter class [the laborers]."

The decision of the Mississippi court remained unchallenged so that it was not carried to the Federal Supreme Court. Moreover the spirit of this decree lived and prevailed among the judiciary of the state of Oregon in the following year.[1]

Thus in 1914 the Oregon court sustained a ten-hour law for employees in factories.[2] Justice Cooley, delivering the opinion of the majority, said,

> Obviously, in addition to the reasons declared in the law, it was in the legislative mind that the regular employment of persons for longer hours in factories where different kinds of machinery and facilities are operated under the present-day high pressure power would tend to increase danger of accidents, and to a greater extent jeopardize life and limb, thereby increasing demand for compensation for such injuries, a portion of which under certain circumstances would be borne by the State . . . here (referring to the act) mills and factories in which machinery is used are classed as places of hazardous occupations.[3]

[1] In Louisiana in 1913 a law which limited work to eight hours a day for stationary firemen was declared unconstitutional. (State *v.* Barba, 132 La. 768). The basis for invalidation was class legislation and violation of freedom of contract.

[2] Three and one-half hours overtime was allowed for extra pay.

[3] State *v.* Bunting, 71 Ore. 259 (1914).

Just as workmen's compensation acts stimulated the "safety first" movement as they were introduced into the several states, here is the further pressure of responsibility upon industrial employers giving a fillip to the movement for a shorter day. The court continues in its appreciation of the needs of a better society:

A certain minimum of physical well-being is necessary in order that social life may exist, the usefulness and intelligence of the citizens be increased, and the progress of civilization accelerated: Freund, Police Power, §§ 8, 10 . . . The required minimum of well-being varies in different periods, but rises with advancing civilization until it includes a certain standard of comfort . . . it is an undeniable fact that prolonged and excessive physical labor is performed at the expense of the mental powers, and it requires no argument to show that a man who day in and day out labors more than 10 hours must not only deteriorate physically, but mentally. The safety of a country depends upon the intelligence of its citizens, and if our institutions are to be preserved and (*sic*) the state must see to it that the citizen shall have some leisure which he may employ in fitting himself for those duties which are the highest attributes of good citizenship. . . . In view of the well-known fact that the custom in our industries does not sanction a longer service than 10 hours per day, it cannot be held, as a matter of law, that the legislative requirement is unreasonable or arbitrary as to hours of labor. . . . It is urged . . . that if it is possible for the legislature to make the declaration that to work in a factory more than ten hours in one day is injurious to the health, then that body can make four hours a day's work, and require two hours of the work to be performed before 8 o'clock A. M. It is sufficient to say that the question of four hours constituting a day's labor, or when any part of it shall be done, is not now before this court.

Following this decision, suit was brought before the United States Supreme Court on writ of error from the supreme court of Oregon. The case was argued in April,

1916, restored to docket for re-argument in June 1916, and re-argued in January, 1917. In the following April, the affirmation of the state court decision was made in the case of Bunting *v.* Oregon, Justice McKenna delivering the opinion for the majority. This case was notable in that the judgment of the court was reached as a result of the commanding weight of counsel's brief (prepared by Mr. Louis D. Brandeis and Miss Josephine Goldmark). A systematic review of scientific evidence amounting to more than a thousand pages was presented to show the effects of overwork upon the physical and moral health of the worker and thus upon the welfare and prosperity of the nation.[1]

In the opinion of the court in this case, conscious recognition was made of the importance and power of facts:

The subject is one for scientific scrutiny and critique, for authoritative interpretation of accredited facts. To this end science has been devoted all over the world. Particularly in the last decade science has been giving us the basis for judgment by experience to which, when furnished, judgment by speculation must yield. . . . It is now demonstrable that the considerations that were patent as to miners in 1898 are today operative, to a greater or less degree, throughout the industrial system. . . . Inasmuch as the application of the contending principles must vary with the facts to which they are sought to be applied, of course new facts are the indispensable basis to the determination of the validity of specific new legislation. . . . .

New policies are usually tentative in their beginnings, advance

[1] It may be noted in passing however, that, successful as it was and although more than six years have elapsed since its occurrence, this is probably the only instance in this country where evidence of this sort has been used in favor of a statute for the protection of men in non-hazardous industries. (The case of the New York bakers is perhaps a partial exception.) On the other hand, care has been given repeatedly by the advocates of special laws for women to present reasons why such laws should be upheld by the courts and the result has been that these laws have been more frequently sustained.

in firmness as they advance in acceptance. They do not at a particular moment of time spring full-perfect in extent or means from the legislative brain. Time may be necessary to fashion them to precedent customs and conditions and as they justify themselves or otherwise they pass from militancy to triumph or from question to repeal. But passing general considerations and coming back to our immediate concern, which is the validity of the particular exertion of power in the Oregon law, our judgment of it is that it does not transcend constitutional limits.[1]

Justice McKenna explained that, while it is not binding upon the court to accede to the statute as a matter within the state's police power, "there is no reason to question the sincerity of the legislature and impute to its members the intent to cloak beneath ordinary words an illegal and sinister design."

This decision remains powerful in the recent history of labor legislation. It would seem to be the crystallization of slowly accumulating conviction in favor of protective hour-laws for employees regardless of sex or age.[2] As such, it is a remarkable encouragement to those who still see a need for further application of its principles.

An interesting example of the failure to carry on these principles of legislation regardless of sex occurred in the territory of Alaska in 1918. In 1917 (Ch. 55) a law was

[1] Bunting *v.* Oregon, 243 U. S. 426 (1916-1917).

[2] The supreme judicial court of Massachusetts annulled a nine-hour act for baggagemen at railroad stations in 1915. (Commonwealth *v.* Boston & Maine Rr., 110 N. E. 264). The decision against a shorter day for the New York bakers was cited as precedent, and the statute was declared to be "an illegal interference with the rights of individuals, both employers and employees, to contract freely and therefore void." This ruling occurred prior to the federal decree in the Oregon case however, and it followed an argument unsupported by statistical or other data. It is of course impossible to tell whether the decision would have been different otherwise, but there seems an even chance that it would have been.

enacted by the Alaska legislature limiting to eight hours the working time of all wage earners and salary earners in the territory "except in cases where life and property is in imminent danger," with penalty for violation. This act was passed with peculiar assurance on the part of the legislature as a result of its having received the expressed favor of a large majority of the people in a referendum vote. Provision had been made for the referendum by special legislative act two years before.

When the supreme court of the territory reviewed the act upon complaint of violation thereof, it refused to declare it valid chiefly on technical grounds. The charge was that there was no provision in the "Organic Act" [the constitution] for obtaining expression from the people regarding proposed legislation, and thus the act of 1915 was "wholly unauthorized" and should not be presumed to bind the courts. Aside from this and other technicalities the court dwelt upon the weakness of the act in its failure to state the reasons for which it was passed. In neither title nor body was it premised "upon any theory that labor of all kinds is injurious to health and dangerous to life and limb," nor that "more than eight hours is inimical to the peace of society or morals of the people, a menace to the cause of education or generally antagonistic to the welfare of the community." [1]

Comparing the Oregon act, as judicially affirmed, with the case in point, the court said, "this act is as different from the act in question as daylight is from darkness." In that case the action was based upon the exercise of the police power of the state and beneficial laws of this sort are rightly upheld by the courts. "But this does not mean that it is fundamentally correct to say that every man, irrespective of the nature of the work he follows, shall be precluded from selling more than eight hours of his labor in any one day

[1] U. S. *v.* Northern Commercial Co. *et al.*, 6 Alaska Reports 94 (1918).

except in cases of emergency." "If a law is needed in any other industry," the court continued [a protective measure for miners was already in operation], let the premises be stated and its enactment be another step in our onward march toward the betterment of social and economic conditions." But it is not possible to take teamsters, fishermen, cooks and other kinds of laborers and "bind them in the same bundle." The case of Lochner *v.* New York was cited therefore, and the act was declared a breach of the right of freedom of contract.

Thus the Alaskan court appeared ready to receive social and economic enlightenment concerning the need of protective legislation. The act failed to pass the constitutional test primarily not because it interfered with liberty and property rights, but because it was not presented in customary form and with sufficient proof of its desirability. Here then is further encouragement to those who would shorten the working day, with scientific facts as a basis for their program.

PUBLIC EMPLOYEES

Wages and Hours of Labor

Modern judicial interpretation regarding restrictive laws for public employees has developed favorably. New York State has a history all her own in this respect. Decisions adverse to statutory regulations of hours and wages of laborers on public works (those employed by the state or municipality or by contractors for public work) was rendered in 1901.[1] Another unfavorable opinion followed in 1903[2] and a fourth in 1904. The grounds of invalidity were that

[1] People *ex rel.* Rodgers *v.* Coler, 166 N. Y. 1; Treat *v.* Coler, 166 N. Y. 144.

[2] People *v.* Orange Road Construction Co., 175 N. Y. 84 (1903); People *ex rel.* Cossey *v.* Grout, 179 N. Y. 417 (1904).

the laws were an "unconstitutional interference by the legislature with the right of the municipality" or state in the matters of hours and wages—that the acts had no relation to the public health, morals, or order. In 1905 a constitutional amendment was adopted taking effect January 1, 1906, enabling the legislature to regulate and fix wages, hours and protection of public employees for the welfare and safety of the people. An act passed the next year, reinstating the invalidated provisions, received sanction by the court in October, 1908,[1] first by the appellate division of the supreme court, and then by the court of appeals. No further appeal was made and the law stands to-day upon this decision.

Kansas laws relating to public employees were also contested in the courts at the beginning of the century. The decisions were uniformly favorable—two in the courts of the state and one carried to the United States Supreme Court.[2] In Ohio a similar measure was declared unconstitutional in 1902.[3]

Since the favorable action of the Federal Court in the Kansas case there has been little challenging of the right of the state legislatures to enact statutes controlling the work of these classes of employees. Constitutionality is not so much awarded on the grounds of an exercise of the police power as on the grounds of the right of the government as an employer.

WORKMEN'S COMPENSATION

Cases testing the constitutionality of workmen's compensation laws compose the most recent species of litigation concerning protective legislation for all industrial workers, and

[1] People *v.* Metz, 193 N. Y. 148.

[2] *Re* Dalton, 61 Kan. 275 (1899): State *v.* Atkin, 64 Kan. 174 (1902); Atkin *v.* Kansas, 191 U. S. 207 (1903).

[3] Cleveland *v.* Construction Co., 67 Ohio 197 (1902).

the courts have generally favored this type of protection. The experience of New York and Washington states will be presented because it is more extensive.

As the first commonwealth in this country to enact compensation legislation to apply generally to industrial workmen, the New York court was also first to pronounce judgment thereon. And the judgment was adverse. The act had been passed in 1910 as an outgrowth of an organized investigation [1] into the facts of industrial accidents, but the opinion of the state's highest tribunal was that the constitution of the state could not be interpreted to justify a provision of this sort. The document presented by the majority was written by Justice Werner annulling the award on the grounds that it was repugnant both to the Fourteenth Amendment of the Federal Constitution and to the state constitution. The case of Noble State Bank *v.* Haskell was cited in defense of the act in which the Federal Supreme Court sustained an Oklahoma statute that required compulsory contribution by banks to a fund for the guarantee of deposits.[2] Justice Werner declared however, that "we cannot recognize them [the Noble Bank case and one other [3]] as controlling of our construction of our Constitution" even though they were thought "to be greatly and immediately necessary to the public welfare." Continuing with his comparison of the two cases, the justice said:

How far these late decisions of the Federal Supreme Court are to be regarded as committing that tribunal to the doctrine that any citizen may be deprived of his private property for the public welfare we are not prepared to decide. All that it is

[1] The Wainwright Commission was a creature of the legislature provided by law of 1909 (chap. 518) and named after Senator Wainwright, chairman.

[2] Noble St. Bk. *v.* Haskell, 219 U. S. 104 (1911).

[3] Assaria State Bank *v.* Dalley, 219 U. S. 121 (1910).

necessary to affirm in the case before us is that in our view of the Constitution of our state, the liability sought to be imposed upon the employers enumerated in the statute before us is a taking of property without due process of law, and the statute is therefore void.[1]

Following this rebuff from the judiciary, a special enabling amendment to the state constitution was adopted in 1913, and a new compensation law was enacted in the following year. In 1915 the new statute was carried into the court for testing. The court of appeals again heard the argument and delivered the opinion—this time a favorable opinion declaring the act to be fundamentally fair to both employer and employee. In view of the discussion of the Noble Bank case in the first instance when the compensation act was declared void, it is peculiarly interesting to find the same case cited at this time in connection with the judicial approval of the law. In declaring the opinion for the court, Judge Miller said in part:

This subject should be viewed in the light of modern conditions, not those under which the common-law doctrines were developed. . . . Surely it is competent for the state in the promotion of the general welfare to require both employer and employee to yield something toward the establishment of a principle and plan of compensation for their mutual protection and advantage. . . . The act now before us seems to be fundamentally fair to both employer and employee. . . . It is plainly justified by the amendment to our own State Constitution and the decisions of the United States Supreme Court, notably in the *Noble State Bank* case,[2] make it reasonably certain that it will be found by that court not to be violative of the Constitution of the United States.[3]

[1] Ives *v.* South Buffalo Ry. Co., 201 N. Y. 271 (1911).

[2] Noble St. Bk. *v.* Haskell, 219 U. S. 104 (1911).

[3] Jensen *v.* So. Pac. Co., 215 N. Y. 514 (1915).

The New York judiciary sensed correctly the attitude of the United States Supreme Court as it was expressed twice on the same day upon the acts of New York and Washington.[1] The New York case had been appealed on writ of error from the supreme court, appellate division, and from the court of appeals, as an illegal taking of property and denial of equal protection of the laws. The Federal Supreme Court recalled Holden *v.* Hardy in delivering its opinion, "The whole is no greater than the sum of all the parts, and when the individual health, safety, and welfare are sacrificed or neglected the State must suffer." Compulsory compensation cannot be regarded therefore as repugnant to the Fourteenth Amendment. The provision of the legislature "prevents pauperism, with its concomitants of vice and crime." Exclusion of farm and domestic laborers cannot be judicially declared an arbitrary classification under the "equal protection" clause since "risks inherent in these occupations are exceptionally patent, simple, and familiar." The compulsory clause provides for four ways of insuring, for if the employer is solvent he may self-insure on reasonable terms (upon the deposit of securities). This option given the employer is not unfair to the employee "for there is no presumption that either [method of insuring] will prove inadequate to safeguard the employee's interests."

The Washington award was upheld by a divided bench, four justices dissenting. Mr. Justice Pitney referred to the decision in respect to the New York act as a precedent for compulsory contribution. But the Washington measure reached further—to a compulsory state fund. The state supreme court had held the act to be within the police power, the charges imposed being as a license tax upon occupation, a combined tax for revenue and regulation. The

[1] N. Y. Central R. R. *v.* White, 243 U. S. 188; Mountain Timber Co. *v.* Wash., 37 Sp. Ct. Rep. 260 (1917).

Federal Court sustained the validity of the award in a neutral statement that the burden of proof against it was on those who seek to overthrow it.

These two decisions by the court of last resort, upholding the farthest reach of compensation legislation, gave strength to favorable decisions in other states, and up to the present time the legality of workmen's compensation acts appears to be established.

SUMMARY

To summarize: The judicial interpretation of laws enacted for all persons in this country is fraught with conflict and inconsistency that tend to disguise the long-time movement in the mind of the judiciary. For example, while the New York court failed to recognize that abolition of cigar manufacture in insanitary tenement houses would lead to betterment of the public health, the same court later sanctioned the Sunday closing law for barbers as a health measure, as also did other state tribunals. Moreover, one-day-of-rest-in-seven legislation has been declared sufficiently conducive to public health to be approved. And although in court review of the wage-payment acts the concept of freedom of contract between employer and employee was considered, there also came into the judicial mind a sense of the possibility that the bargaining power between employer and employee may be unequal, and that interference by the state on behalf of the employee may therefore be warranted.

Furthermore there has developed an almost universal acceptance of restrictive measures in hazardous industries. This legislation is held to be valid on the ground that certain groups of workmen are especially in need of protection by nature of their employment. It is made clear however that this is not class legislation in the prejudicial sense of the word, but reasonable classification for both private and public benefit; that in a closely knit society public welfare depends upon private welfare, and that an individual may even need protection against himself for the good of the community in which he lives.

An extension of the meaning of hazardous employment also shows promising signs of development. In the case of the New York bakers, the state's high court held that the commonwealth should protect workers in employment which is "to some extent detrimental to health. . . . regardless of age or sex." When the Federal Supreme Court reversed this decision it brought down vehement criticism on both sides of the Atlantic ocean. In the constitutional test of the Oregon law that limits the hours of men, mills and factories were expressly declared to be "places of hazardous occupations" in which both individual and social vitality are impaired by excessive hours of labor.[1] The strain of modern industry upon machine-ridden workmen is thus recognized as one of the "new facts" which determine "the validity of specific new legislation." In the same vein, compulsory compensation for the disablement of workmen in industry is also declared a legitimate type of state protection,—"the whole is no greater than the sum of all the parts, and when the individual health, safety, and welfare are sacrificed or neglected the State must suffer."

Thus we may trace the slow growth of a new social concept concerning the rights of men in industry, challenged, at times defeated, but coming into fuller recognition as the weight of evidence grows.

PART II: LEGISLATION FOR WOMEN AS REVIEWED BY THE COURTS

Parallel in point of time to the conflict of decisions relating to the labor of adult employees generally, regardless of

[1] This was also the implied basis for the validity of the similar Mississippi law limiting the hours of men.

sex, has run another set of decisions relating specifically to the labor of women. The great body of these cases is concerned with the constitutional right to interfere in the contract for the hours of work and the wages of women because of their sex. In earlier years there was also some litigation over laws that entirely prohibited the employment of women. These will be considered first.

PROHIBITED EMPLOYMENT

Laws prohibiting the employment of women in specified occupations have seldom been contested in the courts. In three western states in the eighties, judicial interpretation was asked upon legislative exclusion of women employed where intoxicating liquors were sold. In California an act of this sort was declared void. The court held that the state constitution established

> as the permanent and settled rule and policy of this State, that there shall be no legislation either directly or indirectly incapacitating or disabling a woman from entering or pursuing any business, vocation, or profession permitted by law to be entered on and pursued by those sometimes designated as the stronger sex.[1]

A similar provision of the city of Cleveland, Ohio, was upheld by the state supreme court as not in violation of the Fourteenth Amendment. The power to regulate such places is expressly delegated to incorporated cities and villages and, the court held, is here properly exercised. The Washington court also affirmed a like statute in 1895:[2]

> There can be no doubt that this statute was contrived because the particular resorts where bar-maids and box-rustlers find regular employment, and may be found in habitual attend-

[1] *In re* Maguire, 57 Cal. 604 (1881).

[2] *In re* Considine, 83 Fed. Rep. 157.

ance, have offended the moral sensibilities of the people. . . . But the constitutionality of a law is not to be tested by questioning its efficacy. Whether well designed to accomplish the purpose intended or otherwise, the law is a police regulation, and clearly within the police power of the state, which has not been taken away by the fourteenth amendment.

HOURS OF LABOR—DAY WORK

In contrast to the absence of litigation in respect to forbidden employment of women, stands the elaborate structure of judicial opinion in respect to their hours and wages. Here are to be found some of the most extreme interpretations of both state and federal constitutions in the history of labor legislation.

Acts restricting the hours that women may work came among the early laws relating to labor and were early challenged. The supreme court of Massachusetts rendered the first important judgment of a state law in 1876, when it acceded to a ten-hour day and sixty-hour week as a maximum working time for women and children in any manufacturing establishment.[1] The issue appears to have puzzled the jurists, who adjudicated it on negative grounds rather than from any positive sense of its necessity. It was an absence of reason for not sustaining the act that resulted in the favorable decision written by Judge Lord:

There must be no doubt that such legislation may be maintained either as a health or police power regulation if it were necessary to resort to either of those powers. This principle has been so frequently recognized in the commonwealth that reference to the decisions is unnecessary . . . the law does not limit her [woman's] right to labor as many hours per day or per week as she may desire.

[1] Commonwealth *v.* Hamilton Mfg. Co., 120 Mass. 383 (1876).

But it prohibits her from working continuously for more than the specified time at factory work.[1]

This Massachusetts case stood by itself for nineteen years. In 1895, an eight-hour law for factory women in Illinois was argued and annulled by the state supreme court. The act was declared unconstitutional not only as class legislation, but also as an interference with the freedom of contract. The court held that sex alone will not justify the exercise of the police power for the purpose of limiting the right of a woman to make contracts.

> . . . It is not the nature of the things done, but the sex of the persons doing them, which is made the basis of the claim that the Act is a measure for the promotion of the public health. . . . There is no reasonable ground—at least none which has been made manifest to us in the arguments of counsel—for fixing upon eight hours in one day as the limit within which women can work without injury to her physique, and beyond which, if she work, injury will necessarily follow.[2]

The New York cigar-makers' case was cited by the court as precedent for its refusal to affirm the act.

The reversal of the spirit of this first Illinois decision was decreed fifteen years later by the same court in what is commonly known as "the second Ritchie case." [3] Here was given staunch judicial sanction to an act similar to that annulled in 1895, except that the limit of daily hours became ten instead of the earlier eight. It will be seen in the pages to follow that this reversal of the earlier annulment, follow-

[1] Professor Ernst Freund (*Police Power*, § 312) comments that the decision should have been interpreted as an intention to limit the hours of factory work only, leaving open the legislature's power to regulate hours of private work. The issue was not clear to say the least, but surprisingly enough it has frequently served as a precedent in subsequent cases.

[2] Ritchie *v.* People, 155 Ill. 98.

[3] Ritchie *v.* Wayman, 244 Ill. 509 (1910), *infra*, p. 68.

ing a federal sanction for the state of Oregon, came in a practically unbroken line of decisions favorable to the restriction of women's hours. The grounds gradually became uniform, namely,—the physical inferiority of women and their special grouping because of their potential motherhood.

To develop the story chronologically the superior court of Pennsylvania appears to have been the pioneer in this line of argument, since developed and elaborated upon with increasing care and precision. The act sustained by the Pennsylvania court was one limiting the hours of women to twelve a day and sixty a week. "Surely an act which prevents the mothers of our race from being tempted to endanger their life and health by exhaustive employment can be condemned by none save those who expect to profit by it,"[1] remarked the court, and the shorter day for public employees was referred to for precedent, as well as that for men on railroads,

> If such legislation savors of paternalism it is in its least objectionable form in that it cares for those who from their own necessities, ambition, or the cupidity of their employees, may be prompted or required to jeopardize their health in unreasonable and dangerous employment, which in the legislative judgment, founded upon statistical experience, injuriously affects their health, and hence the interests of the state itself . . . [Holden *v.* Hardy cited].

Then again the reasoning of the judges takes the new and specific turn,

> It is undisputed that some employments may be admissible for males and yet improper for females, and regulations recognizing and forbidding women to engage in such would be open to no reasonable objection. The same is true of young children whose employment in mines and manufactories is commonly, and ought always to be regulated. . . .

[1] Commonwealth *v.* Beatty, 15 Pa. Super. 5 (1900).

Sex imposes limitations to excessive or long continued physical labor as certainly as does minority, and the arrested development of children is no more dangerous to the state, than debilitating so large a class of our citizens as adult females by undue and unreasonable physical labor. . . .

Adult females are a class as distinct as minors, separated by natural conditions from all other laborers, and are so constituted as to be unable to endure physical exertion and exposure to the extent and degree that is not harmful to adult males. . . .

Here, then, is the beginning of a new judicial philosophy in respect to labor legislation, women being grouped by themselves or with children as a class in need of protection not needed by men.

Two more state judiciaries upheld hour laws for women in 1902.[1] And the reasoning of the courts was a continuation of that of the lower court of Pennsylvania. Judge Brown, writing from the Nebraska bench, justified the statute passed by the legislature in that " women and children have always, to a certain extent, been wards of the state," that women are subject to disabilities under the common law, limiting them in the right to contract, and withholding from them a voice in making laws which govern them.

[Women] are unable, by reason of their physical limitations, to endure the same hours of exhaustive labor as may be endured by adult males. Certain kinds of work which may be performed by men without injury to their health, would wreck the constitutions and destroy the health of women, and render them incapable of bearing their share of the burdens of the family and home. The state must be accorded the right to guard and protect women, as a class, against such a condition; and the law in question, to that extent, conserves the public health and welfare.

[1] Wenham *v.* State, 65 Neb. 394; State *v.* Buchanan, 29 Wash. 602.

And furthermore, the weaker bargaining power of labor was thought to be peculiar to women by Judge Brown as he continued:

. . . we may well declare a law unconstitutional which interferes with or abridges the right of adult males to contract with each other in any of the business affairs or vocations of life. The employer and the laborer are practically on an equal footing, but these observations do not apply to women and children. Of the many vocations in this country, comparatively few are open to women. Their field of remunerative labor is restricted. Competition for places therein, is necessarily great. The desire for place, and in many instances the necessity of obtaining employment, would subject them to hardships and exactions which they would not otherwise endure. The employer who seeks to obtain the most hours of labor, for the least wages, has such an advantage over them that the wisdom of the law, for their protection, cannot well be questioned. No doubt, these considerations were the moving cause for the passage of the law in question.

Judge Dunbar, speaking for the supreme court of the state of Washington (reversing a decision of the superior court of the state), directed his justification of the act specifically to its physiological importance,

It is a matter of universal knowledge with all reasonably intelligent people of the present age that continuous standing on the feet by women for a great many consecutive hours is deleterious to their health. It must logically follow that that which would deleteriously affect any great number of women who are the mothers of succeeding generations must necessarily affect the public welfare and the public morals. Law is, or ought to be, a progressive science. While the principles of justice are immutable, changing conditions of society and the evolution of employment make a change in the application of principles absolutely necessary to an intelligent administration of government. In the early history of the law, when employments were few and simple, the relative conditions of the citizen and the state were different, and many employments and uses which were then considered inalienable rights have since, from the very necessity of changed conditions, been subjected to legislative control, restriction, and restraint.[1]

The court said that this argument flows from the old announcement of Blackstone that man must surrender certain "natural rights" to society when he becomes a member of a group and has society's protection. Then the argument cites as examples of interference by society, government control of transportation companies, and the restriction and control of the practice of medicine. Anti-trust and usury laws might also have been added to the list.

Following upon these decisions of the judiciary came the ruling of the Oregon court in 1906 and its affirmance by the United States Supreme Court two years later, which marks the zenith of judicial reasoning in support of the limitation of hours for women as a class. The act under litigation was that passed by the Oregon legislature in 1903 declaring that "no female should be employed in any mechanical establishment or factory or laundry in this state more than ten hours during any one day." The state court cited as precedents, Commonwealth *v.* Hamilton of Massachusetts, Wenham *v.* State of Nebraska, and State *v.* Buchanan of Washington,[2] observing by the way that Illinois had declared such a law invalid. The act was then affirmed through Chief Justice Bean, with no further question as to the discretion of the legislature,

Such legislation must be taken as expressing the belief of the legislature, and through it of the people, that the labor of

[1] State *v.* Buchanan, 29 Wash. 602 (1902).

[2] Cited *supra.*

females in such establishments in excess of 10 hours in any one day is detrimental to health and injuriously affects the public welfare.[1]

The opinion of the Federal Supreme Court presented by Justice Brewer is familiar to those interested in this type of protective legislation. In spite of that familiarity, the relative importance of this case in the evalution of special protection for women makes it seem best to quote the reasoning at length:

That woman's physical structure and the performance of maternal functions place her at a disadvantage in the struggle for subsistence is obvious. This is especially true when the burdens of motherhood are upon her. Even when they are not, by abundant testimony of the medical fraternity continuance for a long time on her feet at work, repeating this from day to day, tends to injurious effects upon the body, and as healthy mothers are essential to vigorous offspring, the physical well-being of woman becomes an object of public interest and care in order to preserve the strength and vigor of the race.

Still again, history discloses the fact that woman has always been dependent upon man. He established his control at the outset by superior physical strength, and this control in various forms, with diminishing intensity, has continued to the present. . . . Education was long denied her . . . it is still true that in the struggle for subsistence she is not an equal competitor with her brother. Though limitations upon personal and contractual rights may be removed by legislation, there is that in her disposition and habits of life which will operate against a full assertion of those rights. She will still be where some legislation to protect her seems necessary to secure a real equality of right. Doubtless there are individual exceptions, and there are many respects in which she has an advantage over him; but looking at it from the viewpoint of the effort to maintain an independent position in life, she is not upon an equality. Differ-

[1] State *v.* Muller, 48 Oregon 252 (1906).

entiated by these matters from the other sex, she is properly placed in a class by herself, and legislation designed for her protection may be sustained, even when like legislation is not necessary for men, and could not be sustained. It is impossible to close one's eyes to the fact that she still looks to her brother and depends upon him. Even though all restrictions on political, personal and contractual rights were taken away, and she stood, so far as statutes are concerned, upon an absolutely equal plane with him, it would still be true that she is so constituted that she will rest upon and look to him for protection; that her physical structure and a proper discharge of her maternal functions—having in view not merely her own health, but the well-being of the race—justify legislation to protect her from the greed as well as the passion of man.

Summing up what he considered the differences in sex that form the basis of social legislation for women, Justice Brewer concludes:

The limitations which this statute places upon her contractual powers, upon her right to agree with her employer as to the time she shall labor, are not imposed solely for her benefit, but also largely for the benefit of all. Many words cannot make this plainer. The two sexes differ in structure of body, in the functions to be performed by each, in the amount of physical strength, in the capacity for long-continued labor, particularly when done standing, the influence of vigorous health upon the future well-being of the race, the self-reliance which enables one to assert full rights, and in the capacity to maintain the struggle for subsistence. This difference justifies a difference in legislation and upholds that which is designed to compensate for some of the burdens which rest upon her.[1]

It would seem that little remains unsaid in favor of legislation for the special protection of women in industrial work. Thus the argument as presented by Justice Brewer has stood

[1] Muller *v.* Oregon, 208 U. S. 412 (1908).

high and dominant over practically all other discussions of courts in cognate cases. Monumental also, was the preparation for the defence of this act. For the first time in a case of this kind, counsel's brief was weighted with statistical and explanatory data. The material dealt not only with the extent of long working hours of women in Oregon, but with the subject of the effects upon women—physiological, mental, and moral,—as a result of overwork. The brief was the first of those compiled by Mr. Louis D. Brandeis and Miss Josephine Goldmark, and came into standard use thereafter.[1]

Six important decisions validating acts that limit women's hours have been rendered by state and federal courts since 1908.[2] The second Ritchie case of Illinois, before mentioned, heads the list in its affirmance of the " Woman's Ten Hour Law of 1909 ". The court defended its position in reversing the spirit of its former decision, on two counts,—first, the reason of health was not advanced in 1895, and second, even now an eight-hour law would probably not receive judicial sanction whereas a ten-hour limitation may be considered valid. Mr. Felix Frankfurter, in commenting upon this self-defense of the court, writes,—" A heroic effort is made to distinguish the first Ritchie case from the second Ritchie case. It is true that one was an eight-hour law and the other a ten-hour law, but the two cases are, in fact, irreconcilable in their underlying point of view." [3]

Judge Learned Hand delivered the opinion of the Illinois court in this case. Citing the Oregon documents, he ex-

[1] It was a revision of this same brief which furnished the argument used before the supreme court of Illinois in its later testing of the ten-hour law.

[2] " The Women and Children Act " of Colorado passed in 1903 restricting the work day to eight hours in mill, factory, manufacturing establishment and store, was annulled in 1907 on technical grounds, 41 Colo. 496. The court held, however, that " the laundry business must be considered healthful " even if the court had had power to judge the issue.

[3] Felix Frankfurter, " Hours of Labor and Realism in Constitutional Law," *Harvard Law Review*, vol. xxix, no. 4, p. 356.

plained at length his view of the differences between men and women and the special need of guarding the health of women as mothers. In addition he argued,

The differences existing between the sexes has (*sic*) often formed the basis of a classification upon which to found legislation. It is this distinction, when used as a basis for legislation, which authorizes legislation exempting women from military and jury service and from working upon the public highways or working in mines, and which permits men to enjoy, alone, the elective franchise and to hold public office, and fixes their status as the head of the family in exemption and homestead laws.[1]

And here the justice uttered the oft-repeated phrase,

It is known to all men (and what we know as men we cannot profess to be ignorant of as judges) that woman's physical structure and the performance of maternal functions place her at a great disadvantage in life; that while a man can work for more than ten hours a day without injury to himself, a woman, especially when the burdens of motherhood are upon her, cannot. . . .

In 1912, the confectioners of New York State challenged the validity of the fifty-four-hour law for women in factories which exempted canneries. Class discrimination was alleged. But the court, turning for authority to decisions in other states, maintained the power of the legislature to decide in what employments there should be restriction on grounds of health. Judge Blackmar for the court, showed his recognition of the need of adjustment to industrial conditions in the following words:

The development of the industrial life of the nation, the pressure of women and children entering the industrial field in competition with men physically better qualified for the

[1] Ritchie & Co. *v.* Wayman, 244 Ill. 509 (1910).

struggle, has compelled them to submit to conditions and terms of service which it cannot be presumed they would freely choose. . . . .

Laws, which may be meddlesome interferences with the liberty of the individual in a primitive state, may, in a highly organized society, become essential to public welfare or even to the continuance of civil liberty.[1]

A Massachusetts ten-hour law, sustained by the state, was affirmed by the United States Supreme Court in 1914. Justice McKenna, speaking for the court, followed the well established doctrine that governs this type of enactment,

The legislation is purely a police regulation intended to establish the rights of children and women, who are treated as in a certain sense dependent and under an industrial disadvantage by reason of age and sex, to regular hours of employment for limited and designated periods of time, with fixed intervals for rest and refreshment, and to protect them in the enjoyment of the rights thus established, to the end that the health and endurance of the individual may be insured and the ultimate strength and virility of the race be preserved.[2]

An Ohio nine-hour act, declared valid by the Ohio judiciary, was also sustained by the Federal Supreme Court in 1914, taking for authority its prior decision in Muller *v.* Oregon.[3]

Furthermore, while laws thus far upheld had limited women's working time to a maximum of ten hours a day, an eight-hour law was held constitutional in 1915.

This is the most drastic legal restriction of hours in private "non-hazardous" industries yet or since sustained by the judiciary, and it was affirmed by the United States Sup-

[1] People *ex rel.* Hoelderlin *v.* Kane, 79 Misc. 140 (1913).

[2] Riley *v.* Mass. 232 U. S. 671 (1914).

[3] Hawley *v.* Walker, 232 U. S. 718 (1914).

reme Court in an appeal on writ of error from the California decision. The act prohibits the employment of females for more than eight hours a day or forty-eight hours a week, in manufacturing, mechanical and mercantile establishments, laundries, hotels, restaurants, telephone and telegraph establishments, offices, and in express and transportation service provided the act does not apply to women employed in harvesting, curing, canning or drying of any variety of perishable fruit or vegetable. In his expression of the court opinion, Mr. Justice Hughes quoted the arguments of Justice Brewer regarding woman's physical structure and the vigor of the race, and continued in a generous defence of this act of the legislature:

> It is manifestly impossible to say that the mere fact that the statute of California provides for an eight-hour day, or a maximum of forty-eight hours a week instead of ten hours a day or fifty-four hours a week, takes the case out of the domain of legislative discretion. This is not to imply that a limitation of the hours of labor of women might not be pushed to a wholly indefensible extreme, but there is no ground for the conclusion here that the limit of the reasonable exertion of protective authority has been overstepped.[1]

Justifying the exemptions made by the legislature as properly within its jurisdiction, Justice Hughes recalled

> the well-established principle that the legislature is not bound, in order to support the constitutional validity of its regulation, to extend it to all cases which it might possibly reach. Dealing with practical exigencies, the legislature may be guided by experience. . . . It is free to recognize degrees of harm, and it may confine its restrictions to those classes of cases where the need is deemed to be clearest. As has been said, it may 'proceed cautiously, step by step,' and 'if an evil is specially ex-

[1] Miller *v.* Wilson, 236 U. S. 373 (1915).

perienced in a particular branch of business' it is not necessary that the prohibition 'should be couched in all-embracing terms.' [Cases cited]. If the law presumably hits the evil where it is most felt, it is not to be overthrown because there are other instances to which it might have been applied.

The thought that springs anew from an analysis of this doctrine, coming as it does from the court of last resort, is that the class legislation *bête noire* is gradually being vanquished, that when there is adequate review of laws enacted in sincere attempt to ameliorate economic pressure upon a group of industrial workers, the constitution need not stand in the way, but may expand to receive it.

A second eight-hour law found its way from the California legislature to approval by the United States Supreme Court in 1915.[1] This was a provision for women in hospitals with the case of Miller *v.* Wilson, just reviewed, applied as precedent for sanction. It has been cited [2] as noteworthy, however, that in this case the court relied not upon judicial precedent but upon a bulletin of the United States Bureau of Education [3] for its acceptance of the discriminatory classification in the statute, by which the working hours of students were limited while the hours of graduate nurses remained unrestricted.

HOURS OF LABOR—NIGHT WORK

Curiously, the three important court decisions in this country concerning night work prohibitions have occurred in respect to the New York statutes. The contest over con-

[1] Bosley *v.* McLaughlin, Labor Commissioner State of California, 236 U. S. 385.

[2] 3 Calif. Law Rev. 323, 324.

[3] "Educational Status of Nursing," *Bulletin No. 7*, United States Bureau of Education, 1912. The bulletin turns to Oregon's Industrial Welfare Commission which regulates hours and minimum wages, as being a possible way of obviating constitutional objections.

stitutionality did not reach the United States Supreme Court until 1924 when, in March, there was a unanimous decision in support of this restriction upon woman's work. Of the two state decisions, the one, in 1907,[1] annulled such interference, and the other, in 1915,[2] declared it valid. The recent federal decision in the Radice case about to be discussed has affirmed the second opinion.

Here is another clear case of the weight of a compilation of arguments influencing the judicial mind. In the earlier state case the reasoning was based upon common law precepts, while an extensive brief prepared by the Factory Investigating Commission as *amicus curiae,* which set forth the bad effects of night work, dominated the court in its second hearing on behalf of women workers. The decisions of the judiciary on the two occasions are in spectacular contrast. Judge Gray gave the opinion in 1907, the other six justices concurring:[3]

It is to be observed that it is not a regulation of the number of hours of labor for working women; the enactment goes far beyond this. It attempts to take away the right of a woman to labor before six o'clock in the morning, or after nine o'clock in the evening, without any reference to other considerations. In providing that [act stated], she is prevented, however willing, from engaging herself in a lawful employment during the specified periods of the twenty-four hours. Except as to women under twenty-one years of age, this was the first attempt on the part of the state to restrict their liberty of person, or their

[1] People *v.* Williams, 189 N. Y. 131 (1907).

[2] People *v.* Charles Schweinler Press, 214 N. Y. 395 (1915).

[3] Probably it should not be overlooked that this opinion was given in the interim between the two Oregon decisions—after that of the state court and prior to the federal decision. Professor Ernst Freund suggests that the opinion in the Williams case was in submission to the "supposed doctrine" of the United States Supreme Court. See "Constitutional Limitations and Labor Legislation," *supra, cit.*

freedom of contract, in the pursuit of a vocation. I find nothing in the language of the section which suggests the purpose of promoting health, except as it might be inferred that for a woman to work during the forbidden hours of night would be unhealthful. If the inhibition of the section in question had been framed to prevent the ten hours of work from being performed at night, or to prolong them beyond nine o'clock in the evening, it might, more readily, be appreciated that the health of women was the matter of legislative concern. . . . If this enactment is to be sustained, then an adult woman, although a citizen and entitled as such to all the rights of citizenship under our laws, may not be employed, nor contract to work, in any factory for any period of time, no matter how short, if it is within the prohibited hours; and this, too, without any regard to the healthfulness of the employment. It is clear, as it seems to me, that this legislation cannot, and should not, be upheld as a proper exercise of the police power. It is, certainly, discriminative against female citizens, in denying to them equal rights with men in the same pursuit.

Continuing, the Judge insisted upon drawing the distinction between adult women and children in their economic relations to the State—a distinction which has seldom been made by the judiciary.

The right of the state, as *parens patriae*, to restrict, or to regulate, the labor and employment of children is unquestionable; but an adult female is not to be regarded as a ward of the state, or in any other light than the man is regarded, when the question relates to the business pursuit or calling. She is no more a ward of the state than is the man. She is entitled to enjoy, unmolested, her liberty of person, and her freedom to work for whom she pleases, where she pleases and as long as she pleases, within the general limits operative upon all persons alike, and shall we say that this is valid legislation, which closes the doors of a factory to her before and after certain hours? I think not.[1]

[1] People *v.* Williams, 189 N. Y. 131 (1907).

Justice Hiscock, in unequivocal support of the principle of prohibiting the night work of women in 1915, explained that, in the earlier case, the fact had not been impressed upon the court that the act was a health measure as was expressly stated by Judge Gray, but that it is now plain that night work has a deleterious effect upon women, and that the decree is thoroughly justified.

Before reaching the court of appeals for which Judge Hiscock spoke, the case had been heard both in the court of special sessions and in the appellate division. In the first instance a motion in arrest of judgment was granted, while in the second instance, the bench decided in favor of the act. Justice Ingraham, who spoke for this majority, praised the thoroughness of the investigation of the factory commission which had been the basis for the enactment of the law. He declared that "the report . . . is startling both in regard to effect on the physical well-being of the night workers and the moral effect upon the women who are employed in factories at night."

Mr. Justice Hiscock, sustaining this decision, also clearly reflected the findings of the commission in his reasoning,

> Impairment caused by exhaustion or even ordinary weariness must be repaired by normal and refreshing sleep and rest if health and efficiency are to be preserved. . . . surely it is a matter of vital importance to the state that the health of thousands of women working in factories should be protected and safeguarded from any drain which can reasonably be avoided. This not only for their own sakes but, as is and ought to be constantly and legitimately emphasized, for the sake of the children whom a great majority of them will be called on to bear and who will almost inevitably display in their deficiencies the unfortunate inheritance conferred upon them by physically broken down mothers.[1]

[1] People *v.* Charles Schweinler Press, 214 N. Y. 395 (1915).

A second testing of this night work law was made by the New York court of appeals in the same year;[1] and upon request of Joseph Radice, in 1918, the municipal court of Buffalo was also asked to decide its validity as it applied to women in restaurants in first and second class cities. In both cases the law was promptly declared constitutional on the authority of the Schweinler Press case.

And now it is the prolongation of the Radice case, carried from one of the lowest courts in the state to the highest court in the country, which has given security to night work prohibitions for women. The decision of the federal judges, delivered on March 10, 1924 by Mr. Justice Sutherland, was unanimous in the belief that convincing facts had been submitted which show that women, because of their "more delicate organism," are injured by night work to the extent that they are entitled to special protection from it. On these grounds the earlier decision of the Supreme Court in Muller *v.* Oregon regarding women's daily hours was declared to be controlling.

The New York law had been attacked on two grounds,—first, that it violated the right of contract, and second, that it made unreasonable and arbitrary classification in that only first and second class cities were within the law's ambit and that women dancers and singers in restaurants were entirely outside of it.

In meeting the first accusation, Justice Sutherland pointed to the great force of the evidence submitted by the Factory Investigating Commission, which had won the affirmance of the act in 1915. He said:

The Legislature had before it a mass of information from which it concluded that night work is substantially and especially detrimental to the health of women. We cannot say that the

[1] People *ex rel.* John Krohn *v.* Warden and Keeper of City Prison, Brooklyn, 215 N. Y. 701 (1915).

conclusion is without warrant. . . . The injurious consequences were thought by the Legislature to bear more heavily against women than men, and, considering their more delicate organism, there would seem to be good reason for so thinking. The fact, assuming it to be such, properly may be made the basis of legislation applicable only to women. Testimony was given upon the trial to the effect that the night work in question was not harmful; but we do not find it convincing.[1]

With recognition of the traditional distinction between courts and legislatures which we have seen is not always observed, the Justice then continued,

Where the constitutional validity of a statute depends upon the existence of facts, courts must be cautious about reaching a conclusion respecting them contrary to that reached by the Legislature; and if the question of what the facts establish be a fairly debatable one, it is not permissible for the judge to set up his opinion in respect of it against the opinion of the lawmaker. The state Legislature here determined that night employment of the character specified was sufficiently detrimental to the health and welfare of women engaging in it to justify its suppression, and, since we are unable to find reasonable grounds for a contrary opinion, we are precluded from reviewing the legislative determination.

In his defense against the charge of unequal protection of the statute, the Justice quoted from an opinion delivered earlier by Mr. Justice Hughes, " that the Legislature is not bound, in order to support the constitutional validity of its regulation, to extend it to all cases which it might possibly reach."

This decision of the United States Supreme Court has been acclaimed country wide by those who believe that women in industry should have special protection. The opinion came with particular welcome because of the adverse

[1] Radice *v.* People, 264 U. S. 292 (1923).

decision of the same highest court a year earlier declaring invalid the District of Columbia minimum wage law for women. Because of that decision, advocates of legislation have keenly feared that the Muller *v.* Oregon case of 1908 concerning women's hours might cease to control, but these fears have now, for the time being at least, been quieted.

Thus in this long line of decisions, the courts have, with few exceptions and with striking uniformity, favored limiting the working hours of women. Prior to 1900, one tribunal had affirmed this legislation, and one tribunal had set such a statute aside, on the grounds that sex alone was not justification for special protection. The Pennsylvania case in 1900, however, marked the beginning of a new judicial philosophy in regard to women—a philosophy based upon "physical inferiority" and "potential motherhood." The courts stressed their belief that certain employments are harmful to women and not to men, and that women like children are "wards of the state," that for both of these reasons they are in peculiar need of legislative supervision.

In the Oregon cases of 1906 and 1908, women were no longer designated as wards of the state, but the stress was placed more directly upon their differences from men physically, and their function as mothers. These conditions, together with our folkways—which have reduced the self-reliance of women and made it usual for them to be dependent upon their brothers—seem to have become justifications for their special protection.

SUMMARY

In summary of the analysis so far made of the attitude of the courts regarding protective labor laws for men and for women, some observations may well be drawn.

Except for decisions regarding minimum wages which are about to be discussed, wage-payment acts sustained by the courts have applied alike to all workers, as also have one-day-of-rest-in-seven laws and acts limiting hours in extra-hazardous industries. In a few cases the courts have arbitrated controversies respecting prohibited employment of women and have sustained such prohibition; and now the prohibition of women's night work appears to be constitutionally secure. In "non-hazardous" industries statutes limiting daily working hours have been sustained more often when they have applied to women than when they have applied to men, but a tendency toward the convergence of the respective arguments is perceptible. For example, we have noticed that while the extensive brief which convinced the United States Supreme Court in 1908 that a ten-hour law especially for women was necessary to public welfare, a second extensive brief less than a decade later and chiefly by the same authors, convinced the same high court that a ten-hour law for men as well as women is not unconstitutional. In the interim between these cases, Judge Learned Hand for the Illinois court followed the lead of the earlier brief and decision, and declared that "it is known to all men . . . that while men can work for more than ten hours, women cannot."

This is but one instance among many others which has led some people to have a growing sense that "common knowledge" is not adequate knowledge—that it is too often an expression of tradition or mere emotion rather than of fact. And the corollary to this view is a growing recognition of the need of more facts covering the entire field of human physiological depreciation under overstrain for the enlightenment of the judiciary, as well as for the use of the legislature where the statutes are formed. Also, as facts are accumulated, there appears to be a widening conviction that men as well as women must have protection from the ravages of modern industry. One authority has ventured the following prediction:

. . . in view of our increasing knowledge of the dangers of overwork, especially in continuous industries, the principle of hour restriction, first established for women and children, may eventually be extended to cover all wage-earning men. The laws for one day of rest in seven, and the favorable decision of the United States Supreme Court on an Oregon law for ten hours in manufacturing, make it not unlikely that a period of hour regulation for adult male workers has begun.[1]

MINIMUM WAGES

Minimum wage legislation has been defeated in the constitutional test by the highest tribunal of the country. Although the issue divided the judicial bench and the vote of five to three has been the target for sharp criticism, the decision stands—powerful, if, by many, unaccepted as final.

Prior to this decree of the Federal Supreme Court which invalidated the law of the District of Columbia, and the annulment in the lower court which led to the appeal, minimum wage laws for women so far tested had been uniformly countenanced in the higher courts. An explanation of this growth may be that the minimum wage is a very recent type of legislation in America which did not make its appearance in the courts until after the magic effect of statistical data had been recognized. Though still relatively rare, statistical data have been increasingly presented to the courts for their enlightenment in the review of specific cases, with the effect, almost unfailingly, that the decision has been made on the side upon which the data threw weight. Moreover, the special commission, which is practically indispensable for the administration of a minimum wage law, makes a practical organ for the collection of material regarding the need of such legislation and its operation.

An historical analysis of the attitude of American courts in minimum wage cases does not lead us back very far. The

[1] Commons and Andrews, *op. cit.*, p. 248 (1920).

state of Oregon again furnishes the first judicial contests, beginning in 1914, though the initial act providing for a minimum wage was passed in Massachusetts in 1912. The Oregon act of February 17, 1913 was entitled "An act to protect the lives and health and morals of women and minor [all under 18 years of age] workers, and to establish an industrial welfare commission and define its powers and duties, and to provide for the fixing of minimum wages and maximum hours and standard conditions of labor for such workers, and to provide penalties for violation of this act." The duties of the commission were stated to include that of declaring what hours of labor are unreasonably long, what working conditions are detrimental to health or morals, and what wages are inadequate for a respectable living. Orders of the commission resulting from the act were a nine-hour day and a fifty-hour week, with forty-five minutes for the noon meal and a minimum wage of $8.64 for women in Portland manufacturing establishments.

Ensuing from the orders of the Oregon commission, came the protest of proprietor Stettler alleging deprivation of property and the right to contract, and the denial of equal protection of the laws.[1] All contentions were set aside on the grounds that the act was a proper exercise of the police power of the state and not subversive of the constitution of the United States. Other restrictive measures within the meaning of the constitution were cited, as maximum hour provisions for employees on public works and in mines, and for women and children in manufacturing, mercantile and mechanical establishments. The creation of the industrial welfare commission was held to be a legal delegation of administrative authority to secure compliance with the orders of the legislature and not, as alleged, to act as a substitute for the legislature. The only allegation that

[1] Stettler *v.* O'Hara *et al.*, Ind. Welfare Com., 69 Ore. 519 (1914).

the court recognized for debate was whether the regulation and the object proposed were sufficiently related, or whether "so utterly unreasonable and extravagant" as merely to interfere with private enterprise. The Massachusetts minmum wage commission report of 1912 was pressed into use for evidence, and the sanction of the court was given to the act, declaring it of "common knowledge" that low wages demoralize both the public and the individuals immediately concerned. In fact the court attested that all arguments bearing upon the need of restricting women's hours are pertinent in the expression of their need for a minimum wage and that the act was not violative of the due process clause which, it was satisfied to declare, merely requires the usual procedure of a hearing before properly constituted tribunals.

Following the defeat of plaintiff Stettler, the litigation of this case was continued in the same year by an employee of Stettler named Simpson. The statute again stood the constitutional test on the ground that since the regulation of hours and wages was within the police power of the state, "it would follow as a natural corollary that the right to labor for such hours and at such wages as would reasonably seem to be detrimental to the health or welfare of the community is not a privilege or immunity of any citizen." [1] The earlier Muller *v.* Oregon decision of the Federal Supreme Court relating to hours was adopted by the judiciary in this case as final authority.

In December of 1914 these cases in combination were carried to the United States Supreme court, not to be decided until January, 1917.[2] The argument was heard and reheard with extensive testimony for the defendants in error prepared by Mr. Felix Frankfurter and Miss Josephine Goldmark. The final decision came in the form of an

[1] Simpson *v.* O'Hara *et al.*, 70 Ore. 261 (1914).

[2] Stettler *v.* O'Hara, 243 U. S. 629 (1917).

evenly divided bench,[1] no opinions were delivered, and the Oregon court decision stood unchanged.

The steady progress of minimum wage legislation in its early life lent further momentum. The supreme courts of both Arkansas and Minnesota affirmed wage laws in 1917, both decisions being reversals of the dicta of district judges given prior to the federal review of the Oregon case. The Arkansas judiciary, relying upon Stettler *v.* O'Hara, wrote in conclusion:

It is a matter of common knowledge of which we take judicial notice that conditions have arisen with reference to the employment of women which have made it necessary for many of the States to appoint commissions to make a detailed investigation of the subject of women's work and their wages. Many voluntary societies have made this question the subject of careful investigation. Medical societies and scientists have studied the subject and have prepared written opinions. It has been the consensus of opinion and that of medical societies and scientific experts is that inadequate wages tend to impair the health of women in all cases and in some cases to injure their morals. Indeed, it is a matter of common knowledge that if women are paid inadequate wages so that they are not receiving enough food, this state will impair their health as overwork, and someone else may supply their wages.[2]

The Minnesota court emphasized the fact that the question at issue was " not what we ourselves think of the policy or justification of such legislation " but whether there is a reasonable basis for legislative belief that the conditions mentioned exist, that legislation is necessary and can con-

[1] Justice Brandeis not partaking, having been substantially involved in the preparation of counsel's brief. Justice Brandeis, upon his appointment as Justice of the Supreme Court, left his unfinished work in the hands of Mr. Frankfurter.

[2] State *v.* Crowe, 130 Ark. 272 (1917).

tribute to the promotion of the health and morals of the workers and the good order of the public.

> In this economic strife, women as a class, are not on an equality with men. . . . We think sufficient basis exists. It is not necessary that we should hold that statutes of this kind applicable to men would be valid. We think it clear that there is such an inequality or difference between men and women in the matter of ability to secure a just wage and in the consequences of an inadequate wage that the legislature may by law compensate for the difference. (Cases cited.) [1]

The year 1918 added two more high state courts to the list of those affirming the right of the legislature to provide for minimum wages. In Washington, the aim toward public as well as individual protection was emphasized.[2] In Massachusetts the court was intent upon explaining that the act was not mandatory, that is, it did not declare violation a misdemeanor for which criminal proceedings could be instituted.[3] Thus the authorization of the commission to ascertain facts could not be construed as violation of the constitutional security against an employer's "being compelled to accuse or furnish evidence against himself." The court refused to "prophesy" whether a mandatory act would be declared unconstitutional by the Federal Supreme Court.[4]

The constitutionality of these laws was again affirmed in three state decisions in 1920 and 1921, with relatively simple procedure and firm reliance upon previous rulings in other states. The Texas court declared its belief that "the passage of such laws for the welfare and betterment of the conditions of working men, women, and children is matter well

[1] Williams *v.* Evans *et al.*, 139 Minn. 32 (1917).

[2] Larsen *v.* Rice, 100 Wash. 642 (1918).

[3] Massachusetts is the only state which has a minimum wage law of this type.

[4] Holcombe *v.* Creamer, 231 Mass. 99 (1918).

within the province of the Legislature." [1] The supreme court of Washington in meeting a second request for judgment,[2] preserved and strengthened its first by citations of subsequent cases. In Minnesota, the law was again challenged in the courts,[3] and in this case as in that of 1917 beforementioned, an injunction was granted against the enforcement of the order of the minimum wage commission. The order was again reversed by the supreme court of the state and the statute declared constitutional. In this case the court explained,—" the remedy may not be perfect, but it is such as the law gives. A temporary writ should not have been granted."

The progress of this type of special legislation for women was thus marked. In 1921, Mr. Lindley D. Clark of the United States Bureau of Labor Statistics wrote that although the decision of the Federal Supreme Court had "merely permitted the Oregon decision to stand, by an equally divided bench, the conclusion seems warranted that no successful attack can be anticipated upon the principle of these laws in view of the absolute uniformity with which they have been maintained in the different States where pressed to a decision in the court of last resort." [4]

It was at this very time that the minimum wage law of the District of Columbia was hanging in the balance in the courts, after which, despite confident prophecy and courageous effort, it dropped to defeat. The statute of the District enacted by Congress in 1918 in two separate instances was

[1] Poye *v.* State of Texas, 230 S. W. Rep. 161 (1921) affirming decision of 1920. The Texas act was repealed in 1921 however, and a new law enacted in the same year was vetoed by the Governor. Texas is thus without a minimum wage law.

[2] Spokane Hotel *v.* Younger, 113 Wash. 359 (1920).

[3] Williams *v.* Evans, 139 Minn. 32 (1917); G. O. Miller Telephone Co. *v.* Min. Wage Comm., 145 Minn. 262 (1920).

[4] "Minimum Wage Laws of the United States," *Monthly Labor Review*, Bureau of Labor Statistics, Washington, March, 1921, p. 5.

alleged to be a deprivation of property without due process of law and an interference with the right of free contract. One case was that of the Children's Hospital of the District which sought an injunction against the minimum wage board to restrain it from requiring payment of a wage to their employees different from the wage contract which they had made. The other case was that of Willie Lyons, a woman elevator operator, who protested against the wage requirement of the board on the grounds that she desired to keep her position but that she would not be permitted to do so if it was required that the advanced rates be paid to her.

These cases taken together brought two decisions but one year apart pronouncing the act valid,—that by the supreme court of the District on June 2, 1920 and that by the District court of appeals on June 6, 1921. After the latter hearing, Justice Smyth delivered the opinion of the majority with Justice Van Orsdel in hot dissent. Justice Smyth made clear his conception of the function of the court and that this was a time when the court should not interfere with the act of congress.

> For us the question is one of power, not of expediency . . . when Congress legislates for the District of Columbia it may exercise the police power in all its plentitude. . . . [The basis for court review, therefore, is whether] a statute purporting to have been enacted to protect the public health, the public morals, or the public safety has no real or substantial relation to those objects, or is a palpable invasion of rights secured by the fundamental law. [Cases cited.]

In response to the question of relation between statute and object thereof, the Justice resorted to "common knowledge" making a curious comparison in declaring that as stagnant water is a breeding place for malarial bacteria and is removed by an exercise of the police power with sanction of the country's highest tribunal, so,

It is equally well known that if a working woman does not receive a sufficient wage to supply her with necessary food, shelter, and clothing, and she is compelled to subsist upon less than her requirements demand, the result must be that her health would be injuriously affected.

The act was held to be not an infringement of freedom of contract more than many other acts for the furtherance of the public welfare (such as have been reviewed in this chapter). Justice Stafford in a concurring opinion supplemented the argument by adding

that the asserted right of the employer to be served by anyone who is willing to work for him, and at any wage the worker is willing to accept, must be subordinate to the right of the public to see that those women who are obliged to work for a living shall not be obliged to work for less than a living.

The tenor of the dissent of Justice Van Orsdel may be judged by the following exerpt from his opinion:

The tendency of the hour to socialize property rights under the subterfuge of police regulation is dangerous and if continued will prove destructive of our free institutions. It should be remembered that of the three fundamental principles which underlie government and for which government exists—the principles of life, liberty, and property—the chief of these is property; not that any amount of property is more valuable than the life or liberty of the citizen, but the history of civilization conclusively proves that when the citizen is deprived of the free use and employment of his property, anarchy and revolution follow, and life and liberty are without protection.

The Justice had voiced his fear of "sovietism, general price fixing, etc." and declared that the fixing of wages of employees jeopardizes "the most sacred safeguard which the constitution offers. It is paternalism in the highest degree." [1]

[1] The Children's Hospital of the District of Columbia *v.* Jesse C.

The dissenting opinion in this instance became the dominant opinion upon a rehearing held October 10 and 11, 1921, and reported upon a year later, November 6, 1922. The instance of the rehearing was somewhat unique in judicial history. Justice Robb had been absent from the bench on account of sickness at the time of adjudication, and Justice Stafford, according to legal provision, had been detailed from the supreme court bench of the District to take his place. Upon being refused a rehearing by Justices Smyth and Stafford, the plaintiffs plead with Justice Robb to bring about a special hearing that would enable him to vote. The pressure resulted in a re-opening of the case after a judicial "tug of war" between Justices Robb and Van Orsdel on the one side, and Justices Smyth and Stafford on the other, as to the propriety of such a move. Justice Smyth, now in the rôle of dissenter, discussed the struggle over jurisdiction with admirable restraint and vigor,

> It would seem from the foregoing that the appellants, finding themselves defeated, sought a justice who had not sat in the case, but who, they believed, would be favorable to them, and induced him, by an appeal directed to him personally, to assume jurisdiction and join with the dissenting justice in an attempt to overrule the decisions of the court. I shall not characterize such practice—let the facts speak for themselves.[1]

And then having delivered his rebuke, the justice reiterated his reasons for upholding the constitutionality of the law.

Justice Van Orsdel delivered the opinion of the court. He stated again his principles in regard to the supreme place of property and the danger of wage fixing which would deprive wage earners "of the most sacred safeguard which the Constitution affords,"

Adkins *et al.*; Willie A. Lyons *v.* Jesse C. Adkins *et al.* A discussion of these cases may be found in the *Monthly Labor Review*, *op. cit.*, July, 1920, pp. 131-132 and July, 1921, pp. 202-205.

[1] 284 Fed. Rep. 613 (1922).

Take from the citizen the right to freely contract and sell his labor for the highest wage which his individual skill and efficiency will command, the laborer would be reduced to an automaton—a mere creature of the State. It is paternalism in the highest degree and the struggle of the centuries to establish the principle that the State exists for the citizen, and not the citizen for the State, would be lost.

He concluded, sounding his warning,

If, in the exercise of the police power for the general welfare, power lies in the legislature to fix the wage which the citizen must accept or choose idleness, or as in the case of Willie Lyons, be deprived of the means of earning a living, it is but a step to a legal requirement that the industrious, frugal, economical citizen must divide his earnings with his indolent worthless neighbor. The modern tendency toward indiscriminate legislative and judicial jugglery with great fundamental principles of free government, whereby property rights are being curtailed and destroyed logically will, if persisted in, end in social disorder and revolution.[1]

So stood the last word regarding the minimum wage statute in the District of Columbia, until April 9, 1923. On that day the United State Supreme Court sustained the decision of the District court adverse to a minimum wage, surprising both friends and enemies of that law throughout the country.[2] The prevailing opinion of the tribunal was written by Mr. Justice Sutherland who, we have seen, has since then announced the favorable opinion of the court in the Radice night work prohibition case. A two-fold attack was made upon the law,—first upon the very principle of a legal minimum wage which is a " price-fixing law " and an infringement of the right of free contract, and then upon its special application to women " who are legally as capable

[1] 284 Fed. Rep. 613 (1922).

[2] Adkins *v.* Children's Hospital, Adkins *v.* Lyons, 261 U. S. 525 (1923).

of contracting for themselves as men," and therefore a denial of the equal protection of the laws.

The justice cited at length decisions which have declared other restrictive laws to be valid, pointing out constitutional differences between them and the act under discussion. The truck and other wage-payment acts were to prevent "fraudulent methods in the payment of wages and in no sense can they be said to be, or to furnish a precedent for wage-fixing statutes." The eight-hour law for Utah miners was mentioned as one which the legislature had determined to be necessary and reasonable so that "its decision in that respect was beyond the reviewing power of the Federal courts." So also was the Oregon ten-hour law for all persons upheld by this court in deference to the judgment of the state legislature and state supreme court and "in the absence of facts to support the contrary conclusion." Justice Sutherland hastened to add however, that the Oregon statute had been sustained not as "an attempt to fix wages" but "as a reasonable regulation of hours of service." Moreover the fact was recalled that "this court has been careful in every case where the question has been raised, to place its decision upon this limited authority of the legislature to regulate hours of labor and to disclaim any purpose to uphold the legislation as fixing wages, thus recognizing an essential difference between the two." [1] Furthermore, the opinion of the Court in the federal annulment of the ten-hour law for New York bakers was quoted at considerable length and the justice then asserted, equivocally enough, that "subsequent cases in this court have been distinguished from that decision, but the principles therein stated have never been disapproved." (In his dissenting opinion, Chief Justice Taft said he had

[1] Although this difference has appeared baffling and specious to many, the Court has been consistent, to say the least, by recognizing it again in the affirmance of the New York night work prohibition.

always thought this, the Lochner case, had been "overruled sub silentio.")

Prefacing his analysis of the objectionable peculiarities of the act in question, Justice Sutherland declared one of the cardinal governing principles for the court to be "the rule that every possible presumption is in favor of the validity of an act of Congress until overcome beyond rational doubt; but," he added, "if by clear and indubitable demonstration a statute be opposed to the Constitution we have no choice but to say so."

In the exposition, then, of his disapproval of the economics of a "price-fixing law", the justice remonstrated,

> [The law] compels him [the employer] to pay at least the sum fixed in any event, because the employee needs it, but requires no service of equivalent value from the employee. . . . To the extent that the sum fixed exceeds the fair value of the services rendered, it amounts to a compulsory exaction from the employer for the support of a partially indigent person, for whose condition there rests upon him no peculiar responsibility, and therefore, in effect, arbitrarily shifts to his shoulders a burden which, if it belongs to anybody, belongs to society as a whole. . . . The necessities of the employee are alone considered and these arise outside of the employment, are the same when there is no employment, and as great in one occupation as in another.

Further to stress his point, Justice Sutherland resorted to an analogy in the sale of commodities:

> In principle, there can be no difference between the case of selling labor and the case of selling goods. If one goes to the butcher, the baker or grocer to buy food, he is morally entitled to obtain the worth of his money but he is not entitled to more. If what he gets is worth what he pays he is not justified in demanding more simply because he needs more; and the shopkeeper, having dealt fairly and honestly in that transaction, is not concerned in any peculiar sense with the question of his

customer's necessities. Should a statute undertake to vest in a commission power to determine the quantity of food necessary for individual support and require the shopkeeper, if he sell to the individual at all, to furnish that quantity at not more than a fixed maximum, it would undoubtedly fall before the constitutional test.

Turning to the application of the statute to women alone,[1] the court declared that the Nineteenth Amendment which brought full suffrage to women had reduced the contractual, political, and civil differences between men and women almost "to the vanishing point."

In this aspect of the matter, while the physical differences must be recognized in appropriate cases, and legislation fixing hours or conditions of work may properly take them into account, we can not accept the doctrine that women of mature age, sui juris, require or may be subjected to restrictions upon their liberty of contract which could not lawfully be imposed in the case of men under similar circumstances. . . .

And therefore:

It is simply and exclusively a price-fixing law, confined to adult women (for we are not now considering the provisions relating to minors), who are legally as capable of contracting for themselves as men.

Whether or not he was keeping within his jurisdiction, the justice discussed with considerable insight the inadequacy of the minimum wage concept—that an amount that would be a living wage for one person would be less or more than a living wage for another person, and that the economies of living in a family group are not taken into consideration. In respect to the relation between wages and morals, he maintained,

[1] The inclusion of minors in the provision of the law was not discussed.

It cannot be shown that well paid women safeguard their morals more carefully than those who are poorly paid. Morality rests upon other considerations than wages; and there is, certainly, no such prevalent connection between the two as to justify a broad attempt to adjust the latter with reference to the former. As a means of safeguarding morals the attempted classification, in our opinion, is without reasonable basis. No distinction can be made between women who work for others and those who do not; nor is there ground for distinction between women and men, for, certainly, if women require a minimum wage to preserve their morals men require it to preserve their honesty.

And then, after explaining the precaution the court is obliged to take against making "a wrong decision [which] does not end with itself," and in favor of sustaining "the individual freedom of action contemplated by the Constitution," Justice Sutherland for himself and his four associates announced that "the decrees of the court below" were "affirmed."

Three justices dissented from the majority opinion, Mr. Justice Brandeis not taking sides, and two dissenting opinions were written,—one by Chief Justice Taft with which Justice Sanford concurred, the other by Justice Holmes.

Mr. Chief Justice Taft regretted to be at variance with the court in the distinction it made between "a minimum of wages and a maximum of hours in the limiting of liberty of contract," for, he asserted, "one is the multiplier and the other the multiplicand."

If I am right in thinking that the legislature can find as much support in experience for the view that a sweating wage has as great and as direct a tendency to bring about an injury to the health and morals of workers, as for the view that long hours injure their health, then I respectfully submit that Muller *v.* Oregon, 208 U. S. 412, controls this case.

Conscious that this argument might hold equally true for

men, Justice Taft prefaced his remark with an open recognition that he was not "expressing an opinion that a minimum-wage limitation can be enacted for adult men." [1]

In contrast to the view expressed by Justice Sutherland that the Nineteenth Amendment made women the equal of men in the wage contract, Chief Justice Taft remarked that "the Nineteenth Amendment did not change the physical strength or limitations of women" even though it did give to women political power that would make legislative provisions for their protection more certain.

The dissenting opinion of Justice Holmes in dwelling upon this special point, stated, "It will need more than the Nineteenth Amendment to convince me that there are no differences between men and women, or that legislation can not take those differences into account." Considering the general nature of the statute, Justice Holmes then recalled other restrictive laws which had been upheld "that seem to me to have interfered with liberty of contract quite as seriously and directly as the one before us." He mentioned (citing cases) usury laws, Sunday laws, the regulation of insurance rates, certain requirements regarding the method of paying wages and the regulation of hours. And, he urged, "the size of a loaf of bread may be established." He, too, confessed inability to "understand the principle on which the power to fix a minimum for the wages of women can be denied by those who admit the power to fix a maximum for their hours of work." "The bargain," he urged, "is equally affected whichever half you regulate." (Justice Holmes made no recognition of the application of his argument to men as well as to women.)

[1] It may be said that Chief Justice Taft has discussed further the constitutionality of fixing wages by law in the more recent opinion of the United States Court in Wolff Co. *v.* Industrial Court, 262 U. S. 522. This case is discussed in the *Monthly Labor Review* for July, 1923, pp. 208-211.

The dissenting opinions also gave voice to a mass of statistical and other material that had been gathered for the defense of this law. As *amici curiae,* a number of authoritative bodies in California, Kansas, New York, Oregon, Washington and Wisconsin prepared briefs for counsel, and a compendious brief in two volumes and 1204 pages was compiled by Felix Frankfurter, of counsel, assisted by Mary W. Dewson, Research Secretary of the National Consumers' League. However, for the first time in the history of American high court decisions in labor cases, this method of informing the judiciary as to the reasons for upholding the law, failed to win affirmance of that law. Justice Sutherland referred to the " mass of reports, opinions of special observers and students of the subject " as " interesting but only mildly persuasive." He conceded that the earnings of women have improved but urged that " convincing indications of the logical relation of these desirable changes to the law in question are significantly lacking." Wages among men have risen as much or more than among women, he asserted, and " no real test of the economic value of the law can be had during periods of maximum employment, where general causes keep wages up to or above the minimum; that will come in periods of depression and struggle for employment when the efficient will be employed at the minimum rate while the less capable may not be employed at all."

Thus one of the greatest judicial battles ever fought over a law respecting labor, came to a decisive close. " The effect of the decision " according to Mr. Thomas I. Parkinson, chief of the legislative drafting bureau of Columbia University, " is that no government in this country, federal or state, has the power to say that a woman may not be employed unless she is paid a wage equal to that which a government agency has determined is necessary to provide a decent living, protect her health and safeguard her morals." [1]

The effect of the decision in so far as it will alter the working policy of the advocates of special legislation for industrial women cannot yet be forecast. Ways and means of action are being discussed by different groups. Defensive organizations have been formed in some instances such as that among employers in Oregon who have agreed not to let the federal decision affect the operation of the minimum wage law in their state.[2] Members of the Women's Trade Union League feel a new pressure of necessity for organizing women for mutual aid in driving the wage bargain, and "bona fide trade unions" of wage-earning women is the first of three necessities listed by Samuel Gompers as a result of the decree of the court.[3] Other individuals and groups are urging more seriously than ever that the power of the Supreme Court be modified. In a symposium of government officials, business and labor representatives, social workers, and economists conducted by the *Survey*,[4] in which twenty-five prominent citizens discussed the minimum wage decision, nearly all advocated, directly or by implication, some definite action by amendment to the constitution "which would weaken the power of those who are too ready to set aside the decisions of our duly chosen law-makers." Six of the participants in the symposium, including the four economists,[5] recommended

[1] *The American Labor Legislation Review*, June, 1923, p. 136.

[2] See *infra*, p. 414.

[3] "The Minimum Wage—What Next? A Symposium," *The Survey*, May 15, 1923.

[4] *Op. cit.*

[5] Henry R. Seager, Professor of Economics at Columbia University; John R. Commons, Professor of Economics at the University of Wisconsin; John B. Andrews, Secretary American Association for Labor Legislation; W. Jett Lauck, Economist, Consultant to United Mine Workers and Railway Brotherhoods.

an amendment which would require at least a two-thirds majority of votes (i. e. six out of nine) in order to declare unconstitutional an act of Congress or of a state legislature. By some a three-fourths majority was thought not too rigid a requirement.

Along with these recommendations was frequently expressed the confident belief that the interpretation of the Constitution of the United States can be made to meet the demands of the people whose liberty it is bound to protect. Mrs. Florence Kelley wrote:

> I am convinced that the words of the text of the constitution are broad enough to enable the Supreme Court, had the majority so desired, to uphold the federal child-labor laws and the District of Columbia minimum wage law.

Professor Henry R. Seager wrote:

> Judging from the present trend of opinion and teaching in the law schools of the country and from the gradual revival of progressive thinking, after the post-war reaction, in every section, there is good ground for hoping that the next appointees to the Supreme Bench will share the enlightened views expressed by Justices Taft and Holmes on such issues rather than those of Justice Sutherland and his associates.

Miss Mary Anderson, director of the Women's Bureau of the United States Department of Labor, aptly suggested:

> . . . It is also possible that by bending our energies to the accumulation of more fundamental facts on the wage question and its relation to the individual and to industry we may be able to clarify the situation so that there can be no doubt in the judicial mind that regulation of minimum wages is as important a social need as the regulation of hours of work.

In a stirring address to a large annual meeting of

the Consumers' League shortly after the decision of the Supreme Court, Mr. Felix Frankfurter explained that the majority decision of the judiciary had been reached by "highminded" men who are "just as bent on doing justice —*as they see it*—as Chief Justice Taft and his two associates who dissented," that the question is one of "economics, a question of social policy, and the adjustment of social policy to the vague words of the constitution." Recalling a premise to which Justice Sutherland had acceded, that "the ethical right of every worker to a living wage may be conceded," Mr. Frankfurter urged,

> The task before us all is to generate in this country a current of opinion so that men will not see the divorce that Mr. Justice Sutherland now sees between ethical requirement and constitutional propriety. . . . My interest derives from an unshakeable faith that if we care as much about what we believe in as do those who believe the other thing, our ideas will prevail. If we will counter inertia with intelligence . . . we will have a civilization in this country that is worthy of being called a civilization . . . the kind of investigation that has been going on must be fostered. The information gathered must be made living, vivid, and active.[1]

Like a general exhorting his men, Mr. Frankfurter pressed the members of the Consumers' League to

> Make the facts gained through the operation of such a law so vivid and burning that there will be generated those subtle but very solid currents of opinion that will make the Supreme Court on a reconsideration of the question realize that these are facts with which the states must have the right to deal.

He suggested that this decision is a

[1] Cosmopolitan Club, April 20, 1923. Reproduced in part in the *Bulletin of the Consumers' League of New York*, April, 1923.

triumph for the Alice Paul theory of constitutional law, which is to no little extent a reflex of the thoughtless, unconsidered assumption that in industry it makes no difference whether you are a man or woman. . . . The only way to kill a theory, as Huxley said . . . is by a fact. But the fact itself is not sufficient. You must plant that germ of truth into the body of opinion so that it can spread and kill the theory.

In closing, Mr. Frankfurter plead with his distinguished audience, "Do not expect too much from legislators. Do not even expect too much from courts. They are only indices of the state of feeling, thought and determination of the body politic."

This exhortation did not spring from despair therefore. Moreover it is clear that this view concerning the latent possibilities of broader interpretation of the constitution is in harmony with the views of other students of law and economics. On another occasion, Mr. Frankfurter himself wrote,

Intense feeling against the policy of the legislation must inevitably have influenced the result in the decisions. In truth this presents the point of greatest stress in our constitutional system, for it requires minds of unusual intellectual disinterestedness, detachment, and imagination to escape from the too easy tendency to find lack of power where one is convinced of lack of wisdom.[1]

Nor is this only a recent view. Professor Henry R. Seager, twenty years ago, came to a similar conclusion in his analysis of a series of judicial interpretations:

Confused and conflicting as are these decisions, it is believed that a study of them justifies the contention that in the field of labor restrictions the courts will sustain any measure which they think really calculated to promote the public welfare.

[1] "Hours of Labor and Realism in Constitutional Law," p. 363, *supra, cit.*

And again,

> . . . the constitutional and the economic aspects of the question are so intimately related that we may be certain that a court which believes a protective law economically desirable will find it legally admissable.[1]

More recently another authority has stressed the need of properly constituted investigatory bodies to act for the enlightenment of the judiciary:

> For the present, at any rate, it is not so much attacks on the courts that may be expected to bring progressive labor legislation as reliable investigation of actual conditions by competent administrative authorities whose work will command the respect, not only of courts, but of legislatures, of employers and employees, of the people at large. It is this gap in the American system of labor law that is sought to be filled by the so-called industrial commission.[2]

SUMMARY AND CONCLUSION

With this realization that there has not been sufficient effort to enlighten the courts when important issues have been submitted to them for judgment, it is perhaps not surprising that a review of interpretations in respect to protective labor laws (with the exception of the recent night work case) should begin and close with decisions adverse to those laws. For even though our analysis of decisions clearly reveals a growing tendency in the direction of protection, just as clearly has that tendency wavered. Until the recent decision which annulled the minimum wage law of the District of Columbia, there has been much less fluctuation of decisions regarding special laws for women than for men—that is, in

[1] "The Attitude of American Courts Toward Restrictive Labor Laws," *Political Science Quarterly*, vol. xix, pp. 589-601, Dec., 1904.

[2] Commons and Andrews, *Principles of Labor Legislation*, p. 465 (1920).

the so-called non-hazardous industries. In hazardous industries protection of all workers has increased at a fairly steady pace.

In non-hazardous occupations there are so far two lines of reasoning in regard to protection. On the one hand, the welfare of industrial men as well as of industrial women is considered a necessary concomitant of social progress. The masses of workers in modern economic society represent low earnings and weakness while their employers represent high earnings and strength; thus the bargaining power between employer and employee is unequal and the state rightly interferes for the immediate benefit of the workers and the ultimate benefits of all. "The whole is no greater than the sum of all the parts" and when industry is detrimental to the health and vitality of the working population even "to some extent," that detriment regardless of sex or age is destructive of progress. This was the line of reasoning in several cases, crystallized in Bunting *v.* Oregon by which the Supreme Court of the land affirmed a legal ten-hour day for all persons employed in Oregon mills and factories. Here there was seen to be no need of sex distinction.

On the other hand, however, sex distinction has been considered a necessity. The differentiation of women from men in their physical structure and their function as mothers have been regarded sufficient grounds for affirming special laws regulating their work. The recurring decisions in affirmance of these laws, crystallized by the classic case of Muller *v.* Oregon which affirmed a ten-hour law for women, have acted as precedents for other similar decisions, practically without exception. The night work case of Radice *v.* New York is latest upon the list.

The decision of the United States Supreme Court denying a minimum wage to women indicates a possible inclination in the judicial mind to give new weight to the first of these two grounds for legislation. Here the suggestion was made that sex discrimination is no longer desirable—that women of mature age may not be subjected to restrictions upon their liberty of contract when such restrictions may not be placed upon men, that if women require a minimum wage to preserve their morals, men also need such a wage to preserve their honesty. Moreover, the minority of the court took the converse side of this argument, for while the issue at bar concerned a minimum wage for women and not for men, the major part of the reasoning in favor of affirming the act was as true in the case of men as in the case of women. The justices in the minority declared they saw no distinction—constitutional or economic—between prescribing a maximum of hours and prescribing a minimum of wages. Both affected the bargain, they held, and in overwork and underpay alike there was seen to be a direct "tendency to bring about an injury to the health and morals of the workers." The right to a living wage regardless of sex was either expressed or implied in both majority and minority opinions.

Striking as this decision of the court was therefore, and contrary to the precedent, in that carefully marshaled statistical data failed to sway the majority in favor of the statute, it is possible that a new partial explanation is traceable. The need for "more fundamental facts" is a generally recognized need as the decision is analysed in retrospect. But is may also be true that the specialized nature of the statute was partly responsible for its failure. The grounds for this suggestion are these: It is recognized in practically all other countries where a minimum wage exists that economic need demands a legislated wage for all underpaid workers regardless of sex. One of the reasons given by this majority of justices for dissenting from the act was that sex discrimination is out of date, while the minority of justices held that a minimum of wages is as necessary to welfare as a maximum of hours. These facts seem to force the consideration as to whether this minimum wage statute might not have received a less unfavorable hearing had it applied to all underpaid workers in the District instead of to those only who are women. At least such facts give hope that a favorable decision in respect to minimum wage legislation—with Bunting *v.* Oregon as a precedent—is a possibility of the future when more evidence of the need is presented to the judiciary.

CHAPTER II

Protective Labor Legislation in New York State

PART I: LEGISLATION FOR ALL ADULTS

Prior to the year 1899 there were in New York State two classifications of workers for whom protective labor laws had been enacted,—children and adults. Before 1886 legislation was primarily for the protection of children, and from 1886 to 1889 a number of acts were passed for all employees including a few provisions especially for women. Since 1899, along with extended regulations for general health and safety, has developed an increasing body of legislation specifically for women, these acts having developed in some cases out of earlier provisions which applied only to minors. We will consider the earlier forms of legislation before describing separately and in greater detail laws pertaining especially to women.[1]

[1] For purposes of clarity in tracing the history of labor legislation in New York State, it may be explained that scattered laws attempting to safeguard the interests of working people began to appear in the early 1850's; but it was not until 1886 that a factory act was passed. This first act was on behalf of minors and children. Extended by amendment in the following years, this act together with various other statutes affecting the interests of working people was gathered into the first general Labor Law of 1897 (ch. 415, ch. xxxii of the General Laws). In 1909 (ch. 36), the Labor Law of 1897 and all subsequent legislation relating to the employees and their relations to employers were consolidated into what became known as the Labor Law, constituting chapter 31 of the Consolidated Laws. That is to say, all live provisions were included and all defunct and obsolete acts were struck out through repeal at that time. In 1921 (ch. 50), the Labor Law was completely rearranged and

INDUSTRIAL HOMEWORK

Those problems which are now concerned with so-called "homework," in which women and children are chiefly involved, were in their earlier form largely problems of tenement house manufacture in which whole families were employed. The year 1883, when the first tenement house act was passed, has been given as the year in which labor legislation received its initial momentum in New York State.[1] The beginning should be traced back not to the tenement house law, but to the creation of the State Bureau of Labor Statistics which, though varying in form, has grown to be one of the most important departments of the State. Nevertheless, the enactment of these two provisions in the same year was not a mere coincidence, for they were both the result of the redoubled efforts of organized labor, which had gained sufficient strength to exert political power. The work of the Bureau of Labor Statistics will be discussed later. Our present interest is to trace briefly the course of tenement house laws, the first of which was born to die a memorable death.

This legislation was aimed at the abolition of tenement house cigar manufacture which was a family occupation in the early days. According to Professor F. R. Fairchild[2] the

recodified with the aim of simplification by classification, continuing to constitute chapter 31 of the Consolidated Laws. The Labor Law stands to-day in its recodified form, modified and amended by the subsequent acts of the legislature. With amendments, additions and annotations, it is presented each year in convenient bulletin form by the State Department of Labor, and may be secured upon request. References in this chapter to the Labor Law, unless otherwise stated, are to the edition of the Labor Department.

[1] Adna F. Weber, *Labor Legislation in New York*, 1904, p. 3.

[2] "The Factory Legislation of the State of New York" by F. R. Fairchild, *op. cit.* A full and interesting account of these early attempts at legislation has been given by Mr. Fairchild which has been freely drawn upon in this study.

custom was for the manufacturer to rent tenement houses and sublet the separate apartments to families who agreed to make his cigars. The manufacturer was thus both landlord and employer and reaped his profits both in the form of rent and the sale of his product. Any lack of docility on the part of those employed was likely to result in their dispossession as is said to have been the case in 1877 in the instance of 1000 families during the strike of the New York City cigar makers. At the time of the abolition act of 1883, the New York *Times* reported the existence of 127 houses in New York City in which cigars were manufactured by 1964 families consisting of 7,924 persons. Nearly one-fifth of the cigars manufactured in New York City were made in tenement houses.[1] And along with this peculiar growth of the cigar industry, immigrants poured in from Europe congesting the tenements and leaving nothing to prevent unhealthy conditions of life and work from growing progressively worse.

Thus the act of 1883 was fathered with a double motive by the cigar makers' union. The announced motive was that of protecting the health and morals of the makers of cigars as well as the health of the public. "The second and doubtless the stronger motive was the desire of the leaders of the Cigar Makers' International Union to control the trade". The board of health opposed the bill from the beginning, resolving, in spite of the obvious insanitary conditions, that "the tenement population is not jeopardized by the manufacture of cigars in such houses," that the measure "is not a sanitary measure and has not the approval of this board."

Owing in part, at least, to this continuous assault from the board of health, the act was declared unconstitutional as was also the revised statute of 1884 (ch. 272). The second

[1] *Ibid.*, pp. 13-18.

decree was that in the well known Jacobs case which was discussed in the preceding chapter.

With this sharp rebuff from the state's highest court, the attempt to abolish tenement house cigar manufacture or any other type of manufacture was abandoned.[1] Efforts to avert the evils of homework have since been clothed in pleas for the public health and welfare and even so have made only qualified progress. Until 1892, however, homework as such was entirely without supervision, although the regular workshops, including sweated tenement shops, became subject to inspection under the factory law.

The act of 1892 was the initial step toward the *regulation* rather than the *abolition* of tenement-house labor. Here, homework on 24 specified groups of articles chiefly wearing apparel, artificial flowers, and tobacco products, was limited to the members of the family and the worker was required to obtain a license for the apartment in which he lived and worked. Certain prescriptions were also made for air space according to the number of persons employed. Amendments were made to this act from time to time, making the conditions more exact upon which licenses would be granted. The conditions were such as, (1) that the premises be kept in a sanitary condition, (2) that there be a minimum of 250 cubic feet of air space to each worker, and (3) that no work be done when a contagious disease existed.[2]

In 1899 (ch. 199) while the list of articles which could not be manufactured without a license remained, the manufacture of certain other articles was expressly excluded from regulative measures. These were goods such as collars, cuffs

[1] Fairchild notes in passing that this particular era of tenement house evil when manufacturers were both landlords and employers, was coming to a close, that only two such factories existed when his book was published in 1905.

[2] Governor Roosevelt took an active interest in improving these regulations in those years.

and shirts "made of cotton or linen fabrics that are subjected to the laundering process before being offered for sale."

By the law of 1904 (ch. 550), responsibility was placed upon the owner of the house for the maintenance of sanitary premises; the requirement was made and is still made that the owner must obtain a license before any manufacturing or finishing can be carried on in his house. By 1911, seventeen more articles were added to the list, making 41 in all which could not be manufactured in tenements without an owner's license, labor on all other articles remaining quite free from legal interference.

In 1913 a bill introduced by the Factory Investigating Commission advocated the prohibition of manufacturing certain articles. The provision was that "no article of food, no dolls or doll's clothing and no article of children's or infants' wearing apparel" could be worked upon "in any portion of an apartment any part of which is used for living apartments" (ch. 260). The bill was passed by the legislature and remains on the statute books without having been challenged in the courts.

The tenement house law has been amended further from time to time but with no radical changes from these earlier provisions. Licenses are now required both from the owner or operator of the factory by whom homeworkers are employed, and by the owner of the tenement house in which the workers live and work. Explicit conditions to assure at least a stated minimum of air, light, and sanitation are the bases upon which licenses may be secured, (500 cubic feet of air are now required per person instead of 250 cubic feet as before). A register of names and addresses of all employees who work at home must be kept in each factory, and all goods sent out for home manufacture must bear a factory identification. All registers must be open for inspection by the commissioner of labor at any time, and all licenses are revocable.

Homework is still restricted to members of the family residing therein, with the chief exception of dressmakers' shops located on the first or second floors. Such shops may employ persons other than members of the family, if there is air space equal to 1000 cubic feet per person and if no children under fourteen years of age are so employed. Articles may not be manufactured in the basement or cellar of a tenement house if these rooms are below the ground more than one-half of their height.

The responsibility of supervision and inspection of homeworkers lies with the Department of Labor. Goods unlawfully manufactured may be withheld from sale by the commissioner, and tags labeled "tenement made" and not to be defaced, may be attached thereto. The inspector may demand the disinfection of articles at the owner's expense, or he may destroy articles if the owner fails to comply with orders. Periodic inspections are required to be made not less than once in every six months.

Thus the regulations of homework in tenements have been developed in careful detail,[1] but the reader should not be misled by the thought that homework is really conducted according to the law. For never at any time has the state been able to supply enough inspectors to enforce the requirements. The problems of enforcement will be discussed in a later chapter.

[1] It must be kept in mind however that the law even yet applies only to tenement house work and a tenement house is defined as one in which three or more families live. Thus homeworkers in one or two family houses are quite outside the ambit of the law.

HOURS OF LABOR

1. *Adults*

The earliest protective labor legislation in New York State was on the subject of hours and was enacted in 1853 (ch. 641). At this time, and more forcibly in 1867, (ch. 856), eight hours were declared a legal day's work for all day laborers employed on public works where no contract existed to the contrary. Overtime was permitted, "as many hours as he or she may see fit" with compensation to be agreed upon by employer and employee. These acts did not apply to farm labor, and, by act of 1870 (ch. 385), domestic as well as farm labor was excluded from the meaning of the law.

These regulations obviously were spineless because of their qualifying clauses, but this fact did not prevent others like them from being enacted. Similar to these were two acts passed in the nineties pertaining to brickyards. In 1893 (ch. 691) brickyard employers were forbidden to "require" more than ten hours of work a day from their men, or their employment before 7 a. m. The regulation was emasculated by the amendment of 1896 to the effect that "over work and work prior to seven o'clock in the morning for extra compensation may be performed by agreement between employer and employee." This act thus became worthless along with the earlier statute.

Some understanding of the reason for the weakness of these regulations is suggested by the fact that a less flabby regulation pertaining to bakers was declared unconstitutional. This was the act of 1896 (ch. 672) which declared that employers in bakeries and confectionery establishments could not be "required or permitted to work more than ten hours in any one day unless to make a shorter work day on the last day of the week, nor more hours in any one week than will average ten hours a day for the number of days these persons have worked." The act was passed by the legislature and sustained by the state court of appeals, following upon evidence of the sharp health hazards to which New York bakers were constantly exposed. The reversal of the state court's decision by the United States Supreme Court in 1905 on the grounds of unconstitutionality was discussed in the preceding chapter (Lochner *v.* New York), and the hot criticism that followed the decree will be recalled.

With the exception of this invalidated provision for bakers, legislation thus far enacted was carried into the labor law of 1897 in which was also included a provision for a ten-hour day for railroad employees. These acts as amended are to be found in the labor law of 1924, a summary of which follows.

At present eight hours constitutes a " legal day's work for all classes of employees in this state except those engaged in farm and domestic service unless otherwise provided by law " Overtime for extra compensation is legal except " upon work by or for the state or a municipal corporation, or by contractors or subcontractors therewith and except as otherwise provided in this chapter." [1] An exception to this rule is made in case of " extraordinary emergency." Also certain public employees are exempted from the eight-hour law, such as stationary firemen in state hospitals and other persons employed in the state institutions (except mechanics), those needed during legislative sessions and those at work on highways outside city and village limits.

Ten-hour laws for employees on " street surface and elevated railroads " and on " steam and other railroads " appear in the latest law [2] very much as provided for in the law of

[1] The continuance of the regulation of hours of public employees was made possible by a constitutional amendment in 1905. This legislation had been declared unconstitutional in 1904 (People *v.* Grout).

[2] Labor Law of 1924, §§ 164-166, Art. 5. This law has grown through a series of amendments.

1897. The hours of all train signalmen and train dispatchers have been more drastically regulated however. These persons may not be on duty for more than eight hours in any day (except in cases of extraordinary emergency) and they "shall be allowed at least two days of rest of twenty-four hours each in every calendar month with the regular compensation."[1]

The nominal ten-hour law for employees in brickyards still remains on the statute books. By this provision, employees may not be required to work more than ten hours a day nor before 7 a. m., but other arrangements between employer and employee may be made for extra compensation.[2]

Hours of labor in mines have never been limited by law in New York State although this was one of the first important types of legislation in a number of the great coal and metal mining states of the country. The early law in Utah limiting the working day of miners to eight hours a day received the sanction of the United States Supreme Court, as we have seen, and established a precedent. That the mining industry in New York State is relatively unimportant, is the obvious explanation of the absence of hour legislation, whereas there are detailed regulations (initiated as early as 1892, ch. 677), regarding the safety of men at work in mines, tunnels and quarries, and women and children are forbidden to work in mines.

New York State employs more men in tunnels and caissons, where workers are obliged to breathe compressed air, than any other state. In these occupations New York has,

[1] McKinney's "Consolidated Laws of New York," Annotated, Book 30, *Labor Law*, p. 34. Held constitutional where employees work wholly in intrastate commerce. People *v.* Erie Railroad Co. (1910), 198 N. Y. 368. Reversed for employment in interstate commerce which conflicts with the act of Congress, March 4, 1907, and which superseded state legislation, Erie Railroad Co. *v.* New York (1914), 233 U. S. 671.

[2] Labor Law of 1924, Art. 5, § 163.

beginning in 1909 (ch. 291), developed a law framed under scientific advice to give protection to persons so employed.[1] In addition to specifications concerning the equipment of apparatus and the attendance of medical officers and nurses, hours are now prescribed in a schedule of shifts and intervals according to the degree of air pressure. No person may work more than eight hours a day in an air pressure of 14.7 pounds or more, and "the working time in any twenty-four hours shall be divided into two shifts under compressed air with an interval in open air." [2] The total number of hours to be worked per day is as low as one and one-half under air pressure at fifty pounds, under which condition the minimum rest interval in open air is five hours. "No person shall be subjected to pressure exceeding fifty pounds except in emergency." The length of the rest interval varies from one-half hour up to five hours. A corresponding schedule of regulations for decompression—the process of coming out of compressed air into normal air—is also prescribed by law.[3]

2. *Minors*[4]

A general eight-hour law and prohibition of child labor had been agitated by organized labor since the 'fifties, and beginning in 1869 a child-labor law was presented to the legislature for six successive years. In 1877 the abolition of child labor was one of the four cardinal aims of a strong body of workers who had developed a serious "Political Branch" of labor-union activities. The protection of female labor took, for the moment, a secondary place.

[1] New Jersey, Pennsylvania and Massachusetts also have this type of legislation.

[2] *Ibid.*, § 430.

[3] *Ibid.*, § 431.

[4] No attempt is made to discuss thoroughly the protective measures for children, but only to suggest the trend which gradually widened to include women. Professor Fairchild's *Factory Legislation of the State of New York* has again been used freely for this history.

Perhaps the first clear-cut bill to regulate child labor was framed by President Gerry of the Society for the Prevention of Cruelty to Children, in 1882. The bill passed the senate but was believed to have been lost because of lack of time for its introduction into the assembly before that body adjourned. A child-labor bill restricting the working hours of all children under the age of sixteen, and also of women for the first time, to ten hours a day was presented and defeated in 1883. A bill in the following year attempted to concentrate emphasis upon the regulation of child labor by eliminating entirely the clause pertaining to women. The bill provided that no minor under twenty-one years of age should be employed more than ten hours a day or sixty hours a week, and that minors should have a free hour at noon from twelve to one. Provisions were made for enforcement under the direction of the factory inspector, and two assistants were to be appointed by the state board of health. ". . . Officers of any duly incorporated society for the prevention of cruelty to children were also authorized to enter and inspect the premises where children were employed." [1]

This bill passed the senate but was decried as too radical before it came to final consideration in the assembly. A substitute bill was passed by the assembly in 1884 by a vote of 81 to 21, but was in turn killed in the senate. Though defeated, this act is noteworthy in that it marks the first distinction between the sexes among the minors. Moreover, when modified in the direction of less restriction for females, the bill finally passed both houses in 1886 (ch. 409), and it forms the first real factory legislation in New York State to which later laws were enacted as amendments. The provision was that "no minor under the age of eighteen years nor any woman under twenty-one years shall be employed at labor in any manufacturing establish-

[1] Fairchild, *op. cit.*, p. 42.

ment in this state for a longer period than sixty hours in any one week, unless for the purpose of making necessary repairs."[2] Hours of labor were to be posted for each day.

Three years later, in 1889 (ch. 560), the limitation of ten hours a day was recovered for these minor workers, without which there had been nothing to prevent their legal employment over an inhumanly long period of time. The only exception to the new ten-hour day was that for the purpose of shortening hours on Saturday. The night work prohibition was also introduced at this time by which this same group of minors—females under twenty-one years of age and males under eighteen years—were prohibited from working between the hours of nine in the evening and six in the morning.

In 1890 (ch. 398), the restrictions for minors were made less flexible, all exceptions for making necessary repairs being abrogated. Also these young people were allowed to labor no " more hours in any week than will make an average of ten hours a day for the whole number of days " worked in the week. This made it impossible for employers operating their plants less than five and one-half days in the week to require excessive overtime on the plea that it was in order to have a whole holiday on Saturday.

The year 1896 is notable as the year in which legislation respecting mercantile establishments was enacted,—the first other than the 1881 provision for seats which had never been enforced. The act (ch. 384) was entitled " An act to regulate the employment of women and children in mercantile establishments and to provide that the same shall be enforced." The general provisions were similar to those

[1] Although the provision applied only to females under twenty-one years of age, it was entitled—An act to regulate the employment of women and children in manufacturing establishments, and to provide for the appointment of inspectors to enforce the same.

for factories except for a further divergence in the protection offered to boys and to girls. Boys under sixteen years of age instead of eighteen years, were included, while the provision remained the same for girls, including all under the age of twenty-one years. The night work prohibition for this group was from 10 p. m to 7 a. m. instead of from 9 p. m. to 7 a. m. as for factories. Saturdays were excepted from the ten-hour limitation provided that the week's work was no more than sixty hours. The holiday rush period was excluded entirely during the period between December 15 and January 1 inclusive.

This act was a beginning in the direction of protecting employees in mercantile establishments as yet chiefly only for minors. But it is clear that the extensive exceptions made for just those times where the law was most needed, if at all, rendered it practically worthless. The legislation was the result of the investigation of the Reinhardt Committee appointed by the assembly in 1895 but fiercely combated by mercantile employers.[1]

WAGES

Legislation concerning wages in New York State is not extensive and has been enacted for the most part without regard to sex. In spite of the fact that minimum wage bills applying especially to women have been introduced into the legislature repeatedly in recent years, a law of this type has never yet been entered upon the statute books. New York has, in this respect, failed to join some fourteen other jurisdictions that have enacted minimum wage laws for women.[2]

[1] More recent acts pertaining to minors when they are related to statutes concerning women, will be discussed in Part ii.

[2] Arizona, Arkansas, California, Colorado, Kansas, Massachusetts, Minnesota, North Dakota, Oregon, Porto Rico, South Dakota, Utah, Washington, Wisconsin. The minimum wage laws of Texas, the District of Columbia and Wisconsin have been annulled.

Although there are no enforced minimum wage statutes applying to men in this country, there have been sporadic attempts to secure them. Nebraska attempted the enactment of a minimum wage law for all adult workers in 1909 and in 1912 Ohio actually passed a constitutional amendment specifically permitting a minimum wage act for all classes of workers.[1] In neither of these states, however, has the minimum wage machinery been operated for men.

In New York State, wage legislation is in the main confined to measures for the security of wage payment, that is to the time and method of payment and the assignment of wages. One degree beyond this point is that relating to public employees.

1. *Public Employees*[2]

Regulations concerning the wages of public employees are, in New York State, more explicit than for any other group. In the labor law of 1897, it was required that employees on public works receive remuneration according to the prevailing rate of wages.[3]

[1] Commons and Andrews, *Principles of Labor Legislation* (1920), pp. 196-197.

[2] Labor Law of 1924, §§ 220-223.

[3] A definite rate of wages has seldom been attempted except in 1889-1890 when "there was a statute in force providing that the wages of day laborers employed by the state should be not less than two dollars per day" (McKinney, *op. cit.*, p. 26). Also an order for a two dollar a day minimum for canal employees was issued by chapter 467 in 1923, but was repealed by a later act in the same year (ch. 494). Another attempt for a minimum wage was made in 1915 on behalf of the New York City street cleaners who are among the lowest paid employees of the city. Following a thorough inquiry into the income necessary to maintain a family of five "living in accordance with American ideals" the Board of Estimate proposed that the necessary minimum be paid to this class of employees. At that time this minimum was $70 a month and in 1919 rising prices would have increased it to $118 a month. Some advance was secured but the amount fell below the recommendation of the Board (Commons and Andrews, *op. cit.*, p. 195).

And later amendments have been made to this provision to make it more specific. At present the statute applies to employees on public works "or upon any material to be used upon or in connection therewith," and defines the meaning of prevailing rate as that paid "for a day's work in the same trade or occupation in the locality within the state where the work is performed." Cash payments are required and company stores may not be conducted "if there is any store selling supplies within two miles of the place where such contract is being executed."

2. *Time and Method of Wage Payment*[1]

That employees be paid in cash has also been a legal requirement in practically all instances since 1897. By a recent amendment, however, (Laws of 1921, ch. 642) checks were permitted to be used as a legal medium of payment provided the "employer . . . furnishes satisfactory proof to the commissioner of his financial responsibility and gives reasonable assurance that such checks may be cashed by employees without difficulty and for the full amount for which they are drawn."

Time of payment of wages. The attempt to protect workers from inconvenience and suffering entailed by irregular and deferred payment of their wages was made as early as 1890. Except in the case of employees of steam surface railroads, wages have been required to be paid weekly and not more than six days after the wage is due. This provision was declared constitutional in 1914 by the United States Supreme Court in the case of Erie Railroad Co. *v.* Williams, and the general construction of the law by the Attorney General in 1912 was that "the persons employed are not being benefited at the expense of others, but are assured at regular and frequent intervals payment of the

[1] Labor Law of 1924, §§ 195-197.

wages they are entitled to; the beneficial effect intended by the legislature should not be minimized by narrow construction."[1]

Legislation regarding the time of wage payment of railroad employees was enacted for the first time in 1895 (ch. 791). The regulation as amended was carried into the law of 1897 and is incorporated in the labor law of today. The statute provides that employees of steam surface railroads shall be paid bi-weekly—on the first and fifteenth day of each month—and the payment may be regularly delayed for one half month. In her *Handbook of Labor Laws of New York,* Miss Katharine Anthony points out that

> The disadvantages of this delay to the wage-earners, especially at the beginning of their employment, are patent. In the case of the lowest-paid workers, this legalized "holding-out" of wages is often prohibitive at the outset of the work. It presupposes either credit or savings, neither of which the applicant is likely to have. The social and economic unwisdom of infrequent or postponed pay days is apparent. It sets a premium on casual labor in which payment at least is prompt, at the same time that the State through its labor legislation is seeking to reduce this evil.

Assignment of future wages of employees was declared illegal by law of 1897, section 12, and this prohibition is retained in the present law, section 197. Also "charges for groceries, provisions or clothing shall not be a valid off-set in behalf of the employer against wages."

Deductions from the wages of employees also may not be made by employers "for the purpose of maintaining an insurance fund for their benefit," and "garnishment of wages for debt is not permitted if the debtor's wages are less than twelve dollars a week." Also an employee is entitled to two

[1] McKinney, *op. cit.*, pp. 42-43.

hours' absence from employment to vote at a general election without reduction of wages." [1]

REST PERIODS

1. *Recess for meal times*

The requirements of New York State for rest periods alternating with periods of work in compressed air have been mentioned in the section on hours of labor. Another type of recess which appears to be unique in New York State, applying as it does to all persons,[2] is that allowing for meal-time pauses. With but two or three exceptions these statutes have been enacted regardless of sex or age and they date back to the first factory law amendment of 1887 (ch. 465). At that time a 45-minute period was required at noon which was extended to 60 minutes in 1892, a provision for the evening meal being made in the following year. In 1896 (ch. 384) a 45-minute noon meal-time was allowed in mercantile and other establishments such as business offices, telegraph offices, theaters and other amusement places, restaurants, hotels, apartment houses, etc. Permits for granting exceptions in certain cases could be obtained from the commissioner of labor but the permits were revocable at any time.

In 1910 more specific provisions were made for the evening recess. In factories, if employees worked more than one hour overtime, twenty minutes was demanded for their supper. In mercantile and other establishments, if work was to be continued after 7 p. m., twenty minutes was required for lunch between five and seven o'clock. A special allowance for meal time was made for women in 1919 (ch. 583) when employed in connection with street railroads.

At present, therefore, "every person employed in or in

[1] Katharine Anthony, *Handbook of Labor Laws of New York* (1917), pp. 7-8.

[2] Commons and Andrews, *op. cit.*, p. 271.

connection with a factory and every female employed as a conductor or guard" are allowed a minimum of 60 minutes for the noon-day meal;[1] "every person employed in or in connection with a mercantile or other establishment or occupations coming under the provisions of this chapter" is allowed at least 45 minutes for the noon-day meal, except as otherwise provided. Also all persons employed after seven o'clock in the evening are allowed at least 20 minutes for a meal between the hours of five and seven.[2]

It is reported that the opportunity which the law affords for shortening the noon-time recess has been so frequently observed that "in actual practice, the half-hour luncheon period is found in many establishments."[3] Moreover the failure of the law to state between what times the noon-day meal shall be taken or the maximum number of hours of labor to be worked before the meal, makes it possible for employees to be required to work too long before having this recess.

2. *One Day of Rest in Seven*

While Sunday closing laws for barbers and butchers were enacted in New York as early as 1895 (ch. 823) and 1901 (ch. 392) respectively, the weekly day of rest legislation was not introduced until 1913 (ch. 740). Although the early acts were not primarily protective measures, the fact that our custom has "from time out of mind" recognized Sunday as a day of rest and recreation was of no small importance in winning the favor of the courts.[4]

New York is one of the few states that have effective laws

[1] Of the seventeen replies to the questionnaire of the Factory Investigating Commission in 1912, regarding hours of labor in factories in New York City, eleven advocated a mandatory lunch period of one hour.

[2] Laws of 1924, § 162.

[3] Katharine Anthony, *op. cit.*, p. 5.

[4] 43 N. E. 541 (1896). See discussion of the judicial interpretation of these laws in other states, p. 29, *supra*.

requiring the one day of rest in seven in factories and mercantile establishments.[1] Together with Massachusetts, New York in 1913 adopted the "Standard Bill" which had just been prepared by the American Association for Labor Legislation.[2] It was in 1911 that this association created a special committee with Mr. John A. Fitch as its chairman to work out a law which could be adopted uniformly by the states. Full cognizance was taken of the demands of modern industry which renders impossible any strict adherence to the old Sabbath laws. Furthermore the large Jewish population would have made a general Sunday closing law impracticable in New York. A provision was drafted therefore that, "with reasonable elasticity in cases of emergency or unusual industrial conditions, forbids an employer to work his men seven days a week, and yet permits an industry necessarily or desirably continuous to operate seven days a week." "Tired men are partly poisoned men" was the spirit of the legislative campaigns waged for the passage of this bill, as it has since been the spirit behind the doctrine of the shorter working day "on the basis of efficiency as well as social justice." [3]

[1] By 1920, six states and the Federal Government had such laws, namely, California, Connecticut, Michigan, Massachusetts, New York and Wisconsin. Post Office employees only are included in the federal law, the California and Connecticut acts are emasculated by exemptions in "any case of emergency," and the Michigan law applies only to interurban motormen and conductors. Commons and Andrews, *Principles of Labor Legislation*, p. 280.

[2] Chapter 240. Wisconsin also adopted this bill in 1919.

[3] European precedent is abundant in the enactment of the one-day-of-rest-in-seven provision. Beginning in Switzerland in 1890 according to Commons and Andrews, *op. cit.*, pp. 279-280, and in the other leading countries in about 1905, enforceable laws of this type have spread rather generally. Mr. John Fitch also represented the American Association on a special commission on Hours of Labor in Continuous Industries created by the International Association for Labor Legislation in 1910. The Standard Bill drafted for this country was thus in close harmony with the standards abroad. *American Labor Legislation Review*, 1914, p. 611.

The standard law as enacted and amended by the New York State legislature protects all persons in factory and mercantile establishments from a seven-day week of labor. Certain occupations are excluded such as janitors, watchmen, superintendents and foremen in charge, employees engaged in handling milk and cream or their products where not more than seven persons are employed, persons working not more than three hours on Sunday "setting sponges in bakeries, caring for live animals, maintaining fires, or making necessary repairs to boilers or machinery."[1] In 1919 (ch. 671) employees in hotels were also exempted. Before operating on Sunday, every employer is required to "conspicuously post" the working schedules of employees, "designating a day of rest for each." Also a copy of the schedules must be filed with the commissioner and "no employee shall be permitted to work on his designated day of rest." "If there shall be practical difficulties or unnecessary hardships in carrying out the provisions of this section of the rules of the board, the board may make a variation therefrom if the spirit of the act be observed and substantial justice be done."

This discretionary power delegated to the board has been exercised to a considerable degree, according to the report that about 292 variations were granted by it during the first five years of the existence of the Industrial Commission.[2] 146 of these were granted with the understanding that seven-day workers be put on an eight-hour day schedule of work. No variations were allowed for women workers.

There was another clause in the 1913 act which exempted employees at work in continuous industries with the approval of the commissioner of labor "in his discretion," provided no employee was permitted to work more than eight hours

[1] Massachusetts and Wisconsin grant more exemptions than are granted in New York.

[2] *American Labor Legislation Review* for June, 1920, p. 129.

in any day. In 1915, this provision for exemption was declared unconstitutional by the court of appeals on the ground that it was an unlawful delegation of power to the commissioner of labor.[1] The remainder of the act was upheld as a proper exercise of the police power for the protection of the health of employees. Since this decree, the commissioner has granted needed exemptions only in those continuous industries in which the eight-hour shift was in practice; and the legality of these tactics has thus far not been challenged.[2]

There are still a good many occupations in New York, and more elsewhere, to which the weekly rest statute does not apply, for its main application is to factories and mercantile establishments.[3]

HEALTH AND SAFETY

1. *The Industrial Code*

All types of protective labor legislation are in reality provisions for health and safety, for these conditions are the prerequisites both of good work and good citizenship and hence of public welfare. The remaining part of this section, however, treats of acts to protect health and safety in the narrower sense of the words.

With the creation of a state industrial board in 1913 (ch.

[1] See People *v.* Klinck Packing Co., 214 N. Y. 121, p. 33, *supra*.

[2] Commons and Andrews, *op. cit.*, p. 281. The one day in seven provision is contained in the Laws of 1924, § 161.

[3] Laws of 1924, § 161. The Attorney General, "in numerous opinions" held that the law "does not apply to pharmacies or drug stores, to telegraph and telephone companies (except employees working in shops) to railroads or street railways (except employees working in shops or on factory yard engines), to restaurants, lunchrooms or hotel dining rooms, to cold storage plants (except ice-plant, boiler and engine room employees), to farm work, to chauffeurs, or to the drink hall on the Saratoga Reservation." Employees in hotels were expressly brought under the protection of the law by chapter 671 of the laws of 1921, however.

145) came the beginning of a definite attempt to establish a satisfactory means by which rules and regulations for the protection of lives and health could be assured. For it was evident that such protection could not be accomplished by cumbrous and inflexible acts of the legislature. An industrial code thus became the form in which these rules and regulations were drafted by the board and they "have the force and effect of law." The present statute, section 28, reads in part that,

It being the policy and intent of this chapter that all places to which it applies shall be so constructed, equipped, arranged, operated and conducted in all respects as to provide reasonable and adequate protection to the lives, health and safety of all persons employed therein, and frequenting the same . . . the board may make special rules to guard against such elements of danger by establishing requirements as to temperature, humidity, the removal of dusts, gases or fumes, by requiring licenses to be applied for and issued by the department as a condition of carrying on any such industry, trade, occupation or process, by requiring medical inspection and supervision of persons employed or applying for employment, and by other appropriate means.

The Industrial Code is supplementary to the Labor Law and Workmen's Compensation Law and should be read with these to obtain a full sense of New York State's present attempt to protect the health and safety of laborers and the public.

2. *Special Working Conditions*

Among the earlier laws pertaining to working conditions was the act of 1881 (ch. 298) which required "suitable seats" for female employees in mercantile and manufacturing establishments. The act permitted women to use these seats "for the preservation of their health." But despite the fact that the act declared a violation a misdemeanor, it is a matter of common knowledge that the law was ineffective.

Females were prohibited in 1882 (§ 2010) from employment for service in all places of public amusement in New York City, and in 1896 (ch. 112) this provision was extended to make it unlawful for any female not a member of the family to sell or serve liquor upon the premises. Also in 1896 women and children were forbidden to work in basements of mercantile establishments except by the approval of the health department. These acts were the forerunners of the so-called "welfare legislation" for women which has been developed in more recent years.

Another branch of the health provisions is that requiring water-closets and wash-rooms. It was in the first amendment to the factory law of 1886 that a regulation of this kind was made (Laws of 1887, ch. 462). At that time the legislature demanded that properly kept and screened washrooms and water closets for female employees be maintained separate from those for men. This was followed in 1889 (ch. 560) by specifications for sanitation and ventilation in water closets for men as well as for women. These provisions for the personal accommodations of employees were improved and extended by acts of 1914 (ch. 183) and 1919 (ch. 544) and by rules in the industrial code, until at present, in connection with practically all occupations, explicit requirements for proper separate accommodations are made for men and women.[1] The act of 1919 required for elevator operators that "there shall be provided and maintained for the use of all employees, whether men, women or children, adequate and convenient washrooms or washing facilities and a number of suitable and convenient water closets." However, while seats are rather generally required for women employees, the one instance in which they are re-

[1] For example see Laws of 1924, §§ 203, 293, 295, 316, 378.

quired for men is in dressing rooms for men employed in compressed air.[1]

3. *Protection of Life and Limb*

A large body of law has been developed toward greater safety from accident of the working people in New York State,—beginning with the first act in 1885 for the protection of life and limb, down through the employer's liability act of 1902 to the steadily expanding measure of the Workmen's Compensation Law of the present day. The provisions for workmen's compensation have now become so extensive that they form a division of statutes quite separate from those under the labor law.[2]

By the first of the New York safety statutes it was made a misdemeanor for employers to furnish unsafe mechanical contrivances such as hoists, ladders and scaffolding, used in the erection of buildings.[3] This was mostly a paper beginning, however, according to official reports,[4] and numerous amendments were passed during the succeeding years. For example in 1887 (ch. 462) fire escapes were required to be installed, elevators and stairs and machines guarded, and accidents reported. Police were called upon to receive complaints and investigate unsafe furnishings by the law of 1892 (ch. 517), and in 1899 enforcement of these provisions was lodged with the state factory inspector.

[1] Labor Law of 1924, § 426. The New York Bureau of Women in Industry, 120 East 28th Street, New York City, has on file the texts of all laws to date in regard to seating in industry, in European countries as well as in the United States. This material will be furnished to anyone who is interested.

[2] Of the 67 volumes of McKinney's Consolidated Laws of New York of which the Labor Law is presented in Book 30, the Workmen's Compensation Law composes the whole of Book 64.

[3] Laws of 1885 (ch. 314).

[4] Labor Legislation in New York, by Adna F. Weber, Chief Statistician (1904), p. 21.

During these years employers' liability provisions were being developed in European countries and in some of the states of the Union. As early as 1880 the English Parliament prescribed this larger responsibility for employers and employees, and in 1887 Massachusetts adopted a "substantial copy" of the English act.[1] Indiana, Alabama and Colorado also enacted similar measures before the passing of the New York provision of 1902 (ch. 600). Prior to this enactment the common law—the law of the ages—had remained supreme, but the new statute imposed many new duties and burdens unknown to that law. The statute specifically aimed at the abrogation or modification of two defenses theretofore possessed by employers.

In effect it eliminated the so-called fellow-servant rule in certain cases by providing that the employer should be liable to one employee for the default of another employee who was performing or who was intrusted with the duty of performing acts of superintendence. . . . The statute likewise modified the defense of assumption by an employee of risks flowing from the default of the employer by providing that the question of such assumption should not in any case be one of law but should be one of fact.

Thus the act

did not give a new remedy for acts of negligence resulting in personal injuries; it merely extended the liability of employers for negligence of their superintendents, etc., giving an action in some cases where it would not have existed at common law.[2]

Some extensions were made to the employers' liability act by amendment of 1910 (ch. 302) but the entire act was largely rendered obsolete by the introduction of the more

[1] McKinney, *Labor Law*, pp. 265-266.

[2] *Ibid.*, pp. 266-267.

inclusive workmen's compensation law in 1913 with its subsequent amendments. Some few employments are not included in the compensation law, accidents in connection with which may yet be maintained under the employers' liability act, but all the sections in this act which relate to hazardous employments have been formally repealed,[1] since they are provided for under the later provision.

4. *Workmen's Compensation*

European precedent was again followed in this country by the introduction of the legal right of workmen to compensation for accidents incurred during employment, which transcended the fellow-servant and assumption-of-risk qualifications of the employers' liability act. New York State has the distinction of being first among the states to enact this modern type of law.[2] The provision as passed by the legislature was for an elective compensation made compulsory for hazardous employments, but the compulsory feature was promptly declared unconstitutional in the now famous "Ives case" of 1911 before mentioned. The decree of the courts proved but a passing rebuff. The time for workmen's compensation had come, and the state constitution was amended to admit it. The amendment was passed in 1913 forming section 19 of Article I and in that same year, chapter 816, a new act was passed which was reënacted in 1914 (ch. 41). Since that time numerous amendments have been made for the improvement of this statute.[3]

[1] Laws of 1921, chapter 121.

[2] Laws of 1910, ch. 674. A federal act was passed in 1908 granting compensation rights to certain employees injured in the course of employment.

[3] Following the lead of New York, ten states enacted workmen's compensation legislation in 1911, and at the present time all but some half dozen states have this provision for workers in some form. The federal government provides a model measure for its million employees which was drafted by the American Association for Labor Legislation (Stand-

The New York constitutional amendment, passed primarily to make valid a workmen's compensation law, is admirable for its breadth of phrase based upon a sense of growing human needs. It would seem to be capable of more generous interpretations for the protection of the state's industrial workers than has yet been realized. The amendment begins:

Nothing contained in this constitution shall be construed to limit the power of the legislature to enact laws for the protection of the lives, health, or safety of employees; or for the payment, either by employers, or by employers and employees or otherwise, either directly or through a state or other system

ards for Workmen's Compensation Laws, revised to Jan. 1, 1923). Owing to the early adverse decision of the New York courts, however, the majority of the states adopted provisions for elective rather than compulsory compensation. (Commons and Andrews, *op. cit.*, p. 400.)

But in order to encourage employers to elect compensation instead of retaining the old liability act, that act was made less attractive to them. A number of the former defenses such as suggested by the phrases fellow servant's rule, contributory negligence, and assumption of risk were either removed or modified. In 1920 only 14 of the 45 compensation states were compulsory and 31 elective as to compensation provisions, while 39 were compulsory and six elective as to insurance requirements. (*Cf.* Workmen's Compensation Law of the United States and Canada up to January 1, 1920, by Carl Hockstadt. United States Department of Labor, *Bulletin No. 275*, p. 14).

The wide dissimilarity of the compensation laws in the several states is their greatest point in common, according to Hockstadt, authority on this subject (p. 18). The diversity lies chiefly in those points that are concerned with the kind of system—elective or compulsory compensation and elective or compulsory insurance, after the general principle has been accepted; the scope of the law—the industries, occupations and types of cases covered; the amount of compensation paid, including the period of waiting and the maximum and minimum limits of payment; the length of the compensated period; the extent to which medical service is provided; and the administration of the law. There is wide divergence among the states in the administration of the law, as to the agencies of insurance, the injuries included, the security of payments and the promptness and regularity with which they are made.

of insurance or otherwise, of compensation for injuries . . . or for death . . . resulting from injuries. . . .

Some exceptions are mentioned, namely, where the injured worker is intoxicated, and where the injury has been wilfully inflicted by the injured or another.

The new compensation law was made even more secure by receiving the favor of the courts as was seen in preceding pages.[1] One court explained that

injuries sustained by those who perform the manual and mechanical tasks of an industry must be deemed to have been intended by this statute to be made a social risk, a liability of the industry, a charge upon the production cost of the article manufactured or the service rendered.[2]

In 1922, chapter 615, the law was amended generally. As it stands today it is a law of compulsory compensation and compulsory insurance. It includes all hazardous and non-hazardous occupations, except those in agriculture and domestic service, and employment not conducted for gain but not excepting employments for the state and municipal corporations. Of the non-hazardous occupations, industries employing less than four workmen are not included within the law. Specific provisions are made for compensation benefits according to the seriousness of the accident or injury.

The waiting period between the time of disability and the first compensation payment has just been reduced by the 1924 legislature, from two weeks to seven days. This places New York in the group of some thirty-five jurisdictions that have adopted a waiting period of seven days or less in order to lessen the burdens of industrial victims. The American

[1] See p. 52, *supra*.

[2] Rheinwald *v.* Builders' Brick & Supply Co., 168 App. Div. 425 (1915).

Association for Labor Legislation was an enduring and forceful champion of this improvement in the workmen's compensation law which has heretofore been voted down in the assembly.

In the inclusion of occupational disease as a compensable disability, New York has been more prompt. The courts have tended to interpret the law liberally by frequently including such affections as frost bite, gas poisoning, angina pectoris, anthrax, tuberculosis, and ivy poisoning. And in so doing the courts appeared to reflect a growing public opinion, for in 1920 (ch. 538) the legislature expressly included within the list of compensable cases disablement resulting from certain occupational diseases. New York is now one of the twelve jurisdictions (including the federal government) which includes occupational diseases as personal injuries entitling employees to compensation.[1]

There are four kinds of insurance allowed to New York employers against compensation demands: they may be insured (1) through a state fund, (2) through a mutual insurance corporation, (3) through a private insurance corporation, or by self-insurance.[2] Private companies must be approved by the Industrial Board, and, if self-insured, employers must submit to certain definite rules, such as the deposit of securities with the industrial commissioner, semi-annual reports of claims upon oath, examinations of assets and liabilities, and revocation of the privilege of self-insurance.[3]

The administration of the compensation law in New York

[1] *Standards for Workmen's Compensation Laws, op. cit.*, p. 9.

[2] Among the several states, insurance through a state fund may either be exclusive (the sole type of insurance) or competitive as in New York. In 1920 eight states had the exclusive state fund. See Carl Hockstadt, *op. cit.*, p. 16.

[3] Rules for Self Insurance in New York. *Monthly Labor Review* for August, 1923, pp. 472-473.

State, as of the labor law, is under the complete jurisdiction of the Industrial Board, and all settlements of claims must be made through some member of the board or deputy, with power of appeal. The law applies alike to all persons except that double compensation and death benefits are required for minors illegally employed.[1] During the past two years there has been developed, under the auspices of the Women's Trade Union League and through the unflagging leadership of Mrs. Maud Swartz, a special service for women who are entitled to compensation. In numerous instances women who could not speak English or who had not sufficient ability to push their legitimate claims have been assisted by this agency.

PART II: LEGISLATION FOR WOMEN

In the year 1899, legislation for the protection of industrial women in the State of New York took a more serious turn. The history of legislation for all workers has just been sketched wherein it is clear that an increasing effort has been made by the people of the state to secure greater safety, sanitation, and compensation for injuries for all workers. Women in recent years, however, as in other states and countries, have been the objects of legislation additional to that for men, which runs parallel with and is frequently a part of child labor legislation.[2] These special laws for women will be traced in the following pages with consideration of child labor only as it bears upon the subject in hand. A statement of the legislation only will be made at this time, to be completed by the two following chapters which will present some of the influences which

[1] Added in 1923, ch. 572.

[2] Moreover in the laws preceding 1899, while there was little regulation of the work of adult women, there was more legislation for young women than for young men.

brought about these special laws. The four groups of protective acts for women are those pertaining to (a) hours of day labor, (b) hours of night labor, (c) prohibited employment, (d) special working conditions.

HOURS OF LABOR—DAY WORK

Factories [1]

The first law that limited the hours of all women in New York, over as well as under twenty-one years of age, was that enacted for factories in 1899, (ch. 192). By this act no female and no minor under the age of eighteen years was permitted to be employed " more than ten hours in any one day or sixty hours in any week except to make a shorter last day, or more hours in any week than to make an average of ten hours per day for the whole number of days so worked." The factory inspector was to be notified by the employer in writing if the hours were so changed, the names and addresses of the employees retained to be presented on demand, and a printed notice posted according to regulation.

The six-day week for all women in factories appeared in 1907 (ch. 286), amending the ten-hour law. Exceptions for females sixteen years of age and upwards (and males between sixteen and eighteen years) were that they may be employed more than ten hours a day; "(a) regularly in not to exceed five days a week in order to make a short day or a holiday on one of the six working days of the week; (b) irregularly in not to exceed three days a week, provided that no such person shall be required or permitted to work more than twelve hours in any one day or more than sixty hours in any week." [2] Printed notices of the regular hours of

[1] See the New York State Labor Law, with amendments, additions and annotations to August 1, 1924, § 172.

[2] According to the testimony of Miss Josephine Goldmark before the Factory Investigating Commission in 1912, this was the only law of its

work and of the exceptions were required to be posted according to the form furnished by the commissioner of labor. No change could be made in the scheduled hours for the week after the week's work began, without the commissioner's consent.[1] Whenever women or male minors were employed in two or more factories or mercantile establishments it was stipulated that their hours should not exceed the limit for working in one.

The present nine-hour day and fifty-four-hour week for all women and male minors under eighteen years of age was adopted in 1912 (ch. 539). The twelve-hour day exceptions of 1907 being reduced to ten, and the six-day week limit remaining intact. With this enactment New York joined a group of some fifteen states which, by 1912, had set a maximum limit below sixty hours a week for factory women.[2]

1. *Canneries* [3]

Owing to the nature of the industry some exceptions to the factory law were granted to canning establishments. By the same act that introduced the nine-hour day all hour regulations for women and male minors sixteen to eighteen years of age engaged "in canning or pre-

kind in the United States—allowing as it did, overtime both regularly and irregularly to the extent of twelve hours a day. (Report of the New York Factory Investigating Commission, 1912, vol. iii, p. 1605). See page 160, *infra*.

[1] There was an exception to this rule as a result of the claim of some factories, as canneries, that, "owing to the nature of the work" it was at times impossible to schedule hours a week in advance. To meet cases of this kind, special dispensation could be secured from the commissioner of labor, providing the regular hours of labor were posted and a record of the actual working time was kept in a book subject at all times to the scrutiny of the commissioner or his agent.

[2] California, Connecticut, Maine, Massachusetts, Michigan, Minnesota, Mississippi, New Hampshire, New Jersey, Ohio, Rhode Island, Utah, Washington, Wisconsin.

[3] Labor Law of 1924, § 173.

serving perishable products in fruit and canning establishments" were waived during the season from June 15 to October 15.

This blanket release during the height of the canning season was cancelled in the following year however (ch. 465), in so far as it concerned women workers, male minors sixteen years of age and upwards remaining unrestricted. Following the recommendation of the Factory Investigating Commission, the regulation recognized the same months as before as busy ones and protected workers were permitted to increase their working time during this period provided the hours of the women did not exceed sixty in any week nor ten in any one day, and provided there was one day of rest in seven. Nevertheless the force of this provision was more or less weakened by the fact that the Industrial Board was empowered in the act to permit women to work twelve hours a day and sixty-six hours a week during the shorter period from the 25th of June to the 5th of August of each year, but not more than six days in any week. This allowance was made because the extra work was "required by the needs of the industry" and could "be permitted without serious injury to the health of the women so employed."[1] The permits were contingent upon the fulfilment of three conditions, namely: (1) that the daily hours of work be posted and an accurate record be kept for the examination by officials of the overtime work of each individual; (2) that the floors be properly drained, or that slat platforms be laid down, so that women would not have to stand on moist floors; (3) that no woman work more than ten hours in any occupation that required constant standing, or at labeling or packing cans. The last stipulation was

[1] Where quotations from the statutes are given they are taken from the original law or amendment. Where the content of the 1924 law is the same but the wording differs, the new wording has not been given.

made because labeling and packing cans could not be considered momentarily exigent.

The term "women" in this act referred to females eighteen years of age and upwards. Male minors could continue work without restriction of hours during these rush seasons. This amendment relating to canneries remains the same in the factory law of 1924, section 173.

2. *Laundries*[1]

Laundries are also factories and despite a great deal of effort on the part of their owners, they have not been granted legislative exemptions from the factory law as have canneries. However the statute does not include custom laundry work which is done at home for regular family trade, and, more notably, it does not include hotel laundries for the reason that these have been ruled by the attorney general as non-public enterprises.[2]

3. *Newspaper Offices*[3]

Newspaper offices are also factories, but in 1919 (ch. 582) women "engaged or employed as writers and reporters" in such offices were exempted from the limitation of six days of work a week, as well as from the night work prohibition.

Mercantile and Other Establishments[4]

The 1913 legislature (ch. 493), following the recommendations of the factory commission, introduced limitation of hours for all females engaged in mercantile establishments. (The earlier provision had pertained only to female minors between sixteen and twenty-one years of age). A distinction was made in the act between first and second class cities, the maximum number of working hours for all women in

[1] Labor Law of 1924, § 296.

[2] March 5 and Sept. 28, 1906.

[3] Labor Law of 1924, § 181.

[4] Labor Law of 1924, § 181.

second class cities being made fifty-four in any one week while elsewhere it was sixty hours; nine hours in any one day, and elsewhere ten hours, "unless for the purpose of making a shorter work day of some one day of the week." Saturdays were excepted for all employees sixteen years of age and upwards provided the total number of hours for women did not exceed fifty-four in second class cities and sixty elsewhere. The five days in each year preceding the 25th of December in second class cities, and elsewhere between the 18th and 24th of December, both inclusive, were without regulation as to hours.[1]

Discrimination between first and second class cities was eliminated in the following year, 1914 (ch. 331), and the six-day week regulation was added. The maximum hours in all mercantile establishments in the state for female employees over sixteen years of age were made fifty-four a week and nine a day, "unless for the purpose of making a shorter work day of some one day of the week."[2] The period between the 18th and 24th of December, both inclusive, was excepted, but Saturday exceptions were eliminated.

"Two additional days at any time during the year for the purpose of stocktaking" were made free from hour regulation in 1915 (ch. 386). Printed notices were required to be kept posted in conspicuous places at all times stating the specific number of hours each regulated employee was permitted to work each week. The form of the notice was furnished by the commissioner of labor and no changes could be made in the hours, without his consent, after work had

[1] The meal time requirements in mercantile establishments as in factories were made for all employees it will be remembered. *Cf.* p. 119, *supra*.

[2] In the next amendment in 1915 this exception was limited to one day of more than nine hours "for the purpose of making one or more shorter work days in the week," and it is so in the law of 1924.

begun on the first day of the week, except that such employees could " begin their work after the [scheduled] time of beginning and stop before the time of ending " without being guilty of violation.

1. *Restaurants* [1]

In May 1917 (ch. 535) the nine-hour day and the six-day and fifty-four-hour week were extended to females over the age of sixteen years employed in restaurants in cities of the first and second class. The act did not include women employed as " singers and performers of any kind, or as attendants in ladies' cloak rooms and parlors," nor did it apply to " women employed in or in connection with the dining rooms and kitchens of hotels or in connection with lunch rooms or restaurants conducted by employers solely for the benefit of their own employees."

2. *Messenger Service* [2]

Women messengers were brought under the hour regulation in 1918 (ch. 434). Women over twenty-one could not be employed as " messengers for telegraph or messenger companies in the distribution, transmission or delivery of goods or messages more than six days or fifty-four hours in any one week," the nine-hour-day maximum not being included in the provision. By the same act, females under twenty-one years of age were not permitted to be messengers at any time, and males under twenty-one years in first and second class cities were not permitted to work at night (between 10 p. m. and 5 a. m.).

3. *Elevators* [3]

Women running freight or passenger elevators " in any building or place within the state " were, in 1919 (ch.

[1] Labor Law of 1924, § 182.

[2] Labor Law of 1924, § 185.

[3] Labor Law of 1924, § 183.

544), also limited to six days or fifty-four hours in any one week and nine hours in any one day. Any special permits issued by the labor commissioner and notices of hours of employment of women were required to be posted and not changed after the beginning of work on the first day of the week. The act stipulated that "a female of the age of eighteen years and upwards shall be deemed a woman within the meaning of this chapter." [1]

4. *Street Railroads* [2]

With the influx of women employees on street railroads came the limitation of their hours in that field of work. In 1919 (ch. 583), the legislature ruled that no female over twenty-one years of age [3] could be employed "in or in connection with the operation of any street, surface, electric, subway or elevated railroad, or to sell or accept fares or admissions in any railroad station, car or train" of any of the mentioned railroads "more than six days or fifty-four hours in any one week nor more than nine hours in any one day." The daily hours of labor of such female employees should be understood as "the period between the time of reporting for duty at the barn, terminal, car or station and the time" when they were released for the day—the daily hours to be consecutive "except that one hour should be allowed for meals." [4] Permits making exceptions to this provision were to be posted conspicuously in the barns or terminals. Also printed notices of women's

[1] The Industrial Code, Rule 408, fixes the minimum age of eighteen for all elevator operators. This is in addition to the statute enacted in 1919 (ch. 544) forbidding the employment on elevators of females under eighteen years of age.

[2] Labor Law of 1924, § 184.

[3] Females under twenty-one were prohibited.

[4] This appears to be the only legislative provision for meal time specifically for women.

hours were to be posted, and time books kept for the inspection of the Industrial Commission.

The statute regulating the employment of these women was made less drastic in 1920 (ch. 284), at which time all hour limitations were cancelled except those for conductors and guards. For this group the regulation remained as first adopted. The law stands on the statute books today as amended, but it is without function for the reason that the employment of women as conductors and guards has ceased.

HOURS OF LABOR—NIGHT WORK

Factories [1]

Again in 1899 (ch. 192) was enacted the first legislative prohibition against night work for all women employed in factories, the forbidden time being that between the hours of 9 p. m. and 6 a. m. Up to this time night work had been prohibited only to minors,—males under eighteen and females under twenty-one years of age in factories, and in mercantile establishments males under sixteen years of age and females under twenty-one. In 1907 (ch. 286), males not under eighteen years of age were permitted to work in factories up to twelve o'clock midnight and after four in the morning, the restrictions upon the employment of females remaining the same as before.[2]

The inclusion of adult women in the night work prohibition brought about the annulment of the prohibition by the courts in 1907 as was seen in the preceding chapter. As a result of the efforts of the Factory Investigating Commission, however, a new act was passed in 1915 (ch. 83) requiring that a "period of rest at night" for all females in factories be allowed between 10 p. m. and 7 a. m. While the constitutionality of this provision was also challenged, it

[1] Labor Law of 1924, § 172.

[2] See the discussion of this on pages 361-2, *infra*.

was upheld by the courts, it will be recalled, and remains to-day one of the regulations for the protection of working women.

1. *Canneries* [1]

Exceptions to the night work rule were not made for canneries in 1912 as was the case for day labor, though an exemption for canneries followed in the next year (ch. 465). Here, women eighteen years of age and upwards (and male minors sixteen years and upwards) were permitted to work in fruit-canning establishments between June 15 and October 15 with no prohibition of work at night. However, this exception was abrogated by the act of 1921 (ch. 50) at which time all female employees were prohibited from night work at all times of the year in all factories as follows: girls under the age of twenty-one years, from 9 p. m. to 6 a. m., and women over twenty-one, from 10 p. m. to 6 a. m.

2. *Newspaper Offices* [2]

The act in 1919 (ch. 582) which removed the six-day week regulation from women writers and reporters also permitted these women to work at night.

And two years later, 1921 (ch. 489),[3] the night work prohibition for women proofreaders, linotypists, and monotypists in newspaper offices was also revoked. These amendments were championed by the women themselves the story of which will be related in succeeding pages.

Mercantile and Other Establishments [4]

Women were prohibited from night labor for the first

[1] Labor Law of 1924, §§ 172-173.

[2] Labor Law of 1924, § 2, subd. 9; § 181.

[3] This act amended section two of the newly codified law instead of section three which it erroneously cites.

[4] Labor Law of 1924, §§ 180-186.

time in mercantile establishments in 1913 (ch. 493) in the same year that this prohibition was revised for factories. As in the regulation of day labor, the prohibition was at first made more rigid for second class cities than elsewhere, but the differentiation in both cases was cancelled the following year. In second class cities the act prohibited the work of all female employees before 7 a. m. and after 6 p. m., " and elsewhere after ten o'clock in the evening of any day." On Saturdays there were no limitations upon the working time of employees sixteen years of age and upwards, provided the maximum 54-hour week for second class, and the 60-hour week elsewhere, was not violated. The same exception was made for the five days preceding December 25 in second class cities " and elsewhere between the eighteenth of December and the following twenty-fifth of December both inclusive."

The act of 1914 (ch. 331) made the night work regulations uniform throughout the state for mercantile establishments. All female employees over sixteen years of age were prohibited from employment from 10 p. m. to 7 a. m., exceptions being granted between the 18th and 24th of December, both inclusive. Two days for stocktaking were added to these exceptions in 1915 (ch. 386) by the same act that allowed day-time exceptions for this purpose.

1. *Restaurants*

Restaurants in first and second class cities were next included among those places where the employment at night of females over sixteen years was prohibited.[1] The " period of rest " was between 10 p. m. and 6 a. m. The act did not apply to employees who were singers and performers of any kind, nor to " attendants in ladies' cloak rooms and parlors," nor to " females employed in or in connection with the dining rooms and kitchens of hotels, or in

[1] Laws of 1917, ch. 535.

connection with lunch rooms or restaurants conducted by employers solely for the benefit of their employees." This statute has remained as enacted despite this wide list of exceptions which is charged with irrationality by some working women whose attitude in the matter will be described in a later chapter.

2. *Messenger Service*

The employment of women over twenty-one years of age as messengers in first and second class cities before 7 a. m. and after 10 p. m. of any day was prohibited in 1918 (ch. 434).[1] Males under the age of twenty-one were so prohibited between 10 p. m. and 5 a. m.

3. *Elevators*

Women eighteen years old and upwards were not to be employed on elevators between the hours of 10 p. m. and 7 a.m. by act of 1919 (ch. 544). The law provided that, in the instance of the elevator being used "in connection with a business or industry in which the employment of women between six and seven o'clock in the morning is not prohibited, a woman may begin work at six o'clock in the morning." Also women over twenty-one years of age who were in "the care, custody, management or operation of an elevator in a hotel," were not prohibited from night work.

4. *Street Railroads*: Along with the daytime regulations for females on street railroads and elevators in the laws of 1919 (ch. 583), came the accompanying provisions for night. Women were not to be employed between 10 p. m. and 6 a. m. "in connection with the operation of street surface, electric, subway or elevated roads or the selling or accepting fares or admission in any railroad station, car, or train of the same."

[1] Minor females were entirely prohibited. Labor Law of 1924, § 185.

This measure concerning night work was relaxed in 1920 (ch. 284), as it was also for day work, by removing regulations from all of these women except conductors and guards. This action was also prompted by a protest from a body of the women affected.

PROHIBITED EMPLOYMENT

Although an increasing body of legislation has been enacted for the protection of the health and safety of all workers in industry, this has not been considered sufficient for the protection of women, and the legislature has therefore been persuaded from time to time to demand the complete removal of women from certain kinds of employment, or from employment under certain conditions. The modern prohibitions of this type received their direction along with other special laws for women, in 1899.

1. *Polishing and Grinding* [1]

In 1899 (ch. 375), all females and males under the age of eighteen were prohibited from employment in any factory in the state "in operating or using any emery, corundum, stone, or emery polishing or buffing wheel." An attempt to extend this act in 1902 was defeated in the senate, but in 1903 (ch. 561) an amendment was passed adding other materials that were not to be used by women, namely—tripoli, rouge, carborundum, or any abrasive, where articles of the baser metals or iridium are manufactured.

In the reaction of the last few years against so much special legislation for women, this prohibition has been modified among others that have been mentioned. Thus in 1921 (ch. 642), while the statute was retained, an amendment "provided, however, that females more than twenty-one years of age may be employed in operating such wheels for wet grinding under conditions specified by the industrial board in its rules."

[1] Labor Law of 1924, § 146, subd. 8.

2. *Mines and Quarries*[1]

The present statute which prohibits females, and males under sixteen years of age, from employment in mines and quarries was enacted in 1906 (ch. 375), this was an amendment to the former labor law of 1897, sections 120-121

3. *After Childbirth*[2]

In 1912 (ch. 331) women were forbidden employment within four weeks after childbirth in "factory, mercantile establishment, mill and workshop."

4. *Core Making*[3]

The act regarding the employment of women after childbirth was forwarded by the factory commission as was also that relating to core making in the following year 1913 (ch. 464).[4] At this time core making was ruled out as an occupation for women unless the ovens for baking the cores were located and operated in a room so apart from the room in which they are made "that the gases and fumes from the core-oven will not enter the room or space in which the women are employed." The Industrial

[1] Labor Law of 1924, § 146, subd. 6.

[2] Labor Law of 1924, § 148. The present statute reads "in a factory or mercantile establishment." While this provision had been in existence for some years in European countries, Massachusetts was the only other state in America that had adopted it. The scope of the law is not uniform, Massachusetts like the European countries prohibits employment before parturition as well as after, while New York's provision is similar to that of England—concerning itself with the period following childbirth only. A few other states have introduced childbirth protection since 1912, e. g. Connecticut and Vermont in 1913, and Missouri in 1919. (Commons and Andrews, *op. cit.*, p. 348.)

[3] Labor Law of 1924, § 147.

[4] By the same act further prohibitions were made for female minors, namely,—no female under sixteen years of age could be employed in any capacity where the work required constant standing; and no female under the age of twenty-one years (nor male under eighteen) could be permitted to clean machinery while in motion.

Board was here empowered to adopt rules "regulating the construction, equipment, maintenance and operation of core-rooms and the size and weight that may be handled by women" so as to protect their health and safety. The rules thereupon adopted by the board pertained to temperature and weight-lifting. Rule 584 prohibits females from handling cores "which have a temperature of more than 110 degrees Fahrenheit," and Rule 585 prohibits females from handling cores "where the combined weight of core, core-box, and plate at which she is working exceeds twenty-five pounds."[1]

SPECIAL WORKING CONDITIONS

By specific statutes as well as in the industrial code special conditions of work for women include requirements for seats, sanitary basements and proper washrooms and dressing rooms.

1. *Seats*[2]

The early unenforced act of 1881 requiring seats in mercantile and manufacturing establishments has been mentioned. An amendment of 1896 (ch. 384) required employers of women in mercantile establishments to provide one seat for every three women and to make it possible for these seats to be used in front of or behind the counters according to the location of the work.

[1] It is interesting to note the variety of decisions to which different jurisdictions have come in the matter of the weights women may lift and not injure their health. Compared with the 25 pounds in New York State as mentioned above, Pennsylvania and Ohio limit the weight to 15 pounds, while the maximum in Massachusetts is 40 pounds. The Foundry Safety Code of the American Foundrymen's Association and National Founders' Association states, "No female employed in a foundry shall lift any object exceeding 35 pounds in weight unless she uses mechanical means by which her effort is limited to 35 pounds." *The New Position of Women in American Industry, op. cit.*, pp. 108-109. (No mention is made of the frequency with which these weights may be lifted.)

[2] Labor Law of 1924, § 150.

"Employers of females in a factory or as waitresses in a hotel or restaurant" were ordered by act of 1900 (ch. 533), "to provide and maintain suitable seats" for these employees, permitting their use to an extent "reasonable for the preservation of their health." And in 1913 (ch. 197), a further amendment called for proper backs "where practicable," and women were to be allowed to use these seats "whenever they are engaged in work which can be properly performed in a sitting posture." The Industrial Board was given power to determine "when seats, with or without backs, are necessary and the number thereof."

Chapter 544 of the laws of 1919 added elevators to the list of employments in which seats are required for women, to be used "at such times and to such extent as may be necessary for the preservation of their health."

2. *Basements*

Employment of women and children in unsanitary basements had been legally forbidden in 1896 (ch. 384), and in 1908 (ch. 520) more drastic measures were taken against such employment. In extraordinary session of the legislature on June 16 of the same year, a further step was taken by prohibiting the work of women and children in all basements except by permission of the commissioner of labor. This regulation applied to mercantile establishments in cities of the first class, while the board or department of health held authority over similar matters in smaller cities. In 1913 (ch. 145), the Department of Labor was made responsible for this protection of women and children in second class city basements as well.

3. *Wash-rooms, Toilets, Dressing-rooms*[1]

As was seen in Part I there are, pretty generally, specifications for wash-rooms, washing facilities and water closets

[1] Labor Law of 1924, §§ 378-381.

for all employees at the present time. Dressing rooms are seldom required for men however, where they have been required generally for women. For women in factories the act of 1910 (ch. 229) provided that each such room should "have at least one window opening to the outer air and be enclosed by means of solid partitions or walls. In 1912 (ch. 340), dressing-rooms were required to be at least sixty square feet in size, separate from the toilets, properly lighted, provided with suitable means for hanging clothes and with a suitable number of seats. Toilets for females were ordered plainly marked and solidly partitioned.

Regulations similar to those for factories were made for mercantile establishments in 1914 (ch. 183), where more than five women were employed, and similar requirements were made for women employed on street railroads by act of 1919 (ch. 583).

CHAPTER III

INFLUENCES BEARING UPON LEGISLATION FOR WOMEN IN NEW YORK STATE

ONE of the strongest influences that bears upon the enactment of labor laws is unquestionably that of the decisions of high courts regarding the constitutionality of such laws. We have already followed American judicial reasoning in these cases and have observed that precedent has been established for nearly all types of statutes for the protection of industrial workers. Nevertheless, it is also plain that, in labor cases such as we have examined, judicial benches are more often divided than united, that the views of judges conflict. While court decisions influence the enactment of further statutes, those decisions themselves are reflective of their environment, and the reflection is one of contending social forces. Inevitably some judges are more responsive to progressive currents, some to traditional, and the effects of the judicial conclusions to which they arrive are incalculable.

It is thus our further task to analyze the extra-judicial environment which has furnished stimuli for the enactment of protective measures. We shall, in so doing, confine our principal attention to New York State—to the direct influences which have fostered special laws for women as they have been outlined in the preceding chapter. For, having established a working knowledge of the trend of legislation throughout the country, and more especially in New York, we are now in need of an analysis of sources.

In general, the reports of recommendations of state bureaus and the labor unions have been positive influences toward the special protection of women in New York, but perhaps the most potent force has been that generated by philanthropic groups often through the medium of public men.

The first of the modern laws enacted in 1899 to limit the hours of women employed in factories was probably the direct result of Governor Roosevelt's recommendation to the legislature. The governor had for some time been interested in relieving the oppression of wage earners, and his views were strengthened by the report of the Reinhardt Committee, which had been appointed by the state assembly in March 1895, for the purpose of investigating female labor in New York City.[1] The first report of this committee had been submitted to the assembly in May of the same year, and a second in January 1896.

Both factories and mercantile establishments were investigated by the Reinhardt Committee, which included examination of witnesses before public hearings. In its final report the committee stated the gravest evil to be that of child labor, evasion of the existing law having been successfully practiced by employers. One of the early regulative labor bills passed by the legislature, therefore, was that in 1896 applying to children in factories. Measures similar to this one had been defeated in the legislature each session for a half dozen years, but this time advocates of the bill and those

[1] The Bureau of Statistics of Labor in 1890 had given extended consideration to the testimonies of doctors and workmen in European countries as to the effect of labor upon women and their recommendation concerning its restriction by law. France's sluggishness was cited as contrasted with the progress of England and Belgium. This discussion centered in a general consideration of the world's trend toward a standardized working day and a specific treatment of "Female Labor on the Continent—its effects upon Population."

whom it would affect joined forces and the Andrews Compromise Bill was enacted into law.[1]

Along with this special attention to child labor the Reinhardt Committee also observed, recorded, and protested against the long hours of adult women. Moreover, the Bureau of Statistics of Labor and the factory inspector had reported women's excessively long working hours practically from the creation of the bureau, and had recommended restrictive legislation from year to year.

The ten-hour act of 1899 was the first tangible result of this pressure and a great many of the women themselves were reported to favor it, although the former law which restricted only females under twenty-one years of age had led young women to claim that they were older in order to work longer hours.[2]

Perhaps the most potent influence leading to the formulation of the 1907 amendment to this first act, was the grave disrepute into which the law, an attempted remedy, had fallen as a result of its unenforceability. The official and philanthropic parents of the law had brought it into a hostile world. Employers would have none of it. In March, 1902, the provisions for adult women were about to be repealed quietly by amendment when the amending bill was assailed and laid on the table.[3] Mrs. Susan W. Fitzgerald, manager of the West Side Branch of the University Settlement, argued that society had come to a deplorable state if profit-seeking manufacturers could handle a bill of this kind so quietly that no one knew anything about it, that overwork for women affected the community much more directly than overwork for men, that "most factory women over twenty-one are

[1] New York *Tribune*, April 25, 1896.

[2] Fairchild, F. R., "The Factory Legislation of the State of New York," *American Economic Association Publications*, 1905, vol. vi, p. 67.

[3] New York *Tribune*, March 2, 1902.

married with children, and evil effects of having to be at work all day are greatly increased by every hour that their time at home is cut down." The court of special sessions then did its share to emasculate the law. Having declared the act valid in 1906, citing decisions of Massachusetts, Nebraska and Washington, the court failed to honor its own decision. For, when one hundred employers who had been arraigned by the deputy factory inspector plead guilty, they each and all had their sentences suspended by the court! [1]

Thus in 1907 when Commissioner of Labor Sherman derided the provision as "absurd in practice," because it was not compatible with the demands of industry and was therefore not enforced, it was amended.[2] To make the law more practicable then, it was made more flexible, with resulting leniency toward employers; for while it stipulated a new six-day week it permitted irregular employment for twelve hours a day.

This amendment was passed in the face not only of opposition, but of hope on the part of its opponents for an even more stringent measure. In 1904, Commissioner McMackin voiced the desire[3] of "a large body of citizens" in a recommendation for a maximum fifty-four-hour week for women and male minors under eighteen years, a regulation already in effect for minors under sixteen years. The point was stressed that Massachusetts and Rhode Island had previously enacted fifty-eight-hour laws in factories which would allay the fear of bringing injury upon business interests in New York State in her rivalry with sister commonwealths. This was especially true of the clothing industry in which three-fifths of the operatives were employed and in which the women outnumbered the men.

[1] New York *Tribune*, November 1, 1906.

[2] *Cf.* chapter v, p. 310, *infra*.

[3] *Annual Report of the Commissioner of Labor*, 1904, pp. I. 29.

The commissioner explained that,

While we are concerned about the conditions existing in factories where adult males constitute the entire working force, we are required to be more on the alert and watchful of the interests of the women, minors and children wherever they are found earning their living in a factory. They constitute the most helpless class of bread winners and, presumably, it is for this reason the State has undertaken the control and regulation of their labor, in productive industry, in a special manner.[1]

The strict regulation of child labor was more to be desired than all else, and so it was explained that if women were also limited to fifty-four hours a week the labor of children could be more successfully controlled. Thus in order to secure the full force of the law for children it was deemed advisable to limit the hours of women also. But, as has been said, instead of a more drastic regulation of women's work in 1907, the existing statute was relaxed.

In 1911, New York's legislative atmosphere was stirred from several directions. The Consumers' League of the City of New York reported expert testimony of leading physicians abroad to the effect that we now know a "long working day is not only injurious to the working women themselves, but also affects the physical and moral conditions of the future race." And Governor Dix wrote,

There is a growing feeling that ten hours work under abnormal conditions is injurious to the health of women. Modern industry, with its endless specialization and the speeding up which naturally follows, it is said, operates to the detriment of the female worker. The only relief possible lies either in prohibiting female labor in such circumstances, or in the reduction of hours of labor for women generally. The latter seems to me the wiser course.[2]

[1] *Annual Report of the Commissioner of Labor*, 1904, pp. III. 12-13.

[2] *Annual Report of the Consumers' League of the City of New York* for 1911, pp. 19-20. Governor Dix's view regarding exceptions to regulative measures of this sort is discussed on page 206, *infra*.

Consequently a fifty-four-hour bill for women in factories was introduced, though not passed. It had been initiated by the Consumers' League through its committee on legislation with Miss Pauline Goldmark as chairman, and was supported by the State Federation of Labor and the Child Welfare Committee. The bill passed the assembly and became a democratic party measure. But it was opposed and defeated by large manufacturing interests chiefly in the textile industry, whose "underground" opposition together with the "head on" blows of the canners gave it little chance for life.[1]

This single defeat was minor, however, in the eventful year that 1911 proved to be; perhaps the most eventful in the history of New York State from the point of view of crystallizing efforts to protect women workers. Three things happened. The Triangle Shirt Waist fire occurred on March 25; the Women's Trade Union League announced the fruition of its efforts to establish a Joint Labor Legislative Conference; and the act of the legislature which created the Factory Investigating Commission was passed on the 30th day of June.

The Joint Labor Legislative Conferencewas composed from the New York Central Labor Bodies including those of Manhattan, Brooklyn, the Bronx, The United Hebrew Trades, the Socialist Party and the Women's Trade Union League of the state (organized in 1904). The object of the conference was "to endorse, support and agitate for any labor bill which any of the bodies represented proposes and also to originate bills which the conference decides necessary for the interest and protection of labor." It also aimed to be a political force by watching closely the attitudes of legislators and working for the defeat of those who opposed or failed to support labor measures. The first "rehearsal"

[1] *Op. cit.*, p. 33.

was in that same year at the assembly hearing in Albany on the unsuccessful fifty-four-hour bill. Some women unionists spoke, and others made a strong plea "for legislation that would conserve the health of the women workers."[1]

The fire in the Triangle Shirt Waist Factory on Washington Square, New York City, was a terrible holocaust; 143 workers (mostly girls) were killed either from being burned or from jumping from high windows. The chief cause of the heavy mortality, in addition to fright, was discovered to be locked doors! The immediate result of this tragedy was a mass meeting held in the Metropolitan Opera House from which a Citizens' Committee on Safety was formed to make investigation and promote public policies for the prevention of industrial accidents and fires. It was on the basis of data furnished by this committee, of which Frances Perkins was secretary, that the Factory Investigating Commission was appointed in Albany in June. The outgrowth of the extended investigation of the commission was not only a new set of labor laws, but the creation of the State Industrial Commission with broad powers, which in some form is doubtless a permanent fixture in the labor administration of the state. The Industrial Commission and its work will be discussed in a later chapter.

The Factory Investigating Commission was organized on August 17, 1911, with Mr. Robert F. Wagner for its chairman. The commission was composed of nine members, Chairman Wagner and Senator Charles M. Hamilton being appointed by the president of the senate, Assemblyman Alfred E. Smith, Edward D. Jackson, and Cyrus W. Phillips by the speaker of the assembly, and Simon Brentano,

[1] *Life and Labor*, April, 1911, p. 125. The Joint Labor Legislative Conference of these earlier days no longer lives, but, as we shall see, there has developed since that time a new "Women's Joint Legislative Conference" which includes some of the bodies named above and many others.

Robert E. Dowling, Samuel Gompers, and Mary E. Dreier by Governor Dix. Mr. Smith was elected vice-chairman, Frank A. Tierney, secretary, and Abram I. Elkus, chief counsel, with Bernard L. Shientag as his assistant. Advisory experts were engaged and Dr. George M. Price, a New York City practicing physician of experience, was given general charge of the work of inspection and sanitation. The small sum of $5,500 was expended by the commission for the inspection work and fees of the experts, which in itself is testimony of the widespread coöperation and gratuitous services received from many interested people as well as from those officially connected. The commissioners themselves worked without remuneration.

The Preliminary Report of the commission was published on March 1, 1912, and on March 6 the time for investigation was extended by law. The work continued into 1915 whereupon the full report was published in thirteen volumes. Answers to questionaires, public hearings, reports of intensive investigation, and recommendations for legislative action are the outstanding features of the report, made available for ready reference by an extensive digest.

The prescribed scope of the investigation was sweeping, and, although the first act of the legislature limited the inquiry to cities of the first and second class, the commission was given power to investigate further if it should so determine. "The Commission was to recommend such new legislation as might be found necessary to remedy defects in existing legislation, and to provide for conditions at present unregulated." [1] This included hours of labor, safety, ventilation, sanitation, occupational diseases, tenement house manfacture, wages and other items. Attention was thus to be directed to the needs of industrial workers in general with no special request for attention to women.

[1] *Preliminary Report of the New York Factory Investigating Commission*, 1912, vol. i, p. 16.

At an early date the commission issued a carefully planned questionaire with the purpose both of interesting those people who should be concerned with their inquiry, and of receiving help and advice from men and women of experience. There were forty-six reported replies to the questionaire from prominent people and experts, ten of whom were labor union officials, two officially connected with the State Department of Labor, five physicians two of whom were public health officers, two high officers of the State and National Consumers' Leagues, two lawyers, three insurance men, two employers, engineers, educators, and other public spirited people nearly all of whom were men.

The responses to the questionaire regarding "Hours of Labor" are of interest to us at this point,[1] seventeen of the forty-six having included answers to this group of questions. Relative to hours of labor through the day seven of the seventeen had nothing to suggest that applied to adults; five considered that women and children as a class needed shorter hours by law; these made no mention of shorter hours for men. Two of these five recommended an eight-hour day for women and children (one was a physician and one a labor representative); one recommended a fifty-four-hour week; and two (high officers of the State and National Consumers' Leagues) recommended a week of fifty-four hours for the present, looking toward a future forty-four or forty-eight-hour week. Four of the seventeen (one a physician and three labor representatives) advocated a shorter day for all workers regardless of sex,—eight hours a day or forty-eight hours a week. The last of those who gave their views was former Labor Commissioner Sherman, who recommended that the statute regulating the hours of women and children be made more flexible, prohibiting only what is in fact injurious to their health. He held that males over six-

[1] *Op. cit.*, pp. 649-655.

teen years of age should be "left alone," that "such laws are sentimental nullities." [1]

Florence Kelley, secretary of the National Consumers' League, suggested that "night-work and overtime should be the monopoly of men who are better able to protect their interests in regard to it than either women or children, because men can both vote and expedite legislation for their protection, and also organize and thus enforce their demands" (page 652).

In regard to special regulations of women's hours, Mrs. Kelley wrote, according to the digest (page 651), "We recommend making the hours of labor uniform for women and minors . . . the great need is for simplicity and uniformity." She recommended therefore, "a uniform closing hour for the work of the women and minors in manufacturing, commerce, hotels, offices, telephone service, bakeries, restaurants, and laundries," with a working day not to exceed ten hours a day and fifty-four hours a week, that would later be reduced to forty-eight hours a week.

In contrast to these particularistic views regarding women came the physician's testimony by Dr. Delancy Rochester of Buffalo, "eight hours of actual labor is all that should be demanded of any male or female, and sufficient shift (*sic*) should be used as are necessary in those occupations where work has to be maintained for a longer period." [2] And Mr. F. S. Tomlin, Secretary of the Joint Legislative Labor Conference of Greater New York, added that "No man, woman nor child should, under any circumstances work more than 48 hours a week." [3]

Thus the opinions as expressed in the replies to these questionaires regarding a shorter day for women were al-

[1] *Cf.* page 361, *infra*, for an explanation of this view.

[2] *Op. cit.*, vol. i, p. 654.

[3] *Ibid.*, p. 655.

most equally divided. Of the ten out of forty-six who responded on this point, one-half urged special legislation, four of the other half expressed themselves only on the need of a shorter day for both men and women, and the fifth advocated that limitations upon women's work be made more flexible.

At the public hearings held by the factory commission, Florence Kelly and Josephine Goldmark, two of the most influential witnesses, urged special limitation of women's work. In her discussion of proposed new regulations, Mrs. Kelley suggested that New York copy the Massachusetts law which she deemed the most advanced in the East as it applies to the working hours of women and children, that it has the advantage, as has the English Textile Law, not only of restricting the hours of work to fifty-four but of having a perfectly clear closing hour which is 6 p. m. in the textile industry and 10 p. m. in other occupations. " Everyone who has been the head of a Factory Department has a mortal fear of discretion," Mrs Kelley witnessed, " Everyone who honestly wishes to administer his Department in the interest of the public, wants a perfectly clear sailing chart. He wants it stated in perfectly clear language what is forbidden and what is permitted." [1]

Josephine Goldmark, as witness, filed with the commission the brief which had been prepared by Louis D. Brandeis and herself in 1908 in defence of the Oregon ten-hour law, when the constitutionality of that statute was being tested by the United States Supreme Court. She reminded the commission of the wide use to which this brief had been put—having furnished the argument in defense of ten-hour laws in Illinois, Michigan, Virginia, Louisiana, Ohio, and of eight-hour laws in Washington and California. With this evidence Miss Goldmark turned to the existing

[1] *Op. cit.*, vol. iii, p. 1598.

New York law which she declared to be "indefensible on the score of health." She explained that this statute was the "only law of its kind in the United States" in its allowance of overtime regularly and irregularly in addition to the ten-hour day; that nine states had recently enacted "flat" laws, none permitting more than ten hours a day. She urged that the New York provision was entirely too flexible to be enforced, both in the irregularity of the hours allowed to be worked and in the exceptions to the rule for posting notices when the "nature of the work" so demanded.[1] The brief showed that "in all those states and countries where there has been a provision prohibiting employment of women more than a definite number of hours, the tendency has been for work to be regularized and for the employment to be confined to those specific hours," Miss Goldmark attested. This adjustment could be brought about by the education of consumers, for example, so that they would do their Christmas shopping early, and give laundries a little longer time to wash and deliver their clothes.

After a careful and telling explanation of some of the evil effects of fatigue upon health, Miss Goldmark was asked whether her efforts were for the improvement of laws for women only and not for men. Her reply was in the affirmative,—that her efforts had been confined chiefly to the conditions of women and children and minors.[2]

The preliminary report of the Factory Investigating Commission was transmitted to the legislature on March 1, 1912, and on October first the newly enacted limitation of hours for women and male minors took effect. New York thus joined with five other states on the fifty-four-hour week (Massachusetts, Michigan, Ohio, Maine, and Utah), three

[1] It will be recalled that the law had been given this greater flexibility in 1907 because the provision it displaced had not been enforceable. For further discussion of this situation see p. 310, *infra*.

[2] *Op. cit.*, vol. iii, pp. 1605-1609.

states only, at that time, having an eight-hour day (California, Washington and Colorado).[1]

Thus the testimony gathered in New York and the legislative action that followed it blended harmoniously into the national background. For while there was a growing appreciation of the need of a shorter working day for all industrial employees (demanded by labor unions both through legislation and by contract, and urged by scientific men), special stress was laid pretty unanimously upon the needs of women. In 1910 appeared the first ten volumes of the nineteen-volume report of the United States Department of Labor on the *Condition of Woman and Child Wage Earners in the United States*. Here was an unprecedented compilation of historical and first-hand material that has become the standard reference on this subject. Also *Women's Work* was the special subject of investigation and action by a committee of experts appointed by the American Association for Labor Legislation in 1909. With Irene Osgood Andrews, assistant secretary of the association, as chairman, and the eight influential members of the committee,[2] well known for their special interest in the legal protection of women, an increasing volume of such legislation was bound to follow.

Moreover, the accumulating conviction in favor of this type of legislation was reflected in the courts at the same time that court affirmance was giving impetus to further legislation. The inter-stimulation was positive. This we have seen in the preceding pages—in the far-famed Oregon decision

[1] While the New York law as enacted was thus a definite outgrowth of the work of the factory commission, the campaign for its passage was actively augmented by other advocates of protective legislation, including particularly the New York City Consumers' League operating through its committee on legislation.

[2] These were M. Edith Campbell, Mary Dreier, Ernst Freund, Josephine Goldmark, Susan M. Kingsbury, Anne Morgan, Marie L. Obenauer and Mary Van Kleeck. *Cf. American Labor Legislation Review*, 1914, vol. iv, no. 4.

in 1908, in the "second Ritchie case" in Illinois in 1910, and in the affirmance of an eight-hour law in California in 1915. At a meeting of the National Consumers' League following the Oregon decision for which the league had been chiefly responsible, Ida Tarbell assured the members in her address, that "American women are won completely over when you show them a practical method of aiding and protecting those of their number who have been caught in the cruel grind of our present industrial conditions." [1]

It was in these years (1912) that Josephine Goldmark's classic work on *Fatigue and Efficiency* appeared, bringing the contributions of science into that (to the physiologists) "undiscovered country" — the industrial world. Here was presented a notable collection of evidence on the poison of fatigue and its consequences. "The fundamental basis for laws regulating the working hours of men, women, or children in industrial occupations . . . is the common physiological phenomenon, fatigue, the normal result of all human action. For fatigue is nature's warning signal that the limit of activity is approaching" (page 9). Miss Goldmark pointed to "the special susceptibility to fatigue and disease which distinguishes the female sex, qua female," and led to the conclusion that women, therefore, "clearly need the protection of special laws" (page 39).

Material was given in this work to show that "the industrial overstrain of women has commonly reacted in three visible ways: In a heightened infant mortality, a lowered birth rate, and an impaired second generation" (page 91). Dr. Newman was quoted (page 94), in his summary of the effect of industry upon women:

It is the employment of women from girlhood all through married life, and through the period of child-bearing—the continual stress and strain of work and hours and general con-

[1] *Annual Report of the National Consumers' League*, 1907, p. 26.

ditions prevailing in women's labour—that is exerting its baneful influence on the individual and on the home.[1]

Dr. W. Chapman Grigg who had specialized in diseases of women, was also quoted on the injuries of overwork to the health of girls and women employed in stores. He asserted that prolonged hours are injurious to the generative organs of women causing inflammation in the pelvis:

> . . . if the matter could be gone into carefully, I think the Committee would be perfectly surprised to find what a large number of these women are rendered sterile in consequence of these prolonged hours.[2]

Part II of Miss Goldmark's book was devoted to "The World's Experience upon which Legislation Limiting the Hours of Labor For Women is Based," and consisted of the material contained in four briefs prepared by Mr. Louis D. Brandeis and herself in support of statutes limiting working days for women in Oregon, Illinois, and Ohio (1908-1912) before mentioned. A mass of digested references was here presented showing the dangers of long hours and the benefits of short hours both to society and to industry, concluding that, "legal limitation of hours is the most direct, most effective, and most satisfactory method of protection, for all concerned" (p. 328).[3]

The influence of this book, now a standard work, upon special legislation for women, has unquestionably been great.

[1] Newman, George, M. D. (Lecturer on Public Health at St. Bartholomew's Hospital, London; Medical Officer of Health of Metropolitan Borough of Finsbury). *Infant Mortality*, p. 105 (1907).

[2] *British Sessional Papers*, vol. xii, 1895. "Report of Select Committee on Shops (Early Closing Bill)," pp. 219-220. Witness, Dr. W. Chapman Grigg.

[3] The majority of the references given were to nineteenth century materials dating all the way from 1846 to 1899, the latest mentioned was a study of female wage earners in Great Britain in 1909.

Joining as it did with other forces working in the same direction, the result by 1920 was that forty-six states had shortened women's working day, ten of which had adopted an eight-hour day (with some exceptions).[1]

On January 1, 1924, thirteen states had either an eight-hour day or a forty-eight-hour week for women,[2] and there remained but eight jurisdictions which had made no limitations whatever.[3]

Turning again to New York State, efforts have there been made year after year to join the eight-hour states, but up to the present time the statute limiting women's hours in factories to nine a day stands as it was enacted in 1912. The introduction of an eight-hour bill for factories and mercantile establishments began in 1914, and while such a bill has been introduced every year since that time, debate of it has never been permitted on the floor of the assembly.[4]

Moreover, not only has no eight-hour act been passed in New York, but the nine-hour statute has lived in an almost constant state of insecurity. In 1916, the Spring bill (dubbed the Ripper bill by its opponents because it was aimed to destroy so much of the labor law) was introduced and just escaped becoming a law. This bill allowed the Industrial Commission to make "variations" from the women's fifty-four-hour law permitting overtime "where through failure of machinery to operate in any factory because of accidental damage there is loss of time or loss of

[1] Counting for convenience as states, the District of Columbia and Porto Rico. See Commons and Andrews, *Principles of Labor Legislation*, pp. 237-238.

[2] Arizona, California, Colorado, Kansas, Montana, Nevada, New Mexico, Utah, Washington, District of Columbia, Porto Rico, Massachusetts, North Dakota.

[3] Alabama, Florida, Indiana, Iowa, West Virginia, Alaska, Hawaii, Philippines.

[4] The same is true of the bills for a minimum wage commission.

production which foresight could not prevent." This measure had been recommended by a special legislative committee to investigate labor legislation which, it is charged, held no public hearings and gave no opportunity for public opinion to be expressed. "As a matter of fact the measure was framed at a private conference of manufacturers and labor leaders together with the Industrial Council. The action of the labor leaders in agreeing to these amendments was entirely unaccountable, and later, at the public hearing before the Governor was in fact repudiated by the Women's Trade Union League." [1]

The Consumers' League, in attacking the bill, pointed out that no limitation had been placed upon the amount of overtime women might be permitted to work, that it would be difficult to determine the "loss of time due to accidental damage," etc., and that the manufacturer's word would have to be taken as to what would make up for his loss of production, for the commission would have no means of investi ceting each case sufficiently to make such a decision. "Girls can be made to suffer through no fault of theirs, for the breaking down of machinery. They can be inconvenienced by consequent delay usually caused by inefficient management. Since the present limitation of women's hours of work are justified on grounds of public health, as the courts have repeatedly held, it is surely unreasonable, whatever the exigencies of the manufacturers may be, to allow any inroads on the law to be legalized. For this reason the League has always held that it is illogical as well as dangerous to allow any executive officers to grant variations for overtime beyond the stationary limits." [2]

The overwork of women in canneries was particularly

[1] *Report of the Consumers' League of the City of New York* for 1916, p. 17.

[2] *Ibid.*, p. 18.

feared by the Consumers' League. For the Spring bill would make it possible for women to work in canneries 72 hours a week for 20 consecutive days provided they had the sanction of the Industrial Commission. Furthermore the wording of the act was so obscure it was thought even seven days' work might be extorted from the women, making 84 hours a week.

This bill passed both houses of the legislature and on May 10 the governor held a public hearing. "The opposition led by the Consumers' League and the Women's Trade Union League expressed itself in a most spirited manner and as a result the governor vetoed the bill." In the memorandum giving his reasons, the governor said regarding the variations of overtime, "I feel that the privilege granted under this amendment might be continually abused and would make more difficult the enforcement of the Labor Law."[1] The measure was thus defeated.

Again in 1917, the security of the 54-hour bill, as well as that of other protective measures, was threatened. During this session of the legislature there was chaos over the subject of general relaxation of labor legislation owing to our entry into the war, a bill having been introduced by Senator Ottinger giving the Industrial Commission power to suspend all labor laws during the war period. Though English experience was taken as a warning that this type of action was in grave error, legislators, moved to be "patriotic," appeared to conceive this act to be one manifestation of patriotism. The major efforts of advocates of labor legislation, therefore, had to be directed against the passage of this bill. The fight was long and bitter, the opposition again being staunchly led by the Consumers' League.

As in the preceding year, this measure passed successfully through both houses, after which Governor Whitman came

[1] *Ibid.*, pp. 18-19.

to the rescue of its opponents who were anxious about the welfare of women. On May 23, a hearing was held before the governor at which "trade unionists, women of wealth and prominence, social workers, doctors and lawyers came together to insist that this war should not be waged by the unnecessary sacrifice of women and children." On the following second of June the governor issued a memorandum, a part of which was as follows:

Of course, it is of supreme importance that every man and woman shall be willing to make every necessary sacrifice in this great world war in which our country is to take so conspicuous and so unselfish a part, but if we are to attain the greatest measure of efficiency in our preparation and in our prosecution of the war, we must not permit our people who are engaged in industrial pursuits to become apprehensive that the standards erected for their protection will be set aside; and we must not permit our industrial population to have cause to feel that the war's burdens and sacrifices may rest most heavily upon the shoulders of those least able to bear them. To give cause for such an impression would be a grave error. We must do nothing that will impair the confidence or weaken the loyalty of the service of those who are engaged in the field and factory. We should not disregard the errors of other nations with respect to the suspension of their labor laws. On the contrary, we should profit by their mistakes. The bill is disapproved.[1]

The particular enemy of protective legislation in the senate was plainly Senator Ottinger, or at least he was the medium through which opponents operated.[2] Therefore in the November elections of 1917, women's guns were leveled at this

[1] *Report of the Consumers' League of the City of New York* for 1917, pp. 5-6.

[2] Senator Ottinger had also introduced the first bill of the women printers during the 1917 session of the legislature, which provided for the repeal of the night work prohibition. See p. 242, *infra*.

senator and he was defeated in his reëlection campaign by a majority of 5,000 votes.

This defeat seems not to have effected materially the opposition to protective laws in the next legislative session however. In 1918, the eight-hour day (and minimum wage) provision was again overthrown together with a new group of bills "introduced to safeguard women employed on the various transportation lines, girl elevator operators, and girls employed as messengers."[1] The only exception to the general defeat was the measure restricting the hours of women messengers which was enacted into law.

So far nothing has been said of a minimum wage, for this type of legislation has not even yet gained legal support in New York State. However, along with the attempt for an eight-hour day, a minimum wage for women has been ardently striven for in New York ever since the days of the Factory Investigating Commission.

Interest in raising women's wages had become articulate in this country in about 1910 at the time of the publication of the federal investigation of the *Condition of Woman and Child Wage-Earners in the United States* and the establishment of the British trade boards. The National Consumers' League had been watching the English movement and were inspired to plant the seed in this country. Mrs. Florence Kelley with her characteristic energy declared that "after having changed the opinion of the highest court of the United States, we may perhaps take courage, and feel there is literally nothing we may not justly undertake."[2] Massachusetts was the first state to enact a minimum wage statute and nine states had adopted such legislation by 1915. Minimum wage laws in this country differ materially from

[1] *Report of the Consumers' League of the City of New York* for 1918, p. 3.

[2] *Report of the Consumers' League of New York* for 1909, p. 53.

those of England and all European countries, however, in that they provide only for women.

The Factory Investigating Commission gave extended attention in 1914 to the need of a minimum wage in New York State, which led to its recommending legislative action in 1915. In response to questionaires the commission received 76 replies which it published. Moreover 115 economists, social workers, lawyers, representatives of labor and employers and their representatives contributed to a minimum wage symposium. These responses are all contained in the first volume of the commission's reports of 1915. With some exceptions,[1] the trend of the arguments was in favor of a minimum wage provision for women and minors in New York State. The reasons given are well known,—that the majority of women in industry are young and unorganized, that they plan to be in gainful employment for a relatively brief period of time, until marriage, that they are therefore weaker bargainers; that they thus receive wages too low to maintain a decent living and this is a menace to themselves and to society. Professor H. R. Seager recommended a minimum wage as the most effective means of fighting the evils of industrial homework which is now chiefly undertaken by women and children. He cited the experience of Victoria, Australia, which was that " within a few months the system began to have a marked tendency to put an end to home work, and to transfer industry to well organized shops and factories where the workers were as-

[1]For example, the view of Miss Helen Marot, formerly secretary of the New York Women's Trade Union League, was in opposition to state rates of wages for women alone. " If women need State protection on the ground that they do not organize as men do," she wrote, " then also do the mass of unskilled, unorganized men who do not appreciate or take advantage of organization. . . . The reasons for trade unionists to oppose State interference in wage rates apply to women workers as they do to men." *Op. cit.*, page 774.

sisted by power machinery and efficient organization to earn the wages which employers must in any case pay."

A considerable amount of precise data on the actual wages then being paid to women were also collected by the commission. The wages of 105,000 workers in manufacturing and mercantile establishments were recorded from which it was discovered that over half of these women received less than $8.00 a week. (The commission had determined that $9.00 a week, every week in the year, was at that time the minimum for the maintenance of a normal existence for women and girls).

These findings not only prompted the recommendation of a minimum wage bill by the Factory Investigating Commission, but they commanded stirring support from philanthropic and other bodies whose active interest was the welfare of working women. The Consumers' League formed a committee on living wage with Mary Van Kleeck for its chairman, whose expressed purpose was "to do its part in calling attention to the facts, and to use its influence in securing appropriate and effective legislation."[1] The league called conferences in 1914 for the discussion of the desirability of some form of wage legislation and while it was observed that such legislation was not favored by some trade unionists, "the conference showed that this is by no means the attitude of all workers, but that some of the most thoughtful of them are heartily in favor of such protection for women and minors in the sweated industries." Another meeting was held by the Consumers' League at which Mr. Louis D. Brandeis and Dr. Howard B. Woolston spoke (Dr. Woolston had directed the wage investigations in the state), explaining the desirability of helping women to get a decent wage by statutory act. Thus the agitation for

[1] *Report of the Consumers' League of the City of New York* for 1914, p. 39.

minimum wage legislation had strong support from the outset.[1]

Nevertheless the support of the first minimum wage bill, as of those in subsequent years, was not sufficient to effect its enactment into law.[2] In fact the measure met with immediate defeat, not even being acted upon by the labor and industries committee. It was suggested that the defeat was partly owing to the new republican control in the legislature, the bill having been introduced by a commission of democrats.[3]

We have said that the minimum wage bills have been killed each year in company with the acts for an eight-hour day, and that in 1918 a group of other bills were also destroyed. And now, the tangible effect of this repeated rebuff to the champions of these measures was the formation in the autumn of 1918[4] of the Women's Joint Legislative

[1] At the New York State Constitutional Convention held in 1915, Mr. Alfred E. Smith, now Governor, introduced an amendment empowering the legislature or its agent to prescribe living wages to be paid to women and children. At the same convention another amendment was offered "prohibiting the legislature from passing any bill granting hereafter to any class of individuals any privilege or immunity not granted equally to all members of the State." It need not be said that both measures were defeated. *Cf. Monthly Labor Review* of the United States Bureau of Labor Statistics, October, 1915, p. 41.

[2] The act provided for a wage commission composed of three members to be appointed by the Governor representing employers, employees and the public, with power to appoint a wage board in each underpaid industry in which women and minors were employed, and to investigate and determine wages. The Massachusetts precedent was followed in that the recommendations of the wage boards were not to be compulsory for employers. *Report of the Factory Investigating Commission*, 1915, vol. i, pp. 291-298.

[3] *Report of the Consumers' League of New York* for 1915, p. 16.

[4] The Bureau of Women in Industry was also created in 1918, and under the directorship of Miss Nelle Swartz, has since been actively engaged in studying the conditions under which women work in New York State. The bureau has made a number of very valuable studies

Conference. It is this composite body of women which has played the strong, if not the winning hand, in favor of special laws for women, during recent battles in the state legislature. The organizations that made up the conference were the Women's Trade Union League of New York City,[1] the New York State Woman's Suffrage Party, the New York State Consumers' League, the Consumers' League of the City of New York and the Young Women's Christian Association.[2] Miss Mary E. Dreier was made chairman, and later the executive secretary of the City Consumers' League became, automatically, secretary of the conference. Since the first year other women's organizations have joined the conference including the New York State and City Leagues of Women Voters, United Neighborhood Houses of New York, Women's City Club of New York, New York League of Women Workers, Girls' Friendly Society. The program of the conference was further endorsed by such organizations as the Federal Council of Churches of Christ in America and the Women's Christian Temperance Union.

This conference states that it was formed "at the request of the State Federation of Labor, to formulate and push a program of women's labor bills." [3] And since its inception this group of women has been faithful to its principles. As a body they undertook anew the work which theretofore had been carried by separate units, and entered the campaign

which have been published from time to time by the department of labor and have borne more or less directly upon the necessity for special protection of women. These bulletins are used throughout this work and more will be said of the creation of the bureau in a later chapter.

[1] The membership of the Women's Trade Union League is composed of the friends and benefactors of working women as well as of the women themselves.

[2] Pamphlet of the Women's Joint Legislative Conference, *Shackled*, undated, but probably 1920.

[3] *Ibid.*

of 1919 with new courage and the confidence that comes with a united stand. $800 was contributed by the Women's Trade Union League alone for the campaign fund. More than one hundred women went to the April hearings from New York City not to speak of the enthusiasts from the up-state districts.[1]

An eight-hour day for women in factory and mercantile establishments and a minimum wage commission were provided in the two most urged bills submitted to the legislature in 1919.[2] Four other bills completed the conference program,—a fifty-four-hour week and the prohibition of night work for women employed in offices, elevators and on transportation lines, and a health insurance measure. Pamphlets containing both emotional pleas and matters of fact were widely circulated by the conference,[3] showing the dehumanizing effects upon men and women of long hours of work, and the salutary effects of an eight-hour day, and asking the legislature to " give back to the women who work the Spirit of Life." [4]

The hope of decisive progress in this type of legislation was the more confident this year because of the wholehearted endorsement of Governor Smith. It will be remembered that Mr. Smith was a member of the Factory Investi-

[1] *Life and Labor*, April, 1919, p. 100.

[2] In February, 1919, a new study of earnings of women in New York State was published by the State Department of Labor (*Bulletin no. 92*) which gave fresh strength to arguments for a minimum wage. Earnings were compared with those recorded in the same industries by the Factory Investigating Commission about five years before, and while the median wage had increased from 62 to 70 per cent in these industries this wage was still too low to permit of decent self-support.

[3] Others were prepared by the American Association for Labor Legislation, the National, City and State Consumers' Leagues and the New York State League of Women Voters.

[4] Pamphlet of the Women's Joint Legislative Conference. Undated, but probably 1919.

gating Commission which promoted the cause of special protection of industrial women after their extended investigation some five years before. Thus, in his first annual message to the legislature, Governor Smith now brought to bear the pressure both of his own convictions and of his position. Speaking generally of social legislation he wrote,

Of particular importance to the State is the necessity of adequate protection for workers, especially the women and children. We should constantly strive to better their conditions. For just as we have maintained in the realm of international relations that right and not might should prevail, so in our economic life the weak and helpless should be protected against exploitation and oppression and given the opportunity to enjoy those material and spiritual blessings which alone make life worth living. Such beneficent measures are dictated not alone by sentiments of humanity and fair play, but the welfare of the State demands them and they must be adopted for us to continue and develop as a nation of sound and virile men and women. . . .

Recommending the establishment of a minimum wage commission, Governor Smith declared that,

The justice and necessity of a law of this kind are manifest. It is just as cruel to underpay a woman as to overwork her, and just as harmful and wasteful from the standpoint of the State.

If you believe that the future mothers of this State are a resource that we should conserve, you will give this legislation your most earnest and careful consideration.

Without hesitation the governor then urged further extension of the labor law—that it "should be extended to protect women who have entered new industries because of the war. I refer particularly to the employment of women on surface, subway and elevated railroads, and in the operation of elevators," he said. "Such employment is today unregulated, and the women do not receive the protection and safeguard that the law throws around their work in industrial pursuits generally."[1]

It appears that the cards were stacked against these bills however, despite the exhortations of Governor Smith, for although the elevator and transportation provisions were enacted into law, the others failed to pass. Moreover not only in 1919 but also in the successive following years the eight-hour day and the minimum wage bills have repeatedly failed to meet the approval of the legislature, despite the strongly concerted effort behind them. So-called "welfare bills," they have gone into the fire that destroyed them in pretty much the same way each year. A more powerful machine than that of their proponents has opposed them. In 1919 and 1920 when the support of the bills was strengthened by the insistent endorsement of the governor, the opposing machine on the other hand was operated with a skill not attained before. Illuminating descriptions of the process of defeating the bills were published by the New York State League of Women Voters[2] and by the American Association for Labor Legislation.[3]

According to these reports the opposition to the bills was organized from two coöperating sources, namely; the New York League for Americanism and the Joint Legislative Committee to Investigate Seditious Activities under the chairmanship of Senator Clayton R. Lusk.

[1] *New York Legislative Documents*, 142nd session 1919, vol. i, no. 3, pp. 11-13.

[2] In pamphlet form and reprinted in the *American Labor Legislation Review* for March, 1920, pp. 81-104.

[3] In an article by Frederick MacKenzie, called "The Legislative Campaign in New York for the 'Welfare Bills,'" and quoting from the New York *Tribune* for April 7, 1920. *American Labor Legislation Review*, June, 1920, pp. 136-149.

The New York League for Americanism was said to be the new name of the up-state Associated Manufacturers and Merchants, later called The Associated Industries of New York State. Mark Daly was the leader and lobbyist for this league and contributed to the official organ, *The Monitor*. The active director and promoter was Carleton D. Babcock who, as head of the California Research Society of Social Economics, it is alleged, had been instrumental in defeating the Sickness Insurance bill in that state. Mr. Babcock was also reported to have been in the employ of an influential society of insurance men in Detroit, Michigan, organized for the defeat of any attempt to establish "non-commercial illness insurance and similar humanitarian proposals." Thus the report shows that he was well practised in the game he is charged with having played in New York.

In 1919, reports state, the New York League for Americanism secured thousands of signatures from employees in New York factories petitioning against workmen's health insurance, the signatures then being misappropriated to apply to the whole program of welfare measures. The signatures were said to have been secured under false pretenses, employees being intimidated by individuals who were prejudiced in advance against the proposed legislation. A lecturer for the league was quoted as having explained that the league "was organized primarily to kill off health insurance and other such fool legislation. The Americanism part of it is a catspaw."[1]

Senator Davenport in introducing the health insurance bill in 1919 claimed deliberate poisoning of public opinion in the following unflattering phrases:

A vast organized propagandism, with great expenditures of

[1] *Op. cit.*, March, 1920, p. 97.

money, has been set in motion against it in this instance by designing men. For the time being, many intelligent persons are dupes of this propagandism. Until the hidden and selfish purposes which lie behind the organized and powerful groups are disclosed, the proponents of this bill believe that an honest insurance inside the realm of industry, cannot be obtained. . . . Until the fog of misrepresentation is lifted, and medical and general opinion becomes clarified and formulated, frank and open discussion should continue. . . . It is of far greater consequence to let the light in upon the secret forces of reaction which are really the backbone of the stubborn opposition to this and other proposed measures of social amelioration in the State of New York.

The service recommended by Senator Davenport was performed by the New York League of Women Voters in their above mentioned report and protest to Governor Smith. Wide publicity was given to the exposé by the press throughout the state and in the large newspapers reaching to the Pacific coast.

The other source of opposition, the Lusk Committee, aided by Speaker of the Assembly, Thaddeus Sweet, was the New York State Joint Legislative Committee to Investigate Seditious Activities. Mr. MacKenzie explains that the 1920 bills were killed by the manoeuvres of Speaker Sweet, and his summary of the legislative activity in these two years is worth quoting,

The reactionary leadership that forced this action had announced at the outset its continued and determined opposition to the welfare bills. The "trial" was more than a "red herring" to throw public demand off the trail marked out for the quiet demise of these measures once more in committee rooms; it was an amazing climax to the same ruthless tactics employed a year earlier in withholding them from a vote on the floor of the Assembly. Then the forces in control of the

Assembly drew the issue sharply by blocking progress through orderly legislative processes; here appeared a spectacular flaunting of representation itself. In the earlier case every Assembly constituency in the state was denied its right to the voice and vote of its representative on the welfare bills; in the recent case, five constitutencies were arbitrarily deprived of all right to legislative representation.[1]

Despite the parliamentary trickery in the assembly, the senate had refused to resort to it and the women's eight-hour day and minimum wage bills were passed by that body by a great majority. Moreover the senate's unqualified support of the bills had been in the face of the public charges of Mr. Lusk that the women and all other proponents of these bills were bolshevists and German propagandists

> who advocate the overthrow of the Government of the United States by the confiscation of property belonging to the poor as well as to the rich. You farmers here before me—you will have your very tools stolen from you. These are the people who would overthrow marriages. They believe that every man and woman should consult their own passions. They believe in no future life, no punishment for sin.

And then for climax,

> If Tad Sweet is beaten . . . you'll loose your powerful officer. My God! What a calamity if he were beaten![2]

In the assembly, however, the bills were strangled in committee. Despite the fact that both the eight-hour day and the minimum wage bills had been introduced by republicans, and although republican assemblyman Roosevelt who

[1] *Op. cit.*, p. 144. The reference made above is to the suspension of five socialist assemblymen.

[2] Address of Mr. Lusk at Fulton, Nov. 1, 1920, advocating Mr. Sweet's reelection to the assembly. *American Labor Legislation Review*, 1920, pp. 100-101.

introduced the wage bill was a member of the labor and industries committee to which it had been committed, he could not get his own bill reported out. The chairman of the committee, Mr. George E. Brady, is said to have stated that the committee did not have a quorum at any meeting during both years. The failure of the bills to emerge from committee automatically condemned them to the rules committee where Speaker Sweet presided as chairman, and which was commonly known as "the morgue."[1]

In 1919 Governor Smith did not cease fighting for the minimum wage bill to the very last. As if to bring it back from the dead he plead with the legislature for consideration in a special message dated April 8. He urged that "at the very least the measure should be brought before the floor for discussion," and that the legislature pause to consider the real meaning of a minimum wage—that it is neither a wage fixing measure nor an abandonment of the principle of competition. "In its essence," the governor continued, "the legal or minimum wage is prohibitory, not compulsory in character. The State, in effect, says that to employ women at a wage that is insufficient to sustain them is a public menace, and therefore that danger is prohibited, just as is prohibited the erection of a factory building without proper fire-escape exits or sanitary arrangements."

The governor weighed the individual and social cost of under-payment of women in the following way: "The woman worker pays in reduced health. The employer pays in greatly reduced efficiency. The whole working class to which the woman belongs pays as a result of an unfair and below-the-belt competition. The State pays through its public and private charities, its hospitals, reformatories and other eleemosynary institutions. Heredity pays in the form of

[1] Pamphlet of the Women's Joint Legislative Conference; *Shackled, supra cit.*

poorly nurtured and delinquent offspring; and the nation pays in the impairment and impoverishment of its capital resources." The testimony of a witness before the Factory Investigating Commission was recalled by the governor as having epitomized in a sentence the effect upon health of low wages: "To pay a girl what is below a living wage, is like running a thoroughbred horse without shoes. In order to economize a few dollars at one end of the line, we incur a cost that runs up to hundreds of dollars."

Governor Smith further considered the moral effects of low wages, quoting Dr. Howard Kelly, "the eminent gynecologist," as having said in 1912 that "many girls are driven to a life of shame by low wages." The governor urged that while "excessively low wages may not be a direct or primary cause of a life of shame, indirectly it is inevitably one of the most important contributing factors."

Speaking then in general, Governor Smith despaired of woman's ever being able to "hold off from making a bad bargain." He asserted that the law of supply and demand had been left to regulate wages for more than a hundred years and "the report of the Factory Commission shows how utterly inadequate that is. The results have been highly injurious to social welfare and there are no natural forces to remedy the evil unless the State will, in self-respect, step in. Our whole social progress during the last fifty years has been obtained by limiting and regulating this so-called economic law of supply and demand." [1]

Despite this long and earnest plea from the governor, however, these bills were not even reported out of committee, as we have already seen.

Nevertheless Governor Smith was undaunted by the sweeping defeat of these measures in 1919 and again gave warm and generous attention to them in his second annual

[1] *New York Legislative Documents*, 142nd session, 1919, vol. 36, no. 81.

message to the legislature in the following year. Urging the enactment of the minimum wage provision, he wrote,

> The benefits that will accrue to a large number of women and children in this State by the removal of the industrial injustice that minimum wage boards seek to remedy must not be permitted to be obscured or clouded by smoke-screens from the reactionary interests of the State, who are pretending that it narrows women's opportunities. I have endeavored, with all the powers at my command, to impress upon those Honorable Bodies that this must not be regarded as legislation in the interest of or against any group, but as legislation in the interest of public health and the general welfare, not only of the State as it exists to-day, but for the generations to come. If reactionary organizations are unable to see it in this light, it is most unfortunate, because the arguments which they employ against it could just as reasonably be advanced against every regulatory statute protecting the health of women and minors that has ever been enacted since we have had a State.

Faithful to his constituents, he also tirelessly continued in his endorsement of the eight-hour day for women:

> In recent years experience has taught that excessively long hours do not of themselves insure quantity in production, much less quality. Workers tired and ineffective from fatigue are no good to themselves or the community of which they are a part. It may be old-fashioned to make distinctions in powers of endurance as between the sexes. If so, I plead for place with the most reactionary elements who believe with our noted scientists that women and minors need a health protection in the point of hours of labor that is not necessary to apply to men. I again affirm my belief that the State should move forward and set a new standard of hours of labor for women and minors, based on the maximum eight-hour day, and ask for the enactment of such legislation applied to industrial and mercantile establishments.[1]

[1] *Op. cit.*, 1920, vol. i, no. 3.

At the hearings of the eight-hour and minimum wage bills in the senate chamber on March 23, 1920, another large delegation of women were present from all parts of the state. Miss Frances Perkins spoke for the Industrial Commission urging the passage of the bills. She stated that 53 per cent of the women in New York State were then receiving less than $12 a week. Mr. Sweeney, representing the Retail Clerk's Union in Albany, cited the lowness of wages of retail clerks concluding, " It is plain that this is not a living wage and that it must result in one of two things, either an oppressed and impoverished life, or an escape by means we will not consider." Another witness, Mrs. Stanton, " associated the mentally and physically defective children with the underpaid and overworked women." A number of women wage-earners spoke in favor of the bills as entirely necessary to their welfare. Senator Lowman, employer and contractor who had introduced the 48-hour bill, expressed himself in favor of a 48-hour week for both men and women. His statement was, " I believe that eight hours of labor is long enough for anybody to work a day, man, woman, or child." A witness from Albany, Mr. Huyck, manufacturer, " made a fine witness for our side" reported the Women's Trade Union League. Mr. Huyck expressed his sympathy, likewise, with the need of an eight-hour day for men as well as for women, but his support of this special bill for women was because " Men, through their organizations will get a forty-eight-hour week very quickly. It is going into one industry after another, and women will not get it. . . ."

The Women's Trade Union League then remarked as follows, in concluding its report of the hearings:

It seems a travesty upon representative Government that men who care nothing for social justice, men who have no understanding of the industrial problems, who will not consider these questions on their merit, but who take their orders from a well organized, thoroughly selfish ring of masters, should have in their keeping the health and happiness of hundreds of thousands of working women.[1]

In spite of all, however, the net results of the 1920 campaign were perhaps even more discouraging to the supporters of welfare laws than those of 1919. For, while in the former year all so-called "reactionary" bills were defeated and the "protective" measures relating to women on elevators and transportation lines were enacted, in 1920 all so-called "welfare" bills were defeated and limitations upon hours of women in the transportation service, except for conductors and guards, were repealed. Thus while the outcome was balanced slightly in favor of restriction in 1919, in 1920 weight of legislative sanction had shifted toward release from restriction.[2] It is impossible to measure the significance of this reversal of authority so near at hand, but it is significant that since 1919 no restrictive measures have been enacted for women in New York. On the other hand there have been passed three acts removing such restrictions—for transportation employees, for printers, and for women at polishing and grinding wheels.

Thus during the next two years, and in contrast to those just passed, the legislative horizon reflected but faintly the coloring of propaganda advanced by advocates of welfare legislation. Governor Miller's first annual message to the

[1] *Life and Labor*, May, 1920, pp. 138-140, 160.

[2] On the other hand two other bills removing restrictions introduced in 1920 were not passed. One was the repeal of the elevator bill of the year before which prohibited women operating elevators from night work and from more than fifty-four hours of work weekly. The other was a bill introduced by Assemblyman Betts which repealed all special restrictive measures for women over twenty-one years of age. It is this distinction between adult women and girls that is urged by some groups of working women themselves and these releasing bills were ardently supported by them, particularly by the Women's League for Equal Opportunity.

legislature conspicuously lacked any reference to labor legislation, and in his second message in 1922 the only statement regarding the protection of adults was indirect, negative, and equivocal. This statement was made in connection with his endorsement of child-labor legislation where the governor declared,

I deplore paternalistic tendencies which substitutes (*sic*) dependence upon the State for the self-dependence and self-reliance of the citizen, but it is one of the highest functions of the State to safeguard childhood and to protect the public health and the proper discharge of that function is not paternalistic.[1]

Notwithstanding the unfriendly atmosphere, the Women's Joint Legislative Conference in 1921 succeeded in having their eight-hour day and minimum wage bills introduced into both the senate and assembly by the democrats, Cotillo and Bloch. They were given meager attention on an overcrowded program, however, and again failed to receive a favorable report out of the joint committee. A number of other bills regarding women which the women's conference had refused to endorse were also defeated, some of an indeterminate character but on the general side of restriction, others openly intended to remove restriction. In the former group were hour and wage bills which were introduced into both senate and assembly. These neither stated the maximum hours to be worked nor provided for local wage boards, but they left the onus of fixing both hours and wages upon the Industrial Board.

The second group of bills were in the form of repeals of existing laws. One introduced by Assemblyman Charles H. Betts aimed to annul the 54-hour law for adult women, allowing it to remain for young women under the age of

[1] *New York Legislative Documents*, 145th session, 1922, vol. i, no. 1, p. 26.

twenty-one years. A companion bill was that introduced by Marguerite Smith, planned to annul the night work prohibition for adult women in mills and factories, allowing it to stand for young women under twenty-one years of age. Another bill introduced by Miss Smith released from the night work prohibition women employed in newspaper offices as proofreaders, monotypists and linotypists. Still another bill released women over twenty-one from the prohibition of operating polishing or buffing wheels for wet grinding. The two last releasing measures were enacted into law. The proposals for the general release of adult women from day and night restriction in mills and factories were defeated, along with the acts for women's greater protection—the eight-hour day and mandatory[1] minimum wage bills.

Thus the legislative session of 1921 closed with much less dramatic action in relation to laws for women than in the former two years. This also was the result of the session of 1922.

The legislative year 1923 opened with an entirely new *misè en scene.* The presence once more of Alfred E. Smith in the governor's chair in Albany, gave the women's organizations high hope. And true to his earlier form the reinstated governor again urged passage of the neglected welfare bills. In his exhortations to the legislature on the eight-hour day, he said,

Long ago the State of New York adopted the policy of limiting the hours of labor for women and minors in industry. This was predicated upon the theory that the state should exercise its police power for the protection of their health and welfare. The eight-hour day is well recognized when organized groups are in a position to enforce it. It seems to me that the state is

[1] Making compliance with the mandate of the minimum wage commission compulsory.

behind the time in withholding from the great army of women and minors employed in industry the benefits that grow from the shorter work day which they are unable to secure because of a lack of organized effort.

I, therefore recommend an amendment to the existing statutes that will provide for the eight-hour day for women and children engaged in industry.[1]

Endorsing his former unqualified support of the minimum wage bill, the governor assured the legislature:

For many years we have discussed putting into effect a minimum wage for women and minors in industry established by means of determinations to be reached by a board composed of representatives of the interests involved, the public, the workers, and the employers.

I sincerely believe that the majority of the members of the legislature are in accord now with my views on this subject and I hope that there will be no delay in putting into effect a law embodying in the Department of Labor an unpaid Minimum Wage Board for the establishment of a minimum wage scale for women and minors in industry.[2]

No effort was spared by the Women's Joint Legislative Conference in their preparation for the new joint campaign for 1923. The conference was reorganized with Mary E. Dreier again its chairman, Mrs. Gordon Norrie, vice-chairman, and Clara Mortenson Beyer, secretary. A "Steering Committee" was appointed to handle the legislative program composed of Miss Dreier, Nelle Swartz, chief of the New York State Bureau of Women in Industry, Frances Perkins, member of the Industrial Board, Rose Schneiderman, president of the New York Women's Trade Union League, and Clara Mortenson Beyer, also executive secretary of the Consumers' League of New York.

The organizations that affiliated with the conference and

[1] *Bulletin of the Consumers' League of New York* for January, 1923.

[2] *Ibid.*

pledged financial support, according to the February *Bulletin* of the Consumers' League, were: the American Association for Labor Legislation, Carroll Club, Consumers' League of New York, Girls' Friendly Society, National Consumers' League, New York Child Labor Committee, New York League of Girls' Clubs, New York League of Women Voters, New York Section of the Council of Jewish Women, St. Catherine Welfare Association, United Neighborhood Houses, Vocational Service for Juniors, Women's Christian Temperance Union, Women's City Club, Women's Trade Union League, Young Women's Hebrew Association. Additional organizations which endorsed the two bills were: Citizens' Union, Civic Club of Buffalo, City Club of New York, Joint Legislative Committee of the Ethical Culture Society, Mothers' Club of Great Neck, Long Island, National Council of Catholic Women, New York State Conference of Jewish Women, Women's Municipal League, Women's City Club of Rochester.

The following letter sent to Governor Smith from the first meeting of the conference bears witness to the confidence of victory with which the tireless supporters of these bills entered the campaign this year:

My dear Governor Smith:

In behalf of the Joint Legislative Conference I am authorized to express to you our deep appreciation of your having included the Eight-hour Day and Minimum Wage in your splendid message to the Legislature.

Your interest and support of these measures are a supreme satisfaction to us for they indicate clearly that after years of effort New York will at least be placed abreast of those forward-looking States which already have enacted this legislation.

We send you our warmest congratulation and thanks and offer you our hearty co-operation.

Very sincerely,

(Signed) Mary E. Dreier, Chairman.[1]

[1] *Op. cit.*, January, 1923.

The two bills were duly introduced into the senate and assembly and became known as the Strauss-Galgano bill (eight-hour day) and the Cotillo-Hamill bill (minimum wage commission). All friends of the bills were urged to work as they had never worked before and to write letters urging support to legislators, republicans as well as democrats, and to the members of the labor and industries committee in whose grip the former bills had met their end. The warning was made public that "the women of the State will resent bitterly any attempt to make political capital of this much needed relief legislation for wage-earning women." [1]

A joint hearing of the senate and assembly committees was held on the assembly floor on February 27, and the house was packed to the doors with women enthusiasts, many of whom had come to testify—the others to support the speakers by their presence. A large group of working women were produced as witnesses to show the need of legislation, their expenses being paid out of a fund collected for the purpose. Melinda Scott made an inpassioned appeal for her fellow workers. Bernard Shientag, Industrial Commissioner, and Frances Perkins, member of the Industrial Board, urged the advisability of the passage of these two bills. Miss Perkins recalled the passage of the 54-hour bill twelve years ago and the objections that were made to it at that time—that it would drive industries out of the state because manufacturers could not manage so drastic an interference with the law of supply and demand when they were obliged to compete with others who were not so hampered. She testified that the prophecies of the manufacturers had not come true in spite of the passage of the law, but that on the other hand industries had increased

[1] *Op. cit.*, January, 1923.

in size and in profit making. She implied that the present bills would also bring good effects to employers instead of ill.

But here it is necessary to pause and consider the opposition. For, as has been said, the bills did not pass. Perhaps the political facts explain much of what happened; for while the democrats were in control of the senate, they had only 69 votes in the assembly. And, according to report, the republicans in the assembly took a solid stand behind their leader, Speaker Machold.[1] So from the time the governor's opening message was delivered, it appeared that the bills of the democratic party, including the welfare bills, were insecure. Later on in the session when the air had become thick with conflict, Governor Smith urged his constituents "We are in the right, and being right means being in the majority. . . . There is no reason why you should feel very severely handicapped by being fewer in number when you know the people are with you. They can bring pressure to bear provided you make the right sort of a fight so the State gets to know that a fight is on." [2]

And the state did learn that a fight was on. The Associated Industries with their Mr. Mark Daly again came upon the scene of action, but they found less occasion for extensive manoeuvres than had been necessary in the previous years (1919-1920). For sharp issues develop strange affinities.

As a result of the alleged displacement of thousands of women in New York City owing to the limitations placed upon women's hours in 1912 and 1913 (the maximum 54-hour day and no night work) there grew up an organization of women workers whose aims were crystallized by what they considered righteous indignation. They said they had discovered that protective laws did not protect women, but

[1] New York *Times*, January 10, 1923.

[2] New York *Times*, March 20, 1923.

if anything they protected men by disqualifying a large group of their competitors. The Women's League for Equal Opportunity was the name adopted by this group of women which has grown in numbers since its inception in 1915. Miss Ella M. Sherwin, a printer in Brooklyn, was the first president; and the league is now headed by Mrs. Margaret Firth of New York City, also a printer. The declared object of this organization was, and is, to "make working women see what is happening to them" under the guise of "welfare" legislation. Miss Sherwin's position in part has been stated as follows:

> Welfare legislation, if persisted in, will protect women to the vanishing point. Whatever its intent, it can have but one outcome. It will drain women out of all highly paid and highly organized trades, because the law will prevent them from doing the same work that men do and the unions will prohibit them from working for a lower wage than the men.[1]

In 1917 another group of women formed into an Equal Rights Association whose grievance was practically the same as that of the Women's League for Equal Opportunity. The object of this group has been more generally educational—to broadcast their views concerning the alleged evil effects of protective laws for women not only to the women themselves but to the public. Their official organ is *Industrial Equality* edited by Mrs. Ada R. Wolff, a printer, who is also chairman of the association. "Give a Woman a Man's Chance—Industrially," is the watchword.

These two organizations, working more or less together, have presented themselves at Albany each year during the session of the legislature and have done their part, along with the Associated Industries, to divert the stream of welfare legislation that was being fed by the Woman's Joint Legis-

[1] Quoted in an article by Anne O'Hagan, reprinted from *Touchstone Magazine*, for August, 1919.

lative Conference and men's labor unions. They were ardent supporters of the anti-protection bills introduced by Assemblymen Betts and Smith which have already been mentioned, and in 1920 a well attended dinner was given in New York City in honor of Speaker Sweet in recognition of his successful opposition to the welfare bills.

Since 1921 a new power has come into the scene of which these protesting women's organizations have become allies,—the National Woman's Party. Following the adoption in 1924 of the Nineteenth Amendment to the Federal Constitution which gave complete suffrage to women, the National Woman's Party headed by Miss Alice Paul launched upon a new campaign. It became a permanent organization, retained the old name, and proposed a new federal amendment for the "further release" of women—the removal of all "political, civil or legal disabilities or inequalities on account of sex, or on account of marriage unless applying to both sexes." [1]

Mrs. Oliver H. P. Belmont, who became president, made possible a magnificent national headquarters for the new party in Washington, D. C., situated opposite the Capitol. Alice Paul was made vice-president and active director. Following reorganization the party spared no time in pushing intensive study of the statutes of all of the states, listing those that discriminate against women. Pamphlets were issued as the work of each state was completed, publishing the discriminatory laws. Complementary to this gathering of ammunition, bills have been introduced into the state legislatures for the removal of women's disabilities by amendment to state constitutions. The plan was, and is, to work for individual state amendments simultaneously with the campaign for a federal amendment.

[1] The National Woman's Party issues a weekly paper called *Equal Rights*.

The Achilles' heel of this formidable body of women was its relative indifference to the need of an economic program. The major interest was in the removal of the civil and legal disabilities of women without acting upon the fact that these disabilities rest upon woman's economic status; that there can be no permanent release from disabilities and inequalities until many of the economic problems are solved. Thus in launching their new program, the Woman's Party discovered themselves at once faced with the questions relating to women in industry. They were forced to ask themselves whether they considered special legislation prejudicial to these women and something to be destroyed, or whether they believed that women, being weaker, needed legislation in order to make them equal with men in the earning-a-living world. It was in the state of Wisconsin that this crucial question first arose. The Woman's Party did not take a united stand but permitted the issue to be decided in its name by the interested people of the state. The decision was made in favor of well established " welfare " legislation for women workers which was included in the Equal Rights bill, stress being laid upon the need for special protection in order to make women equal with men. And as a result of this decision, the Equal Rights bill was passed in Wisconsin in 1921.

In New York State, the Woman's Party was plunged into the women's battle over the welfare legislation in 1922 which has been described. It became imperative that an organized position be taken if the party program was to receive support by women in the state, and in other states. Should they decide to endorse the attitude of Wisconsin and make special legislation for women a part of their own program for equality of women, they would receive the support of the thirty or more large women's organizations in New York, most of which were members of the Women's Joint Legislative Conference. If, on the other hand, they decided upon a position opposed to special legislation they were certain to find friends, though fewer in number, and also to find a strongly organized enemy. The issue was as decisive as it was clear-cut. The general program of the Woman's Party was widely accepted among women with the exception of this matter of special protection in industry.

In November of 1922, a national conference of the Woman's Party was held in Washington to draw up its Declaration of Principles. In the form of a resolution, twenty-nine principles were adopted, the fourth of which is as follows:

> That women no longer be barred from any occupation, but every occupation open to men shall be open to women, and restrictions upon the hours, conditions and remuneration of labor shall apply alike to both sexes.

Since the 1922 conference, then, the National Woman's Party has joined and strengthened the opposition to the "welfare bills" for women wherever they have been submitted to state legislatures, unless they were extended to include men.

Little further need be said concerning the legislative session of 1923 in New York State. Despite the large representation of women in support of the minimum wage and eight-hour bills, these bills were defeated again by the stronger opposition. Supplementing the plea of the Associated Industries and other independent manufacturers who operated through the republican bloc, the three women's organizations, the National Woman's Party, the Women's League for Equal Opportunity, and the Equal Rights Association, were strong foes. While the two working women's organizations openly opposed the proposed bills, the National Woman's Party advocated their passage with the word "persons" substituted for the word "women," which method they have adopted for securing an "equal chance" for men and women "before their employers."

Industrial Commissioner Shientag, in his address to the joint legislative committee, explained that he thought these "earnest women" were "unwittingly . . . playing into the hands of an element and group in this State which has always stood against progress, which has always stood against every bit of legislation for the protection of working women and children and for the advancement of the cause of humanity." He continued, in speaking of the minimum wage,

> Why, that is the very thing calculated to bring about the equality that these earnest but, in my judgment, misinformed women are aiming to bring about. . . . It simply means this: That the State says to an employer, "There is a certain point below which you cannot go in paying wages to women, or in employing women." [1]

Before the adjournment of the legislature the minimum wage law of the District of Columbia was declared unconstitutional by the United States Supreme Court. Perhaps this decision was the final blow to the New York bill, which, together with the eight-hour day provision, was tottering.[2] A dramatic week was spent in a breathless attempt by the sponsors of these welfare measures—the Women's Joint Legislative Conference—to secure the discharge of the committee who failed to report the bills out. Seventy-six votes were necessary. But the highest poll was 75 to 72, the roll

[1] *Bulletin of the Consumer's League of New York* for March, 1923.

[2] In an effort to save the minimum wage bill it was changed by its supporters during the legislative session from a compulsory to a non-compulsory measure similar to that of Massachusetts. The hope was that this concession would appease Speaker Machold and the up-state manufacturers whom he represented sufficiently for them to permit it to be enacted into law.

being taken several times upon the charge of jugglery or of absence of pledged voters from their seats.

The Women's Joint Legislative Conference attributed their defeat once more to the Associated Industries machine, one of whose executives, Mr. Charles P. Miller, was chairman of the labor and industries committee.[1] Instead of reporting the bills out, Mr. Miller employed the well known tactics of proposing a new resolution, said to have been formulated by Mark Daly, which the committee adopted. This resolution provided for the creation of a legislative commission whose duties would be to investigate women's wages and hours and the attitude of working women themselves, and to determine whether such bills are economically necessary and desirable. The resolution came to nothing, being defeated in the senate.

The outcome of the 1923 session of the legislature in so far as it affected women in industry, therefore, was entirely negative. The conflicting forces went back to their respective "camps" to gather new strength for the coming year.

In the autumn Governor Smith began with an earnest effort to bring about the election of a democratic assembly for 1924. He declared that the program of the republicans was one of "we will obstruct;" that they had no constructive program and that they refused to permit the people to have popular legislation enacted on the plea that the democrats were wcrking for control of the state. He protested against the iron hand of Speaker Machold in the assembly, and he recalled with implication Colonel Roosevelt's failure to force his minimum wage bill out of committee in 1921. "Let him tell us why he could not get the bill on the calendar when he went to Albany with all the prestige of his illustrious name and the glory of his personal achievements," he de-

[1] *Bulletin of the Consumers' League of New York* for May, 1923.

manded. " Party expedience, party success and party victory are the watchwords of the G. O. P." [1]

All pleas were in vain, however, for the election process again produced a republican majority in the assembly led once more by Speaker Machold.[2] And while some defection appeared at the outset in the republican ranks, the threat was made against Governor Smith's program, that " any foolish Socialist program " would be defeated.

Thus the legislative sky of 1924 was clouded at dawn for the advocates of " welfare " bills. But there were also wide rifts of blue. For one thing, new facts had been gathered since the close of the 1923 legislature. In November was published a comprehensive study of hours and earnings of women in New York, prepared by the Bureau of Women in Industry, Bulletin No. 121. The report included data concerning more than 59,000 women in five industries[3] which indicated that while there has been an improvement in the hours and wages of women in recent years, perhaps 44 per cent of the women whose time was recorded work more than 48 hours a week, and more than twenty per cent earn less

[1] New York *World*, November 2, 1923.

[2] Article iii of the State Constitution prescribes the method of electing legislators in New York State. The system results in the fifty senators being elected approximately according to the census, but it seems this is not true for assemblymen. According to the constitution, one assemblyman is elected from each of the 150 assembly districts, but there must be at least one assemblyman from each county (with one exception) while the remaining number are elected according to the population. This seems to result in the so-called " rotten borough " system whereby up-state electors can retain a majority representation in the assembly while the majority of the people of the state, centered in greater New York, are represented by a minority.

[3] This study has more than usual interest because of its covering precisely the same fields of employment which were investigated by the Factory Investigating Commission in 1913, and the State Department of Labor in 1918. Thus there is an interesting array of comparative data over a ten year period.

than $12 per week; more than one-half of all the women earn less than $16.00 weekly. Since 48 hours is considered a sufficiently long working week, and $16.00 the approximate minimum for a respectable living, these findings gave new strength to the arguments for the 48-hour week and the minimum wage bills.[1]

Moreover, the advocates of these bills felt relatively confident of success this time because, in addition to the staunch friendship of Governor Smith which he again manifested in his legislative message on January 2, Republican State Committee Chairman Morris stated that his committee endorsed the 48-hour bill. The cause of the minimum wage commission also seemed strengthened by the endorsement it had been given by President Coolidge in his message to Congress.

There were two other early features of the 1924 campaign that gave hope to the proponents of the welfare bills. One was the spectacular victory of Governor Smith over Mark Daly of the Associated Industries when the latter failed to substantiate his charge against the efficency of the Department of Labor. We have seen that Mr. Daly represented interests actively opposed to protective legislation; and now it was confidently hoped by advocates of legislation that his power was broken and that a vicious foe was at last vanquished.[2]

Another factor in the campaign that encouraged the welfare enthusiasts was the probable support of Colonel Theodore Roosevelt and his political associates. It appears that Col. Roosevelt has always been sympathetically inclined to-

[1] An important observation made from the data was that in the short hour establishments, a greater number of women worked full time than in the establishments with a longer scheduled week, and furthermore that there is a "decided tendency toward a higher rate of pay for full time work in shorter hour establishments."

[2] More is said of this investigation of the charges of Mr. Daly in a later chapter.

ward welfare measures, and now, it was evident, he was being seriously considered for the next governor. This fact necessitated caution on his part against either active or entirely passive resistance to the measures proposed by democratic Governor Smith. Thus, it was prophesied that the republican campaign methods of 1919, 1920 and 1923 would not be adopted this year. On January 18, cheering headlines appeared in the newspapers such as "Outlook is bright for Smith's laws—bi-partisan agreement to put bulk of program over seems assured." [1]

The second month of the legislative session was not so promising as the first. "Partisan warfare holds sway in the Legislature" was the reflection in the press; [2] "harmony conferences" were admittedly over, and the republican assembly and democratic senate were deadlocked. The eight-hour day and minimum wage bills, among others, appeared to be slated for discard. These bills had been passed in the senate on March 10, a public hearing having taken place on February 26. Cleavage among the senators had developed in the voting, six republicans having broken over party lines to join the democrats in support of the measures.[3] The New York *World* evidenced its friendliness by applauding the rebellious senators, commenting further:

Can there be any excuse for treating measures to regulate the conditions under which women and children work in factories upon a partisan basis? What difference is there between a Republican woman and a Democratic woman, a Democratic child, not yet a voter, and a Republican child, not yet a voter, in industry? Why must such questions, even in the Assembly, be debated or decided upon a partisan basis? [4]

[1] New York Morning *World*, January 18, 1924.

[2] New York Morning *World*, March 12, 1924.

[3] Senators Davenport, Ferris, Lowman, Mastick, Whitley, Hewitt.

[4] *Op. cit.*, March 12, 1924.

Thus the republican party discipline in the senate under Leader Lusk appears to have broken down. In the assembly, however, there was greater solidarity. For, although State Chairman George K. Morris had declared himself in favor of the eight-hour bill and Speaker Machold had said he would not oppose it, a conference of republican assemblymen voted to kill the bills in committee, which, when the time came, was what happened.

On the 7th of March, less than four days before the close of the session, Governor Smith repeated his strong eleventh-hour effort of 1919 to recover his bills. He urged fervently that selfish partisan interests be cast aside and that it be recognized that "the eight-hour day is gradually receiving nation-wide acceptance." As previously, he restated the reasons for this legislation (the eight-hour or Straus bill and the minimum wage or Reiburn bill):

The desire to bring about the forty-eight-hour week is predicated upon the theory of the conservation of the public health. If we are to have a healthy and vigorous race we must look to it by law for the protection of future mothers. It is my very earnest hope that the Legislature will not adjourn without giving to this question the serious attention to which it is entitled.

I would also ask of you to consider the bill already passed by the Senate providing for a Minimum Wage Board to study the question of wages paid to women and children in industry with the power of recommendation as to what constitutes a wage sufficient to enable women and children to maintain themselves in health and comfort.

Such a law has been in force with a great deal of success in the State of Massachusetts for a long period. Employers of female labor in large numbers would welcome any information that would place them in a position to feel that they were doing justice to the women and children they employ.

I can think of no greater asset to the State than healthy

women and children. The life of the State itself is dependent upon them.[1]

But despite all, these bills could not be pried out of the rules committee, and thus they became inert like those in years before. A modification in the 48-hour bill proved of no avail. Introduced by Republican Assemblyman Shonk, this measure was supposed to cancel the chief remaining objections of the canners by permitting fifty-four hours of work a week for a maximum of eight weeks in the year.

The test came before daybreak on the 8th of April when the poll for the release of the eight-hour bill was lost by three votes at 2:30 a. m., and that for the minimum wage was lost by five votes, a half-hour later. The democrats stood solidly for both bills, it is reported, and they were joined by ten republicans for the hour measure and eight for the wage bill. The New York *World* under the title of "Their Master's Voice," narrates that "the remaining Republicans, representing 250,000 fewer than half the votes of the State, killed the bills." And continued,

It might be magnifying his office to call Speaker Machold the leader of this reactionary host. Assemblyman Bloch charges that the master's voice they heard was that of the Albany lobbyist of the Associated Industries, an organization whose cannery complex is known.[2]

But even then oxygen-tank methods were used to revive the 48-hour bill (there was no further hope for the minimum wage measure). Governor Smith issued an emergency message which made it possible for a new hour provision to pass through the senate in order to bring the act again before the assembly. At 3 a. m. on April 11, about five hours before the close of the session, Senator Mastick introduced

[1] *Op. cit.*, April 8, 1924.

[2] *Op. cit.*, April 9, 1924, editorial.

an act corresponding to that of Assemblyman Shonk. It was promptly passed with but five dissenting votes and sent to the assembly. At 6 a. m. the bill's discharge from the rules committee was moved. It was lost by two votes.

Two hours later—at 8:40 a. m. on April 11—the session closed, "with the greatest saturnalia of legislation ever witnessed in the memory of the oldest legislators." [1] A clutter of bills had been disposed of in a most remarkable fashion, and legislators and lobbyists were intoxicated from lack of sleep and the chaos. Clerks and employees are said to have been for sixty hours without sleep.

This brings our legislative story to an end, in its general outline. It is important to say, however, that the battle of 1924 was not all political, but that the cleavage among the women themselves over the "women's bills" had grown fiercely wider. The National Woman's Party, maintaining that "protection" means "restriction," pressed for the passage of twenty-two bills, among which were those aiming for "industrial equality." The League for Equal Opportunity and the Equal Rights League also took a defiant stand against the "welfare bills" and in favor of a repeal of the night work prohibition for women in occupations at which men are employed at night (the Stapley bill). On the other hand, the Women's Joint Legislative Conference, representing about twenty women's organizations, fought hard for "protection," and organized labor is reported to have gone on record as opposed to the anti-night work bill.

The opposing group of women in the contest appeared in large numbers at the February hearings, the women's conference being headed by Mrs. Samuel Bens and supported in its contentions by Industrial Commissioner Shientag, who again urged the need of protection for women. Rose Schneiderman, vice-president of the National Women's

[1] *Op. cit.*, April 12, 1924.

Trade Union League, explained that women must have protection for the short time they are in industry, that they cannot do " the same work as a man " and that " equal rights cannot keep them in work for which they are physically unfit." She continued, " And the women who are strong enough to work beside men, and who want to work at the same hours of the day or night and receive the same pay, might be putting their own brothers, or sweethearts, or future husbands out of a job." [1] Doris Stevens, representing the National Woman's Party, urged that women no longer be linked with children in laws relating to industry, that her party would support legislation protecting men and women alike, and that " it is very gallant of you to offer to give women special privileges, but we are convinced that in the end it will do them more harm than good." [2]

But the New York session closed with no more and no less special protection for women in industry than was on the statute books before it began. The conflicting elements have again become less turbulent, and, as this book goes to print, we are once more in the trough of the legislative wave waiting for another crest in the spring of 1925.

[1] *Op. cit.*, March 16, 19, 24. An interview.

[2] New York *Times*, February 27, 1924.

CHAPTER IV

Influences Continued

We have analysed the influences in New York State which have borne upon the factory law in its restriction of women's working day; and have followed the integration of the social and political machines which have affected the trend of more general legislation for working women. It is evident that the Factory Investigating Commission stimulated the development of this legislation, but while some acts have been passed since the days of this commission, and others have been hotly advocated, much time has been spent in contention against the repeal of statutes already enacted, with relatively small results in the form of new acts.

We will, then, continue the story of influences upon legislation as they have affected more specific occupations. While the daytime hours of women in factories in general (and in mercantile establishments when the proposed regulations affected them also) have been discussed, much remains to be said of particular industries such as canneries, laundries, and homework, and of night work prohibitions; of regulations in restaurants, in elevators, and on transportation lines, of special working conditions, and of the entire prohibition of women's employment in certain occupations.

The subject of daytime hours in factories will be considered first.

HOURS OF LABOR—DAY WORK

Factories

1. *Canneries*

The inclusion of the canning industry in the general factory law of 1899 proved a mistake from the point of view of enforcement, as will be seen in a later chapter. During those years between the hour-limitation act of 1899 which flatly included all factories regardless of their nature, down to 1912 when canneries were completely freed from rules during the rush season, the canners had been actively opposed to any hour limitation and openly violated this provision.

Some canners sought relief by legislative amendment while others adopted the method of passive resistance. And their attitude was rather generally condoned in their communities. In 1907, when the factory law was amended in its hour-limiting provisions in order to effect enforcement, the original bill form followed the English precedent of allowing females over eighteen years of age to work in canneries sixty-six hours a week for a time not exceeding six weeks a year. This was a European custom and it had been permitted by the recent international labor treaty signed at Berne, Switzerland. But in New York, opposition by philanthropic and labor organizations to this exemption for canneries was violent, and the attempt to obtain it was thus temporarily abandoned.

This failure to manifest statutory understanding of the special problem of the canners was sharply regretted by Labor Commissioner Sherman in his annual report.[1] His view was that " Reasonable variations from the more regular limitations imposed upon those industries in which work is or can be made regular should be allowed for those in which

[1] *Annual Report of the Commissioner of Labor*, 1907, pp. I. 50.

it cannot," and that such a provision "would render the law more easily and generally enforceable as to them and would in fact reduce their hours of labor, and it would avoid the danger of an adverse decision from the courts as to the constitutionality of the provisions limiting the hours of women's labor." Contrary to the view expressed later by Florence Kelley in her plea for "uniformity" of regulation as she testified in 1912 before the Factory Investigating Commission, the commissioner expressed his objection to having particular industries "unnecessarily and unreasonably embarrassed for the sole purpose of keeping a regulation general and uniform." He sponsored European provisions which were "based upon necessity and equity and are consonant with health, for the reason that in such industries limited overtime during rush periods or seasons would be counterbalanced by reduced hours in slack periods or seasons."

But those who were eager to protect the women employed in canneries, as well as in other factories, were consistently opposed to making any variations of the rule they had succeeded in getting written into the statutes.

And so the controversy continued. In 1910 the so-called Boshart bill was introduced into the legislature by the canners and opposed by the Consumers' League and other organizations. The bill repealed the sixty-hour provision for women and minors during the height of the canning season—the four months from June to October. As a "camouflage" according to the Consumers' League report, the canners added the clause that overtime should not be required beyond an average of sixty hours a week for the whole period. Despite the precaution of its proponents, the bill made little headway. Moreover, emphasis laid upon the decision of the United States Supreme Court which upheld the constitutionality of the ten-hour law for women in Oregon (Muller *v.* Oregon), together with the pressure brought from the Consumers' League and Child Welfare Committees, led to the withdrawal of the bill by the introducers. Pauline Goldmark, chairman of the league's committee on legislation, raised a warning finger, however, urging that as the canners would try it again: "Eternal vigilance is the price of success in preserving our labor laws against the greed or self-interest of unenlightened merchants and manufacturers." [1]

The warning was a true prophecy, for in 1912 the "interests" became powerful enough to have their way and canneries were relieved of legal supervision regarding women's hours. The 54-hour bill of 1911 is reported to have been killed by the textile industry assisted by the canners. When a similar act was passed in the following year with the cannery exception, it was signed by Governor Dix, but only after considerable pressure had been exercised. His objection was not to the exemption of canneries but to their sole exemption, for he felt that candy and textile industries were as legitimate candidates for legislative leniency as canneries. The governor's view in the matter was interpreted by the 54-hour advocates as a direct diplomatic invitation to these employers to seek exemption from the uniform law at their will.[2] The invitation was promptly accepted by the candy manufacturers, who, a week after the new act went into effect, October 7, challenged the constitutionality of the law on the grounds of class legislation. The result in the courts of this challenge was against the plaintiffs and in favor of the law as explained in the preceding chapter (People *v.* Kane).

The release of the canners won in 1912 proved only temporary. The excessively long hours of cannery em-

[1] *Annual Report of the New York Consumers' League* for 1910, p. 27.

[2] *Ibid.*, 1912, p. 34.

ployees, as discovered by the Factory Investigating Commission, led to the prompt introduction in 1913 of a bill regulating hours of women especially drafted to meet the conditions in canneries. Because of the alleged uncontrollable rush during the four months' season, some concessions were made and the 54-hour regulation was stretched to sixty hours and, during a shorter period, to sixty-six hours for women eighteen years of age and upwards.

According to the report of the commission, there was little difference between men and women in the deplorable conditions of labor under which they worked in these canneries, "the employees are either native American neighbors of the canneries or foreigners imported from cities in family groups of men, women and children." [1] They belonged to "no organizations of any kind," and they worked frightfully long hours (as high as 119 hours a week) and for lower than living wages. "Being scattered units they have no effective means of making public their opinions and wishes."

Notwithstanding the general oppression of cannery employees, the fact that the women outnumbered the men in this industry, added to the greater interest in protecting women, led the commission to make recommendations for the relief of women and children only. Facts concerning women's duties in their houses were submitted to emphasize their need of a shorter day in the canneries,—"of 941 women, 671 or 71 per cent did housework before or after their factory work. These cares must be added to the wear of factory life in measuring the strain under which these women live." Replacement of women by men was also suggested in order that "the most extreme overtime would be eliminated" for women. It was pointed out that those "on the 'capping line,' the can dropper, those who put on caps, the inspector and the syrup maker are among the last to

[1] *Report of the Factory Investigating Commission*, 1913, vol. i, p. 124.

leave, and women are often used for these tasks."[1] Workers who were "employed on the earlier processes finish their work at night and go home before the others." (No data are given in the report regarding the wages received by the women "on the line" compared to those in the earlier processes.)

The report of the factory commission on canneries was concluded by a recommendation in the form of a bill which was that year (1913) enacted verbatim by the legislature. Hearings were held at Albany on February 19 and were attended by enthusiasts from the Consumers' League, child labor committees and the American Association for Labor Legislation. The principles upon which the bill had been drafted were:

First. That no industry should be carried on at the expense of the vitality of the women and children who are employed in it.

Second. That until the sixteenth year is reached it is of the first importance for a child to develop normally, and any occupation which interferes with its normal development physical or mental, is objectionable.

Third. That it is a proper function of the State, through the exercise of its police power, to prohibit any employment of women which saps their vitality and any employment of children which prevents their normal, physical or mental development.

Fourth. That the conditions of labor in factories is a matter of public concern, and that the State through its police power has authority to demand, and should demand, that dangerous machinery be guarded, and that insanitary conditions, especially in factories where food products are handled, be made sanitary.[2]

[1] *Ibid.*, p. 162.

[2] *Ibid.*, vol. ii, pp. 759-760.

Laws relating to canneries in other states had been cited by the commission to show that their recommendations were not without precedent in this country,—"In Illinois the hours of labor of women in canneries are limited to ten hours a day; in Tennessee, to 60 hours a week; in Pennsylvania, to 12 hours a day or 60 a week; and in Wisconsin, to 10 hours a day and not more than 55 hours a week."[1] It was further observed that in Michigan and California similar regulations would doubtless result from widespread state movements toward that end. Despite this testimony, John F. Connor, attorney for the New York Canner's Association, suggested during the discussion of the bill, "that the present statute be given a fair trial before restrictive amendments be adopted. The statute is the same as that found in substantially all the 'Canning States,' and under these circumstances we feel that the Legislature can afford to act conservatively and in harmony with other states."[2]

One of the most significant facts uncovered by the investigation of the factory commission was the grave mismanagement of a great many canneries—the appalling lack of any coördinated plan between the supply of raw materials they undertook to can and the capacity of their plants. The commission concluded that "*Evidently extreme overtime work is due not so much to the character of the industry as to the policy followed in the management of the business,*"[3] a diagnosis that now comes daily from our modern production engineers. That this fact was little understood by the canners themselves was evidenced by the superintendent of a plant in which long working hours were discovered. He explained that, "The way to make money in the canning business is to carry a little larger acreage than you can handle

[1] *Ibid.*, vol. i, p. 169.

[2] *Op. cit.*, 1913, vol. ii, p. 1301.

[3] *Op. cit.*, p. 163.

comfortably, so that you can run pretty steadily throughout the season and your plant won't be idle in slack periods."[1]

The canners did not give up their contention. From the restrictive law of 1913 they promptly sought "honorable" relief through legislation, and the session of 1915 was one of hot contest and acrimony when, organized, the canners presented their program. Three bills to relax the law relating to women employees were introduced by Assemblyman Bewley, a cannery owner. With the plea that canners are quite unable to control the time of the ripening of food and thus the time when food must be canned, even though that time is Saturday night or Sunday, bills for longer hours were presented. Bill No. 1 permitted canning factories to employ women and children seventy-two instead of sixty hours a week; Bill No. 2 permitted canning factories to employ women and children until midnight instead of ten o'clock in the evening; and Bill No. 3 permitted canning factories to employ women and children on Sundays.

According to the New York *Tribune* for April first, a wild scramble into the well of the House occurred when bill No. 1 polled only 72 votes while 76 votes were needed for its passage. New York City republicans were importuned by panting up-state men who beseeched them to change "no" to "aye" in the next voting. In the midst of the pandemonium, the second vote was called for and the clerk announced "Ayes 76, Noes 59." Upon this change of scene,

[1] *Ibid.* One phase of the mismanagement of canneries from a social point of view was the extensive practice of employing children for long hours. This is abundantly described by the factory commission and corroborates the report of the federal investigators in 1908-1909, before mentioned. Children employed at "snipping" beans and husking corn were often found to be working in sheds adjoining the main factory buildings which had been declared by the attorney general not to be included as factories in the meaning of the law. This decision took from these children the protection of the law of 1903 which had prohibited them from work "in connection with any factory."

Minority Leader Alfred E. Smith sprang to his feet exclaiming,

> This is the entering wedge. If you Republicans stay in power long enough you'll tear down the whole law that protects New York's most valuable asset — its womanhood. We on the Factory Commission knew what you canners were doing and we had these laws enacted to stop it, and not only the people of this Commonwealth, but the whole nation applauded our action in stopping canneries from working women one hundred and twenty hours a week.
>
> But you've got to do something to get back to making your 21%. You have the votes and you are going to do it.

Majority Leader H. J. Hinman defended the measure by declaring that the legislation forced upon the state by the Factory Investigating Commission "was a mistake from the outset."

When the second Bewley bill was introduced, Smith did not wait for a vote before he interjected, "All you need is this bill to make you slave drivers." "Its passage means you can work women from six in the morning to midnight. Will humanity and civilization stand that? It's too much." This tirade proved effective—the vote was 60 to 67 against the measure. Of the third bill, Smith cried,—"There is a commandment which says 'Remember the Sabbath Day and keep it holy' and there isn't any clause in it which excepts a canning factory. Are you ready to improve on the handwork of God Almighty?" The roll call this time was 70 to 58 and that bill also was lost.

Heartened by his success, Mr. Smith then contested the vote upon the first of these bills requesting a reconsideration. Hinman objected on the grounds that many of the representatives had left the floor; he suggested that the bill could be brought up for vote again in the morning—but this was not done.

On April 9, therefore, Bewley bill No. 1 became the Thompson canning bill in the senate. Moreover, it was passed by the senate in another lively scrimmage, by a vote of 27 to 15. The most influential republicans were committed to the measure, so the report goes, but Senator Ogden L. Mills was a staunch and outspoken opponent. He stressed the facts of cannery mismanagement by recalling that the factory investigation of 1912 had shown that only six of the canneries in the state regarded it necessary to work women and children seventy-two hours a week, and that such legislation would only "create distrust among laboring people by making this unsound exception in favor of the canners." Senator Robert F. Wagner who, it will be recalled, had been chairman of the Factory Investigating Commission, also attacked the bill in a spirited discussion of more than an hour. He explained that, "This bill is wanted by a few canners with avarice enough to place the almighty dollar above child life and womanhood, who are willing to deify the dollar and sacrifice man on Mammon's altar." Senate Leader Brown returned that the attempt to bar women and children from working at "such gentle and healthful occupations as berry-picking" made "idle citizens." "The sooner you wipe such laws off the statute books the better," he concluded.

The bill was not again introduced into the assembly until April 23, but the Consumers' League was never busier than during this interim. With the Woman's Suffrage Association, the New York Association for Improving the Condition of the Poor, and other women's organizations acting as warm-hearted allies, no stone was left unturned for the defeat of this measure. A carefully appointed hearing was held before Governor Whitman on May 10 with the result that the governor sent a veto memorandum to the assembly stating that he deemed the harm from such a provision to

[1] New York *Tribune*, April 9, 1915.

outweigh the good. Following the final discussion a vote was called for and the bill was defeated by a count of 66 to 70. Thus were killed the three Bewley bills, and the canning industry, at least on the statute books, remained regulated as before.

Comment ran freely in derogation of the action of the legislature on these canners' bills which almost allowed them to be passed. Samuel Gompers, in a *Federationist* editorial in May, emphasized the fact that the legislature has power in sixty days to destroy " laws that were the result of years of struggle." He concluded with the warning, " Put not all your faith in legislation, quoting the New York *World* as follows:

> An eight-hour day for women employees of the Western Union Telegraph Company will be put into effect next week in place of the present nine-hour schedule. A telegraph office, however, is not a cannery, and this eight-hour day is not at the mercy of the New York Legislature.[1]

And so the fight has continued, seldom more fierce than during this 1915 session and often much less so; for, as will be seen in a later chapter, some canners have persisted in violating the law with impunity. Moreover, the State Industrial Commission in 1920 declared that the economic organization of the canning industry would have to be overhauled before exemptions at the height of the season could be abolished. At least two improvements would have to be made, first, the acreage contracted for must be reduced to equal capacity with the plant; and second, cold-storage facilities must be installed to hold crops in the rush period.[2] Wisconsin canneries are said to have adopted this way of holding crops.

[1] The *Federationist*, May, 1915, pp. 353-354.

[2] *Annual Report of the Industrial Commission* for 1920, p. 261.

2. *Laundries*

Laundries are classed as factories in New York State and are subject to all the rules and regulations applying to factories. Nevertheless, here is another industry which has claimed special, if any, attention from the legislature. But their demands have not been heard to the extent of making any general exceptions from the factory law, as in the case of canneries. Certain classes of laundries have managed to secure complete exemption from the law, however. These are hotel and hospital laundries, so exempted on the grounds that they are not public enterprises.

Laundrymen who have been expected to obey the law have protested against it because of the alleged seasonal and sporadic nature of their enterprise, maintaining that in order to meet competition it is imperative to meet the demands for prompt service from customers such as hotels, restaurants and steamboat lines. For these reasons the commissioner of labor in 1906 recommended an exception for laundries from the uniform law, and suggested that some other scheme be devised for checking the overtime work of women.[1]

In this connection it is interesting to know that Curt Muller, of Muller *v.* Oregon fame,[2] was a laundryman. When the decision of the state court was declared favorable to the ten-hour law for women, which had been the subject of Mr. Muller's challenge of that law on the grounds of unconstitutionality, laundrymen of the three Pacific coast states, Oregon, Washington and California, combined and retained distinguished counsel in appeal to the Federal Supreme Court. But they were defeated at that final bar and thus silenced without establishing precedent for making laundries an exceptionally long hour industry.

In 1911 women's organizations in New York State sup-

[1] *Annual Report of the Commissioner of Labor*, 1906, p. 65.

[2] See p. 66, *supra*.

ported a bill amending the factory law to include the outlawed hotel and hospital laundries. The Consumers' League had made an investigation of these establishments and discovered an excess of overwork by their employees showing no basis for their being distinguished from any other laundries. But the bill came to naught. Renewed efforts toward the same end by the Factory Investigating Commission in 1914 also failed, and the factory law, as it concerns laundries and is interpreted by the attorney general to exclude hotel laundries, stands today as originally enacted—impervious to the raids of reformers.

Some of the most notable strikes in New York State in which women have assumed a leading rôle have been in laundries.

The strike of the women starchers in 1905, known as the Troy Laundry Strike, became famous because of its far-reaching results. The governing board of the Consumers' League, having recorded its opposition to the organized laundry employers who refused to arbitrate with organized labor, had been asked to end the strike by conciliation and arbitration.[1] The refusal of the laundrymen to coöperate with the league led to an *impasse*. Spurred by the seriousness of the situation, and believing that only by prompt action could women be relieved from oppression by unscrupulous employers, the industrial committee of the General Federation of Women's Clubs petitioned Congress to make an appropriation for a commission whose task would be to investigate the conditions of female labor throughout the country. President Roosevelt gave the proposal his warm support in his annual message to the Senate. All those who have interested themselves in the facts concerning the conditions of women and children in industry in recent years

[1] *Annual Report of the Consumers' League of the City of New York* for 1905, pp. 19-20.

know the result of this movement,—the classic nineteen-volume report on *The Condition of Woman and Child Wage-Earners in the United States* published in 1910.

Volume XII of this remarkable report is devoted entirely to the employment of women in laundries,—the hours of labor, the general working conditions, the character and the effect of work. The investigators are here shown to have found frequent and very long working days and much consequent ill health [1] among these women, which revelations doubtless increased the pressure of the demand in New York State in the following year for the law to be extended to hotel laundries. But the statute even as it stood was poorly enforced as was witnessed by the participants in an extensive laundry strike in the same year, 1911. "Endless hours" of labor were bitterly complained of on the part of both male and female employees—as many as eighteen to twenty-three in one day! [2]

Mercantile and Other Establishments

Attention to the labor hours of women in mercantile establishments came considerably later than that for factories; the first regulative law came fourteen years later. This has been explained on the ground that conditions in factories were so much worse than elsewhere that, until they were improved, conditions in mercantile establishments, better by contrast, had been overlooked. The movement for improvement in mercantile establishments seems to have been initiated by working women themselves, promptly assisted by philanthropic groups.

In 1890, a group of women employed in shops met to consider the causes of their oppressions and to seek relief through

[1] 129 out of 404 who were examined complained of ill health directly attributable to their occupation, p. 38.

[2] See further reference to this strike in the chapter on Enforcement.

trade unions. They called themselves the Working Women's Society. According to the report of the New York City Consumers' League,[1] these women discovered the widespread character of wrongs done them at their work and determined that an organization among shoppers was necessary to aid them. A joint committee was appointed by the society which, together with Mr. Everett P. Wheeler who acted as chairman of an organized mass meeting, started "The Consumers' League." The principles upon which the league was founded were akin to those of a London association.

The object of the league as stated in its constitution was "To ameliorate the conditions of the women and children employed in the Retail Mercantile Houses of this City by patronizing as far as practicable only such houses as approach in their conditions to the 'Standards of a Fair House' as adopted by the League, and by other methods." The annual publication of a "White List" was begun, with twenty-four houses reaching the required standard.

The general attitude of the league toward its beneficiaries was expressed by Mrs. Charles Russell Lowell, the first president, in concluding her report for the year's work in 1893. It ran as follows:

> Besides our gratitude, however, for the services they [the working women] render, they deserve our pity, because of their helplessness and the peculiar hardships to which they are exposed. They are helpless because they are women, and they are helpless also because they are young, and they are moreover exposed to peculiar temptations from the fact that when wages fall below the living point, the "wages of sin" are always ready for them.[2]

[1] *Report of the Consumers' League of the City of New York*, 1894, p. 3 *et seq.*

[2] *Ibid.*, 1893, p. 8.

Continuing, the report of the following year reads that "this particular class of workers being as a rule, too young and too unskilled to make the formation of trade unions among them either practicable or useful," [1] the league had undertaken to be their official friend.

That statutory regulations be enacted to control the hours of labor and a factory inspector be provided for mercantile establishments as well as for factories was the sense of the bill drafted by the Working Women's Society in 1891 and introduced into the legislature that year—the so-called "Ainsworth Bill." Though the bill was not passed then nor for many years to come, the senate had heard the demands of the women enough by 1895 to appoint the Reinhardt Investigating Committee, before mentioned, "to investigate the conditions of female labor in New York City."

The report of the committee was made in 1895 and 1896 and appears in part in the annual report of the New York City Consumers' League for 1895. Among other criticisms of delinquencies the committee declared that the requirements passed in 1881 for seats in stores had been constantly evaded in spite of the fact that "the importance of providing proper seats and of permitting their use at reasonable times cannot be overestimated;" that the basements of "the mercantile stores were not properly ventilated and lighted," and that the hours of work were excessive. In the same report of the league (p. 13), a unique estimate, showing an inventiveness born of the necessity of other women, showed the extent of extra work which New York City mercantile establishments had filched, in 1895, from shop employees during the holiday season. The number of employees of each of 16 firms times the number of days at holiday season during which, according to advertisements, their shops would be open in the evening, times four (the number of hours

[1] *Ibid.*, 1894, p. 4.

from 6 p. m. to 10 p. m.)=600,200 hours of free labor. 600,200 hours=60,020 working days of 10 hours each= 191 years and some months.[1]

The Reinhardt Committee held hearings on the Ainsworth bill which an association of retail dealers is said to have opposed successfully until that time and which they continued successfully to oppose until 1896, when with substantially fewer restrictions a measure was drafted by the committee and enacted into law by the legislature.[2] The modifications had been demanded by the New York City merchants who succeeded in annulling the force of the statute even in its modified form. For, while the friends of the new act had been able to secure the instalment of salaried inspectors toward the enforcement of the act, the tenure of office of these agents was brought to an early close and with it the life of this first mercantile law. More of the unsuccessful attempts to give the young workers the benefit of this provision will be mentioned in the following chapter.

At this time appeared Florence Kelley's *Ethical Gains Through Legislation* which was widely read by those who were concerned with the lot of wage earners, women wage earners in particular. The book aroused an interest in the legislative method of protecting workers, probably stronger than had ever been felt by philanthropic groups. The Consumers' League became converted anew to this method of protection and subscribed for the service of the legislative bureau of the City Club which furnished the texts of bills and their daily status in the legislature.

In spite of this increased interest in the direction of regulating hours of women's labor, the progress of this regulation in mercantile establishments was slow. Early agitation

[1] *Op. cit.*, 1895, p. 13.

[2] F. R. Fairchild, *The Factory Legislation of the State of New York*, p. 65. See also page 115, *supra*.

for a mercantile law had been limited in the main to children and young people, while the hours of women, it will be recalled, were not regulated until as late as 1913 under the direct pressure of the Factory Investigating Commission. New York thus lagged thirteen years behind Massachusetts in this respect, the State Consumers' League having been more successful there.

Another act restricting the hours of young women and children in mercantile establishments was passed in New York in 1903. This was the Hill bill which called for a compulsory nine-hour day and 54-hour week. The bill was opposed by Senator Brackett who offered a counter amendment requiring the maximum number of hours to be ten a day and sixty a week. Senator Elsberg, the republican party leader, interjected the reminder, however, that the state had already placed itself on record for eight hours for men in public service which made a proposal for ten hours for women and children seem rather ridiculous, whereupon Senator Brackett concluded, "I bow to the will of the party chief. I withdraw the amendment." And the 54-hour day for sub-adult women was won.[1]

The commissioner of labor in his reports for 1907 entered an urgent plea for protective legislation for *adult* women in mercantile establishments. He asked, "Why for instance should women packers be allowed to work 78 and 84 hours a week in ill-ventilated and crowded spaces in department stores if it be a necessary health regulation to prohibit their working more than 60 hours a week in well ventilated and properly appointed workrooms in factories?"[2] He continued that there were few factories in which women's work was as hard, and ventilation as poor, "in short in which the hygienic working conditions are as bad as they are in the

[1] New York *Tribune*, April 15, 1903.

[2] Department of Labor *Bulletin* for June, 1907, p. 199.

average department store." The only adequate explanation, he charged, was that the proprietors of the stores were better organized and had stronger political influence than the manufacturers, that the teaching in schools led to clerical occupation and was silent as to any advantages in factory work. This, he thought, tended to create an increasing aversion in the minds of young people. Recent books and magazine articles had "pandered to the popular appetite for horrors" by discussing factories, he said, and "have clouded the public mind. . . . It is not true that the working conditions in our factories are worse than in other industries or occupations. The contrary is nearer the truth." [1]

The Hooper bill was thus championed in the assembly that year (1908) extending to women in mercantile establishments the provisions of the factory law in the regulation of hours of labor. But the opponents were stronger than the proponents, and the bill failed to pass.

Again in 1909, the Consumers' League instigated the introduction of an amendment to the mercantile law which would apply to women over twenty-one years of age, as well as to those under that age.[2] The act provided a conservative maximum of sixty hours a week and twelve hours a day to relieve the fourteen-hour days that were not infrequent at that time. There was provision also for the repeal of the Christmas holiday overtime allowance, it being declared a disgrace to permit the employment of young women for the excessive hours practised through the holiday season. After a lively hearing in the judiciary committee the bill was favorably reported to the senate, but it failed to be enacted into law. The New York Retail Dry Goods Association was again successful, according to report, as it had been for years.

[1] *Annual Report of the Commissioner of Labor*, 1907, pp. I. 72-73.

[2] *Annual Report of the Consumers' League of the City of New York*, 1909, p. 36.

One of the epoch-making events in the legislative session of 1913 was the passage of the first act that regulated the working hours of adult women in mercantile establishments. The road to this act having been long and rough found its turning in the report of the Factory Investigating Commission. The commission pointed with shame to the mercantile law in New York State as compared with twenty other states in the union which limited the hours of all women in stores. It urged that New York was the only large industrial state which distinguished so sharply between mercantile establishments and factories in their protection of women and children, and that no substantial change had been made since the days of the Reinhardt Committee when the first law was enacted.[1]

The Consumer's League of New York, child labor committees and the American Association for Labor Legislation also worked earnestly for this bill which they supported by a delegation of several hundred representatives at the Albany hearings on February 19.

And so a first step was taken. But even yet the merchants of first-class cities succeeded in staving off the "evil day." The 54-hour provision as finally passed that year was leveled only at establishments in second-class cities which incensed those merchants affected because of the discrimination against them. This discrimination was removed in 1914, when for the first time all women in the state employed in mercantile establishments were included in the statute which limited their working hours. (The effectiveness of this statute is another story, to be told later). But even with this sweeping removal of discrimination between cities there proved to have been a joker in the legislature's pack. A provision introduced by Senator Walter slipped through

[1] *Report of the Factory Investigating Commission*, 1913, vol. i, pp. 286-289.

both houses and received the governor's signature, amending the business law of the state to allow the employment of women and children in drug stores without restriction of hours. This amendment nullified not only the newly enacted statute in so far as it applied to drug stores, but also the earlier provisions of the mercantile law in so far as that law included drug stores.[1]

Following the passage of this mercantile law, recommendations were made practically every year by the division of mercantile inspection that the law should be extended to women in other establishments—as in restaurants, lunch-rooms, theaters, and other places of amusement, in business offices, elevated, surface and railway ticket offices, and at telephone switch-boards. It was asserted in 1916 that "the benefits of this humanitarian legislation are just as essential to the physical and moral welfare of females not legislated for now as for those who are."[2] As the world war progressed the application of the law to women in banks and offices was particularly urged by the mercantile inspector, who held that the hours of labor in these places were longer and that the sanitary conditions often were inferior to those in factories and mercantile establishments.[3] In many cases, it was alleged, women in banks were working eighty-five hours a week;[4] but so far they have not been regulated by law. The annual struggle in recent years to secure an eight-hour day for all women has been described.

[1] In the case of People *v.* Liggett, 227 N. Y. 617 (1919), the state supreme court decided that drug stores selling things besides drugs, medicines, chemicals, etc., are mercantile establishments within the meaning of the labor law.

[2] *Annual Report of the Industrial Commission*, 1916, p. 63.

[3] *Op. cit.*, 1918, p. 14.

[4] *Op. cit.*, 1917, p. 53.

1. *Restaurants*

Early discussion of the limitation of the hours of work of women in restaurants was of unique origin. In 1894 the Department of Labor sent a letter of inquiry to the labor organizations of the state asking for suggestions for needed legislation. The reply of the Magnolia Association of Waiters was as follows:

> There appears to us that there is in the State of New York a great feeling on the part of the bosses to hire women instead of men in our trade, and we do not object to this competition so long as they receive equal pay for equal work, but we find in every instance, that the sole object of the employer is to take advantage of the unorganized condition of women workers and use her [*sic*] as a tool to break up organized labor, by compelling her to work at about one-half the wages paid to men, and as this is such a delicate question to handle, the bosses use the argument that we wish to discriminate against the fair sex, and appeal to public sympathy in the matter. There is a law on the statute books of this State that debars a woman from tending bar,[1] and we are of opinion that this law was passed from a moral standpoint, and we are looking for legislation to have that law amended, so as it will include in its provisions hotels and restaurants where intoxicating liquor is dispensed.[2]

An answer to the same inquiry made from the Brooklyn Branch, No. 4, of the United Silk Weavers read,

> Legislative measures against women and child labor are necessary. Against all these evils and a good many more a trade union alone is powerless nowadays.

Nevertheless, there was a long span of years from the

[1] This probably refers to the enactment of 1882, § 2010 which prohibits females from being employed as waitresses in places of amusement, and later forbade women to serve liquor unless members of the proprietor's family.

[2] *New York Bureau Statistics of Labor*, 1894, p. 386.

time of this plea of the waiters and weavers to the inclusion of restaurants in the mercantile law. Representing a different motive probably from that of these men workers, the commissioner of labor and the industrial commissioner also urged the regulation of women's labor in restaurants for years before its realization in 1917. In 1914, it was explained that the result of the failure to bring about this regulation had encouraged proprietors of bakeries and confectioneries to serve sandwiches and lunches so as to bring their enterprises into the category of restaurants and thus escape the factory law.[1]

But women's organizations were probably responsible, finally, for bringing about this desired legislation. The Consumers' League of the City of New York had made a special investigation before the meeting of the legislature in 1917 so that they were armed with fresh data for the support of the bill. The agents of the league had interviewed 1017 of the female restaurant employers (employed in New York and six other large cities of the state), of whom there were estimated to be between 15,000 and 20,000 in New York State. One-fourth of the 1017 interviewed were under twenty-one years of age, 44 per cent were between twenty-one and thirty years old. Less than one-third were American born. The length of working time in some cases was found to be appalling, for some it was seventy-five hours and over per week. One girl of twenty was reported to be found working 122 hours a week, "longer than the law allows factory employees in two weeks. This, of course, was an extreme case, yet one-half of the 1000 women interviewed by the League worked twelve hours a day, seven days a week, and fifteen hour days were not uncommon." [2]

[1] *Annual Report of the Commissioner of Labor*, 1914, p. 90.

[2] *Behind the Scenes in a Restaurant*. The Consumers' League of the City of New York, 1916, 47 pp. Reviewed in the *Monthly Labor Review* for February, 1917, pp. 258-261; also in the *Annual Report of the Consumers' League* for 1917, pp. 6-7 from which the above quotation is taken.

The "educational campaign," which was based upon these terrific facts, emphasized the health needs of women who handled food not only for their own sakes but in order to protect the public health. The act seems to have been passed that spring with little opposition.

Following the extension of the nine-hour day to restaurants in first and second class cities, the recommendations of the Industrial Commission were shifted to urge inclusion of all restaurants regardless of the size of the city in which they were located. As also were the recommendations of women's philanthropic organizations, who have in late years championed annually a general eight-hour bill for women. The need of such an extension of the statute to include all restaurants was emphasized when conditions in smaller cities and villages were studied. For example the State Bureau of Women in Industry reported inhuman conditions of labor in Niagara Falls, a third class city which is pressed for hotel, restaurant and lunch-room service by streams of tourists. A sample schedule of hours in one restaurant was recorded as follows:[1]

73 hours weekly; 1 day off out of 10 or 12
70 hours weekly; night shift
67 hours weekly; no day off
63 hours weekly; no day off; frequent overtime
56 hours weekly; no day off
71 hours weekly; no day off
84 hours weekly; no day off
105 hours weekly; no day off

All but one restaurant deducted pay for one day's rest in seven. Employers claimed that women had free hours in the afternoon but visitors from the bureau reported always finding women at work in the afternoon.

[1] *Life and Labor* for July, 1919, p. 183.

The plea for this further extension of the law to include all restaurants in the state was again urged from the public health angle as well as for the protection of the women employed, for it was alleged that local health officers were not able to inspect milk and food properly and that the public was thus without protection from the effects upon food of the ill health of restaurant workers. Thus far importunities have been of no avail, however, but if the general eight-hour bill for women is passed according to the plan of its many advocates, restaurants will be included.

2. *Street Railways*

At the entrance of the United States into the world war, women were taken into the transportation service in considerable numbers. Although women had been employed on some lines for years before this time as ticket agents and choppers and car cleaners, their appearance as members of car crews—as conductors and guards clad in cap and khaki coat, breeches and high boots—was an innovation. The exposure of these women to long hours of standing in cold and drafty cars, subjected to the discourtesies of passengers, to necessarily irregular working hours, to the hazards of leaving or arriving at the car stations during all times of the night and day, and to unsatisfactory comfort facilities at barns and terminals,—these conditions under which the women were employed brought their discomforts promptly to the attention of advocates of special protection by law.

Those who desired action on behalf of these newly employed women were not entirely agreed as to the method or degree of action.

Writing for *Life and Labor,* Margaret A. Hobbs, special investigator for the American Association for Labor Legislation, declared that "while theoretically the widest possible range of occupations should be open to women, in

New York at least, the threat to the men's standards and the undesirable characteristics of the work make street railroad work for women a source of injury both to men and women workers. The New York legislature should be asked not simply to regulate but to forbid altogether the employment of women on street cars." [1] Miss Hobbs indicated her sympathy with the report that though the women were declared to be "performing a patriotic service" they had not been hired because of "a real shortage of men, or to replace employes who have gone to war, but to punish the men for their strikes in 1916. The women are being used as a threat to keep the men 'well disciplined' and to prevent the spread of union organization among them." [2] This belief that the employment of women would surely lower labor standards, together with the fact that "women are working ten-hour shifts over a twelve to, in some cases, fourteen-hour period," and that "we find girls in their early twenties beginning their work at ten and eleven o'clock at night and obliged to go through most undesirable sections of the city to reach their cars,"—these conditions were given as reasons for the recommendation of Miss Hobbs that women should be entirely excluded from employment on street cars.

An editor's note appended to Miss Hobbs's article explained that the Women's Trade Union League was not in sympathy with the view that these women should be prohibited from street railway service, for "The League stands for the protection of women in all industries, rather than their prohibition from some industries." [1]

Moreover, at this time the "Lockwood bill" was before the state legislature, inspired by the Women's Trade Union

[1] *Life and Labor* for March, 1918, p. 58.

[2] Mr. Benjamin Squires in a study about to be discussed, reported that the ticket agents of the Interborough Rapid Transit Elevated Lines "voluntarily agreed to work twelve hours per day instead of ten if women were not put on to make up the shortage." *Op. cit., infra.*

League and endorsed by the Consumers' League of the City of New York and the New York Child Labor Committee. The bill provided that,

> no female over the age of sixteen years shall be required, permitted or suffered to work in or in connection with any . . . steam, elevated, subway or surface electric railways . . . more than six days or 48 hours in any one week or more than eight hours in any one day unless for the purpose of making a shorter workday of some one day of the week; or before seven o'clock in the morning or after ten o'clock in the evening of any day.

It should be noted in passing that this bill was all-inclusive of women employed in the transportation service, which made it apply to those female employees of long standing as well as to those who had recently been taken into the service.

Owing to up-state opposition, abetted by the Women's League for Equal Opportunity, the Lockwood bill was defeated and with it the bill regulating the work of elevator operators. In the following year, however, both of these bills were enacted into law. It will be recalled that they were two of the six composing the Women's Joint Legislative Program concerning which the Consumers' League played a prominent rôle.

Moreover, for these advocates of protection fresh ammunition was available this year (1919) in support of the bill regulating women's work in the transportation service. An intensive study of women working on street railways made by Benjamin M. Squires for the United States Bureau of Labor Statistics had appeared in published form in 1918.[1] Here was a carefully presented accumulation of facts of employment on New York street-railway lines which drew from the author the comment that "Whatever the de-

[1] "Woman Street Railway Employees," by Benjamin M. Squires, *Monthly Labor Review*, May, 1918, pp. 1-22.

mand may be for women in the street railway industry, it can not be sufficient to justify their employment under the conditions set forth" (p. 17), and again, "Even under the most favorable conditions, it is doubtful whether the nature of the industry makes it possible properly to safeguard women employees in this respect [referring to adequate toilet facilities]."

Mr. Squires explained the nature of employment on street cars, that it necessitates a list of "extras" which are obviously less favored employees than "regulars" and that on account of their recent appearance in the service many women were obliged not only to be extras but the least favored extras. This was according to the seniority rule which gives the more desirable hours to those who have been longest in the service. "Women take their turn with male employees both as extras and as regulars," and "as regulars some women must have afternoon and night runs, some must have 'night hawks' or 'owls' running into the morning hours, and some will draw day runs, either 'straights' or swings.'"

Types of time schedules of women selected at random were included in the report. The time worked per week for the New York Railways Company was shown to be all the way from 46 hours and 37 minutes to 74 hours and 21 minutes, the time within which the work was completed being from 66 hours to 89 hours and 13 minutes. The average of time worked for the Brooklyn Rapid Transit Company was somewhat higher, from 70 to 80 hours a week, but this was more nearly identical with the time within which the work was completed which ranged from about 70½ to about 80½ hours. Of the total number of 2,196 daily runs made in one week on all lines studied, 73.9 per cent were completed within thirteen hours, the median falling within the group completed in a little over twelve hours' time. In 72 out of 3,744 times, the waiting period between runs or parts of runs fell between the hours of 10 p. m. and 5 a. m. —dreary periods to be spent in deserted car barns.

Moreover, the beginning and end of work frequently occurred during the night hours according to Squires. For example, on the cars of the New York Railways Company, out of 2,127 days worked by woman conductors, 46.6 per cent began between midnight and 8 a. m. and 41.7 per cent ended between the hours of 10 p. m. and 4 a. m. On the Brooklyn Rapid Transit Company cars, of 1,526 days worked by woman conductors and guards, 72.2 per cent began between midnight and 8 a. m. and 18.5 per cent ended between the hours of 10 p. m. and 4 a. m.

This degree of night work was owing in part to the seniority rule which gave the preferable runs to older employees who were more often men. And as has been said, the seniority rule also necessitated some women taking irregular work, that is, work that varied in length of time from less than one hour to more than fourteen hours.

Added to these disadvantages for women were the unsatisfactory comfort facilities. While in most cases perhaps, Squires found the rooms to be clean and adequate in size and, in New York City, to have a matron or janitress in charge, there were instances of shocking absence of proper facilities. It was respecting these conditions in general that the investigators despaired of there ever being a satisfactory adjustment for women.

In concluding his report, Mr. Squires declared, " From the facts brought out in this report it must be evident to any thinking person that it is practically impossible to make the conditions of street railway employment even tolerably endurable to women workers and that the operation of street cars is one of the last occupations into which women should be lured or forced. . . . If the exigencies of the war make it necessary to put women into the less desirable employments such as street railway operation, the public should first oblige such industry to prepare itself for the employment of women by providing the irreducible minimum of decency and comfort before it is permitted to employ them" (p. 22).

This conclusion seems not greatly different from that of Miss Hobbs, suggesting as it did that clerical and factory positions "now filled by men" could as well or better be filled by women instead of their entering transportation service; and furthermore that if those employed on railways were employed at lower wages than men conditions would "result in a lowering of standards of wages and working conditions for both male and female labor." [1]

The bill before the legislature did not call for the prohibition of employment of women on street cars except at night however, nine hours to be the maximum length of the working day. Thus abundantly supported by Mr. Squires and Miss Hobbs on the one hand, and with the opposing employers defeated on the other hand, the bill was enacted into law in this second year of women's employment 1919.

The subsequent release from these restrictions (1920), except for conductors and guards, was granted in direct response to the demands of the women themselves. The effects of the statute were prejudicial instead of protective, they averred, and their counteracting bill drafted by the Women's League for Equal Opportunity with Amy Wren of Brooklyn as counsel, was not forcibly opposed. The expressed view of the advocates of regulation in regard to this modification was that relatively few women were concerned anyway, that the employment of women had been a war measure and would not be continued, so that a relax-

[1] The more recent investigation of women in the transportation service made by the Women's Bureau of the United States Department of Labor advances a view opposite to that of Mr. Squires regarding the desirability of employing women on street cars. This study will be discussed in the chapter on effects of legislation.

ation of the regulations would not in any case make a great difference.

3. *Messenger Service*

The bill regulating the day and night hours of women messengers and prohibiting the service of females under the age of twenty-one, it will be recalled, was the only one of the welfare bills for women which was enacted by the legislature of 1918. The Consumers' League had coöperated with the New York State Committee on Women in Industry in a study of the new occupations opened to women, and found "Little girls as young as 15 and 16 had been employed as messengers. The telegraph companies admitted that there was no way to supervise the kind of a house to which a girl was sent. Because of the serious moral hazard of the industry, the states of Washington, Oregon, and Massachusetts prohibited entirely the employment of women as messengers." It was felt, therefore, that "the moral advantage to the community of the passage of this bill" could "hardly be overestimated." [1]

HOURS OF LABOR—NIGHT WORK

1. *General*

Massachusetts began prohibiting women from night work in 1890. At first the forbidden time was between the hours of 10 p. m. and 6 a. m. in manufacturing and mercantile establishments, but in 1907 the bars were placed higher and women were not to be seen working in textile mills between 6 p. m. and 6 a. m. Even today this is the most drastic regulation in America. And, indeed, Massachusetts seems to have been a pioneer world state in initiating this particular kind of regulation. The International Labor Congresses

[1] *Report of the Consumers' League of the City of New York* for 1918, pp. 3-4.

held in London and Paris in the late eighties expressed pious opinions that there should be no night work whatever except where it was industrially imperative, but only at times was special emphasis laid upon prohibiting women and minors as a class. At the instigation of the International Association for Labor Legislation in Paris in 1900, night work was again stamped as an evil which with wide qualifications should be abolished. However, at the delegates' meetings in 1903 and 1904 the subject narrowed down more traditionally to women and children as subjects of night work prohibition. And in 1905, according to Mr. Iwao Ayusawa, at "the first of the most important international labor conferences in history" held at Berne, Switzerland, eleven countries signed the convention that demanded eleven hours (in some cases ten) of cessation from work at night for women in industrial undertakings. The convention required that the forbidden hours include those between 10 p. m. and 5 a. m. and that "industrial undertakings" be distinguished from commercial and agricultural enterprise. The prohibition did not apply to establishments in which "either less than ten persons or only members of the family were employed." [1]

Fifteen European states were represented at this conference and the subject of prohibiting women's night work had received intensive consideration by a special committee. Wide variations in the current laws for different countries were discovered, but the one significant feature in common was that no country had up to that time prohibited *adult* women from working at night. Belgium and Portugal had made twenty-one years the minimum age of those permitted so to work,[2] "but on the whole lower ages prevailed, . . . The task for the conference was to determine a standard of

[1] Iwao F. Ayusawa, *International Labor Legislation*, pp. 67-69.

[2] *Ibid.*, p. 68.

regulation as high as possible but at the same time sufficiently broad so as to be capable of general adoption."[1]

In 1906 at the call of the Swiss Federal Council a second conference was held at Berne in order to give final authority to the conventions of the previous year. Fourteen countries signed the agreement prohibiting women's work at night. It should be remembered, however, that these international conferences were private undertakings, and thus were of propagandist rather than official character. And moreover they were strictly European, representatives from the United States being conspicuously absent.

Despite this fact America has by no means escaped the influence of European zeal for this form of legislation. At the first International Congress of Working Women held in Washington, D. C. in 1919, the resolution was adopted that "This congress adhere to the Berne Convention of 1906 prohibiting night work for all women in industrial employment."[2] And, more important, national sections of the International Association for Labor Legislation, composed of public officials, economists, physicians, social workers, employers, and employees, began to be established at once after the European conferences, the American Association for Labor Legislation being organized in the same year of the second conference, 1906. Since its inception there has been no greater force in this country toward labor legislation than this association. And while, as has been seen, it endorses and actively helps to secure special protection for women, one of its principles is not to duplicate effort. Therefore since other organizations give their major effort to women, this association gives its greatest weight to general legislation such as workmen's compensation and health insurance.

[1] *Ibid.*, p. 68.

[2] *Monthly Labor Review*, December, 1919, p. 288.

The State of Massachusetts, then, stood first and stands yet, in advance of all other jurisdictions in the country in the prohibitions it has placed upon its women to keep them from the night occupations. Massachusetts has long been taken as a model state in this respect by groups who have tried to introduce these prohibitions in other states. Her statute was threatened in 1924 by advocates of a bill legalizing the work of women and children in textile mills until 11 p. m. instead of 6 p. m., but the bill was defeated and this long standing provision remains secure at least until the next legislative session.

In New York State, aside from these general influences which have set a precedent, practically the same immediate influences have borne upon night-time prohibitions as upon daytime regulations of hours. And in more cases than not, especially among the earlier bills introduced into the legislature, there have been night work clauses contained in provisions to regulate daily and weekly hours. Nine years following the first Massachusetts law, Governor Roosevelt, in his opening message to the New York legislature in 1899, included the recommendation that both day and night work of women and minors be regulated. This was the year that marked the beginning of protective legislation for adult women in New York, it will be remembered, and the exact provisions suggested by Governor Roosevelt were that year enacted into law.

The early proposals of the National Consumers' League, organized also in 1899, provided for a *generally* prohibitory night work law, but pressure from both home and abroad pointed the easier way of limiting the prohibitions to women and minors, and the Consumers' League became converted to this modification.

There was quiet question in the minds of New York labor officials from the start as to the right of the legislature to prohibit *adult* women from working at night. In 1905 with this question in mind, Commissioner of Labor Sherman objected publicly to the unsuitable statutory grouping of females—that there was no intervening group between children and adults. "The absence of this connecting link might become a serious defect and weakness under a certain contingency," he said.[1] The commissioner gave the warning that "Should the law be tested and a decision rendered adverse to the State, night work for females over sixteen years of age would be unrestricted and we would be in the anomolous position of affording better protection to males between sixteen and eighteen years of age than to females of the same age." He recommended that the section be redrawn and amended to contain separate provisions, one applying to all minors and one to females of any age. He added, however, that

Except for the administrative reason that it makes it easier to enforce the prohibition against overtime, there is no present necessity in this state for the prohibition of night work by adult women. On the other hand, if enforced, it would deprive some mature working women, employed at night only, at skilled trades, for short hours and for high wages, of all means of support. And the prohibition, in its application to factories only, seems rather one-sided when we consider that probably the hardest occupations of women, those of hotel laundresses and cleaners (charwomen) are not limited as to hours in any way.[2]

The commissioner's presentiment was accurate. It was only the next year that the court of special sessions pronounced the night work prohibition invalid in its application to adult women—the identical year of the Berne Conference in which fourteen countries had approved of this prohibition. In the following year (1907) the ruling was upheld in the

[1] *Annual Report of the Commission of Labor*, 1905, p. II. 25.

[2] *Ibid.*, 1906, p. I. 60.

state's highest court, in the case of People *v.* Williams already discussed. This decision was deplored from as many directions as influences had come for its passage, and from many more. The American Federation of Labor voiced its protest through its president Samuel Gompers in an editorial entitled "The Comfortable Bench and the Women Night Workers." [1] Gompers censored the judges with asperity for ruling in a case that they "don't know anything about," thus invalidating acts "based on inquiry and knowledge." He concluded that "the New York 'night work' case is, as we have said, typical and characteristic. It will devolve upon organized labor and other thoughtful and human elements of the country to agitate for a change in policy of the corporation-trained judges toward legislation enacted for the protection of the young and the innocent—for the women and children—for labor and for the rights of the people."

The press joined in the loud protestations. Putting its finger upon the very catastrophe against which Commissioner Sherman had warned, the New York *Tribune* [2] explained that the great body of women in factories are young, a large proportion under age, and that the state should properly care for the health and morals of these young women. It urged that though some women, as those in their homes whom the law does not cover, injure themselves, the state should not be prevented from dealing with "a real and menacing industrial evil." And the fact that women want to work at night in factories should be no deterrent to legislation, "for the State should protect them against their own ignorance and their own necessities, which make the exploiters of labor able to command night work."

Commissioner Sherman in discussing the annulment of the act, said,

[1] *The Federationist*, 1907, pp. 174-176.

[2] *August* 5, 1906.

. . . if the regular employment of large night gangs of women in mills does become an established practice, and it be demonstrated that the health of the women thus employed is thereby generally injured, it would seem to the writer that the prohibition although now not necessary for the public health would then become so, and that the courts would then not logically be bound by the decision in the Williams case, based as it is upon different conditions and a different assumption of facts.[1]

The New York City Consumers' League, through its committee on legislation with Frances A. Hand as chairman, declared that the annulment of the night work prohibition had struck a blow at the health and morals of women wage-earners throughout the country. The league saw two particular reasons why the decision of the courts in this case was gravely to be deprecated. First, because with no "fixed limit" of time in which women should work, the sixty-hour law limiting day work would be very difficult to enforce, and second, because of women's morals. The annual report of the league argued in these words,

Moreover, it is a far greater menace to society for women to be turned into the streets at a late hour of the night or at early dawn than for men. Transit facilities are at their worst and any lingering on the streets during those hours is apt to involve a woman in arrest. When men and women work together at night, the ordinary restraints of conduct during the rest hour at midnight are not liable to be observed as they are during the rest hour at noonday.[2]

It was the Factory Investigating Commission that revived the prohibition against the work of women at night. The report on this subject which led to the drafting of the bill that became law in 1913 was prepared by Dr. George M.

[1] New York Department of Labor *Bulletin*, September, 1907, p. 342.

[2] *Annual Report of the Consumers' League of the City of New York* for 1906, p. 19.

Price, director of the investigation. In his opening sentence Dr. Price submitted the well known attitude toward the woman worker,

> Next to child labor, night work of women is the greatest evil of modern industrial life. The participation of women in industry, although so general, has never been regarded as an entirely normal condition of society . . . [1]

He then summed the results of his investigation as follows:

> The objections to night work of women are many. Among the principal ones are the following: lack of sunlight; lack of normal sleep; no compensation in the restless interrupted sleep of day for the sleeplessness of night; the abnormality of sleeping by day; abnormal change in daily life; the destruction of home life; impossibility of properly caring for home and children; lack of restraining influences; day work besides the arduous night tasks.

Dr. Price continued, in an argument against night work in general, that

> It has even been claimed that night work is economically unnecessary, and does not compensate for the evils which result from it. Night work of men is prohibited in a number of Continental countries. As the law relates to bakers, night work is prohibited in Italy and Sweden, in certain cantons of Switzerland, and in several other countries.

Dr. Price's report for the commission embodied both fact and theory regarding women who worked at night. For example, the histories of one hundred night workers in a cordage mill were taken; of these seventy-seven were married and five were widowed, seventy-five had children; and among them there were ninety-seven babies. These

[1] *Second Report of the Factory Investigating Commission*, 1913, vol. ii, p. 439 *et seq.*

women had on an average about four and one-half hours of sleep in the daytime after their night of work in the mill; for they also were obliged to carry on the duties of housewives and mothers. They prepared three meals for the family each day, including breakfast, they did the family washing, and many of them nursed their infants.[1] Four principal explanations were given by these women as to the reasons for their night work, namely,—(1) so they could care for the children in the daytime, (2) because the "boss" had said that they should work at night or "go home," that they couldn't get the men to work for the same wages; (3) because their husbands were sick or over-worked; (4) to increase the family income.

The bill restraining women from night work, as drafted by the Factory Investigating Commission and enacted by the legislature, was expressly a health-and-morals measure, and as such, was declared by the courts to be a sound and legitimate use of the state's police power.[2] In addition to the recommendations of the commission, and wide newspaper publicity of an article written by the American Association for Labor Legislation in defence of the law, an elaborate brief was organized for the instruction of the judges. The work was prepared by Louis D. Brandeis and Josephine Goldmark, a summary of which, 452 pages in length, was published by the National Consumers' League under the title of *The Case Against Nightwork for Women.* The international conference at Berne in 1906 was cited as having set the precedent, as it had also been by Dr. Price and the association for legislation. This book has come to be

[1] A study of women night workers employed in thirty-nine textile mills in Rhode Island made by Florence Kelley in 1918, shows conditions corresponding to those given above. See *Wage Earning Women in War Time. The Textile Industry.* Reprinted from the *Journal of Industrial Hygiene* for October, 1919, by the National Consumers' League.

[2] People *v.* Schweinler Press. See discussion, p. 74, *supra*.

considered a standard work on the subject, but, though it is packed with valuable arguments against the economy of night work, opponents of special legislation for women charge that it does not give the conclusive evidence its authors supposed it to give—that night work is peculiarly harmful to women. The brief, together with the recommendation of the factory commission, was sufficient to convert the judges, however, and a reversal of the former decision was effected.[1] With some modifications, which are discussed elsewhere, and with other modifications threatened, the night work prohibition has remained on the statute books as enacted.[2]

2. *Newspaper Offices*

In addition to the transportation workers, women printers were another group who protested against being forbidden to work at night and who also received release therefrom, in 1921. These women began their agitation in earnest in 1917 by sending a committee to the legislative session to present their argument. An amendment was introduced by Senator Ottinger which passed both houses of the legislature but which received a veto by Governor Whitman because of its being too inclusive.

The next year the amendment was made less general, pertaining specifically to women in newspaper offices. On February 27, 1918, a brief was drawn up by the women printers in support of this bill and endorsed by Typographical Union No. 6, New York, to which the majority of the women belonged. Here it was explained that the chances for day

[1] See page 75, *supra* for recent decision of the United States Supreme Court which made this decree final.

[2] Prohibition against the employment of women at night in the transportation and messenger service were discussed with the regulations of daily hours, *supra*. In 1916, a bill allowing women employed in selling soft drinks and light lunches to be employed until midnight was defeated.

work compared with those for night work are about one in ten, owing to the preponderance of morning newspapers. Also that night work is frequently more desirable to newspaper women. In the words of the brief:

6. We get more sleep than do day workers. Leaving the office at three o'clock in the morning, we can sleep from four o'clock until noon—eight hours' rest—and have all the afternoon to spend in the fresh air and sunshine. We travel to and from work *against* the crowded transportation systems; we have the daylight in which to shop, go to the beaches, etc., whereas a day worker has but one day—Sunday—for outdoor recreation and must go about at night for amusement. In summer night workers have an additional advantage, as after an afternoon spent in park or at beach they work a short shift in a temperature many degrees cooler than that of the day. Evidence that this mode of living is beneficial is furnished by the number of hale and hearty men on morning newspapers, some of them having been employed for thirty years in this work.

7. Since the shifts are shorter and the wage higher for night work no employer would "exploit" women should the restriction against night work be removed, and only those women who desire to work at night would seek such work. At the same time, women holding day situations would be able to work overtime occasionally; thus women printers would regain and retain their "place in the sun"—the trade for which they have qualified by years of hard work, study and experience . . . .

9. Compare the very desirable working conditions and hours of the woman printer, now being driven from the trade by the strict enforcement of the 54-hour law and the "night work" law, with those of the woman canner, who is permitted by specific exemptions to these very laws to work sixty-six hours a week at some seasons of the year! Neither man nor woman is ever asked to work such hours in a printing office.

10. Objection to amending the law as it now stands to exclude woman printers from its provisions comes from two classes only: Women who do not understand our work or our

capabilities and do not care whether we are driven from a skilled to an unskilled occupation; and male printers (a very small number of them, it is true), who claim that amending the law for us will break down labor safeguards. We maintain that it is uneconomic to deprive skilled craftsmen of the benefits of their years of training by leaving unamended a law not meant for them; and also that *a law is strengthened by wise exemptions.*

As fellow citizens with full responsibilities, no longer wards of the state, we ask your full co-operation in the securing of such amendments to the " night work " and 54-hour laws as will permit women printers of this state to work at their trade.

Signed—Authorized Signatures:

Committee of Women Printers:

ELLA M. SHERWIN,
LYDE HARLOW MARTIN,
MARGARET KERR-FIRTH.

LEON H. ROUSE,
President, Typographical Union No. 6.

JOHN S. O'CONNELL,
Secretary-Treasurer.

SIGMUND OPPENHEIMER,
Chairman Executive Committee.

This plea of the newspaper women had to be repeated three more years, however, before it secured for its advocates what they considered to be the privilege of working at night. During the interim, some facts regarding the effects of the prohibitory law were gathered by the New York Bureau of Women in Industry which appeared to furnish material for both sides of the question. These will be discussed later.

INDUSTRIAL HOMEWORK

In homework is seen more clearly than in any other occupation the burden that modern industrial life has placed upon woman. Tied as she is by the complexities of family life, she makes a pitiful and even menacing attempt to adjust herself to the demands of the factory.

This type of employment is now almost entirely the work of women and children. Time was when this was not the case. The war of the cigar makers' union in the eighties to prohibit tenement house manufacture and its end in the courts will be remembered. In those days whole families eked out their living in their work-shop homes. These were for the most part newly arrived immigrants who crowded into New York City tenements which soon became known as "sweat-shops" because of the filthy conditions and the suffering from overwork and underpay. The need for relief was dire. As for cigar manufacture, a gradual adjustment was developed through the increasing and embittered energies of the unions, which took that particular industry out of the homes for the most part. And the men followed it to the factory. This would have left thousands of women who took care of their children and did the housework stripped of gainful employment, had not the clothing and other manufacturers reached out an employing hand. Many of these women were widows, and many of them were required to care for sick and overworked husbands as well as their children, with the economic pressure persistent in any case. This condition furnished, and has continued to furnish, a limitless supply of cheap labor to manufacturers, and they have never ceased to improve their advantages.[1]

Following the rebuff from the judiciary in the legislative attempt to prohibit cigar making in tenement houses, homework was subject to no supervision whatsoever until 1892.[2] In the clothing industry there was little use for factory buildings except for cutting. The ceaseless toil of women and children in their homes, sewing on articles that were

[1] *Cf.* Fairchild, *The Factory Legislation of the State of New York*, *op. cit.*, pp. 11-23.

[2] It has been explained before that homework is a more inclusive phrase than tenement house work, for tenement houses, legally defined, do not include one and two family houses.

sublet to them by sweatshop contractors, was the process by which thousands of garments were made.

About 1890, strongly directed attempts began to be made to regulate the work of tenements through a licensing system. At that time the New York *Tribune*[1] wrote of Helen Campbell's work as an able reformer and lecturer on the Chautauqua circuit, in making the public aware of the menace of the tenement house evil. Mrs. Campbell met the charge of "paternalism" by rejoining that such had been the objection to "all the excellent labor legislation" that had been passed in New York State, but that it was no more paternalistic than to regulate powder-house construction against explosions, or to quarantine against plagues.

Discussion of this kind induced the licensing system of 1892 which was made more inclusive in 1899 upon the recommendation of Governor Roosevelt. The further requirement in 1904 that licenses must be procured by owners of tenement buildings instead of by the separate tenants, had been urged by Commissioner of Labor John McMackin to reduce the municipal proportions of this branch of work for the Department of Labor. And Governor Roosevelt urged it. He had more than once gone through the tenement districts and had learned something of the conditions there. His theory was that owners of congested, unsanitary, and ill-kept tenement houses should be placed at a disadvantage as compared with those where "law and decency prevailed;" that requiring owners to ask for a license would accomplish this point.

In 1906, Commissioner Sherman held[2] that all homework in tenements was not to be condemned, for some of the work was skilled and done under good conditions. He expressed a growing conviction, furthermore, that conditions of the

[1] New York *Tribune*, August 25, 1890.

[2] *Annual Report of the Commissioner of Labor*, 1906, p. 43.

poorer workers would not be improved by absolute prohibition of homework in tenements. Nevertheless, only in the following year he reported[1] that a "group of sociology students are strongly advocating absolute prohibition of homework," all except domestic dress-making. Their principal reasons were those of congestion, lack of sanitation, lack of regulation of child labor, and low wages and long hours that made effective regulation of women's work in factories impossible.

This conflict of opinions among some of those best qualified to judge as to advisable methods of relief, more or less typifies this knottiest problem of protective labor legislation. Since entire prohibition was declared unconstitutional, there has never developed a way to legislate directly for this class of toilers. Abolition has continued to be advocated not always for the relief of the women themselves, for Commissioner Sherman's theory is supported by some others—that the women would be the greater sufferers by being thus deprived of employment—but abolition has frequently been advocated as the only device by which laws restricting women's work in factories could be enforced. As will be considered more fully in pages to come, the possibility of getting their work done for a pittance outside of the factories makes it impossible to force employers to observe limitations of hours of women employed at similar work in factories. And again, this unregulated work at low pay stands as a formidable deterrent to an effective attempt to provide minimum wages.

However, it is not on these grounds that homework has been free from attack by the legislature. Largely for reasons of public health, to protect the consumers from unsanitary goods that may carry disease, and to prohibit the work of young children,—this is the cautious ground, safe from the

[1] *Ibid.*, p. 57.

courts, upon which legislation has been built thus far. The findings of the Factory Investigating Commission in 1913 prompted that body to introduce an amendment to the tenement house law that contained prohibitory measures which the legislature adopted. The protection of the public health is a legitimate exercise of the police power, and abolition of the manufacture of foodstuffs and of articles of children's and infants' wearing apparel was advocated on these grounds. This was the first step to recover the ground lost in the Jacobs case.

Florence Kelley, as a witness before the commission, advocated the sweeping abolition of tenement house work,[1] and supported her view by prophesying that such a step would send the children to school, the sick to hospitals and the able-bodied to work in lofts under better conditions. She thought the change would not affect the status of widows and children under charity, they would remain under charity as before. Mothers could better care for their children and no longer would there be an invasion of the kitchen and bedroom by the factory.

Dr. Annie S. Daniels declared she had approved of abolition of homework since 1888. She saw no reason why it would be any great hardship for women and children. "I am sure it would not," she continued, "because these women are strong, able and capable of working in factories, and their children would be taken care of in kindergartens, and day nurseries. They always have room for children whenever they ask to go in. And the women would work in factories and get better pay. I am pretty sure it would result in making the husbands work in some cases."[2] Rose Schneiderman, speaking for the Women's Trade Union

[1] *Preliminary Report of the Factory Investigating Commission*, 1912, vol. iii, pp. 1592-3.

[2] *Op. cit.*, 1913, vol. i, p. 113.

League, said, "If we can prohibit homework entirely, it would force employers to engage the amount of people that they need in their factories and not avoid the responsibilities of having employees . . . . and it would also perhaps give the employees a chance to get a living wage for the work that they do." [1]

Lillian D. Wald of the Henry Street Settlement, Pauline Goldmark, and Maud E. Miner were also prominent witnesses who advocated complete abolition of this kind of work.

Two manufacturers of neckwear maintained that abolition would harm two classes of workers, namely, married women who have children to care for and husbands to cook for, and those living at a distance (as Hoboken) who would lose two hours in transit if they had to commute to the factory each day.

It was pretty conclusively stated by the factory commission that tenement workers were in the main driven to their employment by economic pressure—because of the low earnings, sickness or unemployment of the father. This was particularly true of the Irish and Americans who did homework only as a last resort. 78 per cent of the homeworkers were discovered to be Italians, who usually came from rural districts and knew little of factory work and organized industry. The men were unskilled workers who often fell into seasonal trades "where wages are small and irregular and must be supplemented." The condition was intensified because Italians cling to their family customs; they expect their daughters to marry young and object to their going out into factory life. The commission discovered that homeworkers are much younger women than many had thought, and that "almost 63 per cent of the fathers of the families doing homework are between the

[1] *Op. cit.*, p. 115.

ages of twenty and forty-five, an age that represents the best years of a man's life and a time when his economic value to the community should be greatest."

Thus the efforts of social workers have been continued towards further prohibition of work in tenements, toward the inclusion of more prohibited articles within the ambit of the law. At the present time many more articles are permitted to be made than prohibited, but many hope that a more enlightened judiciary will allow at least the reversal of this condition. Some yet more optimistic groups hope to effect complete abolition. For instance, the Women's City Club and the City Club of New York are reported to have united in 1920 to further a bill to prohibit in tenement living rooms all work let out by factories." [1]

In view of a recent investigation of homework by the New York Child Welfare Commission, in which overwork of children was discovered to be widespread, State Industrial Commissioner Shientag advocated further extension of the law by the 1924 legislature. This would be a more practicable next step than an attempt for total elimination of manufacturing in tenements, he thought, because the system has become so deeply intrenched. A bill was introduced late in the legislative session, therefore, adding toilet articles, artificial flowers, feathers, hat ornaments, and portions of pajamas to the list of articles that may not be manufactured in tenements. But the act was not passed.

Finally, recommendations are unceasingly made that all homework on goods for sale should be regulated with no

[1] Commons and Andrews, *Principles of Labor Legislation*, p. 368, footnote. On the other hand, a bill was introduced by Senator Meyer in 1922 advocating that a tenement family be permitted to employ a tailor, seamstress, or milliner, and that a person may be employed in a tenement house who is physically handicapped "to the extent of disqualifying him from employment in the normal channels of endeavor, and whose product is sold through a benevolent or charitable society, association, or corporation approved by the state board of charities."

reference to the size of the house in which the work is done. (The present law includes only tenement houses which are defined as houses containing three or more families.) For, in the words of the factory commission, it is clear that the "evils in connection with homework are not created by the type of house or building in which the work is done, but very much depends on the habits or conditions of the people doing the work." The first deputy commissioner, in 1919, declared that there is no valid reason why the law should not be extended except the old one of cost of inspection, but he urged that even this is not a valid reason when the public health is involved. Also the deputy suggested the fear that the underlying reason why the extension of the statute has not been made to include all homework is the objection on the part of large mill owners who are making much use of dwelling-house homeworkers in many places and in many lines of industry outside of New York City.[1]

PROHIBITED EMPLOYMENT

Selling liquor and working in mines were occupations early prohibited to women in New York, and in other states, to protect their morals and their health respectively. There seems to have been little need of urging legislation in favor of these acts. Their desirability was obvious under our present *mores*.

With the exception of employment in basements and polishing and grinding wheels, the other laws that prohibit the employment of New York women have been enacted since the investigations of the Factory Investigating Commission. The commission gave special attention to the suitability of work for women and submitted bills prohibiting core making except under certain circumstances, employment after childbirth and, for young women, employments requiring constant standing and the cleaning of moving machinery. All these measures were passed as submitted.

[1] *Annual Report of the Industrial Commission* for 1919, p. 58.

One of the methods of discovering opinions in regard to such legislation was by questionnaire as already stated, forty-five replies to which were received. Eleven of the forty-five responded to the inquiry regarding the general subject of "Employment of Women and Children," [1] We may pause a few moments over these replies. It is interesting that five of the eleven had nothing to say in regard to the employment of women; three would prohibit women from employment in certain occupations (mines and all employments after 6 p. m. were specified by one), three were opposed to women being employed in any occupation in which there is a severe strain on their constitutions. One of these was a physician who was sweeping in his recommendation for prohibitions for women,—"The employment of women should be prohibited in these industries requiring speeding-up, heavy manual labor, and in such further industries as physical examination shall show to be undesirable for the employment of women." (p. 646) Prohibitions according to this view would, of course, disqualify women from a great many occupations in which large numbers are employed to-day.

Three who replied suggested the need of restricting the employment of pregnant women, and two advocated night work prohibitions (others who were not reported to have expressed themselves on these points, however, are known to be advocates of them). Ex-Labor Commissioner Sherman thought women should be refused employment immediately before and after childbirth, but further than this he recommended that the responsibility of prohibiting their employment be lodged with the board of medical advisers.

The opinions regarding children were interesting and

[1] These were composed of two physicians, three labor representatives, two representatives of philanthropic organizations, an ex-commissioner of labor, and three others. *Preliminary Report of the Factory Investigating Commission*, 1912, vol. i, pp. 646-649.

more freely expressed. Seven out of eleven replies recommended special legislation for boys and girls under sixteen years of age regardless of sex; three would prohibit the employment of this group; three would require physical examinations for all boys and girls under eighteen years; one would increase the number of legislative prohibitions then listed for boys and girls under sixteen years, three would prohibit girls from employment, making no recommendations regarding boys. Two of the three who thus discriminated between boys and girls were labor union representatives. The third was the president of the Consumers' League of New York, who advocated the prohibition of all physically unfit children, while she added that all girls should be prohibited from employment in stores and factories regardless of their physical fitness. Dr. Rochester of Buffalo wrote, as quoted in the digest, " it would be better that no one, male or female should be employed in factories of any sort under the age of eighteen years; that the employment of all under sixteen years should be absolutely prohibited " (p. 649).[1]

1. *Employment after Childbirth*

Although the law that prohibits women in New York from gainful employment for four weeks after childbirth was the

[1] It is pertinent at this point to state the views of Dr. Teleky of the University of Vienna as given by the Commissioner of Labor of New York in his annual report for 1912, p. 74. Dr. Teleky explained that the development of the organism in young people is rapid until the seventeenth and nineteenth year of life; that it is not possible to indicate any sharp boundary line from which any labor should be permitted, but that tuberculosis mortality and accident statistics show that the child of fourteen to fifteen years is not equal to the demands of industrial labor, so that the prohibition of gainful occupation before the sixteenth year is completed seems desirable from the hygienic point of view. The youth of sixteen to eighteen years also needs special protection in respect to the hours of labor. Night work and labor in industries dangerous to the health should be forbidden. Young females in particular need extended protection.

direct proposal of the Factory Investigating Commission, there had been considerable agitation in this direction for some time before. This type of legislation had been of long standing in European and other foreign countries, and Massachusetts alone set the precedent for the states of the Union.

These laws have been enacted on the assumption, which many believed had been substantiated by facts, that there is causal connection between infant mortality and the employment of mothers as evidenced by the fact that infant mortality is highest in towns where women are employed in large numbers. But opinions as to the degree of causation have varied. Sixty years ago Sir John Simon wrote that "in proportion as adult women were taking part in factory labor or in agriculture the mortality of their infants rapidly increased." In 1907, Dr. George Newman concluded his study of this subject in England stressing poverty and ignorance of hygiene as important conditions of infant mortality, as well as the employment of the mothers. He wrote that in addition to "the direct injury to the physique and character of the individual caused by much of the factory employment of women" and "the indirect and reflex injury to the home and social life of the worker, . . . infant mortality . . . is . . . as much a financial as a hygienic question," quoting an experienced medical officer of health. He continued, "Why do married women work in the mills? is the question this medical officer has reached. His answer is that 'a weaver's wages will not allow of the wife's remaining at home, considering the high rents and rates, and so both go—which is the rule—and a hand-to-mouth existence results even for themselves, let alone the little ones, who are left in the intervals to the mercies of the nurse, who, as a rule, takes in the babies to eke out her husband's wages. Much good may be done by hygienic tuition, but I am certain that the root of the whole matter with us is, as I have said, comparatively low wages and high rents and rates.' "[1]

Further, the thirteenth volume of the federal study of the conditions of woman and child wage earners was devoted to this subject with conclusions that appear, in general, to emphasize even more strongly unhealthy influences upon infants other than those of gainful employment of mothers. The results of analysis of available statistics for Massachusetts, as well as of the original study of infant mortality in Fall River, showed that the proportion of women engaged in extra-domestic occupation is "associated very uncertainly, to say the least, with the infant death rate." For Massachusetts as a whole, the analysis "clearly disproves the contention that the extra-domestic employment of women is the dominant factor in determining the infant death rate so far as Massachusetts cities are concerned." In Fall River, the cause of the excessive infant mortality "may be summed up in a sentence as the mother's ignorance of proper feeding, of proper care, and of the simplest requirements of hygiene. To this all other causes must be regarded as secondary." [2]

Studies in seven different cities of the causes of infant mortality which have been made in recent years by the Children's Bureau of the United States Department of Labor, are more or less in agreement with these conclusions, but the emphasis is again shifted. The effects of employment of the mother away from home have been considered positive and serious in all of these reports. A recently published study was that made in Baltimore based on births in one year, 1915. Here the conclusions again are that poverty and artificial feeding are two major causes of infant

[1] Both of the above mentioned studies are discussed by Dr. G. M. Kober in his *Industrial and Personal Hygiene* published in 1908.

[2] *Summary of the Report on Condition of Woman and Child Wage Earners in the United States; Bulletin no. 175* (whole number), United States Department of Labor, pp. 337-359.

mortality; but from this study, perhaps more than from any preceding it, the bureau states that it is satisfied that the mother's employment away from home is a causal factor in infant mortality. Concerning the employment of mothers before childbirth, the report states,

> The variations in still birth rates and the mortality from early infancy in relation to the interval of rest before confinement indicate the importance of the mother's ceasing her employment outside the home at least two weeks before her confinement.

Of the effect upon the infant of the mother's gainful work after parturition, the bureau continues,

> Employment away from home during the baby's first year increased the hazard to the baby. This increase in the hazard was especially marked when the mother took up her work before the baby was 6 months old. The mothers employed away from home resorted largely to artificial feeding for their babies, but the greater prevalence of artificial feeding accounts only in part for the special hazard. The actual number of deaths was greater than the number that would have occurred among them if these babies had faced the average hazards to all babies of their nationalities and their economic status who had the same high percentage of artificial feeding.[1]

This verdict had not been made when the Factory Investigating Commission presented its bill to the legislature in 1912. However the New York medical inspector of factories in 1910, had urged the prohibition of women's work after childbirth for two reasons; first, because the health of children depends upon the health of the mother and the care she can give them, and second, because the stability of the state depends upon the healthfulness of its citizens. The

[1] Publication of the Children's Bureau, U. S. Department of Labor, *Bulletin no. 119*, p. 130.

causes given for the evil effects of the mother's employment were,—(1) overwork of the expectant mother or exposure to industrial poisons which affects the vitality of the child; (2) the substitution of artificial feeding for breast feeding; and (3) the necessary neglect of the child by the mother who is employed away from home.[1]

Furthermore the Brooklyn Pediatric Society, after a discussion of "The Causes and Prevention of Premature Birth," sent its official endorsement of the plans of the factory commission. A resolution was sent in response to a letter from the commission's counsel, Mr. Elkus, as follows:

> Whereas, the statistics collected by many investigators, both in this country and abroad, conclusively prove that factory labor is responsible for a large percentage of prematurity and infant mortality; Be it resolved, That the Brooklyn Pediatric Society heartily endorses the efforts of the Factory Investigating Commission to regulate, by law, the employment of women immediately before and after childbirth.[2]

However, despite precedent and recommendations for prohibitions both before and after parturition, the factory commission's final bill, as drafted and passed, required prohibition of work following childbirth only. Perhaps this compromise stand was taken pragmatically, but it will be seen in a later chapter that even this minimum provision has been impossible to enforce.

[1] *Annual Report of the Commissioner of Labor*, 1910, pp. 78-79.

[2] *Preliminary Report of the Factory Investigating Commission*, 1912, vol. i, p. 807.

2. *Core Making* [1]

The prohibition of core making as an occupation for women where the cores are baked in the making room had an interesting inception. Pronounced opinions were expressed by the witnesses of the Factory Investigating Commission which brought weight in drafting the bill for the legislature. One witness, a manufacturer of harvesting machinery, testified that his theory was that foundries should be so constructed that men as well as women were protected from unhealthy fumes and gases by a proper ventilating system, and that without proper ventilation to carry off fumes neither men nor women should be employed in the core room.[2] On the other hand a doctor who was also a health officer in Buffalo testified that he did not think women should be employed to work in foundries because " it is no place for them." [3] He seemed unable, however, to substantiate his views to the satisfaction of his examiners on the basis either of exposure or offensive fumes. On the one hand, he thought employment of women in slaughter houses was not unadvisable, even though standing in water was necessary. His suggestion was that they could wear rubber boots. On the other hand, when asked to explain why the fumes in foundries are more offensive than those in garbage crematory works where women are employed, the

[1] Cores are parts of molds which fill the spaces that are to be left hollow in finished castings. Sand mixed with molasses or other adhesive material is rammed into the mold or core-box to be given perfect form, then turned out into a metal plate for baking. Small cores one inch or more in size are made and lifted by hand, while a carefully balanced hoisting system is used for the heavier work, some cores measuring many feet.

The fumes that ensue during the baking of cores are obnoxious and deleterious to the persons employed unless they can be carried off by a well regulated process of ventilation.

[2] *Report of the New York Factory Investigating Commissions*, 1913, vol. iv, pp. 1806-7.

[3] *Ibid.*, p. 1786.

doctor refused to respond.[1] The simple statement that women should not be permitted to work " in foundries generally, unless wrapping small pieces of iron," was the theory to which he clung.

The testimony of labor representatives was unequivocal. But before representing them it is worth while to consider the attitude of organized molders in general toward women core makers. In the constitution and rules of order of the International Molders' Union of North America, article 13, section 6, page 37, is included the following:

> Any member, honorary or active, who devotes his time in part or in whole to the instruction of female help in the foundry or at any branch of the trade shall be expelled from this union.

On page 66 are found three resolutions passed at the 25th convention and included in the constitution and rules of order, as follows:

> 13. *Resolved,* That the decision of this convention be the restriction of the further employment of child and woman labor in union core rooms and foundries, and eventually the elimination of such labor in all foundries by the example set by union foundries in the uplifting of humanity.
>
> *Resolved,* That we appeal to the workingmen of both countries when depositing their ballots to vote for the candidates who will pledge themselves to vote for measures and legislation which will eradicate this evil.
>
> *Resolved,* That the incoming officers be directed to, either by themselves or in cooperation with others in the labor movement, give their best thought and effort in opposing the employment of female and child labor in jobs recognized distinctively as men's employment.[2]

[1] *Ibid.*, p. 1800.

[2] Reproduced on page 158 of *The New Position of Women in American Industry*, by the Women's Bureau of the U. S. Department of Labor, *Bulletin no. 12*, 1920. It is explained by the Bureau (p. 109) that the

According to authority the molders' union has steadfastly frowned upon the employment of women in or about the foundry, but though women were employed in Detroit foundries as early as 1884, they did not become a fully recognized "industrial problem" until 1907. At this time the policy of fining members, "honorary or active," was established. The fine was not to be in excess of fifty dollars, but for a second offence the penalty was expulsion from the union. Strikes ensued against the increasing number of women core makers who, in 1912, numbered 1,039 in ninety malleable iron shops. "In order to reach establishments where labor organization would prove very difficult, the Molders endeavored to secure restrictive legislation. In 1910 a bill to prohibit the employment of woman core-makers was introduced in the New York legislature but failed to pass. At the next session of the legislature the bill was reintroduced and the International sent a lobbyist to work for its passage." [1]

Thus the molders were certain of their views when asked to give them before the Factory Investigating Commission in 1913. The representative of the core makers' union of Buffalo declared [2] for his union of 167 members that they were opposed "to this women's core maker bill . . . permitting them to work in a foundry. We claim it is not a proper place for women to be employed." He continued, "The way I look at it is, I believe that all of these women who are working in foundries now should be under a doctor's care, a whole lot of them. I know one person in particular

molder's union considers core making as one part of a molder's apprenticeship and that women core-makers cut men off one step in their training.

[1] Frank T. Stockton, "The International Molders Union of North America," Johns Hopkins University *Studies in Historical and Political Science*, 1921, pp. 61-62.

[2] *Report of the Factory Investigating Commission*, 1913, vol. iv, pp. 1808-1809.

has worked at the business for 16 years, a lady core maker . . . . I don't believe that this woman is physically or morally fit to work in a foundry . . . She is just dodging an undertaker, that is about the size of it, from the fumes and gases of the foundry." Upon being asked if a certain ventilating system would not make the place safe for women, the labor witness rejoined "It may be safe, but I don't believe i would be the place for them anyway. . . . I don't believe it is a proper place for them at all. The only reason I can see that women are employed in foundries in core making is because it is cheaper for the employer."

The witness's true grievance emerged in clearer form as the hearing proceeded. Upon being queried as to what would become of those girls who were core makers, should the legislature prohibit their employment, the witness replied,[1] "That would be easily taken up. All you would have to do would be to look at our Buffalo Evening News and see the Want Ad. column for girls in housework where they belong. I don't think they should be employed in factories. I think the men should be left to make living wages to support the girls and their families." And again, "We know it is no place for them, and one well-known fact I know is that some women—I have worked with women nineteen years—that they could not boil water without burning it, and to become the wife of a man they should have a training at home and learn housework."

Another union representative explained, "You touch dirt and it will stick to you, is the old saying. The moulders are a pretty rough class, as a rule, and if we put the women in there to work they will get rough too. And all foundries are rough, and you can't get out of that." [2]

In its preliminary report of general conditions in foundries the factory commission stated in review [3] that, "the

[1] *Op. cit.*, vol. iv, p. 1810.

[2] *Op. cit.*, 1913, vol. iii, p. 939.

[3] *Op. cit.*, vol. i, 1912, p. 107.

occupation is an arduous one, and the workers during the day are exposed to marked changes in temperature. The washing facilities are bad. The system of ventilation in many of the foundries is entirely inadequate. The result is shown by the number of moulders suffering from rheumatism, pulmonary diseases and kidney trouble." It was observed that the women " work under exactly the same condition and with the same surroundings as the men . . . and altogether the occupation seems to be a most dangerous one for a woman in so far as her health is concerned. . . . The Commission is of the opinion that the employment of women in work of this kind in foundries in the State should be prohibited. Their employment in that industry is not only a great injury to themselves, but it is a menace to posterity, and should not be tolerated by any civilized community." Unwillingness was expressed, however, to recommend legislation at that time because of the lack of " opportunity to gather all the necessary facts in connection with such employment." [1]

The two acts of 1913 were proposed by the factory commission after another year's investigation including foundries, the hearings relating to women having just been described.

Bill No. 25 was concerned with general working conditions in foundries, the commission having been satisfied that requirements further than those for ordinary factories are necessary for the protection of foundry workers. As a result of careful consideration and consultation, therefore, the bill called for both general and specific provisions concerning the heating of foundries and the prevention of drafts, proper ventilation, measures to prevent accidents, washing facilities, passage-ways to outside waterclosets, the milling and cleaning of castings.[2]

[1] *Op. cit.*, 1912, vol. i, p. 107.

[2] *Op. cit.*, 1913, vol. i, pp. 389-391.

The employment of women in core rooms was then given separate attention, and the prohibitory regulations mentioned in Chapter II were contained in a separate bill, No. 26.[1] Repeating the words of the molders' union representative, the commission came to the conclusion that "the foundry is no place for women:"

We believe that it would have been far better if women had never been originally allowed to enter this employment.

There are to-day, however, about three hundred women earning a livelihood from this work upon which they are dependent for their support. Many of these have appealed to the commission not to deprive them of what they, in small country towns, consider their only means of earning a living.

We cannot say that work in a core room as such, is under all circumstances and conditions absolutely detrimental to a woman's health. Although we should like to see this work stopped, and believe that its suppression would be beneficial to the race, . . . nevertheless we cannot at this time recommend an entire prohibition of work that would result in throwing the three hundred women now in the industry out of employment. We believe that work by women in core rooms should be strictly confined to its present limits, and should be gradually eliminated. It should be discouraged and ultimately suppressed. Every obstacle should be thrown in the way of its increase and expansion.

. . . If it is impracticable, as some of the foundry owners have testified, to separate the room in which the women are employed from the core oven by a substantial partition, so as [to] prevent the core-gas from escaping into the room in which the women work, these owners should cease to employ women in work never intended for them. We have no sympathy for the foundry owner who appeared before us and said that so far as work in the core room was concerned, there should be no distinction as to sex.[2]

[1] *Ibid.*, pp. 391-393.

[2] It will be recalled that this witness claimed that there should be good working conditions for men as well as for women.

. . . Nature itself has made the distinction which the foundry owner has said should not be made. Instincts of chivalry and decency as well as concern for the preservation of the race, demand that we should not permit women to engage in work detrimental to their health, that overtaxes their strength, and impairs their vitality as wives and mothers.[1]

The Commission has received descriptions of the abuses that the employment of women in core rooms has led to in other states. We have been told that the cores on which women originally began to work were of a small size but that to-day the women are making cores with a rammer and the size of these cores is such that they have to be hoisted by a derrick.

. . . We believe that these opinions are shared generally by the people of the state who do not wish to see their women employed at manual labor in foundries.[2]

The commission seems to have considered it not worth while to consult " their women " themselves about whether they wanted to be removed from the work which they " in small country towns consider their only means of earning a living," and it would seem that the voluntary opposition to exclusion from foundries raised by these women was given scant attention. The bill was finally submitted by the commission and passed by the legislature, requiring women to be prohibited from employment in core making where the ovens were in the same room in which the cores were made and empowering the Industrial Board to prescribe the size and weight of cores that may be handled by women.

Though the first of the four recommendations of the commission for remedial legislation was that men and women core makers should not be employed in the same room, it

[1] This statement might seem to overlook that made above, that work in the core room is not absolutely detrimental to woman's health.

[2] *Ibid.*, pp. 261-263.

was evidently decided not to include such a provision in the bill.

In the last analysis, then, the strongest influences that bore upon the prohibition of core making as an occupation for women were, firstly, the persistent objection to their employment by the Molder's Union and, secondly, "the instincts of chivalry and decency." It was not shown that women's health need be menaced by this occupation [1] and the opinions of the women themselves were practically ignored. Nevertheless, it was decided that "every obstacle should be thrown in the way" of their employment.

3. *Polishing and Grinding*

The inquiry of the New York State Department of Labor, in 1894, regarding needed legislation which brought the reply of the Magnolia waiters, before mentioned, also brought response from the brass polishers and platers. Differing from the former instance, however, this reply suggested general health legislation:

In our judgment, the best legislation for our trade would be the

[1] Moreover, modern foundries furnish an example of the possibility of making industry safe for its workers. The Federal Women's Bureau in *The New Position of Women in American Industry*, published in 1920 (page 109), says that,

Advanced foundry men recognize that such a condition (core making in heat, smoke, fumes, and dirt or poor ventilation near a bake oven) entails needless exposure for either men or women core makers. The zinc oxide fumes arising from molten brass cause "brass colic" in both men and women, although it is claimed that women and boys fall victims to the disease more readily. The smoke in the malleable and gray iron foundry and from bake ovens is irritating to many workers of both sexes. Modern foundries have their core rooms entirely cut off from the melting and baking rooms. The atmosphere is as free of disturbing or harmful elements as an office room. The sand is fed through a chute to each worker and the plates are carried to and from her bench on an overhead trolley or on moving belts. The noise of machinery of the usual factory is absent.

placing of blowers behind the grinding and buffing lathes, as the dust which flies from the wheels is detrimental to the health of the men.[1]

This was a direct answer to a direct question. Nevertheless, the legislation that followed was not that requiring the scientific improvement of these conditions, but, five years later, the prohibition of females and male minors from employment in polishing and grinding operations. In retrospect this act appears paradoxical because it left those upon whom women and minors were 'dependent' quite exposed to the destruction of their health—a calamity from which they had asked to be saved! The statute was in the spirit of the time, however, as the foregoing pages have shown,—the year 1899 having marked the beginning of modern legislative stress upon the special protection of women in New York State. As time passed, more of these occupations were prohibited to women and minors, but in 1911 the medical inspector of factories expressed his anxiety over the still too narrow scope of the law in its protection of minors and children. He reported finding "eighteen year old boys, who physically looked only fifteen engaged at dusty occupations fit only for strong adults," and children were carrying too heavy loads. Both of these groups "were legally employed." The inspector advocated the entire prohibition of children under the age of eighteen years and of all females from employment in dusty occupations and where acid fumes rose from poisonous materials.[2]

It was not until the Factory Investigating Commission lent a firm hand towards the correction of this unnecessary evil in general, however, that a scientific attempt was made to abolish it. With the preliminary report in 1912, the commission proposed a bill that contained specific require-

[1] New York *Bureau Statistics of Labor*, 1894, p. 397.

[2] *Annual Reports on Factory Inspection, etc.*, 1911, pp. 38-39.

ments for the disposal of dust, fumes and gases by the use of hoods, pipes and exhaust fans. But the legislature was not ready for so far-reaching an act and the bill failed to pass. The next year, without specific changes, responsibility was lodged with the Industrial Board for making rules and regulations to guard against danger " by establishing requirements as to temperature, humidity, the removal of dusts, gases or fumes." Here at last, nearly twenty years following the request of the polishers and platers, came a general provision for the protection of the workers employed in these unhealthy occupations.

This step in the way of progress brought two more or less direct results. One was the valuable bulletin on the subject of *Hoods for Removing Dust, Fumes and Gases*, published in 1917 by the division of industrial hygiene of the state through the Department of Labor. The other result was the partial repeal in 1921 of the clause prohibiting women from operating abrasive wheels. This repeal was brought about by the persistent protest of a group of women who were prohibited from polishing and grinding occupations, a prohibition which they considered unnecessary. The new provision made a distinction between women over twenty-one years of age and girls under twenty-one by permitting women to operate such wheels for wet grinding. Dry grinding occupations remained legally closed to all females, however, though the request had been for a general release. The confidence of these women in pleading their cause was doubtless strengthened by the statements of the Federal Women's Bureau the year before, wherein was explained the error of prohibiting the employment of women on grinding and polishing machines " since it has been proved to be possible to have a device which will draw off the dust so that the operator will not breathe it. Moreover, the danger to the lungs is as great for men as for women, and for the protection of all workers exhaust systems of this kind should be required." Stressing the point further, the bureau continued,

It is unfortunately true that it is easier to secure a guard for a machine to prevent an accident than to compel the drawing off of dust to prevent tuberculosis, for the reason that workmen's compensation laws require the payment of money to the employee who meets with an accident, but as yet compensation for disease caused by the work is not required except in a very few States.[1] In the interest of the health of both men and women, safeguards against industrial diseases should be more effectively demanded. When these are secured it will be found unnecessary to prohibit the employment of women. This form of prohibition, however, has never applied to more than one or two occupations, and is certainly not desirable as compared with a more comprehensive protection of health for all workers.[2]

SPECIAL WORKING CONDITIONS

1. *Seats*

Probably none of the earlier protective measures for women received as much spirited support as that for seats. We have said that in New York State the earliest modern legislation for women was of this kind—that seats be placed behind the counters in mercantile establishments. This law (1881) was passed in response to an urgent demand supported by the testimony of some medical men, that "great and lasting injury" often resulted in stores to women and girls who were subjected to continual standing. For example, Dr. Ames[3] of Massachusetts dwelt upon the evil

[1] These States are California, Connecticut, Hawaii, Illinois, Massachusetts, Minnesota, New Jersey, New York, North Dakota, Ohio, Porto Rico, Wisconsin, and in the federal law.

[2] *The New Position of Women in Industry*, *op. cit.*, p. 32.

[3] Dr. Azel Ames, *Sex in Industry*, 1875, pp. 54-59.

effects of woman's standing and quoted Dr. Ely Van de Warker who held that "the knee joint of women is a sexual characteristic" which together with "the delicate nature of the foot as a part of the sustaining column" made it injurious for women to stand for long periods of time. However, the law is reported to have been enacted by men who knew little about the dimensions of store interiors, and room for the provision for seats behind counters proved more frequently than not a physical impossibility.[1] So, for this and other reasons discussed in a later chapter, this provision languished and died.

In the year following this first enactment, the Woman's Suffrage Association, according to the New York *Tribune*,[2] took up the cudgels on behalf of the "sales ladies," and "haled the cruel shopkeepers into police court," appearing in person against them. It was an amusing description of the scene in which the "benches were filled with fair and fluttering" sales ladies, who, it developed, appeared on behalf of their employers, eager to bear testimony that they were treated in a "perfectly splendid" manner. Mrs. Emma Gates Conkling, who represented the Woman's Suffrage Association, protested successfully against allowing these witnesses to speak, on the grounds that they would perjure their "immortal souls for bread."

Again in the middle of the decade a plea was entered "once more" for seats for women in mercantile establishments.[3] The logic of the request was discussed on two grounds—economy for the employers, and economy for society. "Tired out, half fainting women" cannot do the work of fresh vigorous women; the "holiday principle, already accepted is identical with the seat principle . . . too

[1] New York *Tribune*, Feb. 13, 1882.

[2] New York *Tribune*, editorial, March 3, 1882.

[3] New York *Tribune*, editorial, June 23, 1885.

long hours mean langour and inefficiency." And also the likelihood of strains "which may result in fastening incurable and painful ailments upon them" was dwelt upon. Fatigue which is relieved in men by a few hours of rest was held not to be so easily thrown off by women. Constant standing for them is "extremely mischievous," and "for this reason refusal of seats is peculiarly hard and unfeeling." And again such refusal was condemned by the same newspaper as "positive cruelty and inhumanity" and, because of its permanently injurious effect, more important than Saturday half-holidays. The reluctance of employers to listen to this reasoning, it was averred, was their fear that women would develop the habit of taking too much rest, to the extent of injuring the trade. The *Tribune* flaunted the challenge that if women cared enough about the welfare of their own sex they could long ago have convinced employers that it was to their own interest to provide seats for clerks and salespeople.

Whether or not in response to this challenge of the press, the agitation for seats was revived by the Working Women's Society in the early nineties, and was soon ardently aided by the New York Consumers' League and other groups. The league appeared before legislative committees having succeeded in getting signatures of 64 physicians and 218 other prominent members of the community in support of the bill, "but the bill failed of passage as during the three years previous." [1]

In the report of the president, Josephine Shaw Lowell, the league expressed its aim to create public opinion and "raise the standard of owners of retail shops until men will no more think of keeping women and girls standing from eight in the morning until ten and eleven at night than they

[1] *Annual Report of the New York City Consumers' League* for 1894, p. 11.

would think of doing any other inhuman thing that would bring down public reprobation upon them."[1] Shoppers were pressed to create a customers' demand for better care of the female clerks and to indicate it by making constant inquiries of floor walkers as to the shop's provision of seats and the attitude toward their use. Stores that did not furnish seats were conspicuously left off the "White List" which was regularly published by the league.

Interest in this agitation was manifested by the National Retail Clerks' Protective Association formed in 1890, to the extent that the association included in its Declaration of Principles the use of comfortable seats for "lady clerks" behind sales counters. This action was considered something of a gesture by some, however, for it was felt that if it had come as a sincere demand from a body of this kind it would have brought substantial results. In fairness to the association, on the other hand, there is no indication that it had sufficient strength to enforce this principle, even though advocacy of it may have been entirely sincere.

The Central Labor Union in New York City became sufficiently interested in this agitation, according to the press champion of seats for women,[2] to appoint a delegate to inform them of the facts of the controversy. The appointee first attended meetings of the Working Women's Society where he heard discussion of the inhumanity of merchants in their failure to permit females the use of seats; then he undertook a first-hand investigation. It is not known exactly to what extent this personal investigation was made, nor how it was made, but the nature of the delegate's report came as something of a surprise. For as submitted to the Central Union the delegate had found favor with the merchants who had "shown him every courtesy" and, from

[1] *Ibid.*, p. 14.

[2] New York *Tribune*, January 13, 1896.

his observations, had given satisfactory treatment to women and child employees. The report said that seats were furnished in the big establishments and that the condition of females was much better than in factories. It explained that merchants opposed the bill then before the legislature providing that mercantile establishments be brought under the factory act, because the factory inspectors "were a poor class of men, receiving appointments generally through peanut politicians." After discussion, the Central Labor Union adopted the report of their delegate by a large majority.

These findings were offset by the official reports of the Reinhardt committee which, aided by continued propaganda, brought about the amendments of 1896 and 1900.

By 1911, the fact that all sorts of improvised seats were pressed into service by those who feigned observance of the law, brought the commissioner of labor to recommend a standard seat. He asserted that in place of boxes, barrels, boards and stools, the bureau should be authorized to order a properly adjustable seat permanently secured at a definitely prescribed location, that it should be so adjusted that when an employee sat the soles and heels would rest comfortably on the floor, also that the seat should have a back at an angle of not less than one hundred degrees.[1]

Accordingly, in the first group of bills submitted to the state legislature in 1912 by the Factory Investigating Commission was included an amendment to the provision for seats, requiring that "every person employing females in a factory or as waitresses in a hotel or restaurant shall provide and maintain suitable seats *with backs at an angle of not less than one hundred degrees* for the use of such female employees, and permit the use thereof by such employees"

[1] *Annual Report of the Commissioner of Labor*, 1911, p. 77.

whenever practicable.[1] This bill was too precise to meet the approval of the legislature, and was rejected. It was presented in revised form in the following year and passed—the definite requirement concerning backs being omitted. The successful bill made the more general stipulation that employers provide "suitable seats, with backs wherever practicable," the Industrial Board to determine when this provision was necessary.

The vagueness of this law, however, together with the lack of scientific knowledge of what constitutes proper seating, rendered the provision unsatisfactory to all who concerned themselves with the importance of saving women workers from unnecessary fatigue in this way. The recommendations of the commissioner of labor in 1913 and 1914 again included the precise specifications that seats be eighteen inches from the floor, or, if necessary to be at a greater height, that a proper foot rise be provided eighteen inches below the seat, that the minimum size of the seat be twelve inches in diameter, and that when backs could be used they be at a proper angle. These recommendations were not acted upon by the legislature, and, while interest in the whole question of industrial posture has become more general each year, it has not yet been crystallized into law.

The nature of the progress in this matter is epitomized in an admirable bulletin published in 1921 by the New York Bureau of Women in Industry called *Industrial Posture and Seating,* which would seem to supply influential data toward the improvement of this phase of the working conditions of industrial employees. Aside from comprehensive references to other studies of this subject, the bulletin is eminently successful in setting forth some of the problems of seating, and in establishing the fact that proper posture at work is important for all workers from the point of view both of pro-

[1] *Op. cit.*, 1912, vol. i, pp. 832-833.

duction and of health of the employees. The United States Public Health Service is cited [1] as pointing out that fatigue is regarded as the " greatest obstacle to maximum output," that four out of eleven ways outlined " to reduce fatigue, deal directly with posture. This is but an indication of the importance which is being attached, as a result of scientific study to something which a few years ago was regarded as a trifle or mere detail."

Thus it seems probable that more specific regulations regarding seats would find their way into statute books or industrial codes as further knowledge is acquired through experience.[2] And while stress has been laid chiefly upon the special need of women workers, the New York bureau says " it is more and more true that the determining factors are the demands of the particular occupations, rather than the sex of the worker " (pp. 9-10).[3]

2. *Wash-rooms, toilets, dressing-rooms*

The absence of anything approaching decent sanitary conditions for men and women in many industrial establish-

[1] United States Public Health Service. *How Industrial Fatigue may be Reduced.* Reprint no. 482, 1918.

[2] The New York *Call* claimed in a 1921 circular letter, however, that " because some years ago we fought hard for a law providing seats for salesgirls when not busy has meant that to this day we have no big department store advertisements."

[3] On this point, G. M. Kober is cited who reports varicose veins and deformities of foot and knee among men who are obliged to stand for long hours, as motormen, conductors, machine tenders, etc. (Kober, G. M. and Hanson, W. C., *Diseases of Occupational and Vocational Hygiene* (1916), pp. 444, 445). Also the effects of a constrained position combined with a sedentary life are shown to be very injurious to workers, as weavers, shoemakers, engravers, etc. Internal congestion from constrained attitude, and phthisis, constipation, etc. from interference with normal respiration is common among these groups among whom there is "a low average of life." (Kober, G. M., *Industrial and Personal Hygiene* (1908) p. 54.)

ments was pointed out repeatedly in the reports of the bureau of labor statistics before the first law regarding them was enacted in 1887. Cheaply constructed buildings had been put up in which the crudest of accommodations had been provided. Toilet facilities were meager, and, in not a a few cases as women were introduced into the shops, the same facilities had to be used by both sexes.

In 1881, Commissioner Peck reported the results of an inquiry concerning this state of affairs.[1] 126 out of 810 replies to the question as to whether separate waterclosets were provided were in the negative, 509 answered yes and 175, suspiciously, made no answer to this question. Commissioner Peck urged immediate reform. And in addition to this particular demand he urged the necessity of properly screened waterclosets. "A modest girl will not run the gauntlet of male eyes on the way to the watercloset, and many of them risk their health on this account. There is the highest medical authority for this statement."

The first, in 1910, of the more recent series of acts providing for better accommodations was probably a result of the recommendation of the factory medical inspector. He urged better dressing-rooms for women, not merely closets, but reasonably comfortable rooms lighted by the sun and equipped with couches and medical appurtenances.[2]

Nevertheless, while better rules for fresh air ventilation and privacy were enacted that year, it was not until bills were proposed by the Factory Investigating Commission in 1912 and 1913 that the more nearly comfortable accommodations of today were required by law.

Further improvements have been made by the Industrial Board in the industrial code which has the force of law, rather than by the legislature. Since these enactments,

[1] *New York Bureau of Statistics of Labor*, 1885, pp. 146-152.

[2] *Report of the Bureau of Factory Inspection*, 1909, p. 39.

stress laid upon the necessary minimum of requirements, joined with the recurring recommendations of inspectors, have leaned in the direction of improved facilities for each of the sexes wherever both are employed.

3. *Laundries*

Working conditions in laundries have received a great deal of attention in recent years as the need for their improvement has been increasingly realized. Through a series of investigations made in 1909, 1912, 1917, and 1919, the Consumers' League of New York, whose initial interest had been in reducing women's hours of labor, discovered other exceedingly injurious conditions of labor.

The last of these investigations included both steam and hand laundries, two of the agents being reported to have entered about eighteen laundries as actual workers in order to get first hand information. "Their accounts of working at mangles in rooms often too thick with steam to see across, of standing on wet floors, of their clothing becoming saturated with steam until they were soaking wet, of eating lunches on the tables where laundry was done, of inadequate dressing rooms, unsatisfactory lighting and ventilation, of overcrowding and long hours, indicate the necessity of bringing the rank and file of small laundries up to the standards of a few excellent ones." [1]

These conditions were said to be a result, in part, of failure to enforce existing laws, but also of "the lack of itemized provisions which can be secured only through a complete laundry code." Convinced of this need, the league submitted to the State Industrial Commission a summary of its findings together with "request for a special code of regulations to cover laundry workers." [2] The commission wel-

[1] *Annual Report of the Consumers' League of New York* for 1920, p. 14.

[2] *Ibid.*, p. 15.

comed the report of the league but deferred action until further information concerning laundries could be gathered by state investigators. Follow-up action was interrupted thereafter by the reorganization of the Industrial Commission, and was not revived until 1922. A special advisory committee with a view to preparing a laundry code was then formed within the State Department of Labor. The committee was composed of a representative of the New York State Laundry Owners' Association, the manager of the Laundry Board of Trade of Greater New York, the secretary of the Associated Industries of New York State, a representative of the American Laundry Machine Company, a representative of the United Garment Workers' Union, a representative of the shop committee of the Pilgrim Laundry of Brooklyn and a representative of workers employed in manufacturers' laundries. In addition to these, there were on the committee two heating and ventilating engineers and three representatives of the State Department of Labor.[1]

This committee is still at work, having held hearings on the proposed code in the principal cities of the state during the first week in February of 1924. Evidence will be submitted to the Industrial Board for final action.[2]

[1] *Bulletin* of the Consumers' League of New York for November, 1922.

[2] *Ibid.*, February, 1924.

CHAPTER V

Enforcement of Legislation

PART I: GENERAL ADMINISTRATION

We have seen that the enactment of protective legislation is frequently a very difficult matter; but we have further to see that the enforcement of such legislation is far more difficult. And, obviously, the matter of enforcement is one of major importance. After the enactment of laws, the courts determine whether they *may* live, their enforcement determines whether they *do* live.

The difficulties in the way of administration of labor legislation are numerous and complicated; they are probably the most frequent cause of the failure of legal efficiency. The analysis of these difficulties assumes a three-fold aspect, namely: the degree to which the statute is approved by those concerned; the nature of the statute itself; and the nature and adequacy of the machinery for administration.

Law enforcement is perhaps as much a creature of the determined attitudes of special groups, as is the enactment of the legislation. Acts are adopted or rejected as a result of legislative hearings, with lobbyists playing an active rôle. If the two opposed groups are well matched, the act is likely to be passed, but with some omission or modifying clause that renders it practically impotent. The New York act regulating the hours of men in brickyards is a case in point, by which men may be permitted but not "required" to work more than ten hours a day. Again, if the forces are poorly matched, or if the influence is entirely one-sided, the act may also be passed. If the pressure that brought its enactment was fairly solid and representative, its chances for effective life are high. The prohibition of employment of children in factories at night is an act of this type, for public opinion is strongly opposed to child labor. But if a law has few champions and those few are more or less dissociated from the persons affected by its provisions, the act is likely not to live. Some would cite the prohibition of night work of women in restaurants in this connection. Whether an act has general, or limited and external endorsement, then, is an important condition of its enforcement.

And moreover, loose phrasing has brought about the practical annulment of many a law. Acts purporting to be for the protection of women were long ago exposed as useless, where the expressions, "wilful violations" or "compelling" a woman to work more than a certain number of hours, were used. An eight-hour law in Wisconsin exacting a penalty for "compelling" a woman to work remained a dead letter from 1867 to 1911. The provision was then changed to read that no woman "shall be employed or permitted to work" beyond the legal period. The device of posting notices stating legal regulations for workers is practically useless where the inspector is obliged to prove that a woman has been working "in excess of" the number of hours posted. Substitution of the words "outside of" specified hours goes far to obviate the difficulty. Another instance of failure because of bad wording was the New York law providing for "protection from dust." Until 1910, it was necessary for inspectors to prove that material thrown off by grinding and buffing wheels was technically "dust." In that year the phrase was clarified so that the act provided for an equipment "to remove all matter thrown off such wheels in the course of their use."

Lack of definition of such key words as factory, factory

building, and mercantile establishment has caused no end of embarrassment to inspectors. It has also been the cause of flagrant lack of uniformity in enforcing the spirit of the law. For example, in New York it was not until 1913 that sheds, in which a part of the progress of canning fruit and vegetables was conducted, were included within the meaning of the word " factory " and " factory building." Until this redefinition, small children could be employed with impunity in sheds at " snipping beans," while the law struck hard at an employer who gave them work within the main building just adjoining. A tenement house, for the purpose of administering the regulations of " home work," is defined as a building occupied by three or more families, although the one and two family dwelling house may be the scene of more work than that of the tenement.

Many a law has been completely devitalized by such phrases as " where there is no contract or agreement to the contrary," or " nor shall any person be prevented by anything herein contained from working as many hours overtime or extra hours as he or she may agree." The Illinois law of 1867 establishing eight hours as the legal working day in certain employments contained these " life savers " for the employers. Statutes regulating hours in New York State in 1867 and 1870 were of this type and therefore unenforceable. Specific hour provisions in New York's first Labor Law of 1897 relating to employees in brickyards and on railroads were paralysed in this way. Overtime for extra compensation " by agreement between employer and employee " was permitted by these acts. It will be recalled that this provision relative to brickyard employees stands lifeless on the statute books today, while that for railroad employees has been energized.

The technical phrasing of the statute is, therefore, another important condition of its enforcement. Sometimes the difficulty arises from careless drafting, and at other times the act is consciously rendered ineffective by trickery, partisanship or fatal compromise,—the fault may not be fully discovered until attempts at enforcement are made. When an act is found by the bureau of inspection thus to be unenforceable, it is given no further attention, until such time as it may be amended. Some acts which do not fall entirely into this class, limp along and supply a perpetual source of trouble to administering officials; others, well drafted and well approved, bring prompt and relatively general compliance.

We have seen that the human equation forms an essential part of law-enforcing, as of law-making. In the main, perhaps, officials strive to enforce and proprietors are willing to obey the labor law. (It should be said at this point however, that the third group, the employees, whose first concern the law should be, cannot always be relied upon to demand its observance unless they are combined in strong labor organizations. Complaints of violations are not frequently reported by them, the explanation most commonly made for this is the employee's fear of losing his job. Sometimes, doubtless, the reason lies in ignorance and apathy). However, there are some acts which it is the policy of the official administration not to enforce fully. As, for example, that regarding revocation of contracts for public work in New York State. For, in spite of the clear provision of the law that such a contract shall be revoked upon discovery of an employee's working illegal hours, such action, when a large contract is involved, is considered too heavy a penalty to exact. There are other acts which it is the policy of employers not to have enforced fully. For example, the statute restricting the working time of women in canneries is ignored by some manufacturers during the peak of the season. And in this particular case, as will be seen in pages to come, community opinion, as well as the opinion of the women concerned, has served to strengthen the hand of the offender. The process of annulling the operation of a law may be carried all along the line,—from the putting in readiness of establishment and employees upon the approach of inspectors so that no evidence of violation will be seen, and long protracted delay in responding to warnings, to dismissals of prosecution proceedings by sympathetic police magistrates, suspended sentences, or remitted fines. The greater the lack of coöperation for enforcement on the part of employers and employees, the more persistence and efficiency is required of the agents, if an attempt to gain compliance with the act is to be continued.

We must distiniuish, then, between the two clearly different methods of enforcing the labor law, which are, enforcement by inspection, order, and compliance; and enforcement by inspection, prosecution, and penalty. It is plain that both of these methods should be in ready use,—the one of an educational nature, the other punitive but looking toward education. The latter method, however, relies for its full effectiveness upon the courts and police magistrates; and when courts and magistrates fail to respect the law by carrying prosecution proceedings through to the end, the administrative force is both embarrassed and rendered impotent, irrespective of how faithful and how expert it may be.

The problem of enforcement is also a financial problem. Highly tinged as it is with a political hue, there is an ever present inadequacy of appropriation for the work. Act upon act is passed by state legislatures with not a cent of financial provision for administration. It is a matter of present as well as past history in New York State at least, that at no time has there been an inspecting force adequate to its task, in numbers, salaries, or expertness; and first-rate officials and inspectors frequently have been forfeited owing to a lack of a respectable salary or a possibility of promotion. This condition is, of course, a destructive handicap in the administration of laws and it has incalculable effect upon the morale of the agents at work.

Thus the problem of law enforcement is inherently complex. And the increased mechanization of industry attended by a growing sense of the need for protecting the workers has forced a marked development in the technique of administration in the past dozen years. It was recognized that acts of the legislature, in order to live, required discretionary power on the part of the enforcing agents when general words like "suitable," "reasonable," "proper," "sanitary," "clean," were used. Thus, gradually there has come the realization in some states that specific regulations often cannot be made without current knowledge of exact needs based upon ascertained facts. Legislatures meet but once a year and they are not acquainted with the varying conditions of industry. The need for a body of experts whose continuous attention would be given to the labor law, became clear.

Thus there are today three types of labor law administration. First, there is the old type, common in most of the non-industrial states, requiring the enforcement of specific statutes by authorized officials. The second is like that adopted in Wisconsin in 1911, whereby an industrial commission is created with few specific acts to enforce, and vested with authority to "investigate, ascertain, declare, and prescribe what conditions shall be required for the proper protection of workers for their safety and welfare, the law having been laid down by the legislature only in broad outlines. The third type is that of New York State initiated in 1913, after the preliminary work of the Factory Investigating Commission, and recognized since that time. This was a combination of the first and second types, by which an industrial board was given definite laws to enforce, but was further intrusted to formulate supplementary rules which, after public hearings, became part of the labor law. Ohio and Pennsylvania created industrial commissions similar to that of Wisconsin in 1913, and Colorado, Minnesota, Utah and Massachusetts have, since that time, followed with this general method of administration. Also California, Michigan, Washington, New Jersey, and Illinois have approached the industrial commission type of administration by consolidating their machinery, and other states have moved in that direction. More will be said later of the industrial commission as it has been developed in New York State, but it is important first, as New York is the center of our discussion, to understand something of the earlier problems of its law enforcement, as well as those of more recent date. The development of New York's plan of administration will be followed briefly.

The Administration of the Labor Law in New York State

The machinery for the enforcement of the labor law in New York before 1913 was undermanned, disorganized, and relatively inefficient. And before 1883, there was no enforcement, practically speaking. Some acts had been passed, with the provision that their violation was a misdemeanor, but there was no penalty provided, and no machinery for inspection and enforcement. Any attempts to keep these acts alive were made voluntarily by philanthropists and they usually ended in failure.[1]

[1] In truth, this is the early history of practically all protective labor legislation. Advocates and proponents of laws have, at first, ignored the necessity of specific accompanying provisions for inspection and enforcement of compliance. In England, the first attempt to establish a department of factory inspection was in 1833 even though 1802 marked the beginning of factory legislation. In the United States, there was a parallel lag, provision for factory inspection not having been established until 1886, first in Massachusetts and New York, and within the next five years in New Jersey, Wisconsin, Pennsylvania and Illinois.

The New York State Bureau of Labor Statistics was created in 1883, the result of overwhelming labor union pressure, and was charged with some perfunctory duties of enforcement. The commissioner of labor was given no authority to enter factories and other premises if opposed by the owners, nor could he demand answers to his questions. After persistent reports of the futility of his office as it stood, the legislature in 1886 authorized the commissioner to enter premises and compel bona-fide answers to questions. This appears to have been the first serious provision towards law enforcement in New York, and it was embodied in the same chapter with what has been called the first factory act, before mentioned. The custom of posting in factories public notices of the special acts relating to women and minors was inaugurated at this time; also a factory inspector with an assistant on a small salary was provided for. It was his express duty to enforce the labor laws and make an annual report of progress to the bureau of labor statistics. Penalty for violation ran from fifty to one hundred dollars or from thirty to ninety days' imprisonment.

Amendments were made by the legislature in 1887 to cover some readily observed omissions and errors in the new law. They followed the first of the long line of recommendations of factory inspectors made each year as a result of the attempt to perform their official duties. A copy of the factory law was required to be posted in every work room for the information of the workers, the factory inspector was given a force of eight deputy inspectors to be appointed by himself, and, for convenience of administration, the state was divided into eight districts with one deputy in charge of inspection for each district. The office of factory inspector was severed completely from the bureau of labor statistics and the annual reports were thereafter to be submitted directly to the assembly.

Eight woman deputies were added to the inspection force in 1890. This was accomplished, it is said, in the face of active opposition on the part of the factory inspector and his assistant, which succeeded in defeating the first bill in 1888. The proponents of this innovation were philanthropic women in conjunction with the Working-women's Association, who were convinced that laws would be better enforced if the staff included a contingent of women. There have always been some women deputies since that time; but for many years, not more than ten. The law, while it provided for a larger and still larger force of deputy inspectors, rigidly specified that no more than ten should be women. The total force was increased to twenty-four inspectors in 1893, to twenty-nine in 1896, to thirty-six in 1897, and in 1899 it reached fifty. But this increase did not continue with any steadiness. In 1902, the force was reduced again to 37 and to 34 in 1905, although new acts were being passed which increased the volume of work. Today there are a little less than 200 inspectors, some 30 of whom are women; but even this number, according to the director of inspection, is only one-fourth of the number necessary for proper law enforcement.

The State Department of Labor was organized in 1901, consolidating the bureau of labor statistics, the office of factory inspector, and the board of mediation and arbitration. The three executive bodies concerned with industrial labor were thus brought under one jurisdiction, and the chief was the commissioner of labor. The desirability of this consolidation, it was agreed, was uncertain. It achieved financial economy which was the most that could be claimed for it. Reports of the commissioner that followed the consolidation testified to the difficulties of combining the two unrelated types of work now required of the department,—the collection of the facts of industry for statistical record, and inspection for the discovery of violation of the law. Manufacturers being pressed by inspectors to comply with the law were unwilling to coöperate in gathering facts for record. For this reason a recommendation for reorganization of the department appeared in the commissioner's report for 1906. But this was not effected.

Thus the bureau of factory inspection lived a stormy life during these years. Preceding the creation of the bureau of mercantile inspection in 1908, it was the sole police force of the State Department of Labor. In 1905 there were 35,000 factories and 15,000 tenements subject to inspection. The inspection force numbered only thirty-four and their annual salaries were $1200 each, fixed by law with no provision for increase or promotion.[1] In addition to their own duties, the inspectors were charged with the complicated and time-consuming task of investigation and prosecution for violations of the statute regarding public employees! The consequence was that they were directed hither and thither, meeting the needs of the hour in a few instances, with no pretence at enforcing the laws in general. For many weeks in 1904, for example, they were diverted to investigations on one large contract in New York City relative to the "alien labor" law. And the eight-hour law for public employees kept them active in response to complaints.[2] This act seemed popularly to have been construed, the commissioner of labor explained, to mean that anyone could enter any number of complaints of violation, all of which the factory inspectors were obliged to investigate. This privilege became a convenient instrument of spite in labor disputes as well as a means of "harassing and discrediting" the department of labor at election times.[3] When, driven to action,

[1] *Annual Report of the Commissioner of Labor*, 1905, pp. I, 19.

[2] *Op. cit.*, 1906, pp. I. 25.

[3] *Ibid.*, pp. I. 26.

Labor Commissioner Sherman as director of factory inspection insisted that complaints regarding public employees be filed in writing as was required for all other complaints and await their turn for attention, he was charged with an attempt to annul the force of the law.

The year 1908 marked a brief period of optimism. The department was extended to include a bureau of mercantile inspection at this time, with the duty of enforcing regulations applying to mercantile establishments in first-class cities (meaning New York, Buffalo and Rochester). Heretofore—as continued to be the case in 1908, in all but first-class cities—the mercantile law had been entrusted for administration to the local boards of health, and was practically lifeless.[1] Moreover, there was a fresh interest in enforcement of the labor law generally at this time. Commissioner Williams in his annual report wrote that there had never been "as grim a determination to enforce respect for the requirements of our labor laws."[2] Stress was laid upon the intention not to be "too drastic with violators" but "to safeguard the moral and physical welfare of all factory employees." (Here we find a commissioner openly showing his plan to use his discretion in the degree to which he proposes to apply the law.) The number of prosecutions was increased; but here, unfortunately, it is necessary to remember that prosecutions were "not a reliable barometer of efficiency," then or now, and that, while they may result in conviction and penalty thus stiffening the force of the law, they result more frequently in dismissals or suspended sentences. This will be a subject of fuller discussion later.

Nevertheless, in spite of discouragements, the growing

[1] It was not until 1919 that all mercantile establishments in the state were brought under the supervision of the division of mercantile inspection.

[2] *Annual Report of the Commissioner of Labor* for 1908, p. 17.

realization of the need of protecting workers, with proper laws properly enforced, continued. It came to a head in the appointment by the legislature in 1911 of the Factory Investigating Commission whose work has already been described. This body, whose completed reports fill thirteen heavy volumes, was delegated "to inquire into the conditions under which manufacture is carried on in the cities of the first and second class of the State," and others if deemed desirable, with a view to making recommendations for the welfare of the operatives.

Some of the earliest discoveries of the commission concerned the organization for law enforcement, which was found to be inadequate and inefficient; duplication of work was responsible for inefficiency in large part, it was claimed, there being at least eleven different bodies or officials directly concerned with enforcing the labor law, with little coöperation among them.[1] Furthermore, the work of the inspectors, far greater than they were able to accomplish had inspection alone been their duty, was more and more neglected because of the necessity of spending time on cases where orders were not obeyed. Many re-inspection visits to secure compliance with orders had to be made, series of warnings given, accompanied by sufficient evidence of violation if prosecution was to be instituted, warrants obtained, and finally, numerous hours spent in court as witnesses. Thus an elaborate and troublesome technique was rendered more seriously inefficient by paucity of employees.

The Reorganization Act of 1913 was a result of the findings of the Factory Investigating Commission.[2] This act was an epochal event in the history of the New York State Department of Labor. An industrial board was created as

[1] *American Labor Legislation Review*, 1913, pp. 485, 504.

[2] Reorganization had also been recommended by the Wainwright Commission, mentioned in a previous chapter, a few years before.

a special legislative agency whose duty was to be the formulation and passage of an industrial code of rules and regulations which should have " the force and effect of law." The commissioner of labor at a salary of $8,000 was made chairman of the board, and the four associate members appointed by the governor were paid annual salaries of $3,000 each for full-time employment. A secretary was provided for and the board was given power to engage experts and necessary clerical assistants. Counsel to the Department of Labor was also counsel to the board.

The most comprehensive survey ever made in the state by the Labor Department was immediately planned by the new Industrial Board and there was "a new era in prospect." A " rule of reason " was instituted with the purpose of making the law as effective and as just to all concerned as possible. Provision for appeals from the orders of inspectors to the department was made possible and the following memorandum was stamped on all orders sent to manufacturers:

Important—If you believe these orders are unreasonable or unnecessary, and you desire to have them changed, modified or waived, you are not required to employ or retain a lawyer, architect, engineer, building expert or fire prevention expert. Make written protest within five days to the Commissioner of Labor, when, if the facts justify, a reinspection will be made and such action taken as the later inspection warrants.[1]

Here, then, was a specialized body established to insure effective as well as fair application of fundamental principles to varying conditions and circumstances in widely different industries, communities and plants. The use of delegated

[1] *Annual Report of the Commissioner of Labor*, 1914, p. 15. The practice of including this memorandum proved to be undesirable and was abandoned after a few month's testing. It was considered bad practice in that it suggested appeals to employers who would otherwise not have thought of appealing, thus overburdening the commissioner with unnecessary work and delaying compliance with orders.

regulatory power proved sound, and the Industrial Board did good pioneer work during 1914.

But the year's experience uncovered the desirability of further reorganization. The greatest efficiency could not be secured, the Factory Investigating Commission and others urged, so long as there were two "great state departments dealing in an intimate way with the industries of the state." [1] (The Department of Labor and the Industrial Board were coördinate bodies.) The factory commission declared that a close unification was essential. Consequently, in 1915, a newly organized Industrial Commission assumed charge of the Department of Labor. The commission was composed of five members appointed by the governor, one of whom was designated chairman; and no more than three of whom might be of the same political party. The annual salary of each member was $8,000, and a secretary was provided. The duties of the commission were greatly extended by its authorization to administer the labor law, the workmen's compensation law, and the state insurance fund—the old Industrial Board and the workmen's compensation commission being abolished. Deputy commissioners were to be appointed by the commission, each at an annual salary of $6,000; the first to have charge of the bureau of inspection, the second to have charge of the workmen's compensation bureau, the third to have charge of the bureau of mediation and arbitration. The commission was to develop the beginning made by the Industrial Board, "It being the policy and intent of this chapter that all places to which it applies shall be so constructed, equipped, arranged, operated and conducted in all respects as to provide reasonable and adequate protection, to the lives, health and safety of all persons employed therein, and frequenting the same and that the commission shall from time to time make such rules and regulations as will effectuate such policy and intent." [2]

[1] *Annual Report of the Industrial Commission*, 1915, p. 9.

[2] Chapter 674 of the Laws of 1915, § 51, subd. 2c.

And furthermore, to guard against any outcropping of bureaucracy and to assure proper representation of those immediately affected, an Industrial Council was introduced into the organization. Ten members equally representing employers and employees were thus to be advisors to the commission, all rules, regulations, amendments, or repeals to be submitted to them for consideration and advice before enactment. No compensation or appropriation for traveling expenses were provided for this council, as it was assumed that the privilege of giving advice in these vital matters would be sufficient remuneration.[1]

An important new bureau was created by the Industrial Commission in the third year of its administration, July 16, 1918. This was the Bureau of Women in Industry,—the first body of its kind in the New York State Department of Labor. The immediate supervision of the bureau was to be in charge of a chief "appointed by the Industrial Commission and responsible directly to the Industrial Commission." The functions were described as follows:

Further resolved, The functions of the Bureau of Women in Industry shall be to make investigations and reports upon the conditions under which women are employed in industry, wages, and hours of labor and working conditions; also for the employment of women in industry, and to that end such bureau shall cooperate with the Bureau of Statistics, the Bureau of Inspection, the Bureau of Employment, and any other bureau or agencies of the State Industrial Commission.

Further resolved, That the commission shall define the duties of the members of this bureau and may from time to time modify or change their duties and that no member of the bureau shall assume any functions or responsibility other than those

[1] This provision was amended however, under chapter 355 of the laws of 1918 to provide a compensation per member of $10.00 per diem for each day spent in the work of the council. Necessary traveling expenses were also defrayed by the state.

delegated by the commission, and all questions of policy and all questions of publication shall be determined and approved by the Industrial Commission.

Resolved, That Nelle Swartz[1] be, and she hereby is, appointed chief of the Bureau of Women in Industry.[2]

One looks for an almost magic increase of accomplishment in the enforcement of laws as a result of this thoroughgoing reorganization. With well paid commissioners and deputy commissioners, and with clerks, inspectors, and assistants, the future was promising. A Monthly Bulletin was published by the commission giving statistics of inspection the value of which was at once manifest. Formerly, the review of the work of the inspection bureau did not appear in detailed form until the issue of the annual report, long after immediate need of facts had passed. A Safety Manual was also authorized by the commission to be compiled and printed for the use of inspectors and manufacturers of the state. The "block system" of factory inspection was established at this time in New York City, to the end that each block was to be inspected as a unit. This minimized the danger of neglecting any plants and was a way of keeping account of the exact area covered by each inspector.

But though pronounced improvement was made in securing obedience to the labor laws, the reports of the commission as it proceeded in its work indicate many difficulties. The seat of the trouble was not new,—it was the old twofold problem of the conflict of interests on the one hand, and the gross lack of funds for a sufficient force of employees on the other.

By 1917 the block system of inspection had made it pos-

[1] *Monthly Labor Review*, November, 1918, pp. 192-193.

[2] Miss Swartz has remained chief of the bureau through the changes in state administration and the accompanying vicissitudes of the Department of Labor.

sible for the first time in the history of the Department of Labor to inspect within a fiscal year all the factories and factory buildings in the state.[1] (There were 59,978 factories in the state at that time.) But compliance visits as well as inspection visits are always necessary if the law is to be enforced. These could not be made consistently for the corps of inspectors was woefully inadequate and the salaries were not "commensurate with the duties required." This was true not only for factories, but for mercantile establishments and tenement house work-shops as well, while at the same time the bureau of inspection had greatly increased its standards and the amount of work it required to be performed. Requests for relief from this pressure were and have since been made as regularly as the annual reports of the commission were issued, and, in 1917, First deputy Commissioner James L. Gernon reported that,—"Because the present salary for first grade inspectors is less than the salary paid many mechanics, many capable men on the civil service list have refused to accept employment with the State for less salary than is paid mechanics, and thus the State loses the services of persons whose practical training would fit them for the duties of an inspector." [2]

Nevertheless serious and renewed efforts were made by the commissioner and new and encouraging records were made from year to year. For 1919, Deputy Commissioner Gernon attributed the better results in administration of the law solely to greatly improved methods of procedure and loyal assistance of employees in spite of a particularly hard year. Hard because of increased duties due to amendments to the laws with no increase in the working force; hard also because of the severe influenza epidemic which depleted the force, leaving vacancies which could not be filled quickly at

[1] *Annual Report of the Industrial Commission*, 1917. p. 42.

[2] *Op. cit.*, p. 60.

the salaries provided.[1] Also the jurisdiction of the division of mercantile inspection was this year extended to all cities of the state, adding forty-nine smaller cities with a population of 1,500,000 to the four first and second class cities—New York, Buffalo, Rochester, and Syracuse.

Statistical data concerning the work of enforcement form a substantial part of the yearly reports of the Department of Labor from which brief tables have been taken as presented below. But in order for figures of this sort to be correctly interpreted some recapitulation and preparation is necessary.

As has been said, for the majority of legislative requirements, orders are given when inspectors discover violation, and the case is not referred to counsel for prosecution until repeated warnings have failed to secure compliance. When violations of certain laws are discovered, however—notably the child labor law, the provisions regarding the hours of women, the one-day-of-rest-in-seven act, and the prohibition of locked doors—no orders are given but the violation is referred directly to counsel for prosecution. The following tables give general statistics concerning orders, compliances, prosecutions, and fines since the first year of the Industrial Commission, 1915. Some idea of the magnitude of the task of enforcing labor laws may be gained by their perusal. In reading Table I it should be kept in mind that discoveries of violation which necessitate orders for reform, are limited to the number of inspections that can be made, and that a thorough tour of establishments can be made but seldom—for factories on an average of once a year, for mercantile establishments even less than that. This necessarily leaves the greater part of the period of operation of plants entirely unmolested by law-enforcing agents.

[1] *Annual Report of the Industrial Commission*, 1919, p. 31.

TABLE I

LABOR LAW ADMINISTRATION STATISTICS OF THE NEW YORK DEPARTMENT OF LABOR, BUREAU OF INSPECTION, FROM OCTOBER 1, 1914 TO JUNE 30, 1923, SHOWING ORDERS ISSUED TO FACTORIES AND COMPLIANCES SECURED IN EACH FISCAL YEAR *

Fiscal Year	Orders	Compliances
Oct. 1, 1914–Sept. 30, 1915	163,968	135,697
Oct. 1, 1915–June 30, 1916	116,399†	125,889‡
July 1, 1916–June 30, 1917	173,982	206,625‡
July 1, 1917–June 30, 1918	135,703	152,361‡
July 1, 1918–June 30, 1919	160,631	155,746
July 1, 1919–June 30, 1920	187,272	179,688
July 1, 1920–June 30, 1921	190,506	197,034‡
July 1, 1921–June 30, 1922	123,815	132,435‡
July 1, 1922–June 30, 1923	129,812§	130,350§

* *Annual Reports of the Industrial Commissioner* for 1921, p. 100 and 1922, p. 66.

† For nine months, the fiscal year having been changed to begin in July instead of September.

‡ More compliances than orders indicate that some orders issued in the previous year and left outstanding, were complied with in the current year.

§ Taken from the typewritten report of the chief of inspection before its publication, by courtesy of the industrial commissioner and the chief of inspection of the Department of Labor.

Another fact that must be kept in mind in reading Table II is that already suggested,—that the number of prosecutions reported have only a faint connection with the number of fines imposed. For the police magistrates and the courts frequently fail to coöperate in carrying their part of the prosecution procedure, thinking of a case in its separate and individual aspects rather than as an important step in the law-enforcing process. To have recalcitrant employers dealt with vigorously, followed by a fair sentence imposed not only for punishment of the individual but also to foster respect for the law, is indispensable to law enforcement. But in spite of this need, a surprising number of sentences are suspended, and not infrequently (according to unpublished report) are fines remitted!

TABLE II

PROSECUTIONS COMPLETED AND AMOUNT OF FINES IMPOSED IN FACTORIES AND MERCANTILE ESTABLISHMENTS AS SHOWN BY THE NEW YORK STATE BUREAU OF INSPECTION FOR THE FISCAL YEARS FROM 1914-1915 TO 1922-1923 *

	Prosecutions Completed			Fines Imposed			
Fiscal Year	Factories	Mercantile Establishments	Total	Factories	Mercantile Establishments	Total	Average fine per prosecution
1914–1915....	845	876	1,721	$4,387	$5,842	$10,229	$5.94
1915–1916....	1,923	840	2,763	9,856	6,790	16,646	6.38
1916–1917....	2,835	1,617	4,452	25,250	12,385	37,635	8.45
1917–1918....	1,301	934	2,235	13,755	7,950	21,705	9.76
1918–1919....	1,656	1,155	2,811	12,890	7,085	19,975	7.10
1919–1920....	1,661	1,072	2,733	12,720	9,550	22,270	8.11
1920–1921....	1,074	371	1,445	7,985	3,135	11,120	7.69
1921–1922....	523	209	731	4,955	1,515	6,470	8.85
1922–1923*...	765	340	1,105	7,830	2,200	10,030	9.07

* *Annual Reports of the Industrial Commissioner*, 1921, p. 113 and 1922, p. 65. Data for 1922-1923 were taken from the typewritten report of the chief of inspection before its publication, by courtesy of the industrial commissioner and the chief of inspection of the Department of Labor.

The figures showing the average fine per capita in this table are worthless except as they indicate that a high percentage of prosecutions must have been completed each year for which no fines were imposed. As the minimum fine for a first offence is $20, the greatest number that could have received fines in 1915 and in 1923, for example, would be a little over 500, whereas well over a thousand prosecutions were completed in each of these years. This would indicate that from 50 to 70 per cent of the cases went unfined, and much more than that proportion if there were many second and third offence fines which are by law from $50 to $250, and "at least $250," respectively. This, of course, is to say nothing of the extent to which fines were remitted after they had been imposed, which is a difficult fact to secure.

The above tables carry us through political changes in the administration of New York labor laws into the present regime at Albany, which will be described shortly. But here it is of importance to pause for further understanding of the difficulties and discouragements that come to the officials of law enforcement because of lack of coöperation from some of the courts and magistrates. In the January 1920 issue of the *Bulletin* of the New York State Industrial Commission, Bernard L. Shientag, chief counsel, discussed the menace of suspended sentences in labor law cases. In addition to inadequate fines for completed prosecutions which we have just considered, counsel showed that in 1918, sentences were suspended in 58 per cent of the cases of conviction for violating the labor law in New York City, and in 75 per cent of the cases in the remainder of the state. And also that this record was practically repeated in 1919.

Acting upon the necessity of attempting a remedy for this appalling number of suspended sentences, Counsel Shientag advised the Industrial Commission, in 1919, to experiment with a plan of enforcement which was proving effective in New York City, by which "better and more hearty cooperation from employers" could be obtained. The plan was to summon an employer, who was charged with a minor violation of the law and who failed to comply with the order issued by the commission, to appear before the commission and show cause why he should not be prosecuted. The theory was that many of these cases would never have to be carried into magistrates' courts where they have so largely resulted in suspended sentences, and that the personal contact of employers with the commission would bring a better understanding and more respect for the law. Mr. Shientag explained,

The aim of the Commission is to secure compliance with the law through voluntary action of employers whenever possible, and better results will be obtained along these lines, if the Commission itself takes up first offense violations of the Labor Law and explains to employers directly the necessity of complying with the law and the consequences of subsequent violation. This procedure on the part of the Commission is bound to result in fewer suspended sentences when it finds itself obliged to take employers to court.[1]

The notice that was then being sent with successful results to employers in New York City, called the "departmental summons," was as follows:

STATE OF NEW YORK. DEPARTMENT OF LABOR.

In the Name of the People of the State of New York.

To ....

YOU ARE HEREBY SUMMONED to appear before the Industrial Commission of the State of New York at 124 East 28th Street, New York City, 5th Floor, on the .... day of .... 192 ...... at 2 o'clock in the afternoon, TO SHOW CAUSE why a prosecution should not be commenced against you on complaint of Inspector .... for violation of the Labor Law, to wit: ....
....
and upon your failure to appear at the time and place herein mentioned prosecution will be commenced without further notice.

Dated at the City of New York, this .... day of .... 192..

INDUSTRIAL COMMISSION OF THE STATE OF NEW YORK.

Edward F. Boyle,
Chairman

(Seal)

Bernard L. Shientag,
Counsel

[1] *Annual Report of the Industrial Commission*, 1920, pp. 233-234.

This plan was adopted in 1922 in several other cities of New York State, the Industrial Commissioner taking the place of the Industrial Commission in the hearings after the reorganization of the Labor Department explained below. The plan is now referred to as the " special calendar " and its scope has been extended to include first violations of the child labor law, illegal hours, and day-of-rest laws. In the *Industrial Bulletin* for May, 1922, the following encouraging report was given:

Not only has this method been effective in procuring compliance with the law, but it has eliminated to a very marked degree the irritation caused by criminal prosecution for the minor violations of the Labor Laws. The records that have been kept since the plan was inaugurated in the New York City district show that out of 1,500 cases in which summonses have been issued and that have come before Commissioner Sayer for consideration, complete compliance was obtained in nearly all of them, and in less than fifty cases out of the entire number was it found necessary to send the case to the courts for criminal prosecution.

The report also says that the first " calendars " were held in Buffalo, Rochester, Syracuse and Albany in April (1922) " and the outcome in each instance was the same as it was in New York City."

An attempt to assist the Labor Department in reducing the number of suspended sentences and insufficient fines has been inaugurated by the New York Consumers' League which has formed a law enforcement committee. In its December *Bulletin* of 1923 the league announced that,—" Representatives have been appointed by all coöperating organizations, who will attend every session of the courts when labor cases are tried in Brooklyn and Manhattan. . . . The representatives . . . will keep careful records of all cases handled in court and indicate whether or not they agree with sentences imposed." After a six months' study of these cases, the league recently urged reform in the direction of having such cases heard "before only those magistrates who have an intelligent and sympathetic attitude towards the enforcement of labor legislation."[1] The results of this and the other attempts to obtain better coöperation from the courts in their important rôle toward law enforcement will be watched with interest.

Returning now to the political side of our discussion, the year 1921 marked another reorganization of the Department of Labor in New York. This was the time of the defeat by the republicans of the democratic party with Alfred Smith the candidate for re-election as governor. The new republican governor, Nathan L. Miller, in his first message to the legislature, in January, dwelt upon the evils existing in the administration of the Industrial Commission because of the division of authority and responsibility among its five co-equal members. He alleged a certain competition to have emerged among the commissioners that brought a tendency to enlarge their bureaus and activities unduly. A reform of the system was deemed necessary, therefore, which would concentrate authority and responsibility and at the same time carry on the judicial and legislative activities of the department. Thus the representative Industrial Commission was abolished and in its place was appointed a single commissioner with full and complete administrative power. "He was given power to reorganize the entire Department, to abolish bureaus or divisions, or to consolidate them and rearrange their functions, or to create new ones to take their place. He was given power likewise, to abolish positions, drop employees or transfer them from one position to another."[2]

[1] *Bulletin of the Consumers' League of New York*, April, 1924.

[2] *The Industrial Bulletin*, September, 1922, p. 220.

In the reorganization act approved by the Governor on March 9, 1921, provision was also made for an Industrial Board whose function was to hear "appeals from orders of the Commissioner issued by him to employers or factory owners directing compliance with various provisions of the Labor Law, and also applications for variations from the provisions of the Labor Law or of the Industrial Code."[1] Proposed new rules or modifications in the industrial code were also to be considered by the board for adoption.

Three members constituted the Industrial Board, namely: John D. Higgins of Oswego, Chairman; T. V. O'Connor[2] of Buffalo; and Rosalie Loew Whitney of Brooklyn; these took office on April 15, 1921.[3] Each member of the board was to receive an annual salary of $8,000 which was also the salary of the commissioner. One deputy commissioner appointed by the commissioner at a salary of $7,000 was to take the place of the three former deputy commissioners as well as to assume charge of the bureau of inspection, the bureau of research and codes, the bureau of mediation and arbitration. The chiefs of these bureaus were to report to the deputy commissioner until otherwise notified.

Mr. Henry D. Sayer was appointed to the important office of Industrial Commissioner, having formerly been secretary to the Industrial Commission and chairman of the Industrial Council. He appointed Martin H. Christopherson of Yonkers, deputy commissioner—a former member of the Industrial Council. Mr. Sayer expressed publicly his belief in the

[1] *Annual Report of the Industrial Commissioner*, 1921, p. 9.

[2] Richard H. Curran, of Rochester, was appointed upon the resignation of Mr. O'Connor who resigned to accept a position with the United States Shipping Board.

[3] The members of the Industrial Commission which now ceased to function were, Edward F. Boyle, of New York, Chairman; James M. Lynch of Syracuse; Henry D. Sayer of Richmond Hill; Frances Perkins of New York; and Cyrus W. Phillips of Rochester.

new organization and the possibility of its effecting at once greater economy and greater efficiency. The appropriation for the fiscal year was cut $900,000,—from $2,400,000 for the year just passed to $1,500,000 for the present year although the old commission had requested a total appropriation of $3,000,000 for the present year—just double that which was now to finance the work of the department. Nevertheless, the new commissioner exhorted the officers and employees of the department to increase their accomplishments by greater effort and a better sense of coöperation for the common end of enforcing the law. "Let us try by the earnestness of our work to make up for our decreased numbers," he urged. "If each one will try to do just a little more than he or she did formerly, we will not be doing any more than is rightly expected of us, but the total increase in the output of the Department will be tremendous."[1]

Speaking of his achievements about a year later, Commissioner Sayer said with some pride,

> We completed the year within that appropriation and we did all the work that was necessary to be done. True, we lopped off some of the frills, we cut out some of the useless jobs, and we made everyone give an honest day's work for a day's pay. The actual saving over the preceding year was roundly $1,000,000 and over what the old Commission had estimated as necessary of $1,500,000 [*sic*].

Economy at the expense of the work, of course, is not economy but the records of the Department show that the average case is disposed of more quickly, that compensation

[1] *The Bulletin* for July and August, 1921, p. 173. The commissioner's exhortation reminds one of the reasoning of Sir William Petty in the seventeenth century in his suggestion for the increase of the income of the British government. Sir William's plan was to secure the needed revenue through taxation believing that the people could bear a tax one-twentieth greater than before by eating one-twentieth less, and the difference to them would be too small to be felt.

reaches the beneficiary more promptly than ever before in the history of the Department.

While centering responsibility for administration we retained the benefit of collective judgment in matters of hearing and determination of claims, and in the adoption of Industrial Code rules. . . .

This system has worked out very advantageously.[1]

At the time of this report the New York *Evening Post*, which supported Governor Miller for re-election, conducted a "first-hand investigation" of the reorganized labor department which was published in a series of articles by Adele Shaw, November 2, 3, 6 and 7. These articles told a different story from that of Commissioner Sayer,—that the "number of factory inspections has been cut to a point that it is impossible to carry out the provisions of the law," and "even the supervisor of inspection work makes no pretense that the department is able to carry out the law."

The number of inspectors, according to this reporter, was cut 40 per cent—from 213 to 134; New York City with its 35,000 factories was reduced to 43 inspectors from the former 70. Comparisons in the degree and numbers of inspections could not be made with those of the previous year in the case of factories, because the method of taking records was changed at the time the force was cut. The records concerning homework showed 115,000 less inspections than in the year before, and 136 children were found at work whereas 362 had been discovered the year before. In factories only 68 children were discovered at work as compared with 568 of the preceding year. For mercantile establishments the following comparisons were recorded:

	1921–1922	*1920–1921*
Orders issued	74,341	114,282
Compliance visits	28,468	47,709
Compliances	74,123	114,274
Prosecutions	193	313

[1] *The Industrial Bulletin* for September, 1922, pp. 220-221.

While the report of this investigation was not entirely adverse (some economies were noted such as the inspection of mercantile establishments and factories which was now conducted by the same inspector when under the same roof), these records seem to force the conclusion that the inspection work was less thoroughly done than in the previous year. For it is not reasonable to conclude that there grew so much less need of inspection orders, and prosecutions in a single year as are indicated.[1] Moreover, according to another authority, we are informed that "at the same time the civil service was flouted and 'political pressure' was evident in the filling of positions."[2] The State Federation of Labor, keeping in touch with the work of the Labor Department, took the position that "the department as a whole is doing the best it can under the appropriation given to it, but it is obvious that it is a physical impossibility for the inspectors to properly cover the territory assigned to them."[3]

With the return of Alfred Smith to the governor's chair in 1923, the form into which the Labor Department had been reorganized under Governor Miller remained practically the same. The personnel was changed in two important cases: Bernard L. Shientag was made Industrial Commissioner upon the resignation of Mr. Sayer, and Frances Perkins was appointed to fill the position on the Industrial Board made vacant by the expiration of Mrs. Whitney's term of office. Mr. Shientag, it will be remembered, was associate counsel to the Factory Investigating Commission of which Governor Smith was the vice-chairman, and in 1919 he was appointed counsel to the Indus-

[1] Compare also the marked reduction in orders, compliances, prosecutions, and fines for the fiscal years 1921-1922 as already shown in the tables on pages 296-297.

[2] *American Labor Legislation Review*, December, 1922, p. 191.

[3] New York *Evening Post*, November 3, 1922.

trial Commission. Frances Perkins will also be remembered as a member of the Factory Investigating Commission, and later, a member of the Industrial Commission until its dissolution in 1921.

The policy of the new administration underwent a greater change than its form. In his message of greetings to the Labor Department, Mr. Shientag assured his " co-workers " that " the Labor Department will soon be restored to a high level of efficiency, where it can render the maximum amount of useful service to the People of the State."

" The policy of the present State Administration," he explained, " is to give the Labor Department adequate facilities with which to carry on its important work. Lack of help, insufficient appropriations, will no longer be an excuse for the unjustifiable delay in compensation cases and for non-compliance with important Labor Law orders which I find today. . . ." The commissioner warned that no one should be misled by claiming to have a " pull " with the commissioner. There is no such person. If you do the right thing, the Commissioner will stand behind you. You may expect no consideration otherwise." Referring to the substantially increased budget for the new work, Mr. Shientag said:

> Every employee in this department will receive a square deal from the Commissioner and merit and efficiency will be given full recognition. I have tried to do this in the revised budget which I was called upon to submit within a few weeks after I took office. If I have failed to do full justice to individuals, that will be remedied at my earliest opportunity.[1]

We have seen that Commissioner Shientag is receiving coöperation toward better law enforcement from the Consumers' League and other organizations, and that new

[1] *The Industrial Bulletin* for February, 1923, p. 103.

methods of handling violations by employers are being developed in order to minimize court procedure and the embarrassment caused by suspended sentences and inadequate fines.

In addition to these efforts, a return to a representative commission form of labor law administration in New York seems imminent. That is, unless some political machine prevents such a development. The single commissioner plan, introduced in 1921, gives opportunity for personal bias and partiality on the one hand, and to undue criticism on the other. The latter opportunity has recently been realized in the spectacular charge of Mark A. Daly, secretary of the Associated Industries, Inc., that there had been a "break down" of the Labor Department from inefficiency and extravagance. An investigation was demanded, which Governor Smith surprised the "Industries" by conducting himself. The accusers failed to make a case, their charges being proved unfounded.

This type of accusation could not be easily carried to the extent to which Mr. Daly went, were the power and responsibility of administration lodged with a commission made up of employers and employees such as is true of the Wisconsin Industrial Commission. The view of the American Association of Labor Legislation is made very clear in the following lines:

Many conclusions can be drawn from the various destructive, demoralizing effects of political reorganization and of complacent inefficiency even under the not unmixed merits of the civil service. But outstanding and supremely important is the evident desirabilty in the great industrial state of New York of the industrial commission form of administration. The ambitious efficiency engineer, with a "call" to reorganize government departments, in accordance with his own particular symmetrical chart, may consider the commission form less

" efficient ", but, despite this superficial viewpoint, it offers in its own human field perhaps the only plan for highest efficiency. . . . .

. . . In New York State it appears desirable to have a representative industrial commisson not only to protect a good and able administrator from unwarranted interference like the recent contemptible partisan attack by Mark Daly—an authorized attack that could not have happened under the earlier representative commission—but also to keep the administration of labor laws continuously upon the high plane of the welfare of the whole community.[1]

PART II: ENFORCEMENT OF LAWS RELATING TO WOMEN

Some consideration of the practical force of New York statutes that apply to both men and women, or only to men, was attempted earlier when the laws were described. The degree of enforcement of those acts passed by the legislature for the specific protection of women may now receive more detailed discussion. Enough has been said of the difficulties of administering laws, however, to prevent too high expectation of their enforcement. The continuous lack of an adequate force of inspectors and clerical assistants, the recalcitrance of a few large employers, the ignorance, indifference or fear of the majority of employees, the pushing and pulling of special groups, the failure of the courts to demand respect for the law by consistently imposing sufficient penalties; these, and other difficulties, sometimes more pronounced, sometimes less, according to changing political bias, cramp the free life of any laws for the protection of our working people. And special laws invariably bring with them special problems of enforcement.

There are little satisfactory data concerning the enforcement of special laws for women. One is obliged to rely a great deal upon general statements, supplemented by such

[1] *American Labor Legislation Review*, March, 1924, pp. 93-94.

data as the Department of Labor has been able to gather. An attempt will be made to combine information from these two sources as nearly as it can be done at this time, by an analysis of the methods and extent of enforcement of these laws.

HOURS OF LABOR—DAY WORK

Factories

It will be recalled that the 1881 provision for seats for women in mercantile establishments was still-born, and that 1899 marked the first legislation for adult women that survived as effective law.

Reports concerning the enforcement of the act of 1899 that restricted the hours of all females in factories were slow in appearing. There may have been a delay in inspection as well as in reports, as a result of the disruption of the labor offices in 1901 when their consolidation under the Department of Labor occurred. It was with Commissioner Tecumseh Sherman's annual report for 1905 that the story began. And he opened his discussion with a sigh!—"Section 77 of the Labor Law is in bad shape." The regulation concerning the work of children under sixteen years was generally observed, but the ten-hour day for women and male minors under eighteen[1] was "undoubtedly often violated. Slight violations of the ten-hour rule, where they are deliberate and with the connivance of employees, are hard to discover, and it is difficult to obtain the evidence necessary to convict therefore."[2] But excessive violations were traced and the commissioner deemed that the enforcement was sufficient to bring "a general and beneficent shortening of the hours of the classes referred to."

[1] In this instance, as is usually the case, by "male minors" is meant boys between the ages of sixteen and eighteen years, by "children" is meant those under sixteen years, and by "women," all females over sixteen years.

[2] *Annual Report of the Commissioner of Labor*, 1905, p. 29.

By 1907, however, the problem became more grim. Commissioner Sherman again wailed in his opening line,—"This is a most unsatisfactory subject."[1] "Earnest efforts were made to enforce the limitation of ten hours a day and sixty hours a week, but there were so many defects in the provisions of the act and "so much trouble and opposition caused by the least important regulations" that an endeavor was made only to enforce the sixty hour per week provision. Even that proved unenforceable, however, for lack of sufficient evidence. Prosecutions could only be executed for gross or long-continued violations. Toward the middle of the year the inspectors became so exhausted with even this effort that attempts to enforce were relaxed until the 1907 modifications could take effect. In the meantime visits were made to employers in anticipation of the new provisions (a six-day week, and exceptions to the ten-hour limit) and instructions and advice were given or mailed to them. It was hoped that the greater flexibility of the new ten-hour provision would meet the convenience of employers more nearly than the old regulation, and would therefore provoke less opposition on their part. It seemed reasonable that more hours of work a day could be endured without injury or weariness for four or five days a week than for six days. The 1899 statute "was absurd in practice, for it forbade fifty-five hours work in five days if nothing were worked on the sixth day, but allowed not only fifty-five but even fifty-nine hours work in five days if one hour were worked on the sixth." And furthermore, the commissioner was convinced that some manufacturers could not possibly state at the beginning of the week what the week's hours of work for women would be. He welcomed the new provision that permitted a more flexible arrangement for recording hours for these manufacturers, and expressed assurance that evasion could now be prevented.

[1] *Op. cit.*, 1907, pp. 1, 47.

In spite of the greatly increased elasticity in the factory law created by the 1907 amendment, to which the inspectors had pinned their hopes, troubles did not cease. This time provocation to violations arose, for the most part, from conditions of industry outside of the factories affected by the factory law. (1) Mercantile establishments were not subject to like restrictions. During these years the work of women over the age of twenty-one was not regulated by statute; and also restrictions for all minor workers were waived during the Christmas holiday season. Moreover the existing mercantile law was slackly administered by local boards of health, thus increasing the advantages of merchants over manufacturers in their bargaining power. (2) New York manufacturers insisted that they were and would be handicapped in their competitive relations so long as other states, especially New Jersey, had no like restrictions upon the work of females. (3) Though laundries are factories within the meaning of the law, wide exemptions existed for them in practice.

In addition to these external influences against the enforcement of the factory law, there were strongly resisting forces within its own jurisdiction. For example, canners were both gross and overt violators, giving "necessity" as their only and sufficient excuse. Dressmakers, milliners and certain classes of sweat-shops were also persistently lawless and remained more or less unmolested because they were too numerous to be watched by the existing force of inspectors.

Because of this commonly existing lack of enforcement of the law in specific industries, therefore, and because of the absence of similar legislation in other industries and in neighboring competitive states, manufacturers became dulled to the meaning of the law in their conviction that it was unfair discrimination against themselves. Thus the regulations of women's hours in factories became a dead letter.

In 1911 and 1912, witnesses before the Factory Investigating Commission deprecated the form of the New York law in that it allowed overtime regularly and, in certain cases, irregularly, in addition to the ten-hour day. They criticized just those provisions that had been made by the 1907 amendment, after it had been discovered to the satisfaction of the inspectors and the commissioner that an inflexible law could not be enforced. They asserted that the New York factory law was the only one of its kind among the states, and that while uniform laws can be enforced, irregular laws are a failure. This was particularly true of the New York law, Josephine Goldmark held, where overtime work for a certain number of days each week was allowed, and employers were further permitted to dispense with the usual posting of hours when the "nature of the work" makes it impossible to chart them in advance.[1] "Every possible difficulty" was thus put in the way of enforcement.

Florence Kelley, for the same reasons, denounced the law as "non-enforceable and illusory, and therefore demoralizing to everyone concerned."[2] She pointed out that in order to convict an employer of violating the law, it would be necessary for an inspector to be present and watching a particular worker throughout an entire week. "For facility of enforcement," she urged that "the presence of women and minors in a work room at times other than those posted as their working periods should be forbidden, and should be made *prima facie* evidence of illegal employment." This should apply to all work places instead of only to some, as at present. "The great need is for simplicity and uniformity. . . . We recommend making hours of labor uniform for women and minors."[3]

[1] *Preliminary Report of the Factory Investigating Commission*, 1912, vol. iii, p. 1607.

[2] *Op. cit.*, vol. i, p. 651.

[3] *Op. cit.*, pp. 650-651.

Representatives from several different industries bore witness to the impotence of the law. Jesse Walker, Troy textile worker, testified that many of the women in textile mills worked more than sixty hours a week, that upon receipt of their complaints, an inspector would come and stop the practice for a short time, but that they had never been able to secure any convictions of manufacturers. "It seems, according to the law," he explained, "they must have a statement from one of the girls who work that much, and they find great unwillingness to make any statement, therefore we could not get any convictions. . . . They are unorganized and if they make such a statement they will sacrifice their jobs."

Another witness, Bernard Weinstein, secretary of the United Hebrew Trades in New York City, testified to the ineffectiveness of the act regulating hours of women in the fur trade. Especially in the small shops men and women worked ordinarily between ten and twelve hours a day, he said, and in busy seasons—fourteen hours. A factory inspector made them a visit every three years instead of every year. Employers were particular to have on their walls the sheet of rules and regulations which seemed to them to complete their obligations for the protection of their workers. The rules were for display by the employer instead of a guide for the health of his employees. ". . . he does not care anything about them, or whether they get sick or not, because he can get plenty of them," the witness concluded.[1]

Upon further investigation by the factory commission flagrant violations of the regulation of women's hours in book-binderies were also discovered,—"In 152 cases, instances of illegal overtime were found among the bindery workers in 42 binderies. In eighteen per cent. of these cases—almost one in every five—work continued until 10

[1] *Op. cit.*, vol. iii, p. 1627.

P. M. or much later at night, in addition to the day's work." [1] And the report continues, "The detailed reports of working days longer than twelve hours . . . . show appalling conditions. These hours represent actual working time, after deducting the length of noon hours and the time allowed for supper. In four positions the day was 12¼ hours long; in seven, 12½; in three, 12¾; in nine, 13; in one, 13½; in two 14; in two, 15½; in two 16; in two 18: in one, 19½; in one, 21½; and in one, 22."

In October, 1912, the new 54-hour law for women in New York factories went into effect. The Preliminary Report of the Factory Investigating Commission had been transmitted to the legislature on March 1, 1912, and doubtless influenced the legislature directly toward the passage of the stricter law. Nevertheless it would seem that the enforceability of this act was no greater than that of the old statute which the commission had caused to be displaced. For, while the maximum working day was reduced, the clauses were retained which permitted irregular hours of work—the act had become neither "flat" nor "uniform."

The force of the 54-hour law was seen at once to be endangered by the long-entrenched custom of homework by women. Women worked in factories nine or ten hours a day and then took work home for the night and Sundays. The Factory Investigating Commission reported that employers in the embroidery industry said that 90 per cent of their shop hands were obliged to take their work home at night in rush seasons.[2] No legislative regulations of hours are or can be made effective for home workers, and thus as long as homework exists, it would seem to remain a challenge to the enforcement of regulative factory laws.

[1] *Report of the Factory Investigating Commission*, 1913, vol. i, pp. 199-200.

[2] *Op. cit.*, 1913, vol. i, p. 108.

Little has been reported in recent years concerning the enforcement of hour laws in specific industries. But the general trend is surely toward a shorter working day, as we shall see later. And such a trend is, of course, all favorable to better enforcement of a law requiring shorter hours. Nevertheless a recent report of the Bureau of Women in Industry shows that in six of twenty-one shops in the outer wear knit goods industry "*women were found to reach 60* [hours] *a week and over.* In one shop employing 20 women and 10 men, the working hours were from 8 A. M. to 8:30 P. M.—an 11½-hour day." For four weeks, two shops had worked a 65-hour week, and in other shops, hours of some women and men ran up to nearly seventy.[1]

We are not able to say how many times this condition would be found to be repeated were data available. Practically the only regularly gathered data we have in New York State are to be found in the statistical tables of the Industrial Board and Industrial Commission which appear in the monthly and annual reports. It seems best not to include data from these tables in our discussion, however, because of the many variables that have to be considered in their interpretation. Also, any statistics of inspection, at least in New York State, necessarily give an inadequate picture of violations because of the impossibility, so far, of sufficient inspection. As John L. Gernon, chief inspector, puts it, "when four times as many inspections should be made as are made, one has to form his own opinions as to the fullness of inspection reports." Moreover, the working hours of women are treated together in the tables, with no distinction between day work and night work. And, until the 1920 report, there was no distinction made in the tabulations between women and female minors—the two classifications

[1] *The Outer Wear Knit Goods Industry, Bulletin No. 117*, p. 10. State Department of Labor, March, 1923.

given being women and male minors. These deficiencies are probably due, in the main, to continuous insufficiency of clerical service, because of which many valuable figures have remained untabulated.

1. *Canneries*

Canneries are factories within the meaning of the law, but the exceptional conditions of the canning industry owing to its seasonal character have always demanded special attention by those attempting to secure protection for employees. Legislation has become difficult, but enforcement of legislation has been immeasurably more so. Cannery proprietors have been consistent violators of the law, and their position in the matter has been more or less condoned by the public as we shall see.

In 1907, when amendments to the ten-hour law were being introduced to bring greater flexibility and better enforcement, it has been seen that special provisions for canneries were proposed. The European precedent of permitting females over eighteen years of age to work in canneries sixty-six hours a week for a maximum of six weeks a year was urged by the labor commissioner but defeated by philanthropic and labor organizations. The commissioner maintained that in industries such as canneries work would not be regularized, and that enforcement would be more nearly possible if the peculiarities of the industry were recognized in the law. He explained that "overtime during rush periods or seasons would be counterbalanced by reduced hours in slack periods or seasons." [1]

With this publicly announced disapproval of this provision of the law by the chief administrator of the law, it calls for no great imagination in the absence of statistics, to form a fair conception of the force of the factory act as it applied to canneries.

[1] *Annual Report of the Commissioner of Labor*, 1907, p. I. 50.

The open violation of this statute was a cause of active concern to the new commissioner, John Williams, as expressed in his report for 1908. He wrote,[1] "Startling allegations of inordinately long hours for female employees and utter disregard of child labor laws have been made against the proprietors of factories in this group. . . . It is contrary to the spirit of our institutions that there should be one kind of justice for the ordinary manufacturer and another kind for the violator who happens to be engaged in a certain business. Such a state of facts makes for a contempt of all law. It demands thorough consideration with a view to a remedy, so that the obligation to obey statute law may be enforced without discrimination."

While the zeal of Commissioner Williams was praiseworthy, the next few months proved that he was probably farther removed from a realization of the whole truth than his predecessor had been. He ordered an official investigation of canneries in respect to their observance of the law. Prosecutions were instituted contemporaneously with the investigation. But, ironically, prosecutions of even glaring violations proved to be a "waste of time," for in the proceedings brought, though accompanied by clear evidence of guilt, defendants were discharged or acquitted—the grand jury failing to report a "true bill." The commissioner pronounced the situation intolerable, explaining that failure to secure convictions was owing "not to any lack on the part of the officers of the Bureau of Factory Inspection, but to the utter failure of the minor courts and juries to appreciate the significance of their course in respect-thereof." He asserted that there were no such obstacles to the enforcement of the law in factories other than canneries.[2]

[1] *Op. cit.*, 1908, p. I. 30-31.

[2] The obstacles in factories had also been found to be insurmountable, however, as may be recalled by turning back to page 310.

A recognition of this situation was made by the Factory Investigating Commission which reported that the sixty-hour law for women in factories had never been obeyed in canneries up to the year 1911.[1] Practically speaking, there had not been an attempt to enforce it, and if attempts were made they had been successfully opposed or evaded. One investigator visited a cannery which had been in operation six years but had never before seen an inspector's shadow. Another small factory had had no inspection during the full ten years of its canning operations.

In 1912 the canning industry of the state became legally what it had been illegally for many years past, an entirely unregulated industry during the four months of the rush season. This victory of the canners, after a five-year struggle, constituted the first exception made to the factory law. But it lasted for only one year. For there were about 7000 women employed in the canneries of the state, and, in 1913, the Factory Investigating Commission succeeded in retrieving legal regulation of their hours throughout the working year. In view of the seasonality of the industry, however, a special twelve-hour day and sixty-hour week were permitted during the peak season of the pea crop. This, as we have already seen, is the New York law in regard to canneries today. The prophecy was that there would be no trouble in enforcing this measure, for it was fair to industry; also that the public was now aware of the inhuman hours in cannery employment, and would demand prompt and effective enforcement. The supporters of the act believed that no local court or jury would now "lightly disregard the laws the legislature will enact."[2]

To test the enforceability and adequacy of the new act,

[1] *Op. cit.*, 1913, vol. i, p. 169.

[2] *Second Report of the Factory Investigating Commission*, 1913, vol. i, p. 174.

an investigation was promptly made, the report of which composed thirty-three pages of the annual report of the commissioner of labor for 1914. "How did the present law work in 1914?" was the inquiry. Readers of the report found grounds for expecting particularly encouraging, if not representative, returns, for it was announced in the opening that "extraordinary efforts were put forth to secure a thorough enforcement of the law and to afford full information as to results. These efforts included the assignment of a considerable force of inspectors exclusively to cannery inspections with the result that frequent, amounting to nearly daily, visits to a large number of canneries for longer or shorter periods during the canning season were secured. In addition transcripts from time books were procured for the period in which the largest exemption from the general requirements of the law is permitted to canners, as further evidence of the actual results of such exemption."[1]

In summing up the findings of this test year (page 164), the commissioner cited three classes of canning manufacturers "who seem to be revealed quite clearly by the inspectors' reports; first a majority who both endeavored to and did observe the law; second a smaller number whose intent was to observe the law but who violated it under stress of special circumstances; and third, a still smaller number, though embracing a few of the largest establishments, who displayed an inclination to evade the law at will." The commissioner was emphatic in calling attention to the significance of the fact that so many canners had observed the regulations, which argued "most strongly that the law as it now stands is not an unreasonable restriction upon the industry, and it makes clear that violations of the law are chiefly the result of the individual canner's attitude toward it

[1] *Annual Report of the Commissioner of Labor*, 1914, p. 133.

and not of the necessary exigencies of his business." He urged that the provision be retained as a recognized necessity for the health of women and children—being guided by the practice of firms with high standards rather than by the low-standard firms. In the "low-standard" plants 492 women worked in violation of the maximum number of hours permitted during the peak of the season.

Because of the particular problems that canneries have offered to the law-enforcing agents in New York State, the investigation of 1914 showing the nature of these problems may be discussed in some detail,—as to the nature of permits, the cause of violations, and prosecutions.

Nature of permits. The canners applied generally for permits to operate in accordance with the law. The newly created Industrial Board granted them upon the following conditions:

> that the daily hours of labor of female employees should be posted; that floors where women were employed should be drained free of liquids or, if this could not be done, that slat platforms be provided for such floors; and that women should not be employed more than ten hours per day at work which required continuous standing or while engaged in labeling or packing cans.[1]

The last condition of employment was enacted by the board because it was felt there was no necessity for women to work more than ten hours a day on non-perishable materials. Two plants were reported as violating this condition. No violations were reported of the prohibition as to continuous standing. Three plants holding permits infracted the condition of a dry floor or slat platform, explaining either that the women refused to use them, or that they were not practicable because of the constant passing of trucks. The re-

[1] *Op. cit.*, p. 138.

quirement for posting notices and keeping time books where employers were permitted to post daily instead of weekly schedules, was frequently disobeyed. Canners explained that the receipt of raw material was so irregular that even daily notices could not be posted, and that a great deal of piece work made it impossible to keep the time of women workers.

Cause of violations of working time regulations. The reasons advanced by the canners for the overtime work of women were of four kinds, namely; (a) because of perishable materials on hand; (b) because of former loss of time from breakdown of machinery; (c) because of misunderstanding the permit; (d) because they disapproved of the law; (e) because of an inexperienced manager.

Pressure because of materials on hand was most frequently the cause of overtime violation. Specific instances from the note-books of inspectors were described, such as (pp. 142-143),—" Excessive hours up to 16¾ daily and 77 weekly. . . . Manager says storm on day previous caused delivery of peas late on Saturday; peas had to be cared for when delivered. . . . Women worked until 4 A. M. on Sunday and more than 66 hours during the week; berries and cherries would have spoiled. . . . Almost daily violations of hours for females; work after 10 P. M. Company states vinery is 12 miles distant from factory which causes loss of time in deliveries."

The breakdown of machinery was said to explain a number of cases of excess of night work and also,—" Time book shows women worked 15 hours. On reporting for work, found machinery broken which took 3 hours to repair during which time women did not work. Women worked for 12 hours after starting and were paid for 15 hours. All of the women confirm this statement " (page 144).

A number of infractions were explained on the grounds

of misunderstanding of the permits, while there were more than a few clear cases of defiance of the law. In one case,—"Company feels safe as to support of courts if prosecutions are begun. Time keeper says company is trying to make up for last year's losses by 'jamming through a big year regardless of the laws.' More than 66 hours a week worked. August 18, secretary told inspector that there would be no more overtime or illegal labor until corn ripens 'when it may be necessary'" (pp. 144-145).

At one plant it was explained that the excess of sixty-six hours occurred because the manager was not accustomed to this work, and that "lack of knowledge as to general system of handling products was principal cause for overtime" (page 147).

Prosecutions. In addition to these disappointing discoveries came the hardest blow of all to those who had dared to hope that an hour-law for women with "reasonable" exemptions for canneries would be certain to hold its own through the force of public opinion and the grace of the courts. In spite of the unprecedented effort to enforce the cannery regulations in 1914 came the disillusioning report that, "In the 12 cases charging illegal employment of women, no conviction was secured. In 7 of these cases, the charge was employment later than the posted hours, in 4 cases employment in excess of ten hours per day, and in 1 case employment in excess of twelve hours per day." [1] These were twelve of forty-two prosecutions in all, including women and children, brought against six different canneries. Thirty-nine of these forty-two cases were dismissed or acquitted, in two cases fines of $20 (the minimum) were imposed, and one case was pending as the year closed! "In no one of these cases was dismissal or acquittal secured by reason of any lack of evidence."

[1] *Op. cit.*, page 147.

Counsel for the department related the story of two cases alleging employment of women in excess of ten hours after the expiration of the twelve-hour day permit. The first trial resulted in a disagreement. A "not guilty" verdict was rendered in one case at the second trial, the second case was pending at the close of the fiscal year. The counsel's narrative was as follows:

> After a trial of two hours before a jury, which, in my judgment, was as good a jury as I have seen in a Police Court, consisting as it did of two retired merchants, an insurance agent, a banker, a meat market proprietor and a chauffeur, a verdict of "not guilty" was brought in after the jury's being out ten minutes. In this same case, on August 31st the jury disagreed after being out for two hours.
>
> There was no defense entered to the action as far as the facts were concerned, the defendant through its Attorney and President frankly admitting the employment of the women in question 12½ hours a day and their defense was one of sympathetic appeal to the jury and justification by the large amount of beans delivered to them on the day in question. The Attorney for the defendant also before the jury argued against the constitutionality of the law, which argument I met in my summing up to no avail.[1]

In three other cases charging an excess of hours of women,—

> affidavits as to the actual time worked by each of the women were introduced in evidence by the representative of the Department. Acquittal resulted in each case, however, the defense being that the women were allowed to come and go when they chose and were not *required* to work overtime.[2]

A further disillusionment to the investigators of enforce-

[1] *Op. cit.*, pp. 150-151.

[2] *Op. cit.*, p. 149.

ment was that the courts and juries were securely supported by their constituents. The bureau submitted testimony composed of signed statements, in which a department of education, a board of health, a superintendent of schools, boards of charities, doctors and others vouched for the "physically beneficial" effects of this work for children during vacations, or the advantages of so increasing the family income. It is worth while to reproduce the quotation "from a local newspaper" cited as indicative of public opinion in the vicinity toward the not-guilty verdicts rendered:

The action of the jury reflects the general sentiment of the people of this city, which is to the effect that packers of perishable products can not control the weather, consequently are not in position to regulate the amount of products which can come to the factory daily, and as the female employees are not only willing but glad to have the work, all performed under sanitary conditions and such females only performing factory work practically in the outdoor air and for only a short time in the summer, the general feeling is that the company should not be made criminally liable under these conditions. Otherwise, at times, a great amount of raw material would either deteriorate in quality before being canned or be lost entirely.

As some people express it, it is but little less than an outrage for canning factory interests and employees to be bothered as they now are as a result of legislation which is reasonable as applied to general factory work the year round but which is unreasonable as applied to conditions prevailing in the up-state canning business.

Several other alleged violations of the labor law have been instituted against the —— Company in previous years both here and in ———, where the company has a factory, and which cases were also tried before juries, with the same results as in the cases which were tried yesterday and today.[1]

[1] *Op. cit.*, p. 149.

Thus, in view of the fact that very special attention was given to enforcing the cannery law in 1914, the results could not be called successful, although even these results (with the exception of the part played by the courts) were considered encouraging by the labor commissioner.

And recent developments have shown that there was some cause for encouragement. The coming of the automobile and its use by inspectors, according to an informed member of the inspection bureau, has forced somewhat better conditions. In less recent times the inspector came to cannery centers by train of which the time of arrival was scheduled, affording ample opportunity for temporary cessation of violations of the law before his appearance. Nowadays the inspector arrives at his own time in a machine, and "eye-serving" employers run the risk of being taken unawares. It is impossible to say, of course, how much difference this would make in the extent of compliance with the law, but at any rate when the Bureau of Women in Industry investigated conditions of women's employment in the summer of 1919, they discovered that,—"The maximum number of hours, in the majority of instances, fell below the number allowed by law." [1] This is in keeping with the general reduction of hours in the state as will be noted in the next chapter.

2. *Laundries*

The enforcement of the hour law in laundries has offered another baffling problem to administration officials. Laundrymen as well as canners have always claimed a right to

[1] *Annual Report of the Industrial Commission*, 1920, p. 261. The bureau also found that, in the main, the drainage problems peculiar to canneries had been solved. Nelle Swartz, director of the bureau, said in 1922 that many of the canneries now would not be recognized as the same plants as those of 1914, so improved were they. Floors were properly drained, some being pitched on a slant. In other cases wooden platforms were used.

special privileges on the grounds that their enterprises are both seasonal and sporadic. During the old days of the sixty-hour law, factory inspectors discovered what appeared to be a combined movement on the part of a group of large steam laundries in New York City to evade this restriction upon the employment of their women workers. Girls and women from sixteen years upwards were discovered working from ten to thirteen hours a day in overheated rooms for six days a week and sometimes also a part of Sunday. One laundryman who was prosecuted, in 1906, pleaded that the law was unconstitutional, but the court declared it valid in the same year.

In December, 1911, a memorable laundry strike occurred among New York laundry workers against what they termed "endless hours." Their slogan was,—"To wash or not to wash: Ay, There's the Rub."[1] The largest percentage of workers were women, though the sorters, washers, ironers, and drivers were men who suffered from the same kind of oppression as the women. A sorter said he frequently worked from 7 a. m. to 6 a. m.—"twenty-three hours at a stretch!" Drivers' hours were "quite as outrageous." They remarked,—"Of course our brothers still have that freedom of contract which makes such inhuman hours legal, but what about our sisters?" Some women testified to having worked from sixty-two to seventy-five hours a week. One weekly program showed that from sixty-four to sixty-seven hours were worked in five days. One-half hour was permitted each day for luncheon. Several women reported that sometimes they did not reach home until two or three o'clock in the morning, having gone to work at seven the morning before—eighteen or nineteen hours a day with one-half hour off for luncheon.[2]

[1] *Life and Labor*, March, 1912, pp. 68-69.

[2] *Ibid.*

The explanation of the laundry proprietors for their violations of the law in respect to hours has been that the nature of their trade forces them to operate overtime more or less regularly one or two days a week, that their customers load them with work during the first days of the week. And again, they are not able to tell in advance what days will be long and what days will be short because of the prompt service they are required to give, especially to hotels, restaurants, and steamboat lines.

Another grave difficulty in keeping laundries within the law seems directly owing to the fact that hotel laundries are exempted. The ruling of the attorney general in 1906, remains effective today, that ". . . Hotel laundries, no matter of what character or where situated," are " not *public* laundries within the meaning of " the law."[1] Commissioner Sherman, at the time of the ruling, protested against this decision, charging that it was " unjust and absurd " because hotel laundries were some of the largest steam laundries in operation in the state and were often situated far away from the hotel to which they belonged. While on the other hand, small hand laundries employing women in the old fashioned way were obliged to obey the law. Nevertheless, the judgment of the attorney general still stands, which means also that the laundry code, about to be established to improve general working conditions in laundries, will not apply to hotel laundries.

Mercantile and Other Establishments

We have seen that the retarded regulation of mercantile establishments proved to be an obstacle to the enforcement of the factory law. And, prior to 1908, the mercantile law as it existed was notoriously unenforced. Up to that time the administration of the law was in the hands of

[1] *Annual Report of the Commissioner of Labor*, 1906, p. I. 66.

local boards of health who have never been able to give their attention to the labor law. In the early nineties the Working Women's Society backed by the Consumers' League urged passage of a bill providing that factory inspectors should have supervision over mercantile establishments, but the bill failed. In 1898, the New York City Consumers' League reports that Mr. Nathan Straus, when president of the board of health of New York City, dismissed the mercantile inspectors for the alleged cause of lack of appropriation for salaries. This appropriation had been made under the former administration but was not endorsed by the new board. When the league remonstrated that children were being injuriously employed, they were told that "it was an open secret that under the new régime the law was not to be enforced." [1]

Commissioner Sherman, in his report of 1907, dwelt upon the absence of law in mercantile establishments and its consequent challenge to the enforcement of the factory law. Because of this he explained that the desire of factory women to increase their earnings by working "overtime" was easily satisfied. A New York City manufacturer who manufactured and packed goods chiefly for sale in the city could transfer his goods in bulk to a store or stores, "and there, under conditions probably much inferior to those in the packing department of his factory, carry on his packing without any restrictions whatever upon the labor of his female employees." [2]

Mercantile establishments in cities of the first class were brought under the supervision of the Department of Labor in 1908, and a bureau of mercantile inspection was created. Keen opposition arose against the transfer, not from the

[1] *Report for 1898 of the Consumers' League of the City of New York*, p. 19.

[2] *Annual Report of the Commissioner of Labor*, pp. I. 75-76.

health officers whose authority was thus forfeited, but from the proprietors of large mercantile establishments whose power and influence had kept them practically free from regulatiye provisions heretofore.

However, effective enforcement of the mercantile law (still only for children and females under twenty-one years of age it will be remembered) was not possible because of the paucity of inspectors. "Only a fraction of the whole number of places coming under the provisions of the law has been covered," came the report in 1909.[1] During that year there were 6,737 inspections, 598 special inspections and 5,468 "observations" made; 4,419 orders were issued and 3,935 compliances reported.

The next greatest difficulty in securing observance of the rules lay in the lack of coöperation of the employees. Inspectors were obliged to rely upon employees for their knowledge of violations, unless they stood on watch for more than ten hours a day and could prove that they had done so. Employees could not only not be depended upon to volunteer correct, if any, information, for often they were said to have claimed that the hours had been changed in compliance with the statute when there had been no change whatsoever.[2] Fear of provoking disapproval or discharge was considered the reason for this deception. One mitigation noted in the 1911 report of the commissioner was that there had been no violation during the year of more than ten hours a day or sixty hours a week. How this information was verified was not stated.

The mercantile law thus laid itself wide open to attack by the Factory Investigating Commission in 1913. They reviewed the history of its non-enforcement and successfully urged that establishments in second-class cities also be

[1] *Op. cit.*, 1909, p. 128.

[2] *Op. cit.*, 1911, p. 167.

brought under the supervision of the State Department of Labor. It was in this year also that the act was extended to include all women working in mercantile establishments. Failure to include the provision for posting the schedule of working hours of women, as was the provision for factories, kept the law more perfunctory than real, however, until its amendment including this requirement in 1915. It was considered that here at last was a basis for enforcing the mercantile law. Inspectors were heartened. Instead of having to produce an affidavit declaring a violation, they now only needed to find the employee working outside of posted hours.

But as time went on the same old difficulties proved once more insurmountable. Complaints of employees could not be relied upon for the detection of violations, and this made it necessary to inspect completely and separately each establishment. But the chief mercantile inspector stated[1] that if the entire force worked in New York City alone it could not complete one routine inspection of each mercantile establishment in a year's time. Inspection was necessarily limited, therefore, to establishments which conducted some or all of their business on the ground floor. Furthermore, the organization for the work of inspection left much to be desired. There were no maps and no geographical lists to show the times and places of inspection. There was no central record of all establishments under the jurisdiction of the division, which made it necessary to consult at least six different files in order to discover the record of any one establishment. Thus frequent violators were not known. Moreover, the number of early morning and late evening inspections were too few to discover violations of the hours' regulation.

Over the wide area of third-class cities and villages in New York State the law was still almost entirely inert, and women over sixteen years of age were reported to be em-

[1] *American Labor Legislation Review*, 1917, p. 355.

ployed fourteen hours a day and seven days a week in many instances. In 1919, the legislature transferred the jurisdiction over all mercantile establishments in the state from the local boards of health to the State Department of Labor, bringing forty-nine cities with a population of 1,500,000 under the bureau of inspection for the administration of the law.[1] This was the logical step toward better enforcement which had been advocated for years, but, with the corps of inspectors only slightly enlarged, hopeful results could scarcely be anticipated. Tables showing the results of inspection of mercantile establishments by the bureau of inspection of the Department of Labor are presented each year, as they are for factories, in the annual reports of the industrial commissioner. They are interesting but necessarily incomplete from the point of view of a correct picture of the extent of enforcement of the mercantile law, and will not be included for the same reasons that similar data for factories were not included above.

In summary, then, it appears that the general trend toward a shorter working day in America, as in other countries, has probably been a surer force toward the reduction of the hours of women in mercantile establishments, as in factories, than the enforcement of any specific laws. In keeping with the trend, the larger and more progressive establishments of New York State have not only reduced the daily hours of work, but have established the custom of an all-day-closing on Saturdays during the months of June, July, and August. Four reasons were given by the bureau of inspection for the perceptible decrease in the number of discovered violations of the law in 1920, namely: careful supervision, more wide-spread organization of the workers, the marked shortage of labor, and the increasing number of humane employers many of whom have instituted the eight-hour day.[2]

[1] *Annual Report of the Industrial Commission*, 1919, p. 34.

[2] *Annual Report of the Industrial Commission*, 1920, p. 26.

An additional cause may have been that, in 1920, drug stores were obliged to observe mercantile closing hours according to law. Drug stores had grown to be fairly strong competitors in the range of articles they offered for sale, and the Industrial Commission had contended that they were enough like department stores to be regulated by the mercantile law. This view was sustained by a lower court and now it was affirmed by the New York court of appeals.[1]

1. *Messengers*

The Industrial Commission in 1919 reported little trouble in administering the act of 1918 forbidding the employment as messengers of females under twenty-one years of age. The companies who had employed this class of young women readily complied with the law. So far as discovered in this study, no data have been collected on the experience of the commission in applying the hour-regulations to the work of adult women; nor has the success of regulating the working time of young male messengers been announced.

2. *Elevators*

The statute relating to the hours of females on elevators in factories and mercantile establishments was reported enforced in 1920, the year following the enactment.[2] There was said to be little difficulty in securing the coöperation of owners and managers of property in which these elevators were operated.

HOURS OF LABOR—NIGHT WORK

Factories

Night work restrictions for adult women in factories, also introduced by the act of 1899, were openly violated.

[1] People *v.* L. K. Liggett, 227 N. Y. 617 (1920).

[2] *Annual Report of the Industrial Commission*, 1920, pp. 17, 28-29.

Commissioner Sherman in his report for 1906, announced that, while "extraordinary efforts" had been made to enforce the ten-hour regulation, no serious attempt had been made to enforce the night work rule until that year![1] He explained that there were over 25,000 employees whose time had to be watched and regulated for the enforcement of this feature of the law, a task physically impossible with an inspection force of about fifty.

An interesting issue arose in connection with this act. The commissioner in 1905 admitted a fear of testing the possibility of prohibiting the night work of adult women because of its being bound up with the same regulation for male and female minors, and in case of an adverse decision by the courts, "both prohibitions might be held to fall together."[2] A recommendation was made, therefore, and urged for passage by the legislature, that "a separate prohibition of night work for women under 21 be enacted, so that if the general prohibition should be declared unconstitutional *because of its application to women over 21*, the separate prohibition as to minors would remain unaffected."[3] But the advice was not followed and the commissioner's fear was confirmed. Beginning with the annulment of the act in the court of special sessions of the City of New York, first division, the highest state court in 1908 held that adult women were not "wards of the state" and declared the act to be void, therefore, on the grounds of interference with the freedom of the individual to contract.

While the appeal was pending, discussion of this issue was heated. It was held by some that a prohibition against night work for women under the age of twenty-one only could not be enforced because inspectors could not recognize

[1] *Op. cit.*, 1906, p. I. 61.

[2] *Op. cit.*, 1905, p. 30.

[3] *Op. cit.*, 1906, p. I. 59.

the age of twenty-one. The commissioner returned the suggestion that, while it would not be impossible to know the age "absolutely," it could be known about as well as for male minors under eighteen, and it would at least prevent the employment of "large gangs of young women." [1] It was added that were it not for the administrative reason of facilitating the regulation of day work, there was no present need in New York State for prohibiting adult women from working at night. Further elucidation of this argument may be recalled by turning back to page 237 of this study. It was suggested in connection with the form of the statute, that attention be given to the English "Factory and Workshop Act," a more flexible code of over twenty pages, which is "successfully enforced and has produced good results," while our law is "academically disposed of in ten lines of section 77 of the Labor Law." [2]

During the eight-year interim between the 1908 annulment of this act and the 1915 affirmance of the later prohibition of women's work at night, the inspectors were substantially relieved of the attempt to enforce this type of law. Since 1915, there is practically no available information concerning the degree of its enforcement. The official tables that show violations of the hour law give no clue to the degree of infringement upon the law at night.

Mercantile and Other Establishments

The night work prohibition in New York mercantile establishments, as well as the regulation of hours by day, applied only to boys and girls until 1913. The difficulties of administration of the act were not slight however. If inspectors discovered males fourteen to sixteen years of age or females sixteen to twenty-one at work after ten o'clock,

[1] *Op. cit.*, 1906, p. I. 60.

[2] *Op. cit.*, p. I. 63.

the violation was fairly easy to prove. But all sorts of subterfuges were used by employers in defense—that the young workers refused to go home even though their work was over, or that they were waiting for mother or older brother to come for them. The inspector had actually to see the employee selling merchandise to supply himself with the necessary grounds for a violation charge. To lighten the task of administration, the recommendation of the commissioner of labor in 1910 was renewed to amend the statute to read that no female between sixteen and twenty-one years be allowed to work more than six days or sixty hours a week, and that the period in which such female may work on all days other than Saturday be shortened; that notices be posted stating the regulations. It is not clear why this recommendation was made to apply to females only, for there was as much difficulty in enforcing the law as it applied to young males as to females, if not more.

There is no record of the degree of enforcement of the night work prohibition for women. As for factories, the statistics of the Department of Labor do not show separate tabulations for day and night hours. The chief mercantile inspector reported, in 1917, that in spite of many prosecutions, and numerous letters of warning to proprietors, the night work prohibition in his jurisdiction was giving considerable trouble and being constantly evaded.[2]

1. *Restaurants*

The inclusion, in 1917, of restaurants within the mercantile law added about 8,000 establishments to those already under the supervision of the inspection bureau.[3] A number of serious drawbacks have greatly reduced the

[1] *Annual Report of the Commissioner of Labor*, 1911, p. 168.

[2] *Annual Report of the Industrial Commissioner*, 1917, p. 62.

[3] *Annual Report of the Industrial Commission*, 1917, p. 62.

effectiveness of the act. To begin with, the statute included only first and second class cities, causing some ill-feeling because of its lack of universality. And in Syracuse and Rochester it was not enforced because the question of its constitutionality arose. Class legislation was alleged in 1918 on the ground that the act applied to restaurants and not to hotels. It was declared constitutional, however, and, in March of 1924, the issue was cleared finally by the Federal Supreme Court, in the Radice case, as we have seen, in the affirmance of the prohibition for restaurants regardless of the regulation in hotels.

One difficulty obstructing enforcement has been the failure of the act to require the posting of hours of labor, a provision of the mercantile law which was not early extended to apply to restaurants. And, apparently, inadvertance was not the cause of the omission, for a remedial act proposed in 1919 failed to pass, and was not adopted until sometime later. Another difficulty of enforcement, as explained verbally by the director of inspection, Mr. John L. Gernon, arises because of the intermittent hours of restaurant employment together with the fact that many of the women themselves are not in sympathy with being deprived of work at night when tips are higher.

INDUSTRIAL HOMEWORK

While there is double reason for enforcing the regulations of " homework," there is also double difficulty. The practice of giving out work to be done by women at home, where close surveillance of length of hours and conditions of work is far less possible than in factories, diminishes the force of the factory law and jeopardizes not only the health of the public but the health of the workers. Nevertheless there seems no end to the possibilities of evasion of the tenement house law. When one avenue of escape is closed, another opens wide for the offender. The reports of the commissioners of labor reflect the multiplying difficulties. One year, perhaps after a new regulative measure has been enacted or a few new inspectors added, the heartening report will testify that the result has been "quite marvelous," while the following year will bring forth the discouraging statement that the law is "ridiculous," that "the nomads of the tenements" cannot be controlled with three times the existing force.

One great difficulty in the regulation of homework lies in its seasonal character, so that the number of home workers fluctuates from month to month. And perhaps even greater trouble lies in the fact that only tenement houses (i. e. buildings accomodating three families or more) are regulated by law, and in these houses is included in the law only work on specified articles likely to communicate disease.

Homework has been a licensed occupation in New York since 1899, when the office of the superintendent of licenses was created. Licenses first issued to the workers proved to be mere "scraps of paper" however, for the lessees, moving from one house to another, held them for the protection of their employers as well as themselves, in case of detection. Or, if so disposed, they sold their licenses to their tenement successors! In 1904, licenses began to be issued only to owners of entire buildings instead of to individual tenants, with the purpose of throwing the responsibility for a sanitary house directly upon the owner, and with the result of reducing the number of lessees from 30,000 to 3,000. (This provision of the legislature prohibited the giving out of twenty-four specified articles of manufacture to any occupants of an unlicensed building). The plan was not considered wholly desirable, however, for it added 10,000 tenement buildings to the inspection list, bringing in "hundreds" of better-class buildings and apartment houses which required little inspecting, the owners of which would not apply for licenses.

There were but twenty factory inspectors in 1906, whose duty it was to keep 25,000 factories operating within the law, and about 12,000 tenement houses! The duties in connection with tenement house inspection were twofold. Both licensed and unlicensed buildings had to be inspected. The task was to discover the houses in which work was being done, compel the owners to apply for licenses, make a thorough inspection upon such application, compel the securing and posting of the license if granted, and make reinspections twice yearly; and furthermore, to prevent all manufacturing of the prohibited articles specified by law in unlicensed houses. The labor commissioner wrote gloomily in 1906 that the department had accumulated no statistics of any value as to the quantity of work done or the number of homeworkers in the state; the work was "intermittent and irregular" and, while the lists of outside workers furnished by employers offered some clue, frequently there was no distinction recorded between these and contractors or shop workers, and the duplication of inexact records was great. A constant insufficiency of employees was the chief cause of this plight, and now the commissioner explained that there was no clerical force to check up what data were available. "Therefore we have nothing on our records to serve even as a basis for rough calculation." [1]

A more cheerful aspect of homework inspection was shown by Commissioner Williams in 1909, when he reported that in the 9,646 houses inspected, only one person in every ten apartments was found working in violation of the law, and in only nine cases was it necessary to resort to the drastic course of revoking the license for sanitary reasons.[2]

In striking contrast to this testimony came that of 1912

[1] *Annual Report of the Commissioner of Labor*, 1906, p. 50.

[2] *Op. cit.*, 1909, p. 24.

showing that in New York City, in which 95 per cent of the homework of the state is done, "the burden laid upon us [inspectors] is so out of proportion to the resources at our command for regulative purposes, as to make the pretense of supervision on the part of the State seem ridiculous."[1] During the year, ten inspectors only could be assigned to this work and they had visited approximately 13,000 tenement houses and 145,000 apartments. At the time of inspection they found work being done in 13,000 apartments, but this of course was not at all a trustworthy index to the actual conditions of work throughout the year. Commissioner Williams estimated that five times as many inspectors would be required to ensure proper enforcement. He confessed that at present they were only "able to skim the surface—to relieve the strain upon the public mind incident to occasional disclosures. . . . We must go farther and deeper before the dangers are eradicated."[2]

The Factory Investigating Commission declared that there had never been a serious effort to enforce the regulations for homework in the spirit in which they were enacted, that licenses had been issued as a matter of form, and prosecutions for violations had rarely been instituted. The commission emphasized the ruinous effect of this condition upon all legislation which applies to trades that employ homeworkers, and recommended more drastic regulation for a trial period of two or three years, followed by complete abolition, if unsuccessful. This decision was made despite the fact that some of the major witnesses before the commission urged prompt abolition of tenement house labor, because of the impossibility of regulating it. Florence Kelley in her plea for abolition asserted that proper enforce-

[1] *Op. cit.*, 1912, p. 17.

[2] *Op. cit.*, pp. 18-19.

ment would require that there be one inspector by day and another inspector by night for each one of the 13,000 licensed tenement houses, making 26,000 inspectors; that there would have to be other inspectors investigating unlicensed houses to see whether any should be licensed, and others to supervise those houses whose licenses had been revoked! "It is a fatuous undertaking to burden [factory inspectors] with that duty," she concluded.[1] Lillian Wald, director of the Henry Street Settlement of New York City and Rose Schneiderman, organizer for the Women's Trade Union League, also expressed the belief that homework cannot be regulated by law and therefore should be abolished.

The second report of the Factory Investigating Commission reënforced the first in expressing concern in regard to the problem of homework regulation. It was discovered that the number of articles manufactured for which a license was not required greatly exceeded in number the forty-one articles for which a license was required, and also that the number of persons at work on goods not requiring a license appeared to be vastly greater than the 100,000 workers on the lists of manufacturers. Statistics of employment could not be secured because of the nomadic habits of the workers. The commission explained that "When the homeworker's address is listed in the bulletin,[2] the work is given to her, she is registered in the employer's book by number, and never again is an inquiry made as to her place of abode, although she may have moved a dozen times since the first entry, or, as is frequently the case, a friend or even a friend's friend may now be taking out work under the original number entered."[3]

[1] *Preliminary Report of the Factory Investigating Commission*, 1912, vol. viii, p. 1593.

[2] A monthly bulletin first issued in 1908 for the publication of the lists of licensed houses for the use of employers and employees.

[3] *Op. cit.*, 1913, vol. ii, p. 729.

Moreover, inspections were only made from nine to three o'clock each day, when there was the least probability of overcrowding, with children at school, lodgers probably out, and older members of the family, if employed at other occupations, usually away. Persons not members of the family could not be discovered, as they visited from one tenement house to another illegally carrying their work with them. Indescribable violations of the rule against work in the presence of disease were discovered by the commission. Tuberculosis, typhoid fever, and virulent skin diseases did not prevent their victims from intimate work upon articles made for sale. The mature observation of the commission was that "the attempt to enforce the statute has saddled upon the community a continuing expense for the salaries of inspectors incurred in the effort to do that which in the end has failed." [1]

In spite of all these discouragements, there has been a rather steady improvement in homework conditions in recent years. The tag has proved the "most effective argument" in obstinate cases, by which illegally made goods are marked "tenement-made" for the information of all concerned and are not permitted to be sold. Many employers are reported to coöperate in observing the rules even to the point of sending severe warnings to women that they will refuse to give them work to take home if they are discovered to be disobeying the law, particularly in respect to putting their children to work. Women act promptly upon such a warning for in most cases the necessity of work is urgent.[2] Small new contractors give the agents of enforcement a great deal of difficulty. They know little and care less about the

[1] *Op. cit.*, 1913, p. 738.

[2] There has been at times active opposition on the part of employees however, and several times, according to report, inspectors have suffered for weeks from the result of assaults by woman sympathizers.

law. They are transients in the trade and divulge none of their secrets to inspectors; and if their goods are tagged they leave them unclaimed. Custom tailors and dressmakers are also as persistent violators as they are skilled in evasion. It is difficult to make workers[1] understand that the law forbids one to " hire a few helpers " in a rush season.

The greatest recent problem in connection with regulating tenement work in New York State seems to be that there is more work done in homes that do not come under the law than in homes that do, for one and two family houses have never been included in the law. However, it is clear that the " evils in connection with homework are not created by the type of house or building in which the work is done, but very much depends on the habits or conditions of the people doing the work."

PROHIBITED EMPLOYMENT

Employment after Childbirth

This legislative regulation appears to be one of the most difficult to enforce. In fact it is not enforced; nor can it be by the present methods. Administration of the labor laws is necessarily dependent upon complaints from some source for the reason that inspectors are so very few. Two authorities have told me that there are no complaints submitted in regard to women's working after childbirth, but on the other hand, that there are sometimes protests from women themselves if they are not given work within the forbidden four weeks. These facts surely bear silent and convincing testimony to the need of some form of maternity insurance.

[1] There are many more Italians among tenement house workers than people of any other nationality. The 1916 report of the Industrial Commission (pp. 56-57) stated that of the 20,779 workers reported and representing thirty-four races, 10,641 were Italians, 6,367 were Hebrews, 1,140 were Germans, 1,093 were Americans, and 1,538 were miscellaneous. 19,018 of these workers were employed on articles of clothing.

SPECIAL WORKING CONDITIONS

1. *Seats*

The early laws requiring seats for women in mercantile and manufacturing establishments found ardent champions in the New York City Consumers' League, the City Improvement Society, and other philanthropic bodies that worked tirelessly for their enforcement. These organizations collected facts regarding violations and laid them before the district attorney, whose reply was that "in his opinion it would be difficult to secure a conviction under the loosely constructed law." The Consumers' League urged shoppers to make frequent inquiries regarding the proper provision of seats in stores and the encouragement by floor walkers of their use. Failure to comply with this provision kept merchants from having their firm names published in the league's "white list." Proponents of the law were encouraged when Dr. Ernst Lederle became president of the New York City board of health in 1901, and announced publicly that this law should be enforced, that there would be no more "judicious enforcement," no "side door."

There seems no evidence to show the results of efforts to enforce the provision for seats in these earlier years of the century, but, in 1909, the commissioner of labor implied in his report (pages 41-42), that compliance was more or less casual and that the law was very much disregarded in stores during special sales and rush periods for which special counters were set up. Very frequently, also, women were not permitted to use seats that had been provided. Sometimes this denial was discovered to be the ruling of some petty overseer, and a word of warning by the management was found to be sufficient.[1] But the policy of many firms was reported to be that employees should not sit down during working hours even though seats were available.

[1] *Annual Report of the Commissioner of Labor*, 1909, pp. 41-42.

When the statute began to be taken fairly seriously by some employers, the question arose as to the meaning of "suitable" seats. There was a wide difference of opinion on this point. Chairs, stools, benches, boxes, and shelves were used to meet the requirement of the act. The commissioner of labor for 1911 (page 77), reported that very few seats then supplied could be considered suitable or restful, and that portable seats were practically the same as none at all, for they were too easily pushed out of the way. He recommended standard seats with backs. Seats of standard requirements were described by the Factory Investigating Commission and a bill embodying these requirements was introduced for passage by the legislature, but the act was defeated. And so far like acts for standardizing seats have repeatedly failed to pass.[1]

It is difficult to say to what extent the law for seats as it stands has been enforced. With regard to factories, the Factory Investigating Commission complained in 1912 that "in a great many of the [manufacturing] establishments no seats whatsoever are provided. Where they are furnished, the work that the women have to perform does not permit of their use."[2] In 1913, the commissioner of labor reported that "The enforcement of this section of the law for the past five years has changed the attitude of some employers, relative to permitting employees to use the seats after provided. The up-to-date manager realizes the necessity of allowing the females to use the seats at such times as their duties will permit."[3] In 1921, the Bureau of Women in Industry, reporting on *The Employment of Women in 5 and 10 Cent Stores,* (Bulletin No. 109), said

[1] Description of these requirements was given on pages 272-3, *supra.*

[2] *Preliminary Report of the Factory Investigating Commission,* 1912, vol. i.

[3] *Annual Report of the Commissioner of Labor,* 1913, p. 84.

that "the question is not so much whether seats exist or not, but what chance there is to use them. The only real opportunity to be off one's feet comes when the girls are 'off the floor.'"

Another report of the women's bureau in 1921 based upon replies from 103 manufacturing firms in New York State, was that fifty-nine were using "'ordinary chairs with backs' throughout their factories. Stools, apparently without backs, were still in use in some 25 of the plants."[1] But more significant still is the implication in the bureau's statement that "These laws, as they stand, offer little protection to health, because even when a sufficient number of seats is provided, it is practically impossible to see that employees are allowed to use them."[2]

2. *Basements*

It is possible that the absence of statistical data regarding the observance of the law requiring a permit for employing women in basements means that it has been perfectly observed! Although one has learned to doubt, there seems little to prove the contrary. In fact, the commissioner of labor in 1909 (page 41) reported that the specification for ventilation in basements when women and children were to be employed had made basements the best ventilated parts of such premises. He made the recommendation that these specifications be extended to cover the entire premises. Again in 1911 (page 164) the commissioner reported—"We found in basements where there are proper mechanical means of ventilation, that the air was better than on the other floors of the building." But there seem to be no data on the extent to which the provision prohibiting women from working in unventilated basements has been enforced.

[1] *Industrial Posture and Seating, Bulletin no. 104*, p. 40, New York State.

[2] *Op. cit.*, p. 35.

3. *Toilet Accommodations*

There are also scant data as to the observance of acts relative to wash rooms, toilets and dressing rooms for women in factories and mercantile establishments. The difficulties attending the early regulations in regard to this matter were mentioned in the first chapter. The requirements for separate toilets for women was pretty generally met in establishments outside of New York City but widespread violations existed in New York City; the section regarding toilet accommodations being "one of the most difficult parts of the labor laws to enforce in New York City." [1]

Dressing rooms with solid partitions and a window opening to the outdoor air were furnished in response to section 88 of the labor law by factories and large tenant factories, according to the report of the commissioner in 1911 (page 76). In many large plants lunch rooms were also provided and sometimes a surgical room with a nurse. The smaller tenant factories offered difficulties because of cramped floor area and lack of outdoor windows. Here it was almost impossible to secure compliance with orders. The rooms provided were farcically inadequate—used only for rubbish, they were found to be more unsanitary than any other parts of the establishment.

In 1914, data on sanitation in factories were published by the Industrial Board [2] showing orders issued throughout the state for water-closets numbered 38,645, and compliances 21,956; for wash rooms 6,047, and compliances 2,594; for dressing rooms 6,351 and compliances 4,138. This was a general statement of all orders given, with no separate tabulation of orders regarding facilities for men and for women. There were eleven prosecutions, three of which were dis-

[1] Fairchild, F. R., *The Factory Legislation of the State of New York*, 1905, p. 157.

[2] *Annual Report of the Commissioner of Labor*, 1914, p. 66.

missed or acquitted; five were convicted but sentences were suspended, and three were convicted and fined a total of $65.

For mercantile establishments in 1914, there were 11,952 orders relative to water-closets, and 11,480 compliances. There were only eleven prosecutions entered after final notices had been given, five were for failure to provide water-closets, three for failure to ventilate them properly, and three for failure to clean them.

As in former inspection statistics, so here, caution must be taken in interpreting the figures not to allow them to carry a disproportionate weight. A revealing suggestion for their interpretation, which more or less applies to all data on enforcement thus far gathered, was offered by James L. Gernon, then chief mercantile inspector, when he explained the above returns: "This is a large increase over the number of orders issued for the previous year, and was due to the increase in the force of inspectors."[1] In other words, one should keep in mind that with probably no exception more orders issued does not mean more violations, but more violations discovered, and therefore a little better instead of less enforcement of the law. Also it should be explained that the law is defective in that it fails to place the responsibility for violation, so the inspector is always at a loss to know whether to issue orders to the owner of the building or the tenant. Thus many violations of the provision remain uncorrected.[2]

From the foregoing discussion, it is needless to say that the problems of enforcing protective labor laws are tremendous; and that the machinery of enforcement, at least in

[1] *Annual Report of the Commissioner of Labor*, 1914, p. 91.

[2] More recent data regarding the inspection of toilet accomodations might be shown, for they appear each year in the annual reports of the industrial commissioner. However, later figures have not been given for they seem not to differ materially from those for 1914.

New York State, is painfully cramped. New York has, in general, a commission form of administration which means the delegation of discretionary power by the legislature to a body of experts for intelligent application of the meaning of the laws and the establishment of rules for the improvement of working conditions not otherwise specifically provided for. We have seen that recent modifications in the structure of the administrative body in New York are believed not to have proved entirely successful, and it is possible that another reorganization will be developed to re-establish the more typical form of industrial commission which existed before 1921.

There is, perhaps, no other branch of the state government that suffers more from the manoeuvers of politicians than the machinery of administering the laws. The extent to which laws are enforced is almost impossible to trace, so that it is possible for the agency of enforcement to be crippled materially without arousing great public concern. Budgets can be cut and valuable persons discharged on the plea of lightening the taxpayer's burden and saving unnecessary expense, and the consequent effects upon the lives of the workers remain undiscovered.

To form some conception of the difficulties of measuring the extent of law enforcement in New York State, it is necessary to recall that the number of discoveries of violations is limited to the number of inspections that can be made, and that there has never been an approach to a sufficient number of inspectors. The estimate made, by those informed, of the necessary number of inspectors for proper enforcement varies from four to two hundred times as many as New York has ever had. Thus, of the violations of the law which are committed, only a small per cent are discovered. And then, " only a small percentage of violations discovered result in prosecution [from 14 to 56 per cent in

1919] and of these a large number are dismissed by consent on compliance with orders issued by the Commission." [1] Moreover, of this small per cent of a small per cent, there is a large proportion of suspended sentences ranging from 44 to 76 per cent in 1919.[2] And finally, of the sentences which are not suspended, inadequate fines or none at all are imposed by the courts and magistrates; and the proportion of fines that are remitted is unknown.

This is a discouraging state of affairs to members of the Department of Labor whose standards are high in respect to the enforcement of acts that have been passed by the legislature, as well as to others who believe in the necessity of these laws for the public welfare. Where conviction of the reasonableness of the law exists among employers and employees, there is, of course, less difficulty in enforcing it, and where the workers are organized into unions they are able to force compliance with the law in many cases. But unorganized employees, afraid of losing their jobs, are timid and unsatisfactory in the rôle of complainants, and, as in the case of some special regulations for women, we are told that the difficulty of enforcement is frequently owing to opposition of the workers themselves.

This brings us to appreciate the growing conviction that labor law enforcement must come about through an educational process rather than through police force procedure, and that the needs of all workers for protection by the state should be scientifically considered to make a reliable basis for the enactment of laws with which employers and employees can be taught to sympathize. "It is only when employers have become so enlightened and progressive as to accept the

[1] *The Bulletin* of the New York State Industrial Commission, January, 1920.

[2] The "departmental summons" is said to have made some improvement in the way of reducing the number of suspended sentences since 1919.

standards imposed by the State as the basis for efficiency in industry to be adopted willingly and not through the compulsion of threatened punishment that a satisfactory condition can be said to prevail. When this is achieved the inspectors of the State department of labor become advisors in the application of standards rather than policemen."[1] This is the view of the Women's Bureau of the United States Department of Labor, which, we are told, more nearly describes the method of inspection in English factories. Inspectors in such a system would need to be carefully trained and adequately remunerated for their work, so that the dignity of their positions and the value of their advice would be recognized by all concerned. Scientific improvement in the conduct of industrial plants and scientific improvement in the kinds of laws enacted would seem to be a necessary outgrowth of such a program, and they would increase the possibilities of labor law enforcement to an incalculable degree.

[1] *Bulletin no. 10* of the Women's Bureau, United States Department of Labor, March, 1920, *Hours and Conditions of Work for Women in Industry in Virginia*, p. 32.

CHAPTER VI

Some Effects of Protective Legislation for Women[1]

A recent study made by the New York Bureau of Women in Industry of 59,000 women employed in manufacturing and mercantile establishments in the state shows that 56 per cent were scheduled to work 48 hours and under. Only nine per cent were scheduled to work as much as 53 and 54 hours—the present legal maximum of working hours for women in the state.[2] For men, too, daily hours have been reduced until a substantial majority of them are at the 54-hour level and below.[3]

This is the high mark in New York State of a tendency that has been increasing in recent years. In an earlier bulletin of the Bureau of Women in Industry, the observation was made that,

> It is increasingly recognized that the so-called "standards" embodied in the Labor Law are, in fact, only minimum requirements. Many employers are taking the lead in the establishment of fair conditions; many of them have gone far ahead of the requirements of the law. This is true not only of hours and wages, but also of standards of building construction and plant equipment.[4]

[1] The note at the end of this chapter suggests the nature and scope of an investigation which might lead to more real knowledge of effects of legislation than is now available.

[2] *Hours and Earnings of Women in Five Industries*, New York State Department of Labor, *Bulletin no. 121*, November, 1923.

[3] *The Industrial Bulletin* for February, 1924, p. 106.

[4] *Women Who Work*, *Bulletin no. 110*, pp. 25-26, New York State Department of Labor, April, 1922.

These improvements in the lot of the wage earner cannot be traced to any single source. There is little question, however, that labor legislation and trade unionism, with the growing support of production studies and an enlightened public opinion, have been the chief forces in this direction. The health and safety of the working people are each year being placed at a higher value.

But when this is said the question remains—what results has labor legislation itself brought about? We have seen that the testing of the separate acts by the courts involves the attempt on the part of the judges to foresee effects in their broad outlines. A law that would deprive workers of the freedom of contract (of life, liberty or property) is likely to be declared invalid. However, a law that would protect the health and safety of the workers in their relation to the public welfare, is likely to be sustained. As these two important sets of values are weighed against each other, opinions become divided and the decision of the judges frequently is reached by a bare majority vote. It is the method of reasoning that brings these differences of opinion, for, presumably, there is a common aim. The aim is greater justice to wage earners in making the bargain for the sale of their services.

This aim, of course, is the foundation of protective labor legislation. An inquiry into the actual effects of special protective legislation for women leads to the surprising discovery that there exist practically no unquestioned facts upon which to form an impartial judgment. It is evident, therefore, that the continuous enactment of these statutes has been based upon impression and good intention, principally. Views as to their effects are found to conflict. For example, the federal report on *Woman and Child Wage Earners in the United States* says,

The history of woman's work in this country shows that legislation has been the only force which has improved the working conditions of any large number of women wage-earners.[1]

This view is corroborated by federal and state labor bureaus and by unofficial groups and individuals.

On the other hand, smaller groups of working women, such as the printers and street-railway employees in New York, maintain that this legislation in so far as it effects them has brought suffering to them instead of relief.

There are, perhaps, two main factors that have complicated inquiries into the effects of special legislation for industrial women. One is that the status of women is such that their occupations and plans of living are frequently results of a set of circumstances outside of their control and outside of legislation pertaining to them. Another is that the interrelation of forces in present-day society requires expert analysis in order to trace effects from particular causes. The following pages represent an attempt to collect the available information regarding effects of New York State laws, together with some consideration of effects of legislation outside of New York State.

PART I: SOME EFFECTS OF NEW YORK LAWS

HOURS—DAY WORK

Factories[2]

The length of the working day in relation to legislation for women in New York was discussed by the commissioner of labor in his annual reoprt for 1902. (p. III. 24.) There he stated that the ten-hour day prevailed in the majority of industries in the state but that in the paper and pulp industry and in gas and electric plants the working day

[1] *Woman and Child Wage Earners in the United States*, 1910, vol. ix, p. 12. United States Department of Labor.

[2] See Law, pp. 133-6, *supra*.

exceeded ten hours. " One explanation of such excessively long hours ", he continued,

may be found in the almost total absence of women and boys, who are forbidden by law to contract to work at night or for more than ten hours a day. In industries where women and youths are employed, the factory cannot be operated more than 10 hours a day or 60 hours a week unless their places are filled by adult males (those 18 years of age or older). As such substitution is impracticable, the factory closes down at the end of the ten hours and all classes of workers get the benefit of the law.

In his 1906 report, the commissioner recorded results of a different order. He explained (p. I. 64) that

The enforcement of these provisions does not always result in shortening the hours or in ameliorating the conditions of female employees. On the contrary it not infrequently leads to their discharge and to depriving them of all means of earning a livelihood. That is true particularly where a small proportion of women have forced their way into the more skilled and highly paid trades in which men predominate, and in which short hours are the rule and very long hours the exception.

Nothing more recent was found in the commissioners' reports concerning the limited working day in factories. And nothing more exact. The two observations made in this first decade of the century, however, have since then been so commonly recorded that they are worth remembering; First, that the reduction of hours of women and children frequently reduces the hours of men working in the same plants; and second, that a law passed to protect women frequently handicaps or eliminates them, especially in the higher paid occupations where men predominate.

It is interesting if not significant in this connection to compare the distribution of women in factories in New York

State in 1920 with that in 1910. According to the census, the total number of women gainfully employed in the state increased 15.4 per cent during the decade—from 983,686 in 1910 to 1,135,295 in 1920.[1] The increase in the total female population ten years and over during the decade was 14.5 per cent so that the proportion of women gainfully employed to the total increased but slightly—from 26.7 in 1910 to 26.9 in 1920, or about one per cent. The number of women employed in manufacturing and mechanical industries was less than one per cent greater in 1920 than in 1910, increasing from 348,973 to 351,104. This brings a reduction in the percentage of women in factories of the total women employed from 35.5 per cent in 1910 to 30.9 per cent in 1920.

An explanation of this lag in the employment of women in factories may be that the volume of employment in factories as compared with other classes of employment had fallen off generally between 1910 and 1920. But this is not the case. The census figures for men in factories show that the percentage of men as compared with all men employed was slightly higher in 1920 than in 1910, the proportion being 41.0 per cent in 1910 and 41.75 per cent in 1920. Comparing the relative numerical importance of men and women in manufacturing and mechanical industries,—in 1910, 78.1 per cent of all those employed were men and 21.9 per cent were women, while in 1920, 80.0 per cent were men and 20.0 per cent were women.

These figures are even more interesting when it is seen that the changes in the proportion of men and women for all occupations in the state between 1910 and 1920 moved in the reverse direction. That is to say, the proportion of

[1] The word "women" instead of "females" in these data is plainly a misnomer, for all females ten years of age and over are included. It is unfortunate that there are no complete separate data for adult women.

women to men increased. In 1910, of all persons gainfully employed, 75.4 per cent were men and 24.6 per cent were women; in 1920, 74.8 per cent were men and 25.2 per cent were women. Hence the five per cent decrease in the proportion of women employed in factories to the total of employed women appears to represent a slightly diminished importance of women workers in factories as compared with men, while the importance of women in industry in general slightly increased as compared with men in industry.[1]

It is not possible to say at this time whether the development of the factory law for women during this decade has

[1] It is interesting to compare these changes in the employment of women in New York during this decade with those in New Jersey where there was no significant development of protective factory legislation for women, although the difference was not great. In New Jersey the increase in the total number of women employed in the state was 23.6 per cent, compared with the 15.4 per cent in New York. The total female population ten years of age and over increased 25.2 per cent in New Jersey, compared with the 14.5 per cent in New York, and the proportion of women gainfully employed to the total remained practically the same, as in New York. However, the number of women employed in manufacturing and mechanical industries increased 23 per cent in New Jersey where it remained practically the same in New York, and the reduction of women in factories to the total employed was less than that in New York, or from 38.2 per cent to 37.7 per cent, whereas in New York the reduction was from 35.5 to 30.9 per cent.

As the general increase of women in New Jersey was greater than in New York during the decade, so also was that of men; and the percentage of men in New Jersey factories compared with all men employed, increased from 47.9 to 50.9—somewhat more than in New York. The relative numerical importance of men and women in manufacturing and mechanical industries shifted in New Jersey about the same is in New York—from 81.2 men and 18.6 women in 1910 to 82.2 men and 17.8 women in 1920. The changes in the proportion of men and women in all occupations in New Jersey moved in the reverse direction, as in New York, but to a little less degree—from 77.7 per cent men to 22.3 women in 1910 to 77.4 per cent men and 22.6 per cent women in 1920.

Thus the employment of women in factories in New Jersey seems to have kept pace with the growth of female population and of general factory employment rather more nearly than was true of New York.

had any bearing upon their relatively decreased employment. According to the census, women also took a place of diminished importance in agriculture and domestic service where no special laws apply. On the other hand, compared with men women increased proportionately in transportation and trade, in professional service, and to a marked degree in clerical occupations. About all that can be said with reference to these data and the factory law, therefore, is that the law was accompanied by a decreased proportion of women in factories, while the proportion of men in factories slightly increased.

The tabular presentation of this distribution by the State Division of Women in Industry is as follows:[1]

PERCENTAGE OF MEN AND WOMEN IN OCCUPATIONAL GROUPS IN 1910 AND 1920

	1910		1920	
	Men	Women	Men	Women
All Occupations	75.4	24.6	74.8	25.2
Agriculture, Forestry and Animal Husbandry	96.6	3.4	97.1	2.9
Extraction of Minerals	98.9	1.1	98.5	1.5
Manufacturing and Mechanical Industries	78.1	21.9	80.0	20.0
Transportation	95.4	4.6	91.7	8.3
Trade	86.1	13.9	85.4	14.6
Public Service (N. E. C.*)	98.6	1.4	98.3	1.7
Professional Service	58.0	42.0	56.2	43.8
Domestic and Personal Service	37.7	60.3	44.3	55.7
Clerical Occupations	65.5	34.5	53.5	46.5

* Not elsewhere classified.

NOTE: Of the women engaged in transportation, 86.8 per cent were telephone operators. In the clerical occupations, 97 per cent of the women fall into the three following groups—stenographers and typists, clerks (not in stores), bookkeepers and cashiers.

[1] New York State Department of Labor, Division of Women in Industry. *Women Who Work, Bulletin no. 110*, April, 1922, p. 10.

1. *Canneries* [1]

After studying, in a previous chapter, the imperfect enforcement of cannery laws it is needless to say that nothing appears to be on record as to their effects. The one reference I have found to this phase of the cannery situation was made by the industrial commissioner in his annual report for 1915 (p. 199). Here one canner was reported to have expressed the intention " of trying next year to obtain young men to sort peas, doing away with the women entirely. He hoped in this manner to be able to live within the law even at a considerable increase in cost to himself." It had been explained that men are not so skillful as women in this operation, that " picking small bits of refuse from a stream of peas requires a deftness of touch which men do not possess." [2]

Mercantile Establishments [3]

In 1912, the commissioner of labor reported that females under 21 years of age in mercantile establishments found it a hardship to have their working day limited while that of older women was unrestricted. The result was that, in order to be eligible for employment on an equality with their unrestricted sisters, young women frequently insisted before their employers that they had passed their twenty-first birthday. In order to strengthen the law and to eliminate the inequality of opportunity it had created, the legislature, in the very year following, enacted a restrictive measure for all women in mercantile establishments, making their working hours alike regardless of age.

Knowledge of this experience of the younger in respect to

[1] See Law, pp. 134-6, *supra*.

[2] Note in passing that in spite of this conclusion, men's wages for this work were recorded as averaging 50 per cent more than the wages of the women.

[3] See Law, p. 136.

the older women provokes the question as to the experience of the restricted women in respect to the unrestricted men —whether they were handicapped by the law as were the young women before them. One looks in vain for an answer in the form of a corresponding act in the following year. The answer came, however, in the report of the commissioner of labor who explained that the law, "has provided beneficial results for thousands of female employees, and has incidentally extended its benefits to thousands of male employees working" in the same establishments. He continued that, "In reducing the hours to nine per day, the merchants seem to have suffered very little inconvenience and many of the larger stores have changed their opening hour to 9 a. m., having found that a very small percentage of their business was done before that hour."

While there is striking absence of precise data on all of these points, one would gather from these general statements that women in mercantile establishments did not suffer from legal regulation of hours while men's hours were left free, for the reason that the industry demanded the work of both during open hours. The consequence was that the open hours were shortened. Here was a case where women were numerically predominant [1] so that their restricted hours of employment became general for all. This is just opposite to the situation cited in 1906 where, in more skilled and highly paid occupations, men were predominant and their working time became general for all. In that instance the result of the law, preventing the minority from conforming to the majority, was reported to have been that women were forced out of employment.

[1] Owing to the lack of clerical service, data have not been tabulated showing the relative proportion of men and women in mercantile establishments in New York, but I am assured by the bureau of inspection that women form a substantial majority in these occupations.

In 1916 (p. 63) the mercantile inspector reported that the mercantile law in relation to hours " has proved to be a most humane law, many thousands of women workers having benefited by its observance and enforcement." And again in 1920 (p. 16),—" the report shows that there is a marked tendency to reduce the hours of labor of females, and that many establishments are not working the maximum number of hours permitted by law."

As for quantitative data regarding women employed in trade in New York, as compared with men, the proportion increased slightly from 1910 to 1920.[1] In 1910 the proportion of all employed who were women was 13.9 per cent while in 1920 it was 14.6 per cent. This change in the proportion of men and women was in the opposite direction from that for factories. Like the unfavorable variation in factories however, though more slight, the proportion of women in trade as compared with all women employed, diminished from 1910 to 1920. The percentage was 7.7 in 1910 and 7.5 in 1920.[2]

These facts regarding mercantile employments, as those previously cited concerning factories, furnish no conclusive evidence as to the effect of legislation for women. Yet it is pertinent to observe that though the number of gainfully employed women increased during the decade, there was no increase in their tendency to go into trade.

HOURS—NIGHT WORK

As has been mentioned before, the effect of the first night work law for women and girls in New York was to convince the court of its unconstitutionality. The fact that the law included in blanket form all females regardless of age

[1] *Women Who Work*, *op. cit.*, pp. 10-12.

[2] Of the 86,079 women employed in trade, the largest number or 51.4 per cent were saleswomen. The next largest group were clerks in stores. These were 24.5 per cent of the whole.

brought the decision of invalidity on the grounds that it deprived mature women of the right to freedom of contract. Commissioner Sherman in 1906 (p. I. 60) had declared that there was no necessity for the prohibition of night work by adult women except for administrative reasons,[1] and continued that, "on the other hand, if enforced, it would deprive some mature working women, employed by night only, at skilled trades, for short hours and for high wages, of all means of support." He further pointed out that, "the prohibition in its application to factories only, seems rather one-sided when we consider that probably the hardest occupations of women, those of hotel laundresses and cleaners (charwomen) are not limited as to hours in any way."

In this same year and in 1907 following (p. I. 46) the commissioner reported some effects of the night work prohibition upon the work of young men. His explanation ran as follows:

Considerable distress and opposition has been caused by the enforcement of its [section 77 of the Labor Law] prohibition of night work, because it has prevented youths under 18 from learning certain trades, such as brickmaking and baking, which require work before 6 A. M. and after 9 P. M., respectively, and from being employed in certain high-class factories usually operated only by day but which occasionally run over into the evenings after 9 o'clock. To avoid this unfortunate effect, chapter 507 of the Laws of 1907, which amended section 77, following a recommendation of the Department, placed male minors under 18 in a distinct class by themselves, and shortened the prohibited hours as to them to between midnight and 4 A. M.; but on the other hand it forbids the employment of such minors more than six days a week.

[1] It is less difficult to enforce the prohibition of the work of young women whose exact age is not known, if there are certain stated hours within which *no* females may be employed legally.

Here was a specific need for flexibility in the requirements of the law for the sake of the industrial progress of the workers concerned. It was shown that brick-makers nearly always begin work during the summer months in the cool of the morning long before 6 o'clock, and that bakers do most of their work late at night. Thus parents complained that the law as it stood prevented them from teaching their trades to their own sons. "As a matter of common decency" the labor commissioner called for modification, and modification came forthwith.

It is not possible for us to say at this time whether from the point of view of health as well as vocational progress, this submission was the wisest move on the part of the legislature. What is important to emphasize here is the deep concern over the discovery that the economic advancement of these young men was being retarded by a statutory measure which was supposed to protect them and that this discovery was the basis for amending the law.

1. *Newspaper Offices* [1]

As newspaper offices are factories under the New York law, the 54-hour and night work provisions enacted in 1913 included women printers. The most conspicuous effect upon these women was suggested in the amendment of the law in 1921 releasing them from its restrictions. In the July 15, 1923 number of *Industrial Equality,* the women speak for themselves:

Women printers of New York State were so removed from the actual protection enjoyed in well-paid jobs by the theoretical protection of the "police power" invoked by the fifty-four-hour-and no-night-shift law of 1913, that for EIGHT YEARS they sacrificed leisure and savings to secure an exemption from the "protection" of the state law. At last, in 1921, after an ex-

[1] See Law, p. 136, *supra.*

penditure of incalculable energy and sums amounting to $10,000, an exemption clause became law, and women printers returned to their profession as union members, no longer "wards of the state."

It must have been worth while fighting for, this exemption from a "protective" law, when the women concerned, many with dependents and deprived of steady work, kept up the struggle for eight years!

The sum of $10,000 may seem incredibly large in view of the smallness of the minority as seen in the figures to follow, even though it was raised over a period of eight years. The editor of *Industrial Equality* (Ada R. Wolff, printer) explains, however, that many more working women contributed to the fund than those recorded as employees in printing offices. For example, the women in binderies and jobbing plants were contributors. Also it was explained to me that there is always a fluctuating number of women (and men) who are virtually in the industry but who do not appear on the pay roll. These women try to work their way into the industry by acting as substitutes and are paid in the name of the regular employees whose places they fill for perhaps only a day or two at a time. Since there are two shifts at night and one in the day time, the night work prohibition doubly diminished the chances of these women to get substituting jobs. They were, therefore, ardent supporters of the amendment.

We have precise data concerning the effects of the 1921 amendment regarding the women printers [1] in a report which is one of the two valuable studies made in New York State by the Division of Women in Industry on the subject of effects of legislation.

[1] Unpublished report on *The Employment of Women in Newspaper Offices as Proofreaders, Linotypists and Monotypists*. Division of Women in Industry, New York State Department of Labor, November, 1921.

In her introduction to the report on the printers, Miss Nelle Swartz, explained that,

Ever since the enactment of this law [in 1913], a few women employed in these occupations have tried to have the law amended so that they would not be prohibited from working at night. Their plea at each successive session of the Legislature was that they were being discriminated against in the newspaper offices because of this law; that wages of day workers were not as high as the wages of night workers; that because of this law they were losing their places on the seniority lists and were not given the same opportunity for employment as men.

The study was made, therefore, in the November following the passing of the amendment in the spring of 1921. The expressed purpose was that of ascertaining

1. To what extent women were working in newspaper offices at night, and—
2. If the law as it stood from 1913 to 1921 had actually been a handicap to any considerable group of women in these occupations.

The study records that so far women are not generally employed in newspaper offices, that "statements of the union men and foremen" bore witness to their "prejudice against them"; that, "highly skilled, highly organized, mature women as they are, this group still suffers from the limitation of opportunity which has its roots deep down in class custom and social history."

This being true, the readjustments in the employment of women made during the first six months of their release from the law are somewhat striking. The shifts had all been made in Greater New York.

Of the 55 up-state newspapers which were heard from, 29

employed women and 26 did not employ them. In the 29 newspapers there were 68 women working—33 as proofreaders, 33 as linotypists and 2 as hand compositors, all on day shifts.

In Greater New York, 35 women were employed in these three occupations on ten of the fourteen newspapers. Eighteen or one half of these women had changed the nature of their employment as a result of their release from the law.

On one paper, ten women proofreaders, linotypists and hand compositors worked daily from 8 a. m. to 4 p. m. except Saturdays when their hours were now from 6 p. m. to 12:30 a. m. Before the change was made in the law these women had stopped work at 10 p. m. instead of 12:30 a. m.

Five women proofreaders were employed on another large New York City paper regularly from 7 p. m. until 3 a. m., two of whom had formerly worked on the day shift, the other three having been newly taken on as a result of the amendment.

Two women worked on the "lobster" shift in another large daily newspaper office. These hours are from 2 a. m. to 9 a. m. and command higher wages than any other shift—$61 a week by union agreement.

Another paper employed a woman at night who had previously worked on the day shift.

The wages of these women had been increased accordingly. The report quotes the New York wages as fixed by the trade union as follows:

$55 for the day shift.

$58 for the night shift (beginning work at 6 or 7 p. m.).

$61 for the lobster shift.

The women proofreaders, linotypists and hand compositors employed in the up-state offices received a considerably lower wage, some as low as "$15 or less per week." 32 women received less that $27 which, it was concluded, was indicative of their being employed in non-union shops. As before stated there had been no changes from day to night employment among the up-state women.

Judging from the views of the women themselves, we are obliged to conclude that the freedom of contract of these 18 women, who took up or resumed night work in New York City, was made more real by their release from the restrictions of the law. They were thus enabled to offer their services according to the regulations of newspaper offices, as desirable workers rather than as a separate group of women. Nevertheless it was suggested by a staunch supporter of special protection for women, that these women should have been willing to sacrifice their advancement by allowing the 1913 law to stand unamended,—that the minority should be willing to sacrifice for the majority. These two views will be discussed at a later time.

2. *Restaurants*[1]

There are no statistical data available to show the effects of the 1917 act which limited the working hours of waitresses and prohibited their employment at night. The State Industrial Commission made the general declaration the year following the passage of the act that the provision "has produced very beneficial results" although the full protection of the labor law had not been applied to waitresses.

A contrary impression is given in popular form in *Industrial Equality* (July 15, 1923) under the title of "The Farce of 'Protection'." An attempt is here made to present the irrational inconsistency of the act as it bears upon women employed in restaurants, and reveals in its tone a strong antagonism to the law. In the form of a narrative the work of two girls is summarized. The first is a waitress, who supports an invalid mother, and is prohibited from working at night by "protective" legislation. In consequence she

[1] See Law, p. 138, *supra*.

has to pay a neighbor for caring for her mother during the day and also she loses all companionship with the invalid, who must go to bed very early. In addition to this the confinement of the day work deprives her of outdoor exercise, and though modestly dressed, in a waitress's uniform, she is not allowed to wait during the most profitable shifts of the restaurant's service. The second girl, a cabaret dancer, is permitted to dance by night in the same restaurant. The writer goes on to say,[1] "wouldn't you suppose that the law which 'protects' [one woman] . . . . sufficiently clothed, from earning her living after 10 P. M., would do something for [the other] . . . . who twice nightly courts pneumonia and shivers in Coty's *poudre de riz* and a yard of chiffon?"

"The law does do something. It reads after the clause preventing [one] from working when the tips are heaviest . . . . 'This shall, however, not apply to females in restaurants as singers and performers of any kind. . . .'"

PROHIBITED EMPLOYMENT

1. *Core making*[2]

Women were prohibited in 1913 from making cores in foundries if the work was done in the room in which the cores were baked. As the Federal Women's Bureau points out, "The laws do not, however, prohibit the making of cores in such surroundings as long as women are not the core makers."[3] As no official study has been made of the effects of this act upon the employment of women in foundries, one can only form the comments of a non-official investigator. It will be recalled that there was a vehement

[1] Capitalization for additional emphasis is omitted as the irony is sufficiently evident.

[2] See Law, p. 145, *supra*.

[3] *The New Position of Women in Industry*. United States Department of Labor, Women's Bureau, *Bulletin, no 12*, p. 109, 1920.

protest against this prohibition by the women concerned at the time of its proposal by the Factory Investigating Commission (see p. 264 *supra*). They protested on the ground that it would deprive them of continuing to earn their living by the vocation for which they had been trained. Their protest was disregarded by the commission, however, with the frank admission that " we should like to see this work stopped " and that if the requirements of the law could not be met " these owners should cease to employ women in work not intended for them."

The effect of the statute, as desired by its supporters, is said by a man molder to have been realized. " The result of this law was practically to exclude women from the foundry " he says.[1] And again, " this restrictive legislation ' did produce marked effect ', which means that it helped the organization (Molders' Union) in its effort to exclude women from the foundry."

Another effect of the statute, which seems implied in the report of the Women's Bureau, negative in nature, may be suggested. The law was enacted ostensibly because it is considered unhealthy to work in air poisoned by the fumes and gases from adhesive materials used in forming the cores. Employment in such air was not prohibited to all, but only to women, who were but a small percentage of the employees. The act, therefore, by placing the emphasis upon protecting women alone, failed to emphasize the importance of installing exhaust and ventilating systems which are necessary for the protection of all employed.

2. *Polishing and Grinding* [2]

The effect upon the employment of women of prohibiting them from polishing and grinding operations is told in a

[1] James L. O'Donnell in *Equal Rights*, May 12, 1923, pp. 101-102.

[2] See Law, p. 144, *supra*.

general way by the Women's Bureau of the United States Department of Labor in the bulletin on *The New Position of Women in American Industry* already cited (pp. 103-104). The bureau reports that

Fifty-three firms employed women in grinding and polishing metal parts for the first time in 1917 or 1918. In addition to this, wherever it was the shop practice for machine operators to grind their own tools, women did this work with hand grinders whenever their cutting tools were dulled. Sharpening the tools takes but a few minutes during the day, but as the accuracy of the shape of the tools depends entirely on the skill of the hand grinder, when women machine operators accomplish this task successfully, it may be considered a real achievement. Ohio and New York State laws forbid firms to employ women on abrasive wheels, consequently it was not the general practice in these States to teach women the art of tool grinding. These State restrictions serve not only to exclude women from the occupations of grinding and polishing, but act as a handicap to their employment on all machine tools, since in many machine shops it is customary for each machine tool operator to grind his or her tools. In the two States forbidding this, firms must hire extra men to take care of the women's tools. The reason assigned for the exclusion of women from this work by people interested in the protection of the health of women is that the metal dust produced in the operation is more dangerous to women than to men. All modern grinding and polishing machines are equipped with exhaust systems which, according to tests made by Dr. L. W. Chaney, of the United States Bureau of Labor Statistics, an expert in industrial hazards, adequately remove the metal dust from the room. If modern machine builders have eliminated the health hazards on grinding and polishing, it would seem a wiser provision for all States to insist that adequate exhaust systems be installed so that the health of men as well as that of women could be safeguarded rather than that the protection of the health of women be paid for at the needless price of her exclusion from an occupation that is profitable and can easily be made safe and healthful for both men and women.

The poignancy of the effect of this apparently useless restriction upon women is the more to be felt as the bulletin goes on to report that

About 57 per cent of plants in which women operated grinders on parts that were being manufactured reported the output of women to be equal to or greater than that of men. Many of the machines were automatic, but the work had frequently to be ground to a limit of 0.002 inch. These operators took their own readings, set up and cared for their machines, and sharpened their stones. One firm reports that on automatic saw grinding a woman operated 14 machines, while a man of longer experience operated 5 machines. In another establishment the average output per hour of women on rough and finished tool grinding was 14.38 pieces per hour, while the men's output was 8.42 pieces. The women's experience in the factory had not exceeded 4 months; the men's reached 11 months. "Women have better eyes for symmetry," said a manufacturer who employed them to grind the bore of cylinders.

The bureau continues:

A firm that reported a smaller output for women polishers than for men polishers stated that the quality of the work done by women was better than that done by men. . . .

and 22 out of 32 firms stated that they intended to continue the employment of women as grinders or polishers.

The only result discovered in this study of the 1921 amendment to the New York law that permitted mature women to operate wet grinding wheels, is that given by word of mouth by Nelle Swartz of the State Bureau of Women in Industry. Shortly after the law had been modified, Miss Swartz made a visit to Jamestown, N. Y. which is one of the largest centers in the state for this kind of work. She reported that she found but six women employed in the wet grinding of abrasive metals. These women were grinding ball-bearings.

Transportation Service[1]

In the September, 1919, *Bulletin* of the State Industrial Commission, following the entry upon the statute books of the transportation act regarding the employment of women, the Bureau of Women in Industry wrote,

> There was not much apparent opposition to this bill by either employers or employees when it was introduced in the Legislature, but the moment the bill was to become effective, a cry went up from the women employees saying that if the law was rigidly enforced the majority of them would lose their positions.
>
> The great weakness of the bill was that it was to go into effect immediately, without giving the employers ample time for adjustment or employees time to find other positions.

The act, it will be recalled, prohibited the employment of all females under twenty-one years of age and restricted the working day for all women employed as conductors, guards, ticket agents and allied occupations to nine hours to be executed within a ten-hour period, leaving one hour for meals. The maximum working time per week was limited to 54 hours and all night work was prohibited between 10 p. m. and 6 a. m.

Upon the request of the Industrial Commission, the women's bureau set out " to make a careful study relative to the number of women who would lose their positions as a result of this law and just what the policy of the transportation companies was, previous to the enactment of this law, regarding the employment of women." This article in the *Bulletin* included only a part of the report; the remaining part has never been published owing to lack of funds. However, through the courtesy of Nelle Swartz, chief, I was

[1] See Law, p. 139, *supra*.

given access to the unpublished material, a part of which is presented below.

Concerning the attitude of the companies in regard to the employment of women, the bureau found the women's work to have been

very satisfactory. In the handling of money the employers claim that they are more honest than men; there is less absenteeism among women, and their labor turnover is somewhat lower than that of the men. [The New York Railways Company reported a very high labor turnover in general—complete once a year]. It was the claim of the companies that they wished to retain women as far as possible in conformity with the law.

Following this testimony of the employers it is interesting to see what the probabilities were for their being able to retain the women under the law,—whether the protest of the women against the act, on the grounds that it would force their dismissal, was warranted.

The books of the transportation companies in Greater New York were examined on May 1, 1919, shortly after the passage of the act and twelve days before it was to go into effect. The following data were recorded to show how nearly in consonance with the new statute women's employment was at the time.

Total number of women employed			2,924	
Number employed without violation of any section of the law			490	(16.8%)
Number employed in violation of the law:				
Number employed in violation of the night work law	1,427	(48.8%)		
Number employed in violation of the nine-hour provision	498	(17%)		
Number employed in violation of the nine-hour plus consecutive hour provision	260	(8.9%)		
Number employed in violation of the consecutive hours ruling alone	249	(8.5%)		
Total number employed in violation of the law			2,434	(83.2%)

The significant fact that only 17 per cent of the women employed on the transit lines were then within the ambit of the new law, stimulated the bureau to push its inquiry into the problem of making adjustments to the law. After a careful study of the situation the bureau stated that "certain adjustments can be made by the companies that would make it possible to retain a certain number of women and yet conform to the law." The changes suggested by the bureau and the proportion of adjustments they considered it possible to make as compared with the number of women affected were as in Table I (see following page).

This table indicates that according to the estimate of the women's bureau, 84 per cent of all the women employed on the railways of Greater New York would come under the regulations of the law. Of these only four per cent could be continued in the service. In other words 96 per cent of those affected, or four-fifths of the total women employed—in so far as their positions were otherwise secure—would be thrown out of their positions by the enforcement of the act.

The diminution in the employment of women can by no means be attributed entirely to the effect of the law. The companies had been laying off female employees since November, 1918, when the armistice was signed, and men were filling their places. This fact appears to have been taken too generally, however, as a reliable indication that no women were considered permanently employed in the transportation service, and that the law could not be accused, therefore, for forced unemployment.

Because of this confusion of impressions, the figures on the course of women's employment during the time under discussion are given in full. The data were taken from that part of the unpublished report of the Bureau of Women in Industry which was in the form of a "Brief submitted to the State Industrial Commission" in June, 1919. They include both the total number of female employees in the three large companies and their distribution in specific occupations.

TABLE I

POSSIBLE ADJUSTMENT IN THE EMPLOYMENT OF WOMEN IN ORDER TO CONFORM TO THE TRANSPORTATION ACT, AS SUGGESTED BY THE NEW YORK BUREAU OF WOMEN IN INDUSTRY [1]

Company	Number Women Employed	Women Affected by the Law			
		Number	Per cent	No. possible to be retained and occupation suggested	Per cent of those affected possible to be retained
Brooklyn Rapid Transit Company.	1,723	1,265	73.4	13 ticket choppers 54 car cleaners — 67	5.29
Interborough Rapid Transit Corporation	769	769	100	10 ticket choppers 14 car cleaners — 24	3.12
New York Railways Company........	411	400	97.3	7 porters could have 1 hour less per day	1.75
Total..... ...	2,903*	2,434	83.84	98	4.02

* There is a difference of 21 women between this figure and that in the published report in the *Bulletin*, which is given as 2,924 for the total number of women employed. The total number of women affected, however, comes to the same figure in both reports.

[1] This table may be considered roughly to indicate the number of dismissals of women from the transportation service (allowing for the fact that the consecutive hours provision was practically unobserved as explained on page 386 following), although the only available figures are those given in the letters from four of the companies as quoted on page 387, *infra*.

TABLE II

The Course of Employment of Women by the Brooklyn Rapid Transit Company from July, 1918 to May, 1919, by occupations and by months

Date	Total number female employees	Porters	Conductors and Guards	Ticket Sellers	Ticket Choppers	Car Cleaners
1918						
July	1,863	79	792	906	36	50
August.......	1,850	77	802	891	36	44
September ...	1,857	70	815	880	36	56
October	1,848	67	823	868	36	54
November ...	1,792	64	783	856	36	53
December ...	1,750	56	755	858	36	50
1919						
January	1,769	47	710	920	36	56
February	1,737	45	659	942	36	55
March	1,722	44	615	973	36	54
April 30 or May 1.....	1,723	41	567	1,023	36	56
May 30......	1,364	22	432	827	28	55

TABLE III

The Course of Employment of Women by the Interborough Rapid Transit Company from July, 1918 to May, 1919, by occupations, by months

Date	Total number female employees	Porters	Conductors and Guards	Ticket Sellers	Ticket Choppers	Car Cleaners
1918						
July	802	80	..	38	684	..
August	1,104	165	..	96	822	21
September ...	1,356	205	..	122	1,001	28
October	1,596	201	..	128	1,235	32
November ...	1,449	172	..	151	1,099	27
December ...	1,314	109	..	189	989	27
1919						
January	1,104	58	..	227	792	27
February	1,007	42	..	243	697	25
March	929	28	..	240	642	19
April........	882	20	..	250	596	16
May	769	12	..	239	504	14

TABLE IV

THE COURSE OF EMPLOYMENT OF WOMEN BY THE NEW YORK RAILWAYS COMPANY FROM JULY, 1918 TO MAY, 1919, BY OCCUPATIONS AND BY MONTHS

Date	Total number female employees	Conductors	Car Cleaners	Matrons	Janitresses
1918					
July	426	406	14	2	4
August	446	400	40	2	4
September	562	495	61	2	4
October	638	563	69	2	..
November	613	536	71	2	..
December	586	509	70	3	..
1919					
January	552	485	60	3	..
February	519	462	50	3	..
March	477	438	32	3	..
April	455	418	30	3	..
May	411	378	26	3	..

These data show a wide variation of change in employment within the industry. Some occupations show a decided falling off in the number of women employed from November, 1918, to May, 1919, others show practically no change, while the number of women ticket sellers increased. The following table is a summary of the changes in employment in the three companies by occupations. The change in the number employed and the percentage is given. The minus signs indicate decreases in the number or percentage employed from November to May, and the plus signs indicate increases:

TABLE V

SUMMARY OF TABLES II, III, IV SHOWING THE NUMBER AND PERCENTAGE OF CHANGE IN THE TOTAL NUMBER OF FEMALES EMPLOYED IN SPECIFIED OCCUPATIONS BY THREE COMPANIES FROM NOVEMBER, 1918 TO MAY 1, 1919

Company	Change in the total number of female employees from Nov., 1918, to May 1, 1919	Percentnge of decrease in the total No. of females employed	Porters		Conductors and Guards		Ticket Sellers		Ticket Choppers		Car Cleaners	
			Change in No.	% of change	Change in No.	% of change	Change in No.	% of change	Change in No.	% of change	Change in No.	% of change
Brooklyn Rapid Transit Company	— 69	— 3.9	— 23	—35.9	—216	—27.6	+167	+19.5	No change	No change	+ 3	+ 5.6
I. R. T.	—680	—46.9	—160	—93.	..	..	+ 88	+58.3	—595	—54.1	—13	—48.1
N. Y. Railways Company	—202	—32.95	..	..	—158	—29.5	..	..	..	..	—45	—63.4
Total for all Companies..	—951	—32.7	—183	—77.5	—374	—28.4	+255	+25.3	—595	—54.1	—55	—63.6

In other words these tables show that the decrease in the total number of women employees from the time the armistice was signed to May 1, 1919, was about 33 per cent. The number of women porters decreased over two-thirds or 78 per cent, conductors and guards less than one-third or 28 per cent, ticket choppers over one-half or 54 per cent, car cleaners nearly two-thirds or 64 per cent, while the number of ticket sellers actually increased 25 per cent.

In so far as these figures have value, then, it would appear unwarranted to conclude that because one-third of the women had been laid off in the year before the law took effect, the subsequent dismissals were independent of the law. The marked increase in the number of women ticket agents during the year prior to the enforcement of the act would indeed seem strong evidence in the opposite direction. And, too, it will be recalled that only 17 per cent of the approximate 3000 women employed at the time the act became effective were employed in conformity with its regulations.

In contrast to the view that women were emergency employees for the period of the war only, stands the testimony of the companies that "they wished to retain women," as for example that of Frank Hedley, Vice President and General Manager of the Interborough Rapid Transit Corporation. Mr. Hedley represented Joel B. Hedges, receiver for the surface lines at an investigation meeting relative to the employment of women, held May 23, 1919. In part Mr. Hedley testified as follows:

We have 354 women employed this morning as conductors on the New York Street Railways. A week ago I had 365. The difference in these figures represents the women who have resigned in the last few days. In the New York Railways we have great difficulty still in getting a sufficient number of men to equip the cars. We put the women on these as a wartime measure (then we could not get men enough) with the understanding that the women were going to retain their positions, if their services were satisfactory, and with the understanding that their working conditions and their places in seniority lines, would be precisely the same as for the men and the pay exactly the same. These women have been performing very satisfactory service, as far as the Company and the management is concerned, we have no desire whatever to dispense with them. We know we have a number of deserving women. Some have families they must support, some of them invalid parents that they support, and those women start in there at forty-one cents an hour. That is a higher rate of pay than any of them that I know of ever earned until they came in our employ. They are very desirous and anxious to retain their positions. If they are thrown out they will have to secure employment elsewhere and they will have to do it at a lower rate of wage. It is comparatively easy work and their hours are regular; they know exactly what they are going to do. It is far superior, so the girls say, to the ordinary housework of a servant in a rich man's family because they know when they come to work in the morning and know when they are through at night and free after that. The ordinary houseworker starts at seven in the morning and is not sure whether she will be through at ten in the night. The women hold that these positions with the railroad are far superior to the positions quoted.

Whatever was the driving motive in this testimony, Mr. Hedley's array of arguments appears to indicate a desire on his part to retain his women employees. In speaking further he emphasized the expense to which the women had gone to purchase their uniforms at $10.00 each, and to join the Voluntary Relief Association for sick and death benefits. He declared that the morbidity of the women during the influenza epidemic had been lower than that of the men, that women had kept more regularly at work than the men. " The matrons," he continued, " (that is where we get much information) say women are enjoying better health now than they did when they had confining employment." On the financial side, Mr. Hedley explained that a substantial investment had been made in the form of separate comfort facilities for women at every terminal which represented a loss if women could not be retained. Mr. Dempsey of the Brooklyn Rapid Transit Company declared at the same meeting that the sanitation requirements of the law would not act as a prohibition against the employment of women.

Knowledge of the length of service of the women employees is also of help in the attempt to discover whether they were but transient employees on the street railways. Material on this phase of the inquiry, collected by the Bureau of Women in Industry for 1,640 of the more than 2,000 women employed, is shown in Table VI (see following page).

For purposes of analysis, the time when these women were taken into the employ of the three companies has been divided into three periods, namely,—the period preceding the entry of the United States into the war, the period of our war participation, the period after the signing of the armistice. In so far as this sample is representative, the data show clearly that the large majority of women employed on street cars were probably taken on to fill a war emergency (with the alleged promise of being retained if satisfactory, however). These were three-fourths of all the women recorded. Five per cent of all recorded were probably in no way connected with the war emergency, and 20 per cent were taken on after the signing of the armistice. There was variation within the separate companies. On the Brooklyn Rapid Transit lines, 15 per cent of the women recorded had been in the employ of the company before our entry into the war, and about 26 per cent were taken on after the war, leaving 58 per cent who were taken on during the war. Women seem not to have been employed on the Inter-

TABLE VI

NUMBER OF WOMEN EMPLOYED BY THREE SPECIFIED COMPANIES ON MAY 1, 1919, GIVING THE DATE OF THEIR FIRST EMPLOYMENT, BY OCCUPATIONS

Occupation	Date of first employment							Total for the Company
	Prior to May 1, 1917		Between May 1, 1917 and Nov. 1, 1918			After Nov. 1, 1918		
	Before May 1, 1916	From May 1, 1916 to May 1, 1917	From May 1, 1917 to May 1, 1918	From May 1, 1918 to Aug. 1, 1918	From Aug. 1, 1918 to Nov. 1, 1918	From Nov. 1, 1918 to Feb. 1, 1919	After Feb. 1, 1919	
B. R. T.								
Conductors and guards.	0	0	21	45	35	13	0	
Cleaners and porters ..	0	0	5	3	6	0	0	
Ticket sellers.........	61	28	102	68	53	80	60	
Total for periods...	89 (15.3%)		338 (58.3%)			153 (26.4%)		580
I. R. T.								
Porters..............	0	0	0	5	5	2	0	
Ticket sellers.........	0	0	3	85	111	31	4	
Ticket choppers	0	0	3	202	218	47	20	
Total for periods...	....		632 (85.9%)			104 (14.1%)		736
N. Y. Rys. Co.								
All women	0	0	8	175	70	54	17	
Total for periods...	....		253 (78.1%)			71 (21.9%)		324
Total for periods—three companies..	89 (5.4%)		1,223 (74.6%)			328 (20%)		1,640

borough Rapid Transit and New York Railways lines before the war so that a larger percentage of these were given first employment at that time, but even here 14 and 22 per cent respectively were taken on after the fighting ceased.

Does this evidence seem to show that the protest of the women against the law was warranted? Or would they have been dismissed anyway when the men returned from the trenches? Clearly, it is impossible to tell to what extent the new employees would have been dismissed. The testimony of Mr. Hedley would suggest that the proportion dismissed would have been low, and we have seen that the actual decrease in the numbers for all causes before May 1, 1919 was only 33 per cent of the whole. Moreover those 89 ticket sellers who were old employees, some of them in the service up to 27 years (see p. 385 *infra*), would certainly seem warranted in attributing their dismissal to the transportation act and to nothing else.

There is another consideration in regard to these women employees. Except for the 89 ticket sellers, they had appeared in occupations which were deemed "no place for a woman." [1] The deeper running facts of custom and prejudice, of which legislation itself is sometimes a symbol, were at work in the case of these women. For, aside from the restrictive act of the legislature, the men raised their voices. The union of transit employees is not well organized in New York, and opposition to the employment of women was slight compared to that of the union in Detroit and Cleveland. However, the New York men did not fail to throw their weight against the continued employment of the women.

This fact was pointed out by Mr. Squires on page 21 of his report as follows:

The fact that women take their turn with men and do not have

[1] See Report of Benjamin M. Squires, *Monthly Labor Review*, May, 1918, pp. 1-22, also discussed in a preceding chapter.

the easy runs has tended to allay somewhat the fear that women would be used to drive the men out or break down standards. The ticket agents of the Interborough Rapid Transit Elevated Lines, however, voluntarily agreed to work 12 hours per day instead of 10 if women were not put on to make up the shortage. Organized male labor, it may be said, is not opposed to the introduction of women, providing standards are maintained.

Thus it seems evident that the dismissal of the women was, in some part, owing to the opposition of the men to their further retention.

The explanation of the lack of flexibility of employment on the transportation lines, so that adjustments to the law could not be made, was the peculiarities of the industry, namely,—the seniority system and the necessity to accommodate passengers who travel in two peaks daily.

The seniority system is that by which those employees who have been longest in the service receive the first choice of runs. The report of the women's bureau explained that this system prevented the "otherwise simple" solution of the problem of meeting the night work and nine-hour requirements of the law; that if it were not for this system the companies could employ women on the day shifts and men on the night shifts and arrange the runs so that the women would not need to work more than nine hours a day.

Regarding this point some of the testimony of representatives of the railway companies may be quoted. At the aforementioned meeting held on May 23, 1919, Vice President Dempsey of the Brooklyn Rapid Transit Company declared that,

On account of this law, it was necessary for me to make some re-arrangements, which I proceeded to do. The day after, I had a delegation of the representatives of the men, also the women, and it was necessary for a few days to shift some of the men to night work. They agreed to it, for a very few days, but made it very emphatic that if we intended to give these women their [the men's] seniority, it would not be tolerated, and they assured us that if we did it, they would leave their positions in a body. The women are entirely satisfactory to us and the working conditions entirely satisfactory, but some good samaritan in their behalf has put them out of their jobs.

Mr. Arthur G. Peacock, representing the general attorney of the Interborough Rapid Transit, the New York Railways Company, the New York and Queens County Railway, the New York and Long Island Traction Company, and the Long Island Electric Railway Company, continued,

There are approximately thirty women employed in the Borough of Queens on transit lines. We employ about twenty-two of them. There is not a single one of those runs that begins after six in the morning and before ten at night. Most of them begin a few minutes before six and a few minutes after ten. These women want these jobs. One woman has two children and a paralyzed father. Eleven out of the twenty-two are the sole support. We cannot give them any such hours as prescribed. These women make anywhere from 25 to 30 dollars a week. Most of them worked in factories and stores, making ten, twelve and fourteen dollars a week. We cannot give them any nine hour jobs. If we had any nine hour jobs and the men wanted such jobs, on account of their seniority, we would give them to the men. We cannot get away from the seniority rule.

Mr. Dempsey agreed with Mr. Peacock that the law would prohibit the employment of any women in these positions in the future, for " the women would certainly have to take a night tour first."

The fact that the seniority system requires new employees to take night runs does not pronounce so hard a sentence as it first seems to the uninformed. The labor turnover on transit lines is high, some say 100 per cent a year. Hence new comers move up into the senior groups with relative promptness. On this point the state women's bureau explained,

As for example, in the New York Railways Company approximately one-half of the women conductors have day shifts indicating seniority rights, although no women have been with the company more than two years and almost one-half had been there only nine months.[1]

At the same meeting with the companies mentioned above, Mr. Dempsey spoke further regarding the employment of women, as to seniority and permanency of tenure:

On the stations of Brooklyn . . . the women there outrank the men in seniority. We have employed women since the road was constructed. We have, at the present time, women who have worked 25 to 27 years in the Station Department. Out of a total number of 1070 station employees, 1026 are women This law will cause the women to secure positions elsewhere.

We secure these women largely through other employees; they are largely made up of wives of deceased employees or daughters of some of the employees. They are given the preference when we have vacancies in the stations. I should say 60 per cent of our women are supporting children. The new law practically prohibits the use of women.

Thus the seniority system was the insurmountable obstacle in the attempt to adjust the women's work so that they could be retained in the service and at the same time observe the prohibition of night work.

The consecutive hours requirement of the law was even more impossible to meet than the hour restrictions with which seniority interfered. The peaks of travel in New York City during the morning and afternoon hours of the day make employment necessary in two separate periods. This calls very frequently for a split trick arrangement which extends the over-all time of the employee and provides a shorter or longer leisure time in between. Though many of the women employees interviewed preferred this disposal

[1] *The Bulletin* for September 1919, *supra cit.*

of their time for recreation during a pleasant part of the day, or to enable them to go home in the interim, that clause of the law which requires consecutive employment was aimed to eliminate this practice.

The damaging effect of this clause in the statute was so evident to Miss Swartz, that she requested that it be modified. After an interview with several advocates of protective legislation for women, it was agreed that Bernard L. Shientag, counsel to the Industrial Commission be asked to interpret the law as liberally " as is legally possible."

Following soon upon this request, Mr. Shientag wrote his ruling in a letter to John Mitchell, chairman of the commission. The letter ran,

In view of the foregoing, and because of the ambiguous provisions of the present law, dealing with the period during which the hours of the women in question are to be performed and in view of the peculiar operating conditions to which transit companies are subject, I advise

that the time allowed for meals be an unbroken period but if one hour is allowed, the employee must stop work within ten hours of the time of beginning, if four hours is allowed, the employee must be released for the day within thirteen hours after reporting for duty. " In no case however, is the woman allowed to work more than nine hours per day or 54 hours per week, or after 10 o'clock in the evening or before 6 o'clock in the morning."

On September 10, 1919, in accordance with this legal advice, orders were sent to the railway companies by First Deputy Commissioner John L. Gernon requiring them to observe the law as interpreted. The order was to take effect immediately. Thus, practically speaking, the consecutive hours requirement was removed. But the other restrictions upon hours still remained. These, particularly the prohibition of night work, so interfered with the seniority system that the consequences were serious.

For the purpose of discovering just how serious the consequences were, Miss Swartz, on October 6, 1919, wrote letters of inquiry to each of the companies. She asked for explicit information regarding the effect of the law upon the employment of the women—just what proportion of women the companies were compelled to "lay off" as a result of the transportation law. Excerpts from the four letters received are of interest.

From the Eighth Ave. Railroad Company, October 7, 1919:

I am not just clear as to what you request in your letter of the 6th inst., but will state that the operation of the Transportation Law to which you refer resulted necessarily in the discharge, or laying off, or whatever else it may be terminated, of every woman employed in this Company's service with the exception of one employed for part of her time as cleaner in this office. The proportion eliminated is, therefore, 26/27.

(Signed)

From the New York and Queens County Railway, October 7, 1919:

. . . it was necessary for us to dispense with the services of all of the women who were employed as conductors. We were unable to retain any and had none in any other occupation other than that of conductor. Incidentally we dispensed with the services of one woman who was caretaker of the women's room.

(Signed)

From the New York Railways Company, October 22, 1919:

. . . It was necessary for this company to drop from its service all women conductors, numbering 200 in all, and also three other women employees engaged in miscellaneous capacities. The only other employees affected by this law were those employed as car cleaners in our Car Equipment Department and whose working hours we rearranged in order to comply with the law. We have 17 women employees in this capacity.

(Signed)

From the Brooklyn Rapid Transit, November 26, 1919:

. . . I have to advise you that the number of women ticket agents employed prior to the enactment of the so-called Lockwood Bill vary, the greatest number at any one time being 1087. As a result of the enforcement of the transportation law, this number has been reduced to approximately 750.

On April 1st, of this year, we employed 290 female guards, all of whom have been taken out of service as a result of this law.

(Signed)

To sum up the effects of the New York transportation act upon the employment of women in the light of the foregoing data, there seems little question that a substantial number of women employees were dismissed because of the law. Just how many women fell into this group cannot be determined because other forces were at work which materially affected their dismissal. Principal among these forces was the fact that the majority of these women had been taken into employment as a war emergency and were being dismissed at the close of the war.[1] To consider the law itself however, it is clear that it was in marked opposition to present railway service requirements; so much so that there seems a choice of only two explanations for its passage. Either the bill was championed by those who would discourage the employment of women in the transportation

[1] It would be interesting to know what has developed in respect to women's employment on the transportation lines since the return to peace time conditions and the modifications in the law. I have made a serious effort to secure this information but have so far been unsuccessful.

service altogether, as was the case with the legislation affecting women core makers; or else the bill was introduced and fostered by those who had no scientific knowledge of the industry to which it applied.[1] If there was no thought of eliminating women, the assumption was naïve that the factory and mercantile law could be extended to the railway service without regard to the character of that industry. On this point the Bureau of Women in Industry commented as follows:

> However, in drawing up legislation for industries such as the transportation service, which must operate continuously day and night with the familiar rush and the high peaks in the number of cars, it is obvious that different kind of legislation than that modelled after our factory and mercantile acts is required.[2]

PART II: SOME EFFECTS OF LAWS OUTSIDE OF NEW YORK STATE

HOURS OF LABOR—TRANSPORTATION SERVICE

The subject of women employed in the transportation service has been further investigated by the Women's Bureau of the United States Department of Labor.[3] The material was gathered in June, July and September of 1919 and January of 1920; the cities chosen for study were Chicago, Boston, Detroit and Kansas City. Since a good deal of attention was given by the bureau to the effects of restrictive legislation upon women employees the report may be considered in some detail. While some particular facts,

[1] This seems hardly probable, following so closely upon the careful analysis of the transportation industry in New York by Benjamin Squires. *Op. cit.*

[2] *The Bulletin.* New York State Industrial Commission, September, 1919, p. 237.

[3] *Women Street Car Conductors and Ticket Agents.* Bulletin of the Women's Bureau, No. 11. United States Department of Labor, 1921.

such as the number of women employed in different occupations and their length of service, are not given, there are important data on women's wages compared with those of men, the nature of the runs, etc. The material offered in the report is sufficiently analogous to that just given for New York, to be a basis for some noteworthy comparisons.

" The purpose of the investigation," the bureau explained (p. 14),

> was to discover in several localities the hours of work and wages of women street car conductors and ticket agents; the relation of the work of women to that of men, as shown by methods of granting seniority rights to men and women, and by special regulations for women; and the effect on hours and numbers of women employed of the enforcement of legal regulation of hours for women employed in transportation.

In Detroit the women were employed as conductors in the face of opposition of the union; in Kansas City, with its qualified coöperation. The laws for the protection of women were the same for the two cities except that the Michigan law stated the maximum hours to be ten a day and 54 a week, while that in Missouri made nine hours the maximum day with a 54-hour week. Neither state prohibited night work nor prescribed the length of time in which runs should be made. (These are important differences from the New York law for it was these provisions that constituted the greatest obstacles to retaining women in New York.) According to the Women's Bureau survey, women's schedules were adjusted to meet the requirements of the law in these two cities, without seeming to disqualify such women for employment.

In Detroit, the senority list was maintained for men and women together but women were permitted to choose only those runs which did not exceed their maximum hour limit. The result of this order was that while in July 80.9 per cent of the women had week-day runs of 10 or under 10½ hours, in January this number was increased to 98.4 per cent. The hours within which these runs were made were in both cases all the way from ten to nearly fifteen.

The number of women employed in Detroit in January 1920 was a third less than in July 1919, having fallen from 91 to 61, but the bureau believes this decrease was not a result of the ten-hour law which took effect in August, 1919. The explanation was given (p. 23) that it was "probably due to a normal labor turnover and to the fact that the company was not permitted by the terms of its contract with the union to hire any new women."

With regard to wages in Detroit, there was a relatively favorable comparison between those of men and of women. While no trend of wages is shown, the median weekly earnings of women in July were recorded to have been $31.92 and those of men $37.65. In January following, women's earnings were $31.69 and those of men were $39.40. Thus women's wages decreased only 23 cents in spite of the reduction of hours. The smallness of the reduction was explained by the fact that by January these women had been employed over one year which brought an automatic increase in the hourly rate over that for employees of less than a year. This increase was from 55 cents to 60 cents an hour. The increase in the men's earnings was explained by the fact of their making extra runs because of absence of conductors during the influenza epidemic.

The bureau concludes in regard to the effects of the law in Detroit that

The similarity of the median rate for the wages of men and women during January, as well as July, seems to be conclusive proof that the legal limitation of the women's hours has not resulted in discrimination against them, or in any considerable reduction in their wage. The men's higher wage was earned by extra runs and over-time, from which it was the object of the law to protect the women.

Twenty-six women were employed as conductors by the Kansas City Railways Company in July 1919. These constituted only one per cent of the total working force.[1] Special schedules or "swings" were arranged for these women in order to bring their work within the nine-hour day limited by law. This was accomplished by having them relieved before their runs were completed. Data were accessible for only ten of the twenty-six women but these were considered sufficiently representative for analysis. The women worked on only one of the company's lines and their hours were so reduced that the greater number of women were scheduled to work but seven or eight hours on week-days, only one of the ten having a schedule of nine hours. Sunday runs were very short—three or four hours for the most part. The time within which the work was performed was usually 10, 11 or 12 hours, with a little over 13 hours for the maximum. Furthermore, night runs were made much less commonly by women in Kansas City because of the special "swings," than by the women in Detroit whose work was differentiated from that of the men to a minimum degree.

The wages in Kansas City were considerably lower than in Detroit. The average monthly earnings of women were $75. The average is not given for men. Seventy-five dollars a month was guaranteed by the company to both men and women "if they took whatever runs were offered and reported on time." Seven hours and 14 minutes a day for thirty days a month was the working time considered necessary to earn the $75 though this amount was paid if fewer hours were worked. The company asserted that the special schedules which they were required to make for women

[1] *Op. cit.*, p. 72.

made the employment of a woman cost them 57 cents an hour while the maximum earning capacity for individual employees was 40 cents. The Women's Bureau discredited this assertion, however, showing that only two of the "10 representative schedules" showed less than the required number of hours. In receiving $75 a month, then, these two women were said to have been paid more than they earned.

The union in Kansas City is reported to have relinquished its earlier expressed opposition to the employment of women in May, 1918, and to have coöperated since that date in the satisfactory adjustment of women's hours and schedules. The Kansas City example of coöperation between men and women employed in the same occupation is sometimes referred to, therefore, as significant of what can be done. However the Women's Bureau explains that "the Kansas City situation is not reflected in the general policy of the union." The bureau quotes (page 12) a revealing excerpt from a letter received from the international president of the Amalgamated Association of Street and Electric Railway Employees of America, Mr. W. D. Mahon, as follows: "The dispute that was raised by our organization was against women acting as conductors on surface and trolley cars. Our organization took the position that it was no fit place for a woman to work and has decided against it."

The conclusions of the Women's Bureau on the findings regarding the employment of women on street cars in these two cities are noteworthy. In addition to its summary of the relation of legislation to employment, the report of the bureau seems to clear away a misconception as to "woman's place." The conclusion is squarely opposed to the view just given and to the conclusion of Benjamin Squires after his New York study, but it appears to be supported by the evidence presented:

On the whole, the facts reported for these two cities do not show any royal road to ideal conditions for women street car conductors. The Kansas City women had comparatively short hours and no night work, but their wage rate did not compare favorably with that of the Detroit conductors. The Detroit women worked longer hours, at night, and frequently seven days a week, but their pay was good, and each woman who was interviewed found the work congenial, not too taxing physically, and better paid than any work she had ever done before.

Although conditions were not ideal, however, no particular reason was disclosed either through a careful study of hours and wages, or through investigation of actual working conditions or through interviews with the women themselves, to prove that the work of a street car conductor was unfit for women. On the contrary it seemed to combine many advantages not always found in the traditional occupations for women.

Street car conductors do not have to stand continuously, they get plenty of fresh air and variety of employment, there is no heavy work to be done, their wages are good, and their hours are no longer than in many other occupations in which women have worked for years. Forty-six women conductors in Detroit told the investigators of the Women's Bureau that they preferred the work of a conductor to any work they had ever done before. Only one woman, who used to drive a rural free-delivery wagon, liked her previous occupation better. No evidence was found to show that the work on the street cars involved exposure to risks or dangers which women are not facing and coping with successfully in other forms of work. The 10-hour day and 54-hour week law in Detroit, although adherence to it had not been absolute, seemed to have resulted in a considerable shortening of hours for the women without decreasing their numbers or their pay. Whether, under the peculiar conditions incident to the conduct of a transportation system, absolute adherence to an inelastic regulation of hours can be arranged for without handicapping the women can not be asserted from any facts included in this survey.

The difficulties with which both the companies and the women were faced in complying with the law in Detroit and Kansas City emphasizes [*sic*], however, the need for a very careful study of local conditions before any phase of a transportation law is decided upon, with a view to determining possible local adjustments to make compliance more feasible and less likely to wreak disaster upon those it was framed to benefit.[1]

In Chicago and Boston women were employed as ticket agents and collectors in such large numbers that those occupations had come to be accepted as "women's work". No statement is made regarding women as conductors in these two cities. The Illinois law made the maximum working time for women ten hours a day and 70 hours a week, while in Massachusetts, the maximum since July, 1919, has been nine hours a day and 48 hours a week. Here also as in Detroit and Kansas City and differing from New York, there were no restrictions put upon women's working at night nor upon the "over-all" hours.

More or less independently of the laws the women employees in each of the two cities, according to the report, were employed usually on an eight-hour-day schedule. Seniority lists were maintained for both men and women and night work was eliminated for women. In Boston this was possible because the street car lines do not run all night. In Chicago, by agreement with the union, men were employed especially for this work. The Chicago situation would seem to be an outstanding case of successful agreement among the men and women members of a common union whereby the women are flexibly and voluntarily protected from certain kinds of work even to a greater degree than the statutes demand. It must be remembered however that the over-all hours were not prescribed, and what is perhaps more explanatory—men only

[1] *Op. cit.*, p. 24.

were employed as conductors, while the majority of ticket agents were women. Thus men and women were to a certain extent in non-competing groups.

Peculiar circumstances arose in Boston to render the limitations upon women by law less burdensome than was anticipated. The number of women was not curtailed at the passing of the new law, but the company had expected to be obliged to increase the working force because of the shortened day. However, the introduction of the ten-cent fare at that time brought about two counteracting factors: (1) a slight reduction in the traffic, and (2) a reduction in the labor of change-making owing to the absence of pennies in the fare.

The Boston women were found to have been full members of the union since 1912. However this fact was considered less significant than the harmony between men and women in Chicago for the reason that practically the entire force of collectors in Boston were women. The non-competing nature of the separate occupations was more complete.

It would seem from the federal report, then, that the reasons for the more favorable effect of the laws regarding women in the transportation service in Chicago and Boston as compared with New York are three:

1. The occupations were more limited in scope so that the element of competition between men and women was largely reduced in Chicago and Boston, whereas, in New York, the field of women's occupations was broad and the competition sharp.

2. The restrictive measures in Chicago and Boston did not include the most difficult requirements of the New York statute,—the prohibition of night work and the requirement for consecutive hours of work.

3. The union in Chicago and Boston did not oppose the employment of women but on the contrary it coöperated to

adjust it. In New York, what weight the men gave in the matter was in opposition to the women.

In general summary of the effects of special legislation upon women in the transportation service, it must be said that the effects, so far as known, have not been uniform. Where the law demands conditions nearly in conformity with the practices established independently by the company, the effect has been more or less negative. On the other hand, where the law requires drastic changes in the operations of the lines if women are to be retained, women are likely to find themselves without employment. Where men and women belong to the same union, difficulties of adjustment are somewhat simplified. In general, however, women are greatly in the minority in this set of occupations, which fact in itself makes special privileges for them less possible.

HOURS OF LABOR—FACTORIES

An encouraging report on the steady decrease in the length of the working day in manufacturing industries for all employees in the United States, was made in the August, 1922, number of the *Monthly Labor Review* (page 89). Here almost one-half of all wage earners in factories are shown to have been working in 1919 on a schedule of forty-eight hours and under, and the regular hours of nearly two-thirds were under fifty-four hours. This, of course, does not include overtime work. The table in part is on page 398.

As in the case of the general reduction of hours in factories in New York State, so in the whole country there is no single cause of the reduction. Labor unions have played no small part, and now at least an eight-hour day is urged by efficiency experts and probably all who have studied impartially the way of social and economic progress.

The effect of a legally restricted working day for women when the requirement is not also made for men is less certain.

REGULAR HOURS OF WORK PER WEEK IN THE MANUFACTURING INDUSTRIES OF THE UNITED STATES, 1909, 1914 AND 1919

Regular hours of work per week	Wage earners working each specified number of hours					
	Average number			Per cent		
	1909	1914	1919	1909	1914	1919
48 and under	523,652	833,330	4,418,693	7.9	11.8	48.6
Over 48 and under 54	481,157	945,735	1,496,177	7.3	13.4	16.4
54	1,019,438	1,818,390	828,353	15.4	25.8	9.1
Over 54 and under 60	1,999,307	1,543,018	1,248,854	30.2	21.9	13.7
60	2,017,280	1,487,801	827,745	30.5	21.1	9.1
Over 60	574,212	407,973	276,550	8.7	5.8	3.0
Total	6,615,046	7,036,247	9,096,372	100.0	100.0	100.0

Conclusions are at variance on the two sides of the question. Meetings of labor representatives of women have not been able to take an unqualified position in favor of such legislation because there have always been some representatives who objected. This was true of the industrial conference called by the Federal Women's Bureau in January, 1923. At this conference, Dr. R. A. Spaeth of Johns Hopkins University, was asked to discuss the matter from the medical point of view. When Dr. Spaeth came to the specific issue of a shorter legal day for women he questioned its desirability. His view was that apart from the function of women as child bearers, there is not much evidence that industry affects women more seriously than men, and to forbid women to work more than a certain number of hours while men were not so restricted would result in discrimination against the women. He declared that the eight-hour day is "very opportunistic anyway," that this length of day has been chosen because of its convenience rather than for any scientific reason, that work should be done on an hour basis. The implication seems to have been that different individuals can work different lengths of time without injury.

A favorable report of the working of the eight-hour day for women in laundries in the District of Columbia was sent in a letter to a New York newspaper by Ethel M. Smith, secretary of the legislative committee of the National Women's Trade Union League on January 24, 1923. The report maintained that the working day of women had been shortened by the law without resulting in women's dismissal. Miss Smith explained that in the laundry industry during the war with the general expansion of business, and in spite of the fact that this expansion took place after the eight-hour law for women had been enacted, the proportion of women employed remained the same. In other words, while the working force in laundries was increased, the number of women whose legal day was restricted was increased as rapidly as the number of men whose working day was not restricted by law. Miss Smith stated that the increase of employees in laundries in the District after the enactment of the law was from 994 to 1636. "Of these 436 were men and 1200 were women, which was exactly the same ratio of men and women that prevailed before the 8-hour law was passed in the laundries of Washington." [1]

The one intensive study of the effects of a shortened working day for women by law was that published in Bulletin No. 15 by the Women's Bureau of the United States Department of Labor in 1921, entitled *Some Effects of*

[1] It would be interesting to know whether the hours of men were reduced in these laundries also, since so large a majority of the employees were women. It is unfortunate, too, that no data could be given concerning the wages of the women, but the fact that the minimum wage law was persistently opposed by the laundrymen made it impossible to secure reliable wage records.

Legislation Limiting Hours of Work for Women. This is an interesting piece of work but too brief to furnish a basis for forming conclusions. Perhaps its greatest value lies in the fact that it marks a beginning in the analysis of this important question. The possibility that "special legislation regulating their hours and conditions of work might hamper the free use of women in industry" was recognized on the one hand, in the letter of transmittal by Mary Anderson, Director, while, "On the other hand, the beneficial effect of special legislation for women has seemed so great that it would be most disastrous to condemn it without a full and careful examination of the arguments brought against it."

The subject of the survey was a group of rubber and electric appliance factories in Massachusetts and in New Jersey just before and soon after the introduction of the 48-hour week for women in factories in Massachusetts.

The conditions in New Jersey were taken as a basis for measuring the effects of the new 48-hour law in Massachusetts, as the statute in New Jersey limiting women's hours to 60 a week had stood unchanged since 1912. The plants in the two states were considered sufficiently similar in respect to the number, age, and sex of the employees, the absence of labor organizations, the technique of production and the nature of the products. In both cases women were employed in several occupations in which men and children also worked, so that substitution for women by men and children was possible. Moreover, in both cases there was said to be a shortage of women.

The protective law of Massachusetts became effective in July, 1919, and the times chosen for the studies in the two states were one week in April and one week in October of that year. The facts of variation in the employment of men and women in the two states were shown in the survey in a series of tables. From these tables deductions have been drawn and set down in the following columns:

	New Jersey—1919	*Massachusetts*—1919
Plants visited	37	28
Number of employees	24,273	43,662
Men	15,902	31,665
Per cent	65.5	72.5
Women	8,371	12,007
Per cent	34.5	27.5
Number plants reducing hours between April and October.	8	25
Number of employees	8,301	43,572
Men	4,243	31,574
Per cent	51.1	72.5
Women	4,058	11,998
Per cent	48.9	27.5
Variation in total number of workers, April to October	+5.4*	+12.9*
Women	—3.1*	+ 9.2*
Proportion women to men.	—3.1*	— .9*
Decrease in hours per week between April and October where greatest number of women were affected	3 hours and under 4	6 hours and under 7
Number plants reducing hours at another time than between April and October	13	3
Number of employees	10,230	90
Men	7,280	81
Per cent	59.5	88.9
Women	2,950	9
Per cent	40.5	11.1
Per cent of men whose hours were reduced when hours of women were reduced (all factories)	58.9	77.7
Number plants visited which did not reduce hours	16	0
Number of employees	5,742	
Men	4,379	
Women	1,363	

* The sign (+) indicates an increase; (—) indicates a decrease.

That the law in Massachusetts resulted in marked reduction in women's hours is obvious. The hours of three-fourths of the men were also reduced, and a parallel process was going on in New Jersey to a somewhat less degree. The survey does not state what was the length of the working day, as reduced, however, which leaves the reader with insufficient knowledge for a comparison of the final status of the workers in the two states. The cause of the reduction of hours in Massachusetts would seem to have been the law; in New Jersey, the cause as reported by employers was the scarcity of workers and the conviction that a shorter day brings increased output.

The Women's Bureau concludes from the data (p. 14) that

> Clearly the Massachusetts law does not seem to have placed the women of that State in a less desirable relationship to industry than that held by their sisters working in similar industries in the neighboring State. A greater number of women had their hours reduced to a greater extent in Massachusetts than in New Jersey,[1] but in spite of that fact the proportion of Massachusetts women was reduced only nine-tenths of 1 per cent while the proportion of New Jersey women dropped more than 3 per cent during the same six months.

The effect upon wages of the variation in hours in the two states was also considered, but not for men and women separately. The results were given (p. 17) as follows:

> . . . more than one-half of the establishments in each State increased both their time and piece rates when hours were reduced. Seven of the 28 plants in Massachusetts and 5 of the 21 in New Jersey increased only their time rates, expecting the piece-workers to make up the extra wage through an increased hourly output. In one factory manufacturing rubber goods in Massachusetts, when hours were reduced from 54 to 48 an increase of pay was given equivalent to three hours a week, but the workers were expected to make up the other three hours' pay through increased production. Similar arrangements were found in various other factories, but a straight increase in time and piece rates was more often the rule than the exception.

[1] The proportion of women employed in New Jersey was greater than in Massachusetts it will be noticed, however.

It is unfortunate that the report omits specific wage data. It would be pertinent to know in what proportion the wages of women were increased relative to the wages of men; whether the greater falling off in the number of women employed in New Jersey as compared with Massachusetts was in any way connected with a greater increase in women's wages in New Jersey or in the wages of the men in Massachusetts.[1]

Another interesting question arises in studying the report as to why in both New Jersey and Massachusetts the variation in the proportion of women to men employed was in the opposite direction to the trend of their relative numbers in the same factories before the period April to October. In New Jersey the nature of the output in the rubber industry called for heavier work than that in the electric appliance industry, so that the proportion of women was smaller in the rubber than in the electrical plants. But during the period under study the number of women in the rubber industry increased .8 per cent while in the electrical industry the number decreased 3.96 per cent. In Massachusetts the nature of the output was just the reverse, the rubber industry called for the lighter work of the two and had employed proportionately more women than the electric appliance industry. However the women increased only 5.4 per cent in the rubber industry as compared with 15.7 per cent in the electrical plants. Thus in both states there was a marked increase in the proportion of women employed in the heavier-work plants as compared with the lighter-work plants. No explanation is offered for this in the report.

As to whether any discrimination against women was discovered in Massachusetts as a result of the limitation of

[1] It would also be pertinent to know whether there was any variation in the policy of administration of the hour law for women in New Jersey during this period.

their hours, the bureau reports only one instance. It was that of an electrical appliance factory, the manager of which declared that the women were "perfectly satisfactory" but that he would employ no more of them because under the law they could not work overtime. The reaction of the bureau to this instance was expressed as follows:

It would seem that the necessity to forego the opportunity to "work overtime" would not be an insupportable hardship for the women employed in this plant, and that the testimony of many other women who had benefited from the shorter day would offset this one evidence of "discrimination."

There had been no substitution of men or minors for women because of the difficulty of conforming to the act, according to the report of the bureau. "On the contrary, the demand for women workers seemed to exceed the supply in most localities." Many of the women were interviewed during the period of the survey and their response was favorable to the law—that it had been of great benefit to them, and "that the decreased working hours had resulted in only a few instances in reduced pay."

On the whole one would conclude from the data presented that the condition of Massachusetts women in regard to hours had been distinctly improved as a result of the restrictive law. It is noteworthy that the hours of so large a majority of men were also reduced, and that so many changes were made in the state of New Jersey where the lot of the worker has been given scant attention by the legislature as compared with the record of Massachusetts.

MINIMUM WAGES

Minimum wage laws for women in this country have been overshadowed by the decision of the United States Supreme Court for the District of Columbia (April 9, 1923) which held that the District law is invalid because unconstitutional.

"We cannot accept the doctrine that women of mature age, *sui juris,* require or may be subjected to restriction upon their liberty of contract which could not lawfully be imposed in the case of men under similar circumstances," declared the majority opinion. This decision has, of course, more or less jeopardized the minimum wage laws in all other jurisdictions of this country and it is conceivable that the sex basis for wage adjustment by law may be modified. At present the United States is the only important country except Canada in which this basis is used in the protection of underpaid workers and now that this practice is outlawed in one jurisdiction, it may be that the effects of such legislation also are of passing interest. However in America minimum wage provisions still occupy a substantial place in the system of special protection for women and some attempt to analyse their effects cannot well be omitted from this discussion.

As with other types of special legislation for women, so with the minimum wage laws, reports of their effects are conflicting. Facts so far presented in their favor have not been sufficient to quiet the objectors, nor to satisfy the impartial observer. Minimum wage commissions, some employers, and many working women are unequivocal in their endorsement of the minimum wage principle on the basis of their experience. We shall review some of these conclusions.[1]

[1] Since the writing of this chapter an interesting study of *State Minimum Wage Laws in Practice* has been published by the National Consumers' League, prepared by Felix Frankfurter, Mary W. Dewson and John R. Commons. The history and results of minimum wage legislation in California, Wisconsin and Massachusetts are presented in the form of a brief in defense of the California statute before the state supreme court, and for the use of the Ohio Legislative Investigating Commission which looks toward reporting a bill in 1925.

The Industrial Commission of Wisconsin in 1920[1] registered the estimate "that from one-fourth to one-third of the women of the State had their wages advanced as a direct result of" a wage order made effective August 1, 1919, "while sympathetic advances affected a number of higher paid workers." In the telephone industry the increase in wages was reported in many cases to have been more than 100 per cent and, for the industry as a whole, more than 33 per cent. The report declared that, "The law has not interfered with opportunities for employment, though it probably had a temporary effect in reducing the number of child-labor permits issued during the summer and fall of 1919."

The Minimum Wage Board of the District of Columbia arrived at conclusions entirely favorable to the law after four years of its operation, 1919-1922. According to Elizabeth Brandeis,[2] secretary to the board, wages as revealed by surveys, "tend to show that even under favorable circumstances the law of supply and demand does not secure to the majority of women workers wages sufficient to meet the minimum cost of decent living." A pronounced decrease in the number of women receiving less than $16 (the approximate minimum) is shown:

Using the same representative identical establishments for the comparison, we find that under unregulated wage conditions in 1919, 75% of the women in hotels, 82% of the women in commercial printing plants and 75% of the women in stores were receiving less than $16 per week. In 1922, following the establishment of minimum wage rates, these groups of workers had shrunk to 46%, 20% and 10% respectively.

[1] Industrial Commission of Wisconsin, *Biennial Report*, 1918-1920, pp. 57-65, reviewed in the *Monthly Labor Review* for March, 1921, p. 117.

[2] *Bulletin*, The Consumers' League of New York, February, 1923.

The lower decrease for hotel women is explained by the fact that many were part-time workers.

Thus the minimum wage law in the District of Columbia has clearly fulfilled its primary purpose, that is, to raise the wages of the very poorly paid. The question remains whether it has brought attendant evils which would serve to outweigh this benefit.

To meet the contention of some that the effect of the law is prejudicial to women rather than beneficial Miss Brandeis says that

The figures for the District, taking the various industrial groups together, show that in 1922 over 50% of the women and minor workers subject to minimum wage rates were actually receiving wages above those fixed by law. It is clear that the minimum, far from becoming the maximum, is scarcely even the standard wage.

Further it is declared that there was no displacement of women by men but an actual increase in the number of women employed,[1] and that the increase in wages probably did not increase the cost of goods to consumers. The conclusion is drawn, therefore,

. . . that the minimum wage law of the District of Columbia is serving the purpose for which it was enacted. Without bringing to pass any of the evil consequences so frequently predicted, it has effected a substantial increase in wages among the

[1] This deduction appears to stand upon the fact that women did not decrease in *number*, when obviously the *proportion* is the more telling basis for judgment. In an unpublished statement however, Miss Brandeis gave proportionate data for women in hotels and restaurants in Washington. According to the 1910 census, she says that 689 women were employed in these industries, and 1720 men, while in 1920, 1626 women were so employed and 1836 men. This was an increase in the proportion of women to all employed, from 28.6 per cent in 1910 to 47 per cent in 1920.

large groups of women who are found, even at a time of actual labor shortage, to be receiving wages far below the subsistence level.

Some effects of the operation of the California minimum wage law were recently discussed[2] by Mr. Louis Bloch, Statistician, California Bureau of Labor Statistics, on the basis of data gathered by his bureau and by the State Industrial Welfare Commission. An order fixing the wage at $16.00 per week had been issued in June and July, 1920, for women and minors in the manufacturing and mercantile industries and in laundries. In the report of the Industrial Welfare Commission of March, 1922, on 4,350 establishments involving 52,326 women and minors employed as time workers, the following facts were shown: (1) Only eight per cent of these workers were receiving less than the legal minimum wage rate of $16.00. (2) An additional 33 per cent were receiving from $16 to $16.99, and (3) the remaining 59 per cent of the total were receiving $17 or over. The laundry and mercantile industries evinced a little greater tendency to exceed the minimum rate than did manufacturing.

From the twentieth biennial report of the bureau of labor statistics of California, Mr. Bloch shows further data on the favorable effects of the minimum wage law. These are presented in the form of an interesting comparison of the wages of women and minors affected by the law with the wages of males not so affected. The data are as follows:

(1) Adult females: Among the females eighteen years of age and over, 77 per cent earned less than $16 per week in 1918, while only 28 per cent were in this wage group in 1921. In 1921, 72 per cent earned $16 or more per week as compared with 23 per cent in 1918. The median wage in 1918 was that from $12 to $13.99 per week, and in 1921 the

[1] *Monthly Labor Review*, August, 1923, pp. 1-12.

median had moved to from $16 to $17.99.[1] Table VII embodies these data.

TABLE VII

WAGES OF FEMALES 18 YEARS AND OVER IN 1918 AND IN 1921 BY NUMBERS AND PERCENTAGE OF ALL EMPLOYED

Weekly earnings	1918		1921	
	Number	Per cent	Number	Per cent
Under $16	29,678	77.1	10,202	28.2
$16 and over	8,796	22.9	25,870	71.8
Total	38,474	100.0	36,072	100.0
Median wage	$12 to $13.99		$16 to $17.99	

(2) Minors: Of the minors affected by the minimum wage law, 77 per cent of the males and 94 per cent of the females received less than $16 per week in 1918, whereas in 1921, 64 per cent of the males and 69 per cent of the females received less than $16. The median wage for males in 1918 was that between $12 and $13.99 and in 1921 between $14 and $15.99. For females, the median wage was between $8 and $9.99 in 1918 and between $12 and 13.99 in 1921.

[1] Of course the increase in wages may have been due in part to an increased price level. Cost of living figures for San Francisco and Oakland are reported by the United States Bureau of Labor Statistics to have risen some 16 per cent from December, 1918 to December, 1921. However, we are about to see above that there was little change in the wages of lower paid men during this time, so it may be also that the rising price level in itself would have had no effect upon wages of low-paid women.

TABLE VIII

WAGES OF MINORS IN 1918 AND IN 1921 BY SEX, NUMBERS, AND PERCENTAGE OF ALL EMPLOYED

Weekly Earnings	Males				Females			
	1918		1921		1918		1921	
	Number	Per cent	Number	Per cent	Number	Per cent	Number	Per cent
Under $16	2,672	77.1	737	64.0	3,016	94.4	1,133	68.6
$16 and over...	816	22.9	415	36.0	177	5.6	520	31.4
Total	3,488*	100.0	1,152	100.0	3,193	100.0	1,653	100.0
Median wage.	$12 to $13.99		$14 to $15.99		$8 to $9.99		$12 to $13.99	

* The total given in the report is 3,548 which appears to be an error.

(3) Adult Males: Males eighteen years of age and over are not affected by the minimum wage law. Mr. Bloch's study shows, therefore, that the number of men in the lower paid groups remained practically the same during the three years in which the survey was made. In 1918, the percentage receiving less than $16 was 4.3, while 7.4 per cent received less than $18; in 1921, 4.2 per cent received less than $16 and 7.3 per cent less than $18. Comparison of the stationary wages of these groups of men with the relative improvement in the wages of women, suggests that men would have been more likely to receive a living wage had they, too, been included in the decree.

With the higher paid groups of men the situation was different, for these did receive an advance in wages during these years of increased cost of living. In 1918, 63 per cent of the males eighteen years of age and over received less than $30 per week, while in 1921 this proportion fell to 55 per cent. In 1918, 93 per cent received less than $40 and in 1921 this proportion fell to 85 per cent. The median wage for adult males in both years was that between $25 and $29.99.

TABLE IX

WAGES OF MALES 18 YEARS AND OVER IN 1918 AND IN 1921 BY CUMULATIVE NUMBERS AND PERCENTAGES

Weekly earnings	1918		1921	
	Cumulative numbers	Cumulative percentages	Cumulative numbers	Cumulative percentages
Under $16........	7,037	4.3	4,346	4.2
Under $18........	12,108	7.4	7,579	7.3
Under $30........	104,031	62.0	56,240	54.7
Under $40........	153,772	92.9	86,813	84.6
Total	165,378	100.0	102,672	100.0
Median wage..	$25 to $29.99		$25 to $29.99	

As for the numerical importance of women in the three industries before and after the $16 decrees were entered, a true picture cannot be given without comparative knowledge of the change in the number of employed women in the state. Nevertheless, the available figures are interesting. Mr. Bloch shows that in the three industries under his survey the *numbers* of women decreased after the decree was entered, while the *proportion* of women to men increased. 18.9 per cent (38,474) of the total number of adult employees were women in 1918, while this ratio had risen to 25.9 per cent (36,072) in 1921. The same variation was true of minors—47.3 per cent (3,193) were females in 1918, and in 1921, 58.9 per cent (1,653) were females.

Figures are also given to show that there was no substitution of apprentices for women—the proportion of women and minors receiving less than the minimum wage rates having declined since the $16 decree.

Thus it appears that the California minimum wage orders did not bring about displacement of women by men or minors. Also that they have resulted in raising the wage rates of a large number of low-paid workers to whom they apply, that is, all females and male minors under eighteen years of age. It appears, too, that the low-paid males over eighteen years might likewise have been benefited had the orders been extended to include them.

Mr. Bloch states that there are no data for an analysis of the growth of industries in California as related to the operation of the minimum wage law, but he reports "normal growth" of the industries affected. Marked progress in the canning industry is shown as a more particular proof that the law has not injured industry. For, since women are in the "preponderant majority" of all employees in canneries, it was felt that had the statute retarded business the effect would have been registered there.

In corroboration of this report of Mr. Bloch, come some selected testimonies of southern California employers at a public hearing held in Los Angeles on December 11, 1922 by the Industrial Welfare Commission.[1] The subject of discussion was the reduction of the minimum wage from $16 to $15 per week, and the three industries concerned were represented for the southern part of the state. Mr. W. L. Stevens, laundryman, said, "I am delegated to state to your honorable Commission that the laundrymen are one

[1] As reported by the Consumers' League of New York in the *Bulletin* for February, 1923.

hundred per cent opposed to any reduction of the minimum wage at this time." From a representative of the cafeterias and bakeries of Southern California came the statement that, "unless your Commission can find for an absolute certainty that the women can live on a lower minimum than they are now getting, it is our request, by unanimous vote in our organization, that there be no lowering of the minimum scale." The Fish Canners and the Retail Dry Goods Merchants' Association expressed their satisfaction with the $16.00 rate. The Merchants' and Manufacturers' Association of Los Angeles and the Employing Printers' Association through Mr. I. H. Rice stated, "that our policy of good industrial relations and sound management will overcome many of the difficulties of dollars and cents in the wages paid." He believed that the minimum wage should be established in spite of the difficulties involved, and declared that "we would like to see it just a little bit more than liberal."

Employers in other parts of the country have voiced opinions similar to these testimonies of the employers of Southern California. Mr. Edward A. Filene of Boston, employer of three thousand women in his department store, testifies heartily to the greater economy of employing women at a living wage.[1] Mr. Filene foresees a wholesome effect upon business of a rigorously enforced minimum wage law. "We shall (then) be forced to turn to the real remedy," he says,

> the really big source of reduction in costs, namely, the conquering of the enormous waste that is now in all of our businesses, however good a reputation they may have for careful management.
>
> I shall not ask you to take my judgment on this question of waste, but refer you to the report of Hoover's Committee of

[1] *Bulletin* of the Consumers' League of New York, January, 1923.

Engineers on this subject which is published in book form under the title " Waste in Industry."

In his discussion of the *Minimum Wage Laws of the United States*,[1] Mr. Lindley D. Clark of the United States Bureau of Labor Statistics included a long list of expressions from employers in ten states stating their views on the minimum wage law. Many expressions were to the effect that the provision is "No check on business," or that " Such a law is the only thing to have." Mr. Clark summed up the returns in the statement that " the number of employers who expressed actual opposition to the law was almost negligible though some were vigorous in their denunciation of it."

The view of the Manufacturers' and Merchants' Association of Oregon concerning the minimum wage principle, its effects, and the recent decision of the United States Supreme Court was stated recently in unequivocal terms in a bulletin issued by the association.[2] The purpose of the bulletin was,

to plead with *ALL* employers of Oregon to still acknowledge the authority of the Industrial Welfare Commission's rulings, and in no case deviate from them, nor in any instance where a higher wage than the present minimum is now being paid, to reduce such wage to the minimum; but on the contrary where production and efficiency justifies it, rather to *increase the wages.*

The Directors of the Association adopted the following resolution:

Whereas, the Supreme Court of the United States, has recently declared unconstitutional the minimum wage law of the District of Columbia, and

Whereas, the law in question is so similar to the law of Oregon, that if a test case of same was made, our law might be held to be invalid also, and

[1] *Monthly Labor Review*, March, 1921, pp. 1-20.

[2] Reproduced in News Letter No. 26 of the Women's Bureau of the U. S. Department of Labor, September 11, 1923.

WHEREAS, the experience of a great majority (if not all) employers of Oregon who employ women, is that the minimum wage law of this State has been of such material benefit to both employers and employees, (aside from the humanitarian side of the question), that it would be most unfortunate as well as a disgrace to the State to disturb the equitable and harmonious relations now existing where women are employed in our industries,[1] therefore,

Be it Resolved, that the Manufacturers' and Merchants' Association of Oregon pledge to the Industrial Welfare Commission their support and cooperation in maintaining the present status of the Oregon law, and that we will use every effort to discourage anyone from testing the validity of the law in the courts, and will also use every effort to prevent the repeal of the law by the Legislature, should such a thing be attempted, and as an evidence of our sincerity we hereby pledge ourselves to be governed in the future as we have in the past by the rulings of the Industrial Welfare Commission.

In contrast to the staunch support of the minimum wage law by this group of Oregon employers, and to the views of some employers in other states, stands an opposite attitude as given in the recent report of the Special Legislative Investigating Commission of Massachusetts.[2] This commission, appointed to investigate whether the law should be extended, amended, or repealed, states (page 20) that

[1] In her summary of the report of the United States Bureau of Labor Statistics, *Bulletin No. 176*, which was an analysis of the effects of the minimum wage law in Oregon, Dr. Emilie Hutchinson says, "For the total number of women employed, average weekly earnings increased almost ten per cent, yet contrary to the frequent prediction, there was no substitution of men for women at the higher rates. Finally, there was an increase in labor cost, but this was offset to some extent by readjustments in the total employed group of men and women." *Women's Wages*, p. 139 (1919).

[2] *Report of the Special Commission on Unemployment, Unemployment Compensation, and the Minimum Wage*, Massachusetts, February 9, 1923.

With almost united opposition of employers throughout the Commonwealth, the Commission is compelled to recognize the fact that the Minimum Wage Law is extremely unpopular among most employers in the Commonwealth. It is also handicapped in administering the law because of the existing antipathy to it.

The testimony of a former member of the minimum wage commission, a representative of employers, who spoke before this commission, is reproduced in the report (page 19) as follows:

I freely admit the end sought—namely, the amelioration of the condition of many women helpless in the swirl of industrialism—is greatly to be desired. My own arguments . . . are that a minimum wage applied by law in any form is wrong in principle and will not accomplish the object sought, and if it produces any results at all toward that end, will do so at the expense of the law-abiding employer and to the apparent benefit of his unscrupulous competitor.

Continuing, this witness summarizing his views of the law from his experience on the Commission, says:—

Ever since my own experience on the Commission I have felt that the law is neither the panacea its zealous friends imagine or the menace its frenzied enemies assert. . . . The decrees followed by inspections unquestionably improved conditions under some employers; the posting of a notice or the mere imminence of a pay-roll examination tended to make other employers turn from more pressing problems and examine and revise their pay-roll columns. Add to these gains the not inconsiderable benefit to an industry of having a group of fair-minded employers and employees exchange freely across the table their own problems and grievances in the presence of disinterested representatives of the public, and you have summed up, I believe, about all the benefits accruing from the law.[1]

[1] Mr. Charles F. Dutch, former chairman of the commission and representative of the public, testified at the same hearings of the com-

On the other hand, it should be remembered that conditions were then ideal for the law, since wages were rising and help scarce, which meant either that current wages were always safely above the scale of the decree, or business was so rushing and employees so hard to get that no one eared long to quibble over their pay.

It is principally because of this last mentioned state of affairs in industry that the commission feels that the minimum wage law in Massachusetts, during its operation since 1913, "has not . . . had a fair trial." The conclusion was therefore that,

While there is evidence that the condition of women workers has been improved, the good results accruing from the law have not been sufficient to justify the Commission in recommending at this time an extension of its provisions.[1]

Continuance of the "recommendatory law"[2] for a period of five years was therefore recommended, during which time such information shall be gathered as "to make it possible to determine more accurately whether the legislation is justified or required."

In a thus far unpublished presentation of *Some Problems*

mission in terms more favorable to the law, that it is "a protection on both sides"—not only to the worker but to the "scrupulous high-minded employer" against his "unscrupulous competitor."

[1] Mr. J. Healey dissented from this conclusion and submitted a minority report which maintained that the results of the operation of the Massachusetts statute "fully justify, not only a continuation of the law, but an amendment to make it mandatory . . . experience justifies the conclusion that the law is now a practicable and necessary measure."

[2] The Massachusetts legislature has never given the Minimum Wage Commission power to enforce its wage decrees directly, although the commission has power under the law to inspect in order to determine compliance with the decree and may publish the names of employers who refuse to comply. This method is reported to have been effective in the majority of cases.

Connected with Minimum Wage in Massachusetts, Ethel M. Johnson, acting director, presents the view of the present minimum wage commission.[1] Miss Johnson agrees that the recommendatory feature of the law complicates its administration, that it requires "much more time and effort to secure adjustment of non-compliance," but she remarks also that the effort brings about "better understanding of the purpose of the law," and secures "a spirit of cooperation among employers" that makes it "distinctly worth while." In explaining some other difficulties of administration, Miss Johnson says that

> The lack of uniformity in rates for different occupations—the occasional failure of wage boards to function harmoniously, the delay in revising rates to meet changes in the cost of living, the time and expense involved in bringing new occupations under the scope of decrees, the friction sometimes occasioned by the inspection work—these are other difficulties which must be recognized. Their removal, however, involves administrative rather than legislative changes. Some of the difficulties mentioned are necessarily incident to the work. To a considerable extent, however, they are all within the power of the Commission to correct or lessen.

Miss Johnson explains that the occasional indifference on the part of employers, and timidity on the part of employees, "which prevents them from submitting nominations or accepting service on the boards (composed of employers and employees and at least one representative of the public), have at times presented a serious handicap in the work."

Wide variations in the minimum wage rates for different occupations have arisen from three sources. First, because of the fact that decrees were entered at different periods

[1] Some of this material is presented here through the courtesy of Miss Johnson.

when the cost of living varied widely and could not be revised with ease. Second, because of the peculiarity of the Massachusetts law which requires the financial condition of the industry to be considered in fixing the wage. Third, because each industry affected by the minimum wage law has its own separate wage board. Since 1920 it has been within the powers of the commission to reconvene wage boards for the purpose of revising decrees to meet cost of living changes. "Since that time eight decrees have been revised. The six decrees entered in 1922 superseding earlier ones, show a variation of only 50c. a week in place of decrees which varied as widely as $7.25 a week."

In a general review of the effects of minimum wage legislation in Massachusetts, Miss Johnson emphasizes the educational value—the education of public opinion upon which the law depends for its operation.

The revised decrees for six industries entered by the commission upon the recommendation of the respective wage boards are listed in the following table showing the time the decree became effective:

TABLE IX

Industry	Minimum Wage	Time degree became effective
Women's Clothing	$14.00	May 15, 1922
Paper Box	13.50	May 15, 1922
Men's Furnishings	13.75	June 1, 1922
Retail Store	14.00	June 1, 1922
Muslin Underwear	13.75	June 1, 1922
Laundry	13.50	July 1, 1922

Initial inspection of these industries were made by the commission to ascertain to what extent the new minimum wages were being paid. The material presented in Tables X and XI has been collated from the unpublished records of

TABLE X

WOMEN'S WEEKLY EARNINGS IN SIX INDUSTRIES IN MASSACHUSETTS AS TAKEN FROM THE PAYROLLS IN 1922 AND 1923 FOLLOWING A REVISION OF RATES EFFECTIVE IN THE SPRING OF 1922, BY WAGE GROUPS AND NUMBER AND PERCENTAGE OF EMPLOYEES

Industry	Time of Inspection	Number of plants	Number of employees	Receiving under $13		Receiving $13 and under $15		Per cent receiving $15 and over $15	Median Wage	Modal Wage
				Number	Per cent	Number	Per cent			
Women's Clothing	May, '22–Jan., '23..	255	2,739	663	24.2	328	12.0	63.8	$16 and under $17	$15 and under $16*
Paper Box.......	June, '22 through Feb., '23........	172	3,981	1,774	44.6	596	14.9	40.5	$13 and under $14	$12 and under $13†
Men's Furnishings	June–Nov., '22.....	71	2,862	1,265	44.2	444	15.5	40.3	$13 and under $14	$12 and under $13†
Retail Stores	June–Apr., '23.....	1,484	18,218	5,923	32.5	3,771	20.6	46.9	$14 and under $15	$14 and under $15†
Muslin Underwear	May, '22–Jan., '23..	111	2,437	1,188	48.7	411	16.9	34.4	$13 and under $14	$12 and under $13†
Laundries	July, '22–Apr., '23..	280	1,061	570	53.7	195	18.4	27.9	$12 and under $13	$12 and under $13
Total	May, '22–Apr., '23..	2,373	31,298	11,383	36.36	5,745	18.35	45.27		

* While the largest number of women is recorded in the group receiving $21 and over, this is not within a single class interval, so that the largest number of women in a single group is as indicated.

† While the largest number of women is recorded in the group receiving $18 and over, this is not within a single class interval, so that the largest number of women in a single group is as indicated.

the investigation. Miss Johnson warns however, against making too broad application of her data, for they do not "indicate either the wage increases resulting from the decrees or the possible displacements that may have been involved in the adjustments which are made after the decrees have gone into operation." The table shows the time that the survey was made, that is the time period during which the data were taken from the pay-roll records, the number of plants inspected, the number of female employees for whom records were taken, the number and percentages of employees in different wage groups, the median wage, the modal wage, and the number and percentage of employees who earned approximately the minimum, less than the minimum, and more than the minimum.

The inspections were all made during the twelve-month period, May, 1922, to April, 1923. 4,448 establishments were visited and the wages of 53,621 women were recorded. Since the minimum wages set were highly homogeneous, varying only from $13.50 to $14, those women who were receiving from $13 to under $15 have been grouped together as being in the approximate minimum wage groups. (The data were recorded in class intervals of $1.00). It is noteworthy to observe that one-fifth or 19.6 per cent of the employees were receiving this wage at the time of the inspection, that one-third were receiving a wage below the approximate minimum, and that from two-fifths to one-half or 46.7 per cent were receiving more than the minimum. That is to say, considerably more women were being paid above the minimum than below when the inspection was made. In a large majority of cases the median wage fell within the approximate minimum wage—$13 and under $15. In the 280 laundries the median wage fell distinctly below the minimum, and in all of the women's clothing industries the median wage was distinctly above the minimum.

TABLE XI

WOMEN'S WEEKLY EARNINGS IN SIX INDUSTRIES IN MASSACHUSETTS AS TAKEN FROM THE PAYROLLS IN 1922 BY WAGE GROUPS AND NUMBERS AND PERCENTAGES OF EMPLOYEES, WAGE DECREES NOT HAVING BEEN RECENTLY MADE

Industry	Time of Inspection	Number of plants	Number of employees	Receiving under $13		Receiving $13 and under $15		Per cent receiving $15 and over	Median Wage	Modal Wage
				Number	Per cent	Number	Per cent			
Candy	Nov., '21–Jan., '22..	119	6,902	3,567	51.7	1,190	17.3	31.0	$12 and under $13	$12 and under $13*
Corset	March–May, '22....	15	1,187	810	68.2	157	13.2	18.6	$10 and under $11	$9 and under $10†
Hosiery and Knit Goods	Sept., '21–Jan., '22 .	42	1,607	690	42.9	254	15.8	41.3	$13 and under $14	$12 and under $13*
Minor Confec. and Food	Nov.–Jan., '22	37	447	293	65.5	61	13.6	20.9	$11 and under $12	$12 and under $13
Wholesale Millinery	March, '22	59	1,535	548	35.7	181	11.8	52.5	$15 and under $16	$15 and under $16*
Office Buildings	March–May, '22....	246	1,294	943	72.9	165	12.8	14.3	$11 and under $12	$11 and under $12
Total	Nov., '21–May, '22 .	518	12,972	6,851	52.81	2,008	16.25	30.94		

* While the largest number of women is recorded in the group receiving $18 and over, this is not within a single class interval, so that the largest number of women in a single group is as indicated.

† While the largest number of women is recorded in the group receiving under $7, this is not within a single class interval, so that the largest number of women in a single group is as indicated.

For purposes of comparison, Table XI gives data for six industries for which no revision of wage decree was made in 1922. The time in which these records were taken was approximately a year earlier than that for the industries just discussed but this will not interfere with their use for rough comparisons. (The general level of wages as shown for New York State, which was probably not unlike that for Massachusetts, was practically the same in 1921 as in 1922.)

In this group of industries more than one-half or 52.8 per cent of the women employed were receiving less than $13 per week, one-sixth were receiving $13 and under $15, leaving less than one-third of the total or 30.9 per cent who received $15 and above. In other words, substantially more women received below $13 than above $15, which is the reverse of the case for the six industries for which new wage decrees were entered in 1922.[1]

Thus it appears obvious that women's weekly earnings tend to be higher in Massachusetts in those industries for which the minimum wage has been revised, and lower where they have not been so revised. But, as discovered by the special investigating commission, there is no uniformity of response to minimum wage decrees among different employers. Moreover, while Miss Johnson says "a good deal has been accomplished by the law in improving wage conditions for women workers," she implies further that we shall have to wait longer for knowledge of the effects of these decrees upon the broader economic status of women in Massachusetts and upon their opportunities for employment.

This conclusion corroborates that of Professor Emilie J. Hutchinson in her study of *Women's Wages* in 1919. Professor Hutchinson laid stress upon the need of more

[1] The full weight of this comparison cannot be measured, however, without some comparative knowledge of general wage levels in each of these two groups of industries. These data seem not to be available.

specific data, dispassionately gathered. On the side of industrial enterprise, she suggested that it is necessary to know "the effect of minimum rates of pay on output, profits, prices and the management of industry." On the side of the workers, "investigation should be made of the effect, if any, of wage legislation on general conditions of labor, on the matter of employment, trade-unionism, and the general welfare of the workers."

Doubtless it is some such study as this which the Massachusetts Special Legislative Investigating Commission considers it necessary to make before it can be determined conclusively "whether or not the [wage] legislation has justified its mission." While employers have offered substantial opposition to the minimum wage law in Massachusetts, the resolutions of the association of Oregon employers indicate whole-hearted support of the law, and sound no need of further inquiry into its effects upon their industries. In accordance with this view stands the testimony of Edward A. Filene of Boston. In regard to the attitude of employers toward the minimum wage principle, however, it should be noted that their favorable testimony is practically always based chiefly upon the advantage to industry of paying a living wage to the workers on the grounds that such a wage tends to diminish labor costs. This, of course, is an argument against all sub-living wages and applies to low-paid men as well as to low-paid women. Other countries have recognized this fact in their minimum wage laws but it has yet to be recognized in America. Unquestionably the proportion of under-paid women exceeds that of underpaid men, but the reverse is true when numbers are considered. So the question remains as to whether these facts warrant minimum wage legislation on the basis of sex so long as large numbers of both sexes are under-paid. Both men and women need a living wage in order to live, a sub-living wage for men is perhaps the largest single cause of the entrance of their wives and children into gainful employment; thus the argument for prescribing the payment of a living wage by law may prove to be as strong for one sex as for the other.

CONCLUSION

From the foregoing discussion it is obvious that the effects of special protective legislation for industrial women are only partially known—that impressions are many and facts are few. From the data that are available however, certain deductions may, perhaps, be made. These are of two kinds, depending upon whether women predominate in the industries or occupations affected by the law, or whether men are in the large majority—whether the occupations involved are considered " women's work " or " men's work."

In occupations and industries such as in mercantile establishments and some factories, where the majority of employees are women, we have seen that special protective laws, such as those for shorter hours, seem to cause an improvement in their working conditions, that is, provided the requirements do not demand too radical a readjustment in the industry. In enterprises of this kind, the law is likely to cause a revision of schedule for the entire set of occupations or industry—for the men employed as well as for the women. Such regulations sometimes prove a lesson in efficiency from which employers learn the advantages of conserving human labor in general.

Thus in occupations or industries where women predominate, protective laws for women are found to be likely to protect both men and women.

Where men are in the pronounced majority in the industry or occupations in which special restrictions are placed upon women, the effect appears to be somewhat the reverse of protection of women. This appeared to be the case among

New York women printers and street-railway employees, among women in core-rooms and at polishing and grinding wheels.[1] In these cases the positions of the women were jeopardized and, in a number of instances, lost.

Thus in occupations or industries where men greatly predominate, protective laws for women are likely to prohibit rather than protect their employment or, in other words, to relieve men of the competition of women.

The economic consequences for women where legislation proves prejudicial to their employment are obviously grave. Traditionally, women have accepted too small a wage for their labor and have seemed helpless to do otherwise. They have been massed in a limited number of occupations known as women's occupations—overcrowded, overworked, underpaid. Minimum wages and shorter hours have been demanded for their relief. Now, here and there, small minorities of women through superior skill have detached themselves from the mass. They have gained more strength to dignify their relations with their employers in the matter of wages and hours of work. They have entered into occupations which are traditionally known as men's occupations (frequently, only because they require greater skill and higher pay).

For these minorities of women, legislation based only upon sex is of doubtful value. It is an important fact that they are minorities in a double sense—among other industrial women and also among the men with whom they work. The question arises then, should the sex of these minorities be of first consideration, or their economic status? This is a vital inquiry which requires more extended analysis

[1] This was not true in the Massachusetts rubber and electric appliance industries it will be recalled. Here, however, different from the above mentioned occupations, women though in the minority were employed in large numbers. The law did not demand radical readjustment in the plants, and the hours of some three-fourths of the men also were reduced.

than can be given at this point. What may be said at this time, however, is that no person, socially minded and intelligent, would stress economic advancement at the *expense* of health, either for men or for women. For tired and sickly workers are costly to society. Furthermore, it may be that depleted women are at times more costly than depleted men. And in so far as there are actual physiological differences between men and women, economic status could only be enhanced by the recognition of such differences, perhaps by legislation. But the grave danger is that of false physiology —of physiology tinged with prejudice or custom.

That legislation based upon false physiology may prove a menace to the economic status of women has been revealed in the analysis of effects in this chapter. The health of women in printing establishments and in foundries, for instance, was not found to be menaced although regulations including them were said to be health and morals measures. In the case of women in the transportation service, one investigating expert pronounced such occupations no place for women, and in New York State a law prejudicial to their employment was enacted. The Federal Women's Bureau, on the other hand, discovered women in the transportation service to be improved both in their economic status and in their health and happiness, and warns against unscientific legislation "lest the law wreak disaster upon those it was framed to benefit."

Thus while some special laws for women—whether or not they are based upon false sex physiology—have tended to improve the working conditions of both men and women, other laws have tended to penalize women. The penalty falls more sharply upon those significant minorities who have emerged from the mass into a more self-reliant position. Since it appears to be no longer doubted that women are in industry to stay, warning must again be sounded lest the progress of these minorities—the economic standard bearers in the progress of women—be thwarted.[1]

[1] It should be said that this necessary emphasis upon the importance of minorities is probably peculiar to the subject in hand. More frequently the theory of sacrificing the minority for the majority is accepted as desirable today.

NOTE.—Important facts that would be needed in an intensive effort to discover the effects of special legislation for women might be said to fall into two general categories: First, the effects of the law upon industry itself. This would seem to necessitate extended and minute experiment in a large number of plants with control both of workers and working conditions. Or, more easily obtainable, and perhaps for the present almost as valuable if the regulations were enforced, would be comparative statistics before and after legislation was enacted, together with precise and complete comparisons of conditions in regulated industries with those in unregulated industries.

The second part of the inquiry would be the effects of such laws upon the status of women, economic and social. This would seem to require case study of both an intensive and extensive sort. It would require the sort of intensive investigation that Le Play made in the seventeenth century (*Les Ouvriers Europeens*) of carefully chosen families, when he was intellectually curious about their standards of living. He felt it necessary to know his subjects personally, to know what they were thinking and doing and why they did so and when.

This inquiry into effects of legislation would surely require sufficient acquaintance with the women affected by the law to discover the nature of the change in their occupation—whether it is more or less desirable; whether they are receiving as good, better, or lower wages, whether they are more contented or less so, whether their attitude toward their families has changed and what is the nature of the change. One would need to know over a length of time what the attitude of the women toward industrial employment is, what it is where there is no special legislation compared with where there is such legislation (other things like plant organization being equal of course). One would need to know the attitude of both men and women toward women belonging to unions where there is no special legislation, compared with where there is such legislation.

These are unquestionably some of the facts that should be discovered if the effects of this special type of legislation are really to be known. The task would of course be so great that only a well equipped bureau could undertake it with success.

CHAPTER VII

The Controversy

Are there valid grounds for the special protection of women in industry? As the preceding pages have shown, this question has been answered in the affirmative many times by the courts and, although it appears to have long been considered settled, it is the subject of a growing controversy among women themselves. What, then, is the basis for the controversy, why has it arisen, and who take the opposing sides? It is never an easy matter to state accurately what people believe, and it is practically impossible to analyse motives at long range. But because of the importance of the matters in dispute, let us, allowing for a margin of error, make an attempt to discover what the issue really is.

In the tracing of various influences that have resulted in these special laws for women, it has become plain that they sprang from the conviction that in their dealings with employers, women are not so able to take care of themselves as are men. One classic explanation of this inability is the extreme youth of gainfully employed women, and, turning to age records, we find support for this contention. According to the United States census for 1920, we find that, of all gainfully employed females ten years of age and over, a little over one-fifth (21.7 per cent) were under 20 years, and another fifth or 42.8 per cent in all, were under the age of 25. For New York State, the returns were about the same—19.8 per cent of the employed females were under 20 years of age and 42.4 per cent were under 25 years.

The phrase "women in industry" in its common usage, then, includes a substantial number of inexperienced female minors and young women who tend to marry and leave industry and who are likely to do their work in the state of mind of a transient. Thus their union membership is small and their bargaining power weak; they tend to accept passively the work and the pay that is doled out to them.

The consequence of this passivity is that women often become victims of the acquisitive instincts of unscrupulous employers, with danger both to their health and to their morals, and, since they will be mothers of future generations, danger to the health of society at large.

Moreover, married women are in industry in large numbers. According to the last census, there are nearly 2,000,000 married women in the United States who are gainfully employed, and this is more than one-fifth of all employed females. When women return to industry after marriage, usually they are or will become mothers and housewives as well as industrial workers. Judging from local studies that have been made, perhaps it is safe to estimate that one-half of these gainfully employed married women are mothers. Thus, under our present social system, these women are forced to carry a double burden which may seem to put them in need of protection for the sake of their families as well as of themselves.

Women in industry are made up for the most part, therefore, either of female minors who have not reached the strength of adulthood, or of older women who are wives and mothers as well as industrial workers.

To fortify the assertion that women need special protection is presented the fact that there is more sickness among female workers than among males. A study of morbidity in New York State in 1919, for instance, revealed the number of cases of sickness among females to be 50 per cent greater than among males (154 to 1000 females and 101 to 1000 males), and the average number of days lost per employee was almost correspondingly great—1.6 per female and 0.9 per male.[1]

Women are thus believed to be physiologically less resistant to the wear and tear of industrial life, a conclusion which is reached by Dr. Alice Hamilton of the Harvard Medical School in her observation of the greater susceptibility of women to trade poisons. Some recent data, paralleled in other countries, which Dr. Hamilton has gathered from American potteries, show that "The average length of exposure to lead of the men who developed lead poisoning was seventeen years, but the average length of exposure for the women was only 9.3 years."[2]

Because, then, of their youth, their maternity, and their tendency to more frequent ill-health, with all of the accompanying implications of these factors (including immobility), special laws have been enacted for women for shorter working hours, minimum wages, special working conditions, the prohibition of night work, and, in some occupations, for the entire prohibition of employment.

The condition of affairs as thus stated appears convincing and entirely defensible, and well within the established limits of custom. But the facts of experience and the social trend of recent years press the question as to whether in stating the case thus it has been presented completely, or whether a full stop may have been placed where only a comma should have fallen. For we have seen, as the numbers of employed women increase and spread into wider fields of industry, that we are forced to recognize the arrival of new ele-

[1] *Sickness Among New York State Factory Workers in 1919, Bulletin no. 108*, State Department of Labor, August, 1921.

[2] *The Woman Citizen*, "Protection for Working Women," March 8, 1924, p. 16.

ments of difficulty regarding the desirability of their protection when men are not protected likewise. The principle of special protection is being challenged as untenable and irrational—as prejudicial to women rather than advantageous. What, then, is the cause of this protest?

We have seen that certain minorities of women such as those in newspaper offices, in foundries, and some of those in the transportation service, have found themselves out of employment because of legislation which restricted them while their men associates and competitors remained legally free to work. We have seen that these women, who are neither very young nor apparently greatly encumbered by home ties, instead of asking for protection privileges, are asking their legislators to "give a woman a man's chance—industrially." They join with the National Woman's Party in the demand "that women shall no longer be barred from any occupation, but every occupation open to men shall be open to women, and restrictions upon the hours, conditions, and remuneration of labor shall apply alike to both sexes."

And now, while these demands may appear at first thought to be directly opposed to the best interests of women and society, these women insist that upon second thought the case is quite the reverse. They maintain that too much stress is laid upon the *differences* between men and women whence springs the case for legislating for women only, and not enough attention is given to the *similarities* in men and women whence springs the need, perhaps, for legislating for both. Instead of mitigating the whole human burden of industrial hardship, and so improving the family and social condition of workers, this discrimination against woman creates restrictions that make new obstacles for her in finding employment, or in keeping it on terms of equality of pay.

It should be said at the outset that these groups of women

protestants would include *adults* only in this freedom from special protection. Their belief is as firm that minors, both male and female, should be specially protected against the raids of industry upon their minds and bodies, as that adult women should not have such special protection.

For adult women the grievance is that barring them from entering certain occupations or prohibiting them from continuing in skilled occupations for which they are trained, such as polishing and grinding and core making, the effect is not only injurious to themselves but the repercussions of the injury are felt by all other women in industry. For the result automatically throws them back into occupations most of which are already overcrowded by women and in which women, chiefly because of their numbers, are underpaid. The economically necessary result of this increased pressure for employment is depression of the bargaining power which is already weak, rendering women less able to help themselves in the struggle for decent working conditions and a living wage. In turn, it is this very lack of power among working women that forms one of the principal bases of special laws for their protection. Thus, there is formed a vicious circle from which women are not permitted to escape.

That this series of discriminations to which women are found time after time to be victims is a serious matter in their economic life, few who are acquainted with economic facts will deny. The fact that women are commonly considered primarily as mothers of the race has been an unchallenged reason for disregarding the obstacles in the way of their economic progress. It is impossible to say how much of woman's backwardness in industry is owing to the disregard of ways to help her forward—ways which are devised for men, as for example for the sons of bricklayers and bakers in New York who, it will be remembered, were released from the night work prohibition so that they might learn their fathers' trades in the cool of the summer mornings.

But here it is rightly asked, can the health of women be maintained without special protection? We have seen records showing that their morbidity is greater than that of men. Can this fact be denied any more than we can deny that women are by these laws economically handicapped as compared with men? Unfortunately, there is no single answer to this important question and so we must continue the analysis. Sometimes, of course, women's ill-health is that of pregnancy or of permanent injuries from having borne children. Sometimes it is the result of the double strain of housework and a paid job; and sometimes it is the absence of proper maintenance caused either by the lack of regular work which brings regular pay, or, having regular employment, the lack of sufficient pay.

When ill-health is an outgrowth of child bearing, obviously it is peculiar to women, and probably all of those whose views we are discussing, whether or not they believe generally in special protection of women, are agreed that proper provisions should be made for women who are engaged in that hazardous occupation. This is a subject for a separate analysis.

When the ill-health of women is a result of overwork from combining household duties with industrial employment, it is bound up closely with the employment of men who are members of the same family units. We have seen that the cause of children's being pressed into industry, as well as the eagerness of women to work overtime in the shops and factories, is due to economic pressure. The seat of this pressure, doubtless with few exceptions, lies in the inability of husbands and fathers to earn a sufficient living, or to their sickness from overwork or exposure, or to their death. This is true also in the case of industrial homework, where, again, economic necessity is the unrelenting goad to which women and children are forced to respond.[1] Thus while we are stressing the need for vigor in the mothers of the race, the necessity for sound fathers must not be overlooked. For it is not enough for a child to be healthy at birth. Wholesome environment and proper care are necessary to the second important half of the process of its growth. Studies of the Federal Children's Bureau show high correlation between the earnings of fathers and infant mortality, the number of infant deaths decreasing perceptibly as fathers' earnings increase.[2]

Moreover the high death rate of men from tuberculosis is a marked phenomenon in present-day life which menaces the economic status of their families to say nothing of the injury it inflicts upon society at large. Recent compilations show that between the ages of five and 20 years, girls are victims of tuberculosis a little more often than boys, the deaths per 100,000 persons running from 40 to 134 for girls and from 39 to 123 for boys. But beginning with the age of twenty, there is a very marked excess of deaths among men over women, ranging all the way from 20 per cent to 240 per cent. These facts are of such signal importance that the figures themselves may be given for the different age groups as compiled by the New York Tuberculosis Association. The data are only for New York City but since

[1] Fathers of homeworking families, as discovered by the New York Factory Investigating Commission, are in the prime of their working lives, more than 63 per cent of them being between 20 and 45 years of age.

[2] Children's Bureau, United States Department of Labor, *Infant Mortality*, Results of a Field Study in Manchester, N. H., series no. 6, Bureau Publication No. 20, 1917. See also the recent comprehensive study by Robert M. Woodbury which is an analysis of the seven studies of the children's Bureau: Economic Factors in Infant Mortality, *Journal of the American Statistical Association*, June, 1924, pp. 137-155.

tuberculosis is an urban disease they may perhaps be considered fairly representative.

TUBERCULOSIS DEATH RATE * BY SEX AND AGE, NEW YORK CITY, 1910 TO 1920

Age	Rate	
	Males	Females
0-4	157	138
5-9	39	40
10-14	27	48
15-19	123	134
20-24	199	164
25-29	245	182
30-34	323	189
35-39	412	189
40-44	445	175
45-49	458	150
50-54	421	132
55-59	466	137
60-64	380	125
65-69	369	131
70-74	247	120
75-79	195	94
80-84	122	69
85 and over	103	58

* From all forms of tuberculosis per 100,000 persons living at each specified age period. Compiled from statistics of the New York Department of Health and the United States Census by G. J. Drolet, Statistician, Research Service New York Tuberculosis Association.

These conditions and others about to be mentioned seem to suggest that legislation, if it is to be enacted at all, should include overworked and underpaid men if the health and security of their families, to say nothing of the public, is to be guarded; the ill-health and disabilities of wage-earning women in families are bound up with the ill-health and disabilities of family men; that a plan for a minimum wage for these women, or for the restriction of their working hours, or the entire prohibition of their employment, may be treating a symptom instead of the disease. For it is clear that to tolerate underpayment of men or to allot them "a monopoly of overtime and night-work" is likely to allot their families sick fathers and husbands, or none at all.

It is not possible to say as yet to what extent women are inherently less resistant to the strain of industry than men, and to what extent their overfatigue from carrying two jobs is the cause of their greater morbidity. When their remunerated work is inferior to that of men the explanation is sometimes given that, whether married or single, they come to their work tired from housework, a condition less often to be met by men. Moreover the overfatigue factor has been offered as a reason for women's greater susceptibility to trade poisons, and, I believe, no adequate test has been made to disprove this theory. These are some of the conditions predisposing women in industry to illness that should be thoroughly investigated before final conclusions can be safely reached.

It should be said at this point that many advocates of special laws for women meet this general line of reasoning by declaring that they are not opposed to the legal protection of men, that, in fact, they favor it as soon as it can be achieved and accepted by the courts although so far it has been impossible. They believe their course is the practical and desirable method of securing better conditions for all industrial employees—that the attainment of shorter hours for women in factories and mercantile establishments usually means that men's hours also are shortened, because of the interdependence of their work. They believe that the few women who suffer from special protective laws should surrender their individual interests for the benefit of larger groups of women, and voluntarily meet the accompanying personal loss.

This expresses a philosophy of progressive legislation which began with the protection of children, is now being extended to women, and will finally, so far as this is considered necessary, result in the inclusion of all industrial workers. It is supposed to be an educational process—for the workers that they may understand their right to leisure and health; for employers, that they may learn of their obligation to permit if not promote good citizenship on the part of their employees; for legislators, that they may feel their responsibility for utilizing the police power of the state for the wefare of their community; and above all, perhaps, for the ethical enlightenment of the courts upon whose sovereign judgment all legislation for welfare and progress ultimately rests.

This program—progressive legislation which considers special laws for working women as an entering wedge for universal industrial improvement—one which involves great cost to an unknown number of them and which moreover may not result, after all, in general legislation for men and women—is hotly opposed by those whom it has caused consciously to suffer. Also the generalizations made in respect to women are resented as unscientific and untenable. An example of this would be the inclusion of adult women with immature girls which appears to have been injurious to both, depriving girls of the care they might otherwise have had, as in the case of the first New York statute prohibiting night work for young women which was declared unconstitutional because it included adult women as well. The opponents of protection also point out that many women are either not mothers or are mothers of grown-up children, so that legislation for mothers which includes them is inept.

When they have thus eliminated the peculiar disabilities of youth and maternity from their contention, the protestants maintain that they, as mature women, are in no greater need of special protection than the masses of men who are overworked, underpaid and unorganized, that these men need protection quite as much as the masses of women, and that protection could be gained for them and upheld in the courts as it has already been in a number of instances, if there were as much effort made in that direction as for laws for women.

Furthermore, it is repeated, that it is constantly evident that men are not the physical giants that failure to give them legal protection would seem to assume. In addition to what has been said on this point, for example, attention may be called to the numerous cases of inguinal hernia which industrial physicians are discovering. This is an affection as peculiar to men as injuries from child birth are to women, and, while so far it appears impossible to foretell in what men this hernia may develop when heavy work is undertaken, the possibility for it to develop is present. "The hernial sac may fill for the first time when a worker is lifting, pushing, or pulling; the tenseness of muscular strain may coincide with the psychological moment for the filling of a preformed sac," explains Dr. Charles A. Lauffer, author of *Hernia as an Anatomical Defect.*[1]

Thus if men engaged in heavy work are to maintain their physical efficiency it would seem that careful oversight of them by a plant physician is important. And for a man who has developed inguinal hernia there are of course certain kinds of employment which he cannot safely undertake. Dr. Lauffer says that from his observations "data on the physical examination of prospective employees reveal the fact that approximately 3 per cent of the men offering their services to the industries have well-developed inguinal hernias; approximately 14 per cent have incipient hernias,"

[1] *Monthly Labor Review*, September, 1919, pp. 282-286, quoting from the August issue of *Journal of Industrial Hygiene*, 1919; Charles A. Lauffer, M. D., Medical Director, Relief Department, Westinghouse Electric and Manufacturing Company, East Pittsburg, Pa., and Secretary of the Hernia Committee of the National Safety Council, 1917.

and finally that hernia of this kind may "be regarded as the greatest single frailty of the American worker." [1]

And again, contrary to the common belief that lead poisoning among men does not affect their children, Sir Thomas Oliver showed different facts more than a decade ago. He wrote, in part, of men lead workers in Hungary as follows: "Owing to their wives so frequently miscarrying, potters in Hungary have few children, seldom more than one or two, and the children who are spared to them grow slowly, are of short stature, and are frequently almost dwarfs. In some of the villages the majority of the potters have no children at all—not one of the infants born alive had survived . . . the children die from hydrocephalus, from acute meningitis, or in convulsions. . . ." [2] It should not be understood by this quotation that Dr. Oliver denies the likelihood of more serious effects of poisoned mothers upon their children than of poisoned fathers. The proper emphasis seems to be, not that mothers in general *can* work in lead without harming their children, but that fathers in general *cannot* do such work without harming their children.

Thus we may repeat Henry R. Seager's published remarks of eight years ago regarding the social necessity of caring for the health of fathers as well as mothers,

There is no sharp dividing line between women wage-earners and men wage-earners as regards their helplessness in the face of diverse industrial conditions. The Supreme Court of the United States has justified ten-hour laws for women on the ground that they are the potential mothers of the oncoming generation and that therefore the protection of their health and vitality is essential to the welfare of the nation. But is it

[1] *Ibid.*

[2] "Lead Poisoning and the Race," by Sir Thomas Oliver, M. D., British *Medical Journal*, vol. i, pp. 1096-1098, 1911.

reasonable to maintain that the health and vitality of the potential fathers of the oncoming generation are less essential to our national welfare? In arguing that protective laws for women are justified, while protective laws for men represent an unwarranted interference with their liberty, our judges appear to me to have been guided by a somewhat old fashioned attitude toward women rather than by sound reason. Mr. Gompers and those who agree with him that hour laws for adult men not in government employment are undesirable, though hour laws for women are, seem to me to acquiesce too readily with the views of our judges of the old school. Doubtless the proportion of men wage-earners who, through efficient labor organizations, have secured all and more than they could secure through legislation is greater than the proportion of women wage-earners, but there are many women wage-earners who do not need legislative protection, and there are, in my judgement, more men wage-earners who do need it.[1]

In this passage Professor Seager seems to discard the theory that legislation for women should be used as an entering wedge and to imply another objection to such legislation which is held by many women—an objection which cannot be overlooked in this analysis. This is that special protection, not based upon handicaps that are necessarily peculiar to women, places one more obstacle in the way of woman's emergence from the state of bondage in which society has so long held her. There is little question that many individuals, in advocating these special laws are obeying the dictates of a more deep-seated tradition than that which appears on the surface — a tradition which claims that "woman's place is in the home," long after she has been obliged to leave the home. For example, Dr. Price, direc-

[1] "American Labor Legislation," by Henry R. Seager, President, American Association for Labor Legislation, *American Labor Legislation Review*, 1916, pp. 93-94.

tor of investigation of the New York Factory Investigating Commission, opened his report in 1913 by explaining that "Participation of women in industry, though so general, has never been regarded as an entirely normal condition in society." [1] And more recently, United States Secretary of Labor Davis, after asserting that there is no question as to whether women have a right to earn a living, wrote his summary for publication as follows:

At the same time all will agree that women in industry would not exist in an ideal social scheme. Women have a higher duty and a higher sphere in life. Eve was the companion and helpmate of Adam and in every way his social equal, but it was for Adam to protect Eve and provide for their posterity. It is true that later womankind were considered inferior, and became, we might say, slaves of society. All civilized nations are again coming to recognize the equality of women and men and in no country are her rights greater than in America, where her social standing is even higher than man's. With all this, I personally prefer to see a woman guiding the destiny of the nation—in the home.[2]

A step further in this general philosophy of woman's place is taken by the Amalgamated Society of Engineers in England, as quoted by the Women's Freedom League. Plainly these engineers *do* question the *right* of women to work although they are certain of their *ability*. Their statement as quoted is:

Robbed of those deceitful things called percentages which sometimes put a rosy aspect on the worst case, it must be admitted that the enthusiasm for women workers is not very

[1] *Second Report of the New York Factory Investigating Commission*, 1913, vol. ii, p. 439.

[2] "Safeguarding the Mothers of Tomorrow," published as the sixth of a series of articles by United States Secretary of Labor, James L. Davis, in the *Gazette* of Colorado Springs, November 5, 1922.

pronounced. We are not amongst those who regard with astonishment the fact that women are able to do the work that men and boys do. . . . We think that the question of the ability of women may be left out of the argument; it may be accepted without reserve. But it by no means follows that because women can do men's work therefore they should be allowed to do it. Nor does it follow because women are willing and steady workers that therefore they should be employed in factories . . . the employment of women is only desirable when the supply of men is deficient, and when that state arises the question will settle itself.

Another trade journal with tendencies to philosophize on woman's place, contributed to this controversy by roundly assuring its readers that—" The more advanced the stage of civilization the more the male workers keep their women at home the better to fulfil their domestic duties and thus lift the level of the plane of physical, mental and social life." [1]

Statements such as these, of course, are echoes of a passing social order. Fortunately or unfortunately, the apparent facts force recognition by the impartial observer that " women are in industry to stay." One of the favorite subjects of sociological discussion now-a-days is upon the question, what is progress? Is our society advancing or retrograding? We need not participate in this discussion to conclude that whether or not we are moving forward, there is no doubt that we are moving. Social change is inevitable.[2] The machine age is upon us as a result of the invention of the steam engine and the long line of other mechanical devices which have forced industrial and social

[1] The two above quotations appeared in a pamphlet article called " Women's Right to Work," by L. Lind-af-Hageby, published by the Women's Freedom League, 144, High Holborn, W. C. 1, London, England. The date was not given but it was later than 1919.

[2] *Cf. Social Change* by Professor William F. Ogburn, 1923.

readjustment. Without being dogmatic it is as logical to declare that our economic order must return to that of 1750 as to say that women must take themselves out of industry.

Correlative with the contention that women should not be in industry is the position of men's unions regarding women's special protection, which Florence Kelley has discussed in an interesting way,

> Statutes restricting the hours of labor of women and children, while enacted in the interest of health and morality, have often been urged by persons animated by two other motives as well. In many cases, men who saw their own occupations threatened by unwelcome competitors, demanded restrictions upon the hours of work of those competitors for the purpose of rendering women less desirable as employees. In other cases, men who wished reduced hours of work for themselves, which the courts denied them, obtained the desired statutory reduction by the indirect method of restrictions upon the hours of labor of the women and children whose work interlocked with their own.[1]

From this it seems there are mixed motives underlying the advocacy of special laws for women. One of the fundamental motives is not the protection of women's health but the retention either of a tradition or of a job. This motive appears in the form of a health and morals disguise, to use the psychologist's terminology, which forces a reasoning based upon a false theory of physiology. And what is more, this logic has been employed consciously or unconsciously, by practically all groups of people who have been in favor of general protection of women to the exclusion of men. It is the persistence of custom or a shortsighted sense of self-preservation among people, whether they are composed of philanthropic groups, of men's labor unions, or of the mass

[1] *Ethical Gains Through Legislation*, by Mrs. Florence Kelley, 1914, p. 133.

of working women themselves, which leads them to accept the performance of hard domestic labor by women as a necessity and as the will of society, while they frown upon the employment of women in foundries, for example, even though their heavy lifting is done by means of balanced machinery. In New York State, it will be remembered, three hundred core makers protested against being deprived of the work for which they were trained, and although the factory commission declared they could not discover that the work was always and absolutely detrimental to their health, their "instincts of chivalry and decency" dictated that "every obstacle should be thrown in the way" of the further employment of women in foundries. The subscription of the molder's union to this program, and, in fact, its long campaign to bring it into being, has also been described—the testimony that foundries are not a "proper place for women" proved to be thin disguise for the real motive of the molders which was to check competition by women.

Again, it is a matter of history that men successfully opposed the retention of women in the transportation service in some if not all localities in which they were employed during the war. In Cleveland, the last resort in order to end a grave situation induced by a three-day strike on the street-car lines by the men's union, was the following agreement:

> It is hereby agreed by and between the undersigned that on and after this date there will be no more women employed as conductors, that the Cleveland Railway Co. will remove and displace the women that are now in its service as rapidly as possible.
>
> It is further agreed and understood that on and after March 1, 1919, no women will be in the employ of the Cleveland Railway Co. as conductors.[1]

[1] Quoted from the Cleveland *Plain Dealer*, Dec. 6, 1918 in an article in the *Monthly Labor Review* of the United States Department of Labor for January, 1919, pp. 224-230.

According to report, the railway company had strongly urged that the discharge of the women would lower the standard of service, and the women made every effort to retain their positions which they claimed they had secured under exactly the same conditions as the men, with no favors as to wages, hours, or runs.

In New York, the men, less strong than in Cleveland, offered their services for twelve hours a day instead of ten in exchange for the promise of the companies that women should not be employed. About the same time the opinion of an expert investigator in New York was declared in opposition to women's employment in street-car service and a resulting regulation was made by the legislature which, if fully enforced, would have rendered more than four-fifths of such employment impossible. The women concerned protested against the act and later won its partial repeal. Moreover, they felt that their resentment was vindicated by the report of the Federal Women's Bureau that transportation service increased both the health and happiness of the women employed whom they investigated and could not be considered undesirable for them.

Another example of the reasoning of men's unions in the form of a plea for the protection of women's health is that of the Wisconsin Federation of Labor, which, at its annual convention in 1918, passed a general resolution to protect "the interests of the toilers in the State" against the influx of women. The resolution was as follows:

> Whereas it has come to our notice that female labor is sought and has already been found to be working at the polishing and buffing trade, under no better conditions than those which have confronted our members for years and at a much lower rate of wages than is paid to our male members; and
>
> Whereas the polishing and buffing trade is known to be in-

jurious to the health, and wishing to protect our future generations; be it therefore

Resolved, That the incoming executive board of the Wisconsin State Federation of Labor introduce a bill in the next State legislature forbidding the employment of women at the polishing and buffing trade.[1]

It is worth recalling that the New York Factory Commission urged and secured the prohibition of women in these trades in New York State, for which it is now shown there is no physiological basis. For, according to the Federal Women's Bureau, "the danger to the lungs is as great for men as for women, and for the protection of all workers exhaust systems . . . should be required."[2]

English experience adds to this argument that physiological inferences regarding women have been taken too much for granted. For example, a report of the Health of Munition Workers Committee stated that digging and excavating had been looked upon with doubt as occupations for women, but the secretary to the Ministry of Munitions declared later,

The suggestion, so far as it might be applied to the work that they [women] had been doing habitually, was happily contradicted by experience. Some of the best fortifications in the north of England had been excavated by women navvies, formerly fishwomen from Scotland, and it was a matter of common observation that the physical development of [the] women had improved beyond all knowledge since the war, and never had they seemed more fit to discharge all their functions in civil life.[3]

[1] *Monthly Labor Review,* January, 1919, pp. 220-221.

[2] *The New Position of Women in American Industry, Bulletin no. 12,* United States Department of Labor, Women's Bureau, 1920.

[3] Speech of T. G. Kellaway, summarized in *Dilution of Labor Bulletin,* London, June, 1918, p. 122. Quoted in the *Monthly Labor Review* for September, 1918, p. 217.

Some suggestions made by the Health of Munition Workers Committee for overcoming specious objections of employers to the employment of women in certain occupations were also described in one of the reports:

It has often been found effective, when an employer or a works manager pleads the weight of the work as an excuse for not employing female labor, to ask him whether the men lift the work. He usually replies that the men do not do so, that the work is lifted by a crane, but that the machines on which the work is done are very heavy. On this one has to ask him whether he expects the man who is operating the machine to carry the machine about. He will possibly then take refuge in the fact that the cuts on the work are so heavy; and again one can ask whether the cut is taken by the operator or the machine. It will be found, in fact, almost always, that when the management of a factory is driven to pleading the weight of the work, or the weight of the machine, or the heaviness of the cut, as an excuse for not employng female labor, they are really in a bad way for want of an argument.[1]

Many other examples could be given in evidence of the fact that mixed motives supported by tradition, have been conjoined toward "protecting women to the vanishing point" in some occupations, for the sake of their "health and morals." The opponents of special legislation object to the persistently exaggerated concern over women's morals when the source of social danger is more often the morals of men. They rebel against unnecessarily prolonged recognition of the double standard of morality which they allege is encouraged by such laws as those prohibiting night work and requiring minimum wages especially for women. They admit that the immediate results of this and other legislation have, in numerous cases, been beneficial to women and

[1] *Dilution of Labor Bulletin*, London, April, 1918, pp. 99; quoted in the *Monthly Labor Review*, September, 1918, pp. 215-223, 216.

to the working classes in general, but they believe that the *loss to the cause of women in the struggle for a status in present economic society is greater than the gain.* The general attitude may be condensed as follows: In place of protective laws for women alone, the need is for better public police protection, restriction of the work of all minors, more attention to the individual health of all workers, and a conscious attempt to displace rather than inadvertently to foster double standards for adults. Equality of opportunity, so far as it is possible, is requested so that women may develop their economic status according to their capabilities, instead of being expected to conform to the habits of their grandmothers or to respond to the desire of comfortable people for the old type of domestic servitude.

The leaders of these insurgents understand the anxiety of their brothers over the insecurity of their employment in the face of increasing numbers of women, and they urge that organizations into the same unions with mutual instead of divided aims is the only solution. They urgently object to the implication in the view supporting legislation for women expressed by Rose Schneiderman, president of the New York Women's Trade Union League, that "The women who are strong enough to work beside men, and who want to work at the same hours of the day or night and receive the same pay, might be putting their own brothers, or sweethearts, or future husbands out of a job."[1]

The arguments of these protestants are suggestive. They indicate that the problem of women in industry is more acute than ever because more realized, that wholesale legislation for their health and morals is too often based upon opinion and tradition, and may cost them their jobs, to say nothing of the less tangible evils it is sure to foster; that

[1] Article by Mabel Abbott, New York *World*, Sunday, March 16, 1924.

some better informed method of protecting exploited industrial workers must be devised.[1]

Moreover this is not the dictum of a handful of women in this country. It has been a bone of contention at international conferences as well,[2] necessitating the qualification of resolutions from time to time. At the first international congress of working women held in Washington, D. C. in 1919, Miss Margaret Bondfield, a prominent English delegate said, "We are no longer thinking of night-work in terms of sex, but just in terms of using every effort to get rid of night-work for everybody." Following the conference the Women's Freedom League of England wrote, "There is something almost pathetic in the spectacle of women accepting as a boon and a blessing the recent decision of the Industrial Labor Conference at Washington to prohibit night-work for women and employment in unhealthy processes. The result of the decision can only be further sex-exclusion, further degradation of women as industrial units. The enforcement in this country since March, 1919, of the Act which forbids the employment of women on night shifts has been the direct cause of the dismissal of large numbers of women. . . ."[3]

At the women's meeting held preliminary to the third international labor conference of Geneva in 1921, emphasis was laid upon the trend toward protection from harmful working conditions regardless of sex:

[1] See some of the testimonies given at the Women's Industrial Conference held in Washington, D. C. in 1923, as reported by the *Monthly Labor Review* of the United States Department of Labor, February, 1923, pp. 50-51.

[2] For example, see the report of the First International Congress of Working Women held in Washington, D. C. in 1919; *Monthly Labor Review* for December, 1919, pp. 280-290.

[3] Pamphlet entitled "Women's Right to Work" by L. Lind-af-Hageby. Published by the Women's Freedom League, 144, High Holborn, W. C. 1.

The principal importance of the conference which is about to be held lies, as has been shown, not in the special measures that it may adopt for the protection of women workers so much as in the proposal to put men and women on a footing of almost complete equality in all protective measures contemplated. It is in this direction that women desire to see the development of protection for women workers. They no longer ask for privileges—they demand absolute equality.[1]

And again, at the ninth congress of the International Woman Suffrage Alliance held at Rome in 1923, the following resolution was adopted regarding women in industry:

That the right to work of all be recognized, and no obstacle be placed in the way of married women who desire to work; that no special regulation for women's work, different from regulations for men, should be imposed contrary to the wishes of the women concerned; that laws relative to women as mothers should be so framed as not to handicap them in their economic position, and that all future labour regulations should bend towards equality for men and women.[2]

Mrs. Sidney Webb, whom both sides of this controversy claim as a supporter of their cause, has also laid increasing emphasis upon the need for abandoning the traditional notions concerning sex in industry. She lays stress upon the need for an "occupational rate" of payment for work regardless of the sex of the worker, emphasizing that attention be given to the fitness of the individual for the job rather than generalizations concerning fitness and remuneration according to sex.[3] Mrs. Webb is more interested in the proper

[1] *The International Protection of Women Workers*, International Labor Office, Geneva, October, 1921, 14 pp. Studies and Reports, Series I, No. 1. *Monthly Labor Review*, December, 1921, p. 200.

[2] The International Woman's Suffrage News (*Jus Suffragi*), July, 1923.

[3] (Minority) *Report of the War Cabinet Committee on Women in Industry*, Great Britain, 1919.

protection of all workers than of women alone. She is not, however, one of those who would cease to advocate legal protection of women, when they need such protection, if organized men oppose legislation for men. But since male trade unionists in England in recent years, favor regulation for men as well as for women, Mrs. Webb in her own country, is free to take an uncompromised stand according to her convictions.

Thus, we have come to the point where it is clear that there is a growing appreciation of the fact that conservation of our human resources in industry is essential regardless of sex; that we must eliminate unnecessary waste. The need for "industrial physiology," to use Dr. Frederic S. Lee's term, is every day more realized. This is the need for careful observation and experiment in order to determine how the industrial worker actually performs his work and what conditions are most conducive to the combination of effective effort and good health; and then, the development in the factories of those proper conditions.[1] The works doctor is a new institution in industry through whom this procedure may take place with a reduction in the wastes of production and an increase in the welfare of society. A specific example of the application of this plan in connection with our particular subject of discussion was implied by Chief of Inspection Gernon of the New York Department of Labor. When Mr. Gernon was asked by a group of advocates of special protection how heavy a weight he thought women should be allowed to lift at their work, he answered, "Show me the woman." [2]

[1] See "The New Science of Industrial Physiology," Public Health reports (1919), xxiv, pp. 723-728, and *The Human Machine and Industrial Efficiency*, by Frederick S. Lee (1918).

[2] It will be remembered that there has been no single conclusion arrived at in prescribing the maximum weights which women may lift by law, the variation being all the way from 15 pounds in Pennsylvania and Ohio, to 25 pounds in New York and 40 pounds in Massachusetts.

Without attempting to prophesy, compulsory health insurance for all industrial workers seems a certain further development for the promotion of our national welfare. America has lagged behind other modern countries in this particular although the American Association for Labor Legislation has urged it for many years.[1] By an adequate plan for health insurance each worker would receive benefits according to his relative needs, and premiums would be imposed according to probable benefits. Maternity insurance —provision for cash benefits and proper care of women during the period of child bearing—would form a part of a general health insurance program. It may be that women other than those bearing children, would have to draw more heavily upon such an insurance than men, although it is conceivable that the ratio of morbidity may grow less as acute economic pressure is relieved and as the family becomes more nearly adjusted to present-day life. It cannot be repeated too often that the double load that many gainfully employed women now carry, with its accompanying fatigue, is responsible to an unknown degree for their ill-health, their greater susceptibility to trade poisons, and what is often interpreted as physical inferiority. Just how much this condition is responsible for women's ills no one can tell until much more care has been given to tests. But it must always be kept in mind in considering problems concerning women, that one of our very greatest social needs is the readjustment of the family; and compulsory health insurance would powerfully contribute to this end.

In conclusion, it is clear that the advantages to society of protective labor legislation for our working population are being increasingly recognized.

[1] See *The American Labor Legislation Review*, whole number for June, 1916 which includes a discussion of the compulsory health insurance system in Great Britain at that time, and a tentative draft of a bill for this country.

It is also true that where labor organization exists, the need for interference by the state is reduced and the enforcement of laws that are enacted is much more efficient. If all workmen were successfully organized, it is conceivable that there would be little need for their protection by law. But the facts are far from this—perhaps about one-fourth of the organizable workers in the country are members of unions. Furthermore, union membership fluctuates very perceptibly with the course of the business cycle. For an indefinite stretch of time into the future, therefore, our industrial workers, for the most part, will rely upon legislation and enlightened public opinion for the improvement of their state.

It is the view of a substantial number of persons in this country that organization is retarded by legal regulation of wages and hours of labor, that when workmen can rely upon state protection their appreciation of the value of union membership is weakened. These persons therefore, disapprove of protective laws of this sort for workers not in the employ of the government. The late Samuel Gompers, President of the American Federation of Labor for the last nearly forty years, took this view in respect to men but not in respect to women. But this attitude seems, unfortunately, to disregard the persistent fact that there is "no sharp dividing line" between unorganized men and unorganized women wage-earners in their helplessness to throw off the anti-social conditions of industry. Some final observations, that may be made in this study therefore, are:

(1) All children and young people probably under the age of twenty-one years, who are gainfully employed, require action by the state on behalf of their welfare and the welfare of society. In general, there would seem no reason for distinction between boys and girls. However, as further knowledge of physiology is accumulated, should it become

a scientifically established fact that boys or girls require certain protective laws peculiar to their sex, failure to secure such protection would be at the expense of social as well as economic progress. This care could be administered through a system of industrial hygiene superintendence according to an industrial code, better than through the less flexible action of legislatures.

(2) Theoretically, the above suggestions would apply also to the masses of unskilled, unorganized adult workers. Unfortunately, however, considerable education must be acquired before this step can be realized. Education is needed among those labor leaders themselves who fail to consider that minimum comfort standards by law for men as well as for women, by stimulating a desire for still better standards, may increase the possibilities of strong union rather than hinder them. It is a psychological fact upon which we can rely, I believe, that when working people enjoy a little better standard of living than they have had, they yearn for more instead of less of the pleasures of life. The public itself, to say nothing of our judges, must also be educated to realize the need of protecting male workers; that the disease and accidents among tired industrial men are a menace to their families and the public health as well as those of women; that it is not enough to doctor the mothers with laws when all too often only such doctoring of the fathers can touch the root of the evil. Here again, much could be done, probably, with a minimum of legislation and a maximum of health supervision of individual workers.

This educational process should not take a very long time if the emphasis upon the need for protection could be shifted in this direction. State constitutions have been amended to permit the enactment of labor laws when once the necessity became apparent, such as the amendment in New York

State to include workmen's compensation, and, in Ohio, that permitting a general minimum wage law. Also the courts have made substantial progress in upholding the constitutionality of protective laws for men, so that there seems little reason to doubt that acts based upon scientifically determined physiological needs will be passed and supported as equitable.[1] It may develop that such needs will necessitate special laws for women in some cases, and, in some cases special laws for men.

Until this time comes, when more education and further scientific knowledge is attained, should not the choice of occupation among adult women, so far as there is a choice, be left to those supremely concerned—the women themselves? Would not this in itself throw the emphasis upon the need of a plan for progressive legislation *beginning with the most helpless of our workers whether they be male or female;* upon the imperative need for women to organize, thus strengthening the bargaining power of both men and women and making more probable the enforcement of laws which are passed; upon the advancement of intelligent women into skilled trades; and upon a comprehensive plan for health insurance? Does not other action than this seem fraught with the danger of restriction instead of protection? It cannot be overlooked that many so-called protective laws based upon sex appear to serve only as a handicap for those very important minorities of women who have entered the ranks of skilled workers.

[1] The words of Felix Frankfurter to the Consumers' League can give as much hope at this point as when they were first spoken (*cf.*, p. 97, *supra*): "My interest derives from an unshakeable faith that if we care as much about what we believe in as do those who believe the other thing, our ideas will prevail.... The information gathered must be made living, vivid and active."

TABLE OF CASES CITED

INDEX

Bei Fragen zur Produktsicherheit wenden Sie sich bitte an:
If you have any questions regarding product safety,
please contact:

Walter de Gruyter GmbH
Genthiner Straße 13
10785 Berlin
productsafety@degruyterbrill.com